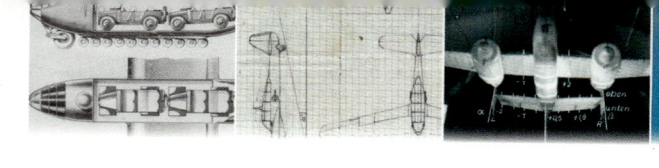

Preface & Contents

It has been nearly a decade since I began to study German Second World War aircraft development through the prism of primary source documents – tens of thousands of archived reports, letters, memos, meeting transcripts and more, written in German, by Germans, for Germans during the war.

Working this way, rather than relying on postwar books, papers and magazine articles, has provided an interesting counterpoint to those sources and an alternative perspective on what actually happened behind closed doors within the German wartime aviation industry.

With *Secret Projects of the Luftwaffe*, I wanted to delve a little more deeply into the history of some well-known 'projects' as well as bringing to light others that have never been made public before. It came as something of a surprise to discover, based on numerous documents, that Blohm & Voss's unusual BV 40 'glide fighter' – a glider that was also a fighter for use against Allied bombers – was only a 'glide fighter' for a little over half of its development, the first half. Thereafter it was developed as a manned missile, a suicide weapon for use by one of the Luftwaffe's most notorious units.

During the postwar period, Blohm & Voss chief designer Richard Vogt and two of his engineers, Hermann Pohlmann and Hans Amtmann, all wrote books about their wartime work and all mentioned the BV 40 as a 'glide fighter'. But all were very brief in their descriptions of it and none of them mentioned that it had become a 'manned missile' intended for KG 200 even before the first prototype flew. Most modern histories of the type are based on an article published in Issue 6 of *Luftfahrt International* magazine, dated November to December 1974. This reprinted some documents from the 'glide fighter' phase of the type's development and mentioned the 'manned missile' as a mere BV 40-based 'project' – a suggestion only.

At the end of the piece, the magazine's editorial team provide a list of 92 BV 40-related primary source "references" – seemingly a cast iron guarantee of accuracy – and thank the press office of MBB Hamburg and Pohlmann for "the support provided". No mention is made of where the 92 source documents can be found.

In fact, nearly all are located together on a single roll of microfilm kept at the National Air and Space Museum in Washington, DC. And actually reading those 92 documents makes the BV 40's post-April 1944 mission abundantly clear, though no drawings appear to have survived showing a Heinkel He 177 with a BV 40 manned missile slung beneath each wing, ready for an attack.

Another discovery made while working on this publication concerns the Focke-Wulf Ta 154, sometimes referred to as the 'Moskito' since it was said to be an analogue for the British-made de Havilland Mosquito – famous for its wooden airframe. While Focke-Wulf factory leader Kurt Tank is generally credited as the type's designer, this is not the whole story. The idea to build it in the first place, based on the wide availability of reliable and moderately powerful Jumo 211 engines, came from Auto Union technical director William Werner.

Werner comes across in contemporary meeting transcripts as an energetic man full of ideas and with the industrial muscle to back them up – Auto Union building Junkers aero engines under licence. His concept was for a twin-engine night bomber or fighter-bomber powered by the latest development of the 211, with Erhard Milch, the man in charge of Luftwaffe procurement, inserting the notion that this would be a wooden aircraft.

With off-the-shelf engines and a basic airframe, the idea was to get this rough-and-ready new machine into production in record time. It would be a proto Volksjäger-like effort, with the design finalised in weeks and with furniture makers press-ganged into manufacturing its components. But who would lead this effort and get the thing done without a fuss? Various names were bandied around: Heinrich Hertel at Junkers, maybe, or Heinkel chief designer Karl Schwärzler. In the end, Tank was picked for the job because he was 'lively' and 'a man of initiative'. Or perhaps because he had powerful friends, needed a 'win' and was not in a position to turn it down.

Also within these pages you will discover exactly why Focke-Wulf's 1936 twin-engine fighter, the Fw 187, was suddenly revived during 1942 and why it was then abruptly canned not long after. You will also learn about Germany's last piston engine fighter design competition of the war – and why it might not have been all that it appeared at first glance – not to mention Messerschmitt's take on the Dornier Do 335.

Finally, you may also notice that more images within this publication are presented at full-page size than was the case with my 'Luftwaffe Secret' series. This is in response to reader feedback and I must confess that, my own eyesight being what it is, I too appreciate seeing drawings presented on a slightly larger scale.

Please enjoy this latest peek behind the curtain of Germany's aero industry circa 1939 to 1945.

- **004** Focke-Wulf bomber-engine fighters
- **022** Focke-Wulf Fw 187 als Höhenjäger, Kampfzerstörer und Nachtjäger
- **044** Focke-Wulf Jäger mit 2 x BMW 801 F
- **058** Messerschmitt Schnellbomber „Do"
- **060** Blohm & Voss BV 40
- **090** Hochleistungs-Otto-Jäger
- **122** Heinkel Ringflügel-Projekte

Author: **Dan Sharp**
Design: **Druck Media Pvt. Ltd.**
Publisher: **Steve O'Hara**

Published by:
Mortons Media Group Ltd, Media Centre, Morton Way, Horncastle, Lincolnshire LN9 6JR.

Tel. 01507 529529

ISBN: 978-1-911703-28-0

© 2023 Mortons Media Group Ltd. All rights reserved. No part of this publication may be reproduced or transmitted in any form or by any means, electronic or mechanical, including photocopying, recording, or any information storage retrieval system without prior permission in writing from the publisher.

Thanks to: Steve Coates, Calum Douglas, Ben Dunnell, Ian Fisher, Steve O'Hara, Carlos Alberto Henriques, Paul Martell-Mead, Jamie McGinnes, Ronnie Olsthoorn, J. Richard Smith, Daniel Uhr, Stephen Walton and Tony Wilson.

Ain't no substitute for cubic inches*

Focke-Wulf bomber-engine fighters

Putting an engine intended for heavy bombers into a lightweight single-seat fighter might seem counterintuitive – but Focke-Wulf persisted with exactly this line of development and produced some truly bizarre-looking aircraft designs along the way.

The overheating issues plaguing BMW's early 801 variants were giving Focke-Wulf a headache during the first half of 1941 and the company had also commenced work on its DB 603 vehicle, the Fw 190 C, to compete with Messerschmitt's Me 309.

With the future of a BMW 801-powered Fw 190 looking less than rosy and with efforts under way to put the longer, heavier 603 onto the 190 airframe, Focke-Wulf launched a wide-ranging study looking at what other fighter engines might be available and whether they might represent an alternative for the 190.

The resulting report, largely complete by mid-June but evidently not published until early August, focused on eight engines: the in-production BMW 801 C (for comparative purposes), BMW 801 E, DB 603, DB 614, BMW P 8019, Jumo 222, BMW 802 and BMW 803.

The BMW 801 E was a variant of the regular air-cooled 14-cylinder radial 801 with improved supercharger, improved pistons and an improved oil system with a defoaming centrifuge. The DB 603 was an inline liquid-cooled inverted V12; the DB 614 was a 603 with two superchargers; the BMW P 8019 was an 801 with two-stage supercharger and intercooler; the Jumo 222 had 24 cylinders arranged in six inline banks of four and was liquid cooled; the BMW 802 was a fuel-injected air-cooled 18-cylinder radial with a two-stage supercharger and the BMW 803 essentially consisted of two 801s back-to-back, liquid- rather than air-cooled, and driving contra-rotating propellers.

Focke-Wulf had requested the latest data from BMW and Daimler-Benz on their respective powerplants, with most of it being current to May or June 1941. The Jumo 222 data, however, came from December 9, 1939. Presumably no 222 update was necessary since Focke-Wulf had been working closely with Junkers on the 222-powered Fw 191 bomber – and must therefore have been well aware of the engine's development status.

Power-to-weight comparisons showed that the DB 614 and BMW P 8019 had the best ratios while the BMW 802, BMW 803 and DB 603 were somewhat less favourable, though the DB 603 performed particularly well at lower altitudes. The report noted that the Jumo 222, "due to its high weight … is the least favourable for installation in a fighter".

With this information in hand, Focke-Wulf's engineers came up with an airframe to suit each engine. It was assumed that each would need one-and-a-half hour endurance at full power, wing-loading of around 210kg per square metre, armament of MG 17s, MG 131s and/or MG 151s, a pressurised cockpit, armour and normal fighter equipment.

The BMW 801 E, DB 603, DB 614 and BMW P 8019 were of a size, shape and weight that made them suitable for installation into something which at least nominally could be called an Fw 190 – albeit with airframe modifications in some cases. The Jumo 222, BMW 802 and BMW 803, however, would need all-new airframes.

The report observed that, "a comparison of the calculated take-off weights against the engine weights shows that the engine weight is almost 56% of the take-off weight. The proportion of equipment, armour, ammunition, armament and crew varies between 14% and 16% of the take-off weight."

The standard equipment amounted to a static weight of 250kg, which meant that "with increasing engine power and the same climb performance or power load, an ever greater weight in kilograms is available for armament and armour. This means that with increasing engine power, the total weight increases, but at the same time the combat effectiveness of the aircraft increases. In this case, either a larger number of weapons and ammunition can be carried, thus increasing the density of fire, or large-calibre weapons with a correspondingly greater effect can be installed. The latter, especially, is necessary when one considers that with the increasing wing loading and physical size of bombers, the cross-section of the load-bearing parts increases sharply, so it becomes more and more difficult to force the enemy aircraft to crash by firing at it with small calibres".

By this rationale, when attempting to shoot down enemy bombers at least, it was more important for a fighter to carry a heavy weapons load than for it to be lightweight and manoeuvrable. This in turn made the Jumo 222, BMW 802 and BMW 803 look increasingly attractive as fighter engines, since although fitting them resulted in a monstrously heavy fighter, it also allowed for some impressive firepower.

EINSITZER MIT JUMO 222

Focke-Wulf's earliest known attempt at designing a single-seat fighter powered by a Jumo 222 was depicted in drawing numbers 0310 207-01 and 0310 207-07. It certainly looked like a regular Fw 190 A at first glance but was actually somewhat larger in every respect – exactly 1m longer at 9.85m and with an 11.50m wingspan compared to 10.50m. Wing area was 22sqm, compared to the 190's 18.3sqm, and the undercarriage mainwheels were set 4.1m apart compared to the 190's 3.5m, presenting a very sturdy-looking stance on the ground. Take-off weight was 4,630kg, compared to the Fw 190 A's 3,770kg, and of that 840kg was available for weapons.

Under 'airframe structure', the report stated: "Pressurised cabin with a compression and control system that delivers a constant air pressure of 0.67 ata at an altitude of between 3.5 and 5.7km and an overpressure of 0.17 ata above the outside air pressure at an altitude of 5.7-12km, so that at an altitude of 12km the pressure is what it would be at 8km.

"Pilot's seat and headrest armoured. Tempered glass front windscreen. Equipment includes the normal flight control and engine equipment, radio system, oxygen for two hours, detection device FuG 25 [IFF

---

* Or in this case, cubic centimetres.

transponder]. The installation of a camera (overload) is possible.

"Armament two MG 17 on the nose with 1,000 rounds each, two MG 151 in the wing roots with 400 rounds of ammunition each. The accommodation of other weapons in the wing outside the prop circle is possible. A bomb load of up to 500kg can be carried as an overload on a rack on the underside of the fuselage.

"Instead of the bomb load, a jettisonable additional fuel tank with a capacity of 300 litres can also be carried."

Projected top speed was 690km/h at an altitude of 6,250m.

EINSITZER MIT BMW 802

In contrast to the Einsitzer mit Jumo 222, the Einsitzer mit BMW 802 depicted in drawings 0310 207-08 and 0310 207-09 bore only a passing resemblance to the Fw 190. It was 2.3m longer at 11.15m – with the cockpit set towards the tail behind an extremely long nose and forward fuselage. Wingspan was 2.5m greater, at 13m (the report text stated 12.5m but the appended drawing showed 13m), and the 190's smooth wing dihedral was replaced with a gullwing effect whereby the inner wing section was perpendicular to the fuselage and only the mid-outer section was angled up. Wing area was 26sqm but due to the inverted gullwing design, with the undercarriage being attached to the short perpendicular wing section, the undercarriage mainwheels retained the 190's track distance at 3.5m apart.

Take-off weight was 5,400kg – 770kg more than the Einsitzer mit Jumo 222 and 1,630kg more than a regular Fw 190 A. But payload

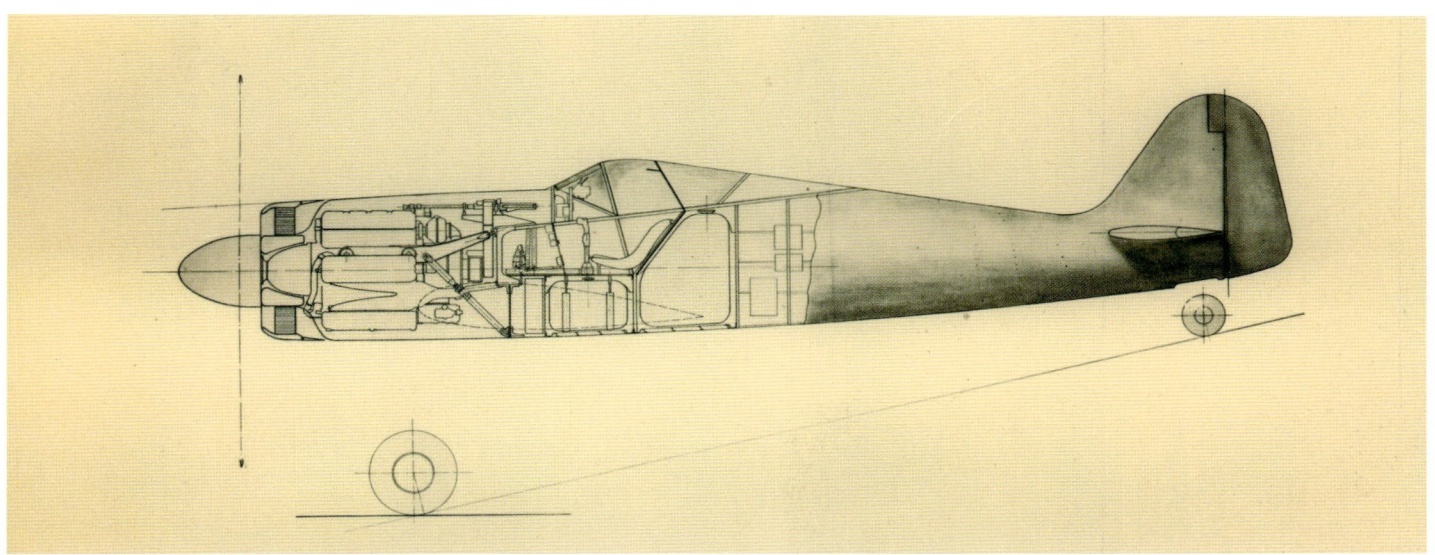

ABOVE: Side view of the Focke-Wulf Einsitzer mit Jumo 222 from drawing number 0310 207-07.

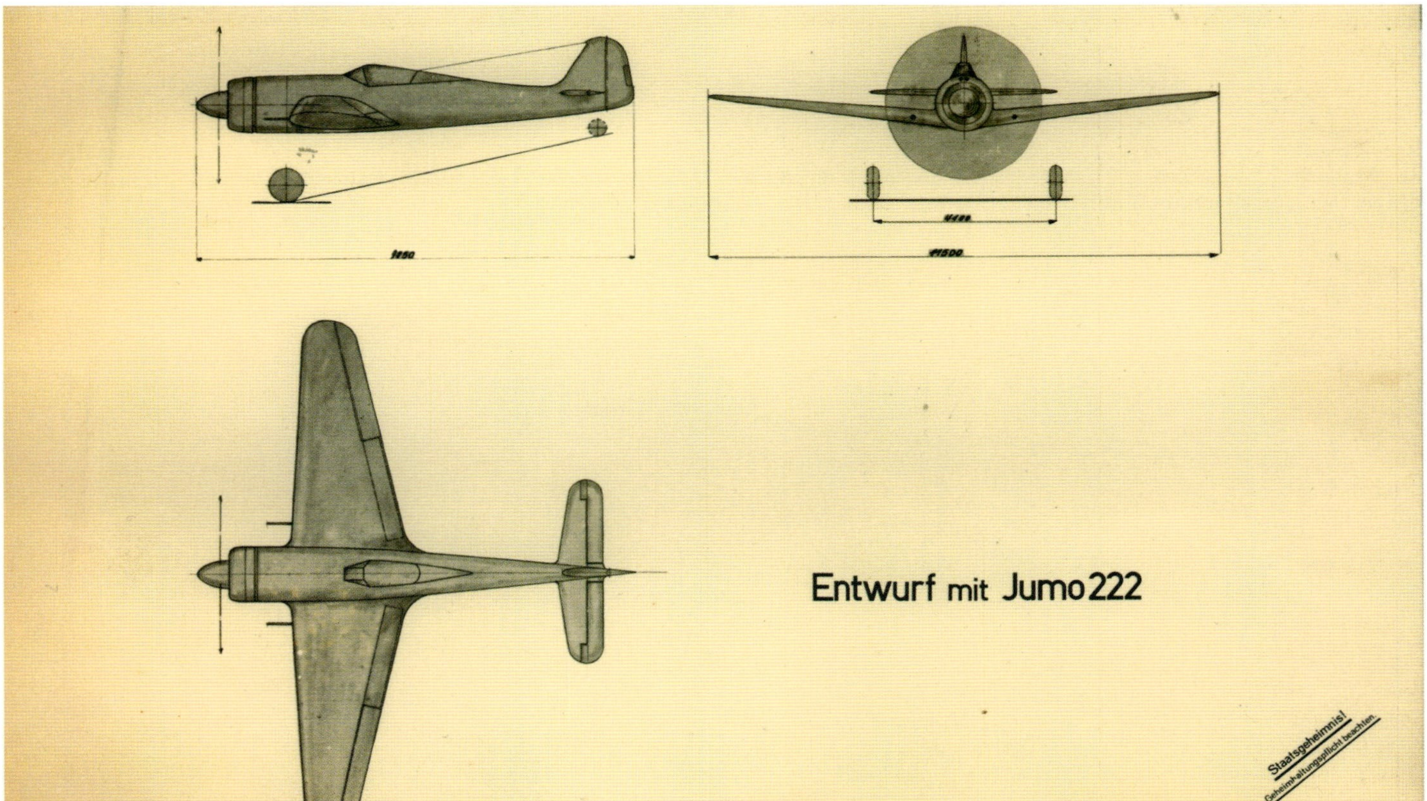

ABOVE: The first of many attempts by Focke-Wulf to design a fighter powered by the Jumo 222 engine, as shown here in drawing number 0310 207-01. The aircraft appears little different from a regular Fw 190 but it is larger in most dimensions. Oddly, now exhaust stubs are depicted.

was increased to 923kg – 83kg more than the Jumo 222 design could manage.

The 802 design's pressurised cockpit would provide 8km altitude pressure up to 14km, the same armour protection was fitted as appeared on the 222 design, and equipment was the same. Armament, however, was increased to three MG 151s with 400 rounds apiece – one on the nose and the others in the wingroots. The nose-mounted cannon could be replaced with two MG 17s with 1,000 rounds each. Again, more guns could be housed in the outer wings if desired.

There was the same under-fuselage 500kg bomb/300 litre drop tank option but now the outer wings could also carry 50kg bombs.

Maximum projected speed was 725km/h at 8,000m.

EINSITZER MIT BMW 803

The BMW 803-powered fighter design completely dispensed with the conventional single-seat fighter layout and adopted something more akin to the Fokker G.I,

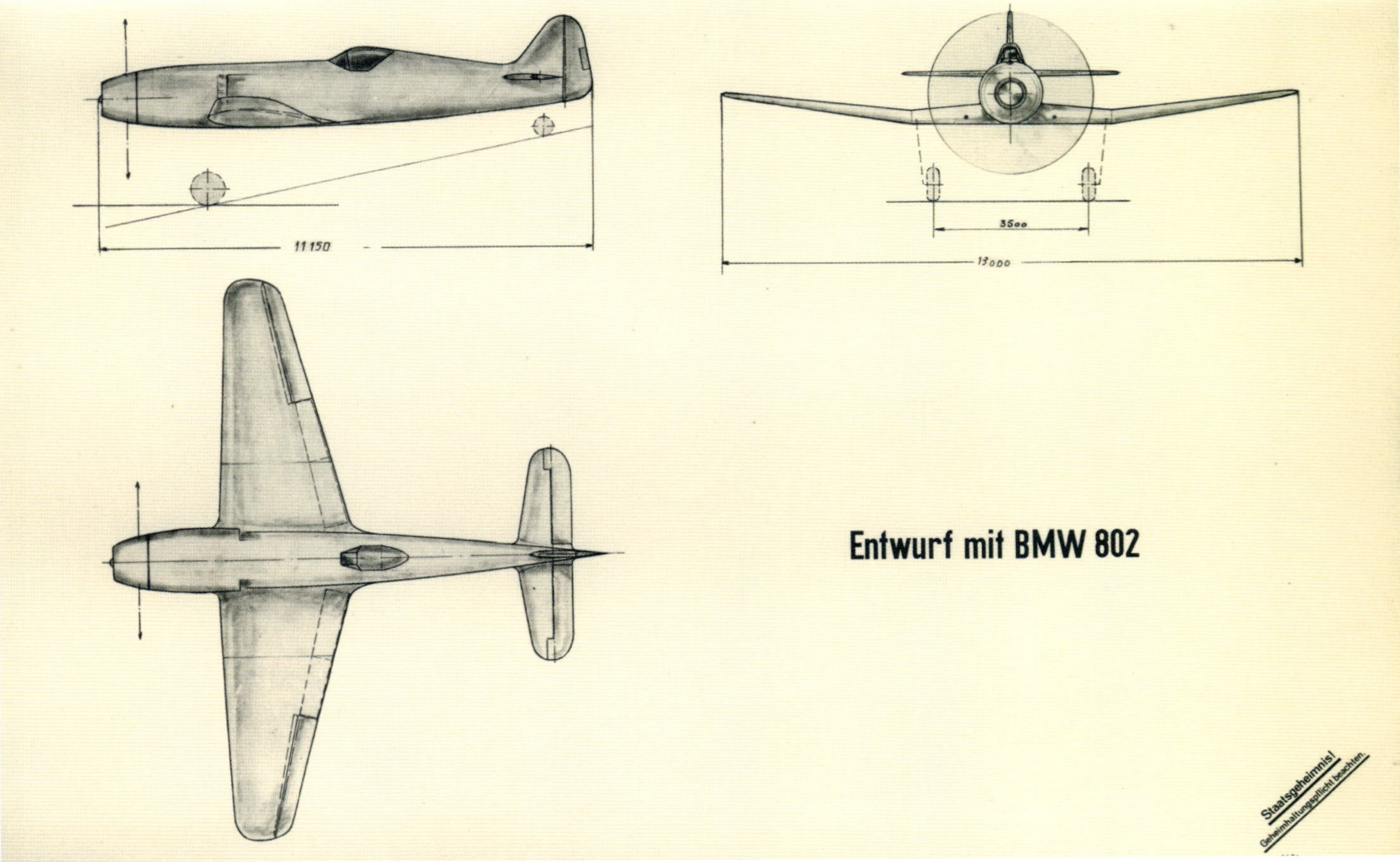

ABOVE: BMW's 802 was never going to fit within the confines of an off-the-shelf Fw 190 airframe. Consequently, Focke-Wulf came up with this bespoke design, with a hugely long nose and inverted gullwings. This is drawing number 0310 207-09.

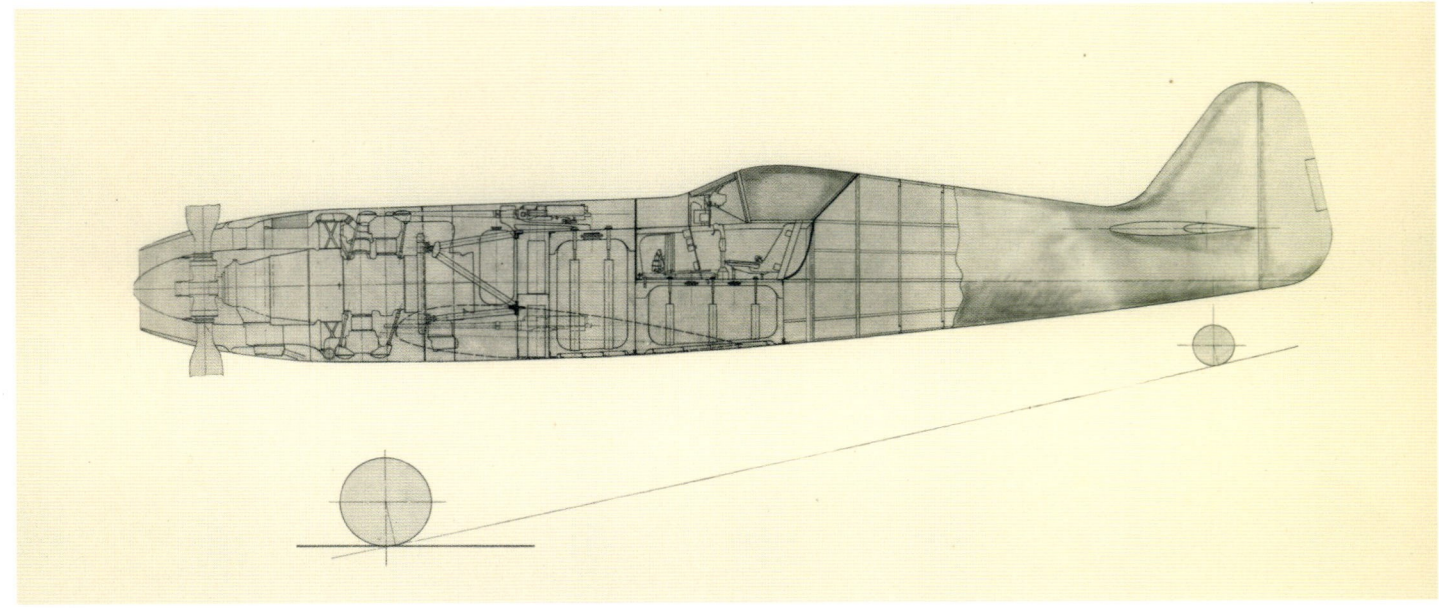

ABOVE: The side view, drawing number 0310 207-08, shows the large space required to house the BMW 802 within the Einsitzer mit BMW 802, the cockpit being relocated almost into the tail.

Fw 189 or Fokker D.XXIII. The enormous engine was positioned at the rear of a central pod-type fuselage, driving contra-rotating pusher props between a pair of tail booms. Attached to the trailing edges of swept wings, these ended in rounded fins connected by a single high-set constant-chord tailplane.

The pilot was seated within a pressure cabin at the front of the central pod, enjoying excellent visibility forwards and down. The nosewheel of the tricycle undercarriage folded up rearwards to sit within the pod between the cockpit and the aircraft's single large fuel tank – which itself sat immediately in front of the huge engine bay. Air was fed to the engine's radiators via inlets both above and below the fuselage.

Dimensionally, the Einsitzer mit BMW 803 was large but not ridiculously so. It was longer than the Fw 189 at 13.8m compared to 11.9m but had a much shorter wingspan thanks to sweepback, at 13.2m compared to 18.4m. Wing area was not dissimilar at 35sqm compared to the Fw 189's 38sqm.

What was dissimilar, though, was the aircraft's projected take-off weight – 7,500kg, which was not quite double the Fw 189's 3,950kg. True to the original proposition however, this yielded yet more payload capacity at 1,160kg.

The aircraft's pressure cabin would function much like that of the BMW

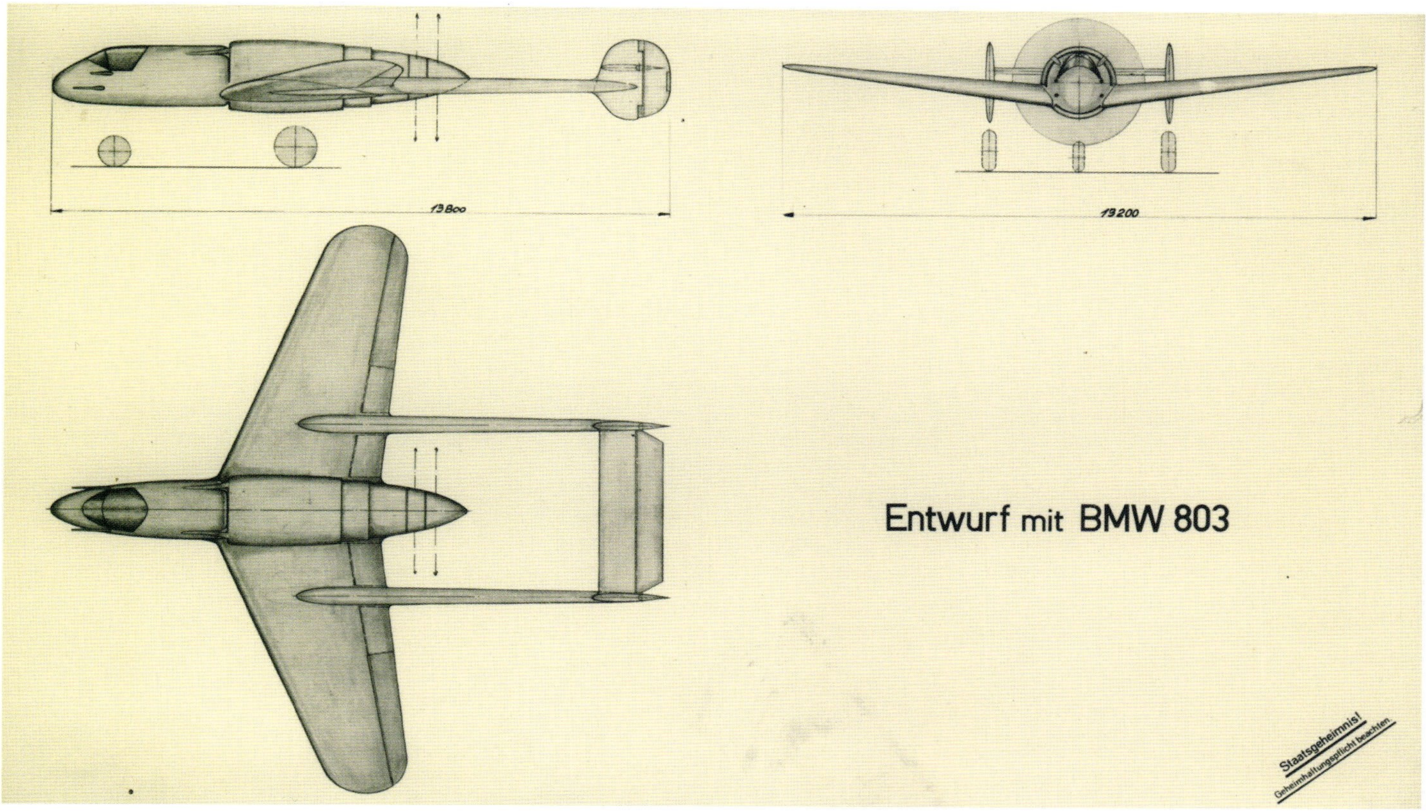

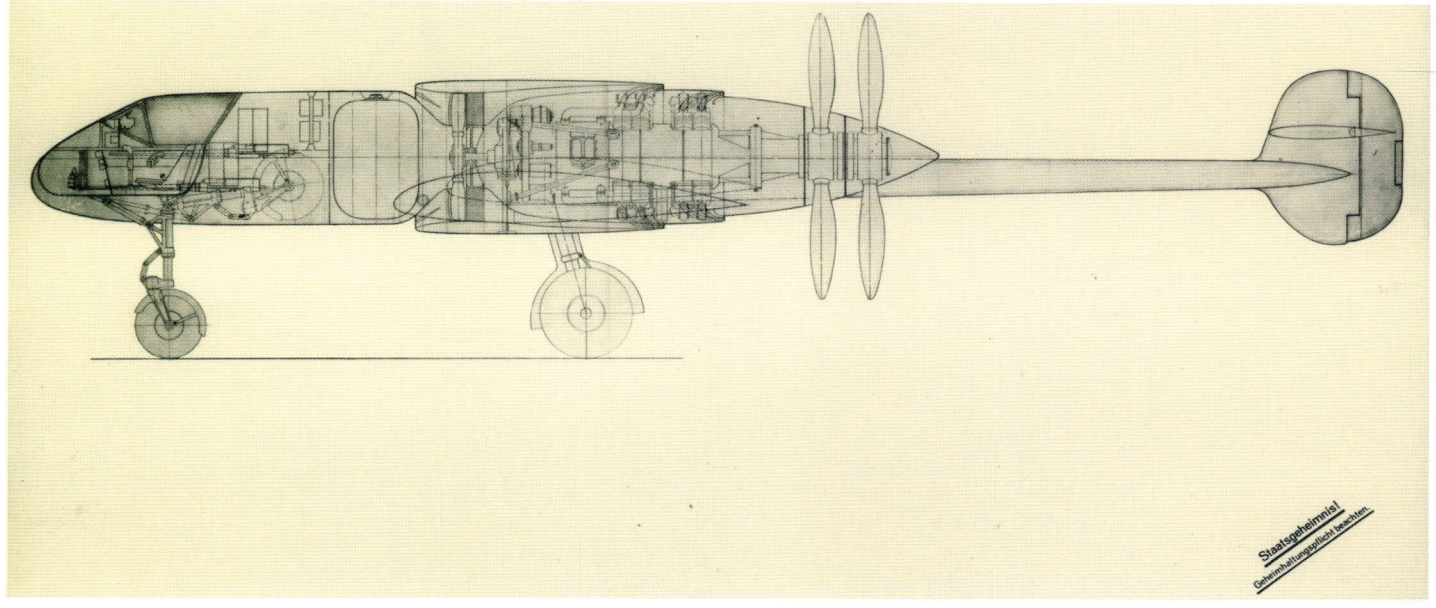

ABOVE: Focke-Wulf's radical-looking Einsitzer mit BMW 803 from drawing 0310 207-02. Coming up with an airframe that could be powered by one enormous engine, when that engine couldn't possibly go in the nose, must have been a real challenge for Focke-Wulf's engineers.

ABOVE: Internal view of the Ensitzer mit BMW 803 from drawing 0310 207-04. This reveals that the unusual segmented look of the rear fuselage was to provide an outlet for the engine exhausts.

Secret Projects of the Luftwaffe

802-powered design but would be made of armoured steel 6-10mm thick, with the pilot's windscreen being made of armoured glass. The usual equipment was fitted but armament could now be four MG 151s with 400 rounds each, two positioned on either side of the cockpit – the pilot having a view of the target unobstructed by a propeller or a lengthy section of forward fuselage. Not only that, according to the report: "The accommodation of two cannon of stronger calibre, about 3-4cm, is possible. At the same time, two or four MGs can be accommodated in the wing roots". A 250kg or 500kg bomb could be carried beneath each boom, below the wing, as an overload. Alternatively, two 300 litre drop tanks could be carried.

Top speed peaked in two areas of the graph – hitting a respectable 720km/h at 3,000m before falling back to 690km/h at 6,000m, then rising again to an overall peak of 730km/h at 9,000m.

TANK'S SPECIFICATION

Three months after this initial round of engine assessment and airframe design concepts, on November 8, 1941, Focke-Wulf's charismatic boss Kurt Tank (his official title being Betriebsführer or 'works leader' – a position specific to the Nazi legislature) drew up an order for further research and sent it to his designers and engineers.

He wrote: "War experience gained to date, both in attack and defence, especially in operational air warfare, shows that it is necessary to seek ever greater altitudes. For the fighter aircraft, getting clear of ground defences and reducing the chances of success for defending fighters are the decisive reasons for seeking greater altitudes. The same consideration naturally applies to carrying out reconnaissance undisturbed.

"For the fighter, of course, the demand for superiority in altitude arises from the need to be able to successfully attack with the element of surprise and from a tactically favourable position, both against the bomber and against any accompanying fighter escort. The question to be answered here is whether all tactical missions from close to the ground up to the highest altitudes can be performed using a single type of fighter aircraft. The engine required for reaching higher altitudes, with the high weight load from the supercharger and intermediate cooling, and the corresponding increase in drag, requires a construction effort that will probably result in very poor flight performance at low altitudes.

"In order to come to a clear judgment about the required design features, a quantitative examination of the task through two extreme projects is necessary: 1) The normal fighter. 2) The high-altitude fighter. The basis for the normal fighter is the normal engine with supercharger but without intermediate cooling, without a pressure cabin and with the best possible armour protection and initial rate of climb.

"The basis for the high-altitude fighter is the high-altitude engine with motor-driven multi-stage supercharger or exhaust gas turbines with intercooling, with high-altitude turbine, with very little armour protection and initially low rate of climb. The wing loads will probably also differ, namely the normal fighter with a higher wing loading compared to the high-altitude fighter. The resulting lower speed of the high-altitude fighter must be able to be briefly increased by additional thrust devices [presumably solid rocket boosters].

"At this point, the question as to which of the two classes the jet fighter will fall into remains unresolved. The following engines are to be provided for the implementation of the project work: DB 605 with multi-stage supercharger, DB 603, DB 614, BMW 802, BMW 803, BMW 804. A twin-engine version of the high-altitude fighter should also be considered."

Work on the BMW 804 engine had evidently begun in September 1941. It was to be a 14-cylinder air-cooled double-row radial with 45.5 litre displacement and was supposed to work in a four-stroke process with direct fuel injection.

In the first development stage, maximum power was supposed to be 2,000hp compared to 1,800hp from the 801 D at the time. With a single-stage three-speed

ABOVE: Focke-Wulf's hands-on Betriebsführer Kurt Tank, photographed at the controls of an Fw 190 on June 5, 1943.

supercharger this was supposed to be achieved at an altitude of around 7-8km, with a two-stage four-speed supercharger it would be reached at 12km.

BMW cancelled it during the spring of 1942, alongside the BMW 802, when the company realised that its development resources were critically overstretched.

At around this time, on April 21, 1942, Focke-Wulf produced another engine comparison report with drawings showing concept aircraft designs – presumably the result of Tank's order. Now, however, the bomber engines were gone; the overall number of options had increased to a dozen but now they were all expected to suit an Fw 190 airframe with no all-new aircraft envisioned: BMW 801 C/D, BMW 801 J, BMW P 8028, Jumo 213, Jumo 213 A-2, Jumo 213 with two-stage supercharger and intercooler, DB 603, DB 614, DB 623 A, DB 609 and DB 624.

The bomber-engined fighter concept may have been shelved but it was certainly not forgotten.

JUMO 222 UPDATE

During the Air Ministry department heads meeting on June 30, 1942, the head of the Technical Office engines department, Generalingenieur Wolfram Eisenlohr, gave a presentation on the development status of the Jumo 222. According to a summary produced after the meeting: "The engine was commissioned in 1937. The first prototype engines were put to the test in early 1939. Despite intensive testing in 1940-41, a number of unexpected technical difficulties could not be completely eliminated. In the autumn of 1941, the engine was therefore initially removed from the procurement programme.

"The development was continued with a simultaneous increase in performance from 2,000 to 2,300 to 2,500hp. On the basis of 2,000hp, nine engines were run for about 1,100 hours on the test bench; on the basis of 2,500hp, a total of 253 test bench hours were achieved with four engines. According to our development plans, the following schedule has been set out: completion of the development and testing up to the series release [approval for production] on April 1, 1943. Start of series production in small numbers in spring 1944. Delivery of the first engines suitable for series production type aircraft from September 1944.

"A prerequisite for adhering to those dates is the fulfilment of the following requirements: a) Reinforcement of the current staff working on the Jumo 222 in the development plant. b) Support for the Junkers company in the procurement of materials and fuel. c) Start of series production in a main Junkers plant. d) Broadening of the flight test base by accelerating the provision of further test-free start-ups of the series.

"It is proposed to release the Jumo 222 A/B engine type initially with a take-off power of 2,300 hp. An increase in performance to 2,500hp can later be carried out in a relatively short time. The Jumo 222 C/D is intended for a further increase in performance to around 3,000hp. The increase in performance is achieved by using C3 fuel, increasing the volume and increasing the speed. The start of this engine can be expected in autumn 1945 as standard. In its entire structure, the Jumo 222 engine is the first organic [presumably Eisenlohr means an engine not composed from parts of other, smaller, engines] engine in the power class between 2,000 and 3,000hp.

"A direct comparison with the DB 610 double engine is hardly possible. The DB 610 represents a quick fix for a large engine unit. The twin engine has heavier weight, greater labour and maintenance requirements, and larger projection of drag areas and vulnerable areas. The production costs of the Jumo 222 are around 30% higher than today's 12-cylinder engine using the same production methods. A further development of the Jumo 222 can be created in the longer term as a six-row radial engine with a starting power of over 4,000hp.

"The engine is absolutely sound in its basic structure and should not have any more teething problems than any other new model, but it is very likely that it will perform better on the basis of the previously conducted tests. The increase in output to 3,000hp aimed at by Junkers is considered achievable. Dr Werner [Dr William Werner was technical director of Auto Union and an industry consultant/troubleshooter working for Albert Speer's war production ministry] reports that the number of pieces is of decisive importance for production. About 700 engines could be built in Magdeburg. However, this means that the Mimo programme has to be increased from 700 to 900 Jumo 213 engines. The production costs here are around 25% higher than for the 12-cylinder engine. The question of series production must be decided as soon as possible, since the machine tools are not available to the required extent."

On the basis that it was absolutely essential not only for the ailing Bomber B programme and possibly also for the Ju 188 and He 177, Generalfeldmarschall Erhard Milch, head of the Air Ministry and in charge of procurement for the Luftwaffe,

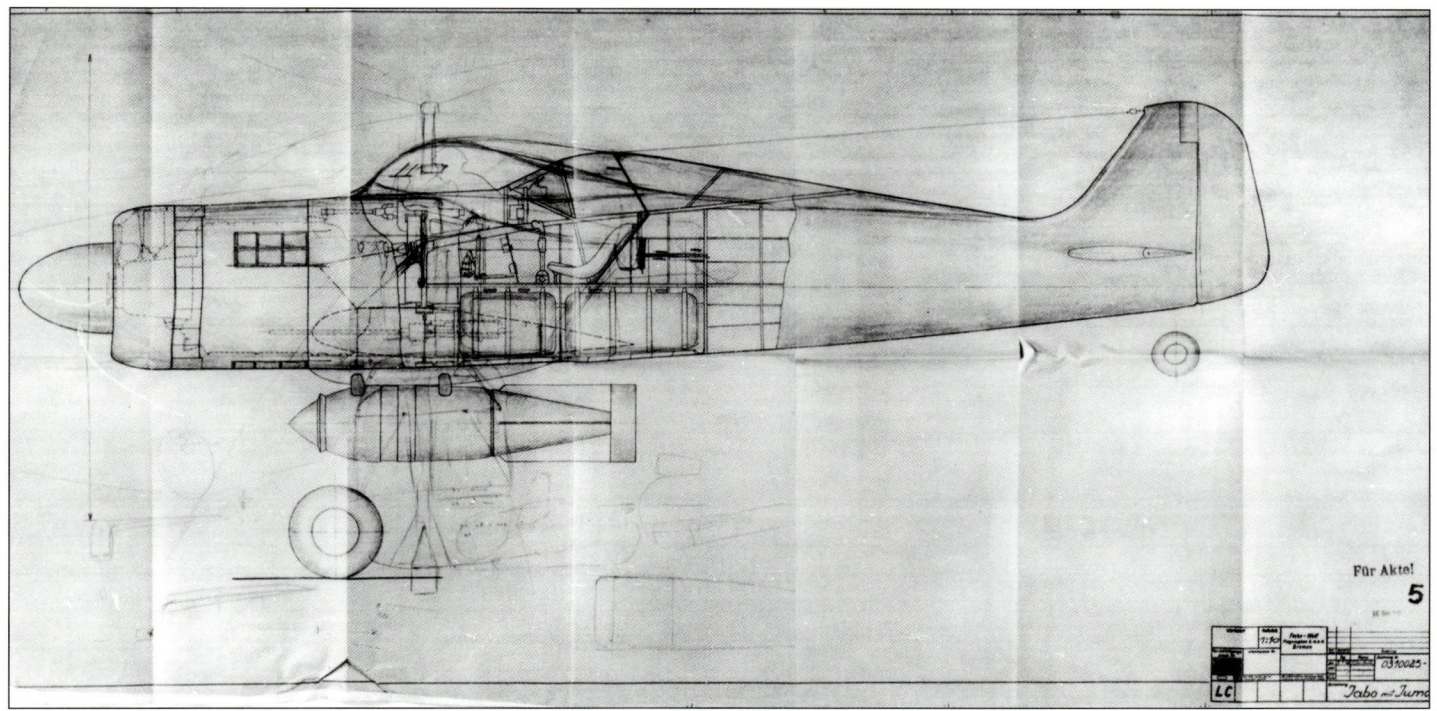

ABOVE: Focke-Wulf revisited plans for a Jumo 222 powered single-seater in July 1942, drawing number 0310 025-553 depicting a 222-powered fighter-bomber or 'Jabo'. Bizarrely, and for reasons unknown, this particular version has been overdrawn to show a prone pilot using a periscope!

"ordered the series production of the Jumo 222".

FORWARD-SWEPT -564

In July 1942 – 11 months after the publication of the report which detailed the Einsitzer mit Jumo 222 – Focke-Wulf engineers began examining work conducted on swept-wing designs by aerodynamicists Albert Betz and Adolf Busemann.

According to a company report dated November 4, 1942, "with currently flown and future expected flight speeds, we are approaching the speed of sound and thus the areas in which the compressibility of the air affects the properties of the wing. First and foremost, when the critical speed is exceeded, there is an increase in drag and a shift in the pressure point. With large Mach numbers, compression shocks occur, which first extend locally and later over the

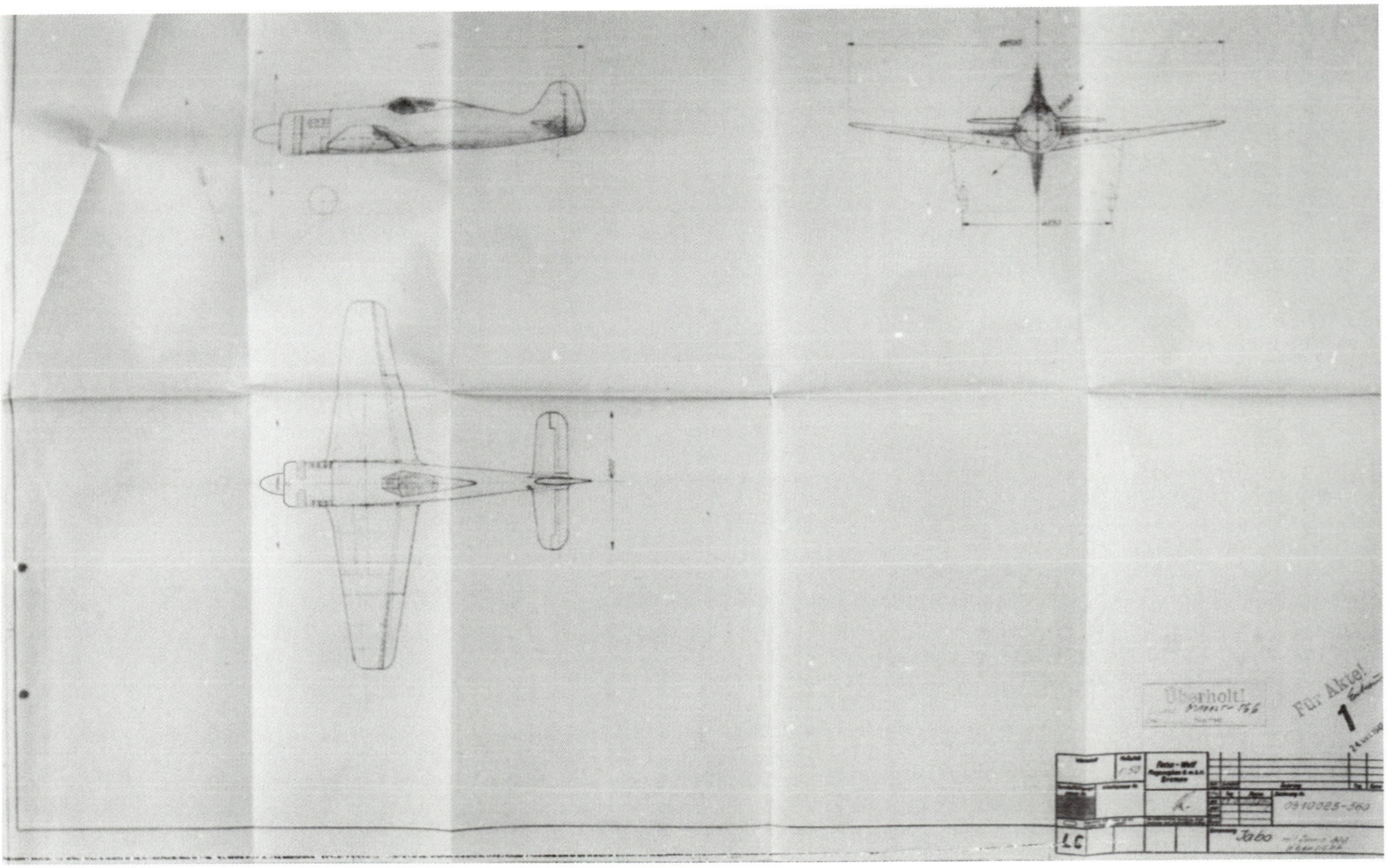

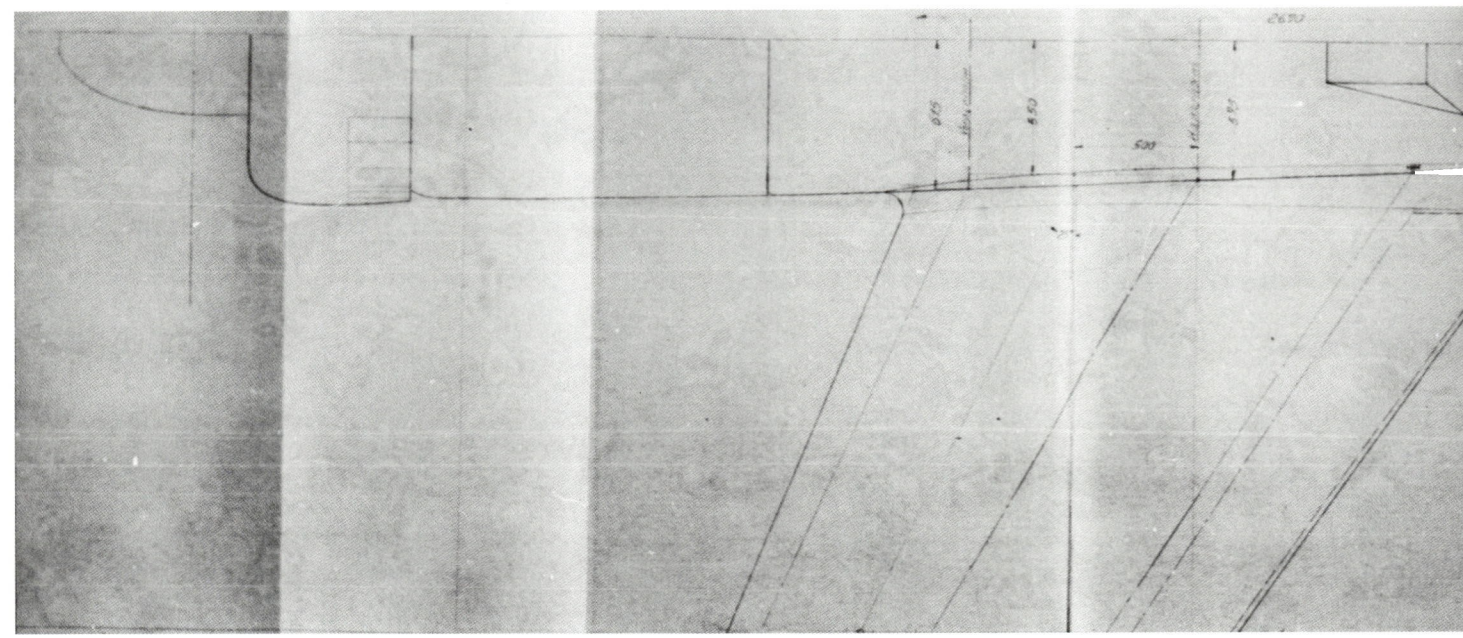

ABOVE: Focke-Wulf design for a Jumo 222-powered fighter-bomber or 'Jabo' from drawing number 0310 025-560, later refined in drawing number 0310 025-566. Oddly, only six exhaust stubs are depicted when the 222 would usually require eight.

ABOVE: Focke-Wulf drawing 0310 025-564 is surely one of the oddest Fw 190-like aircraft designs ever created – with a Jumo 222 engine up front and both forward-swept wings and tailplanes.

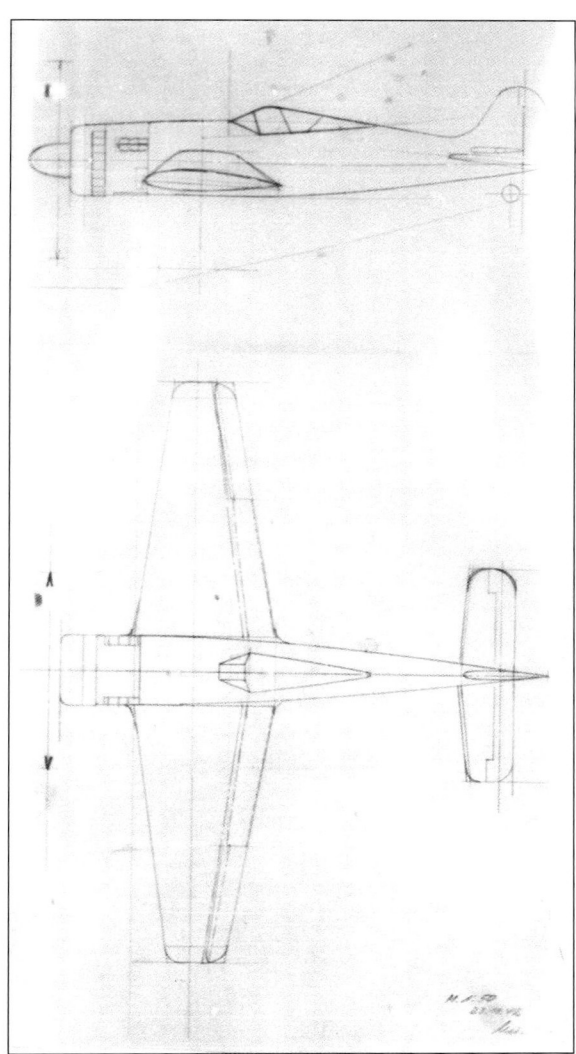

ABOVE: Sketch showing two parts of a three-view dated November 23, 1942. It would appear that this was the basis for the otherwise missing 0310 025-566 of November 29, 1942.

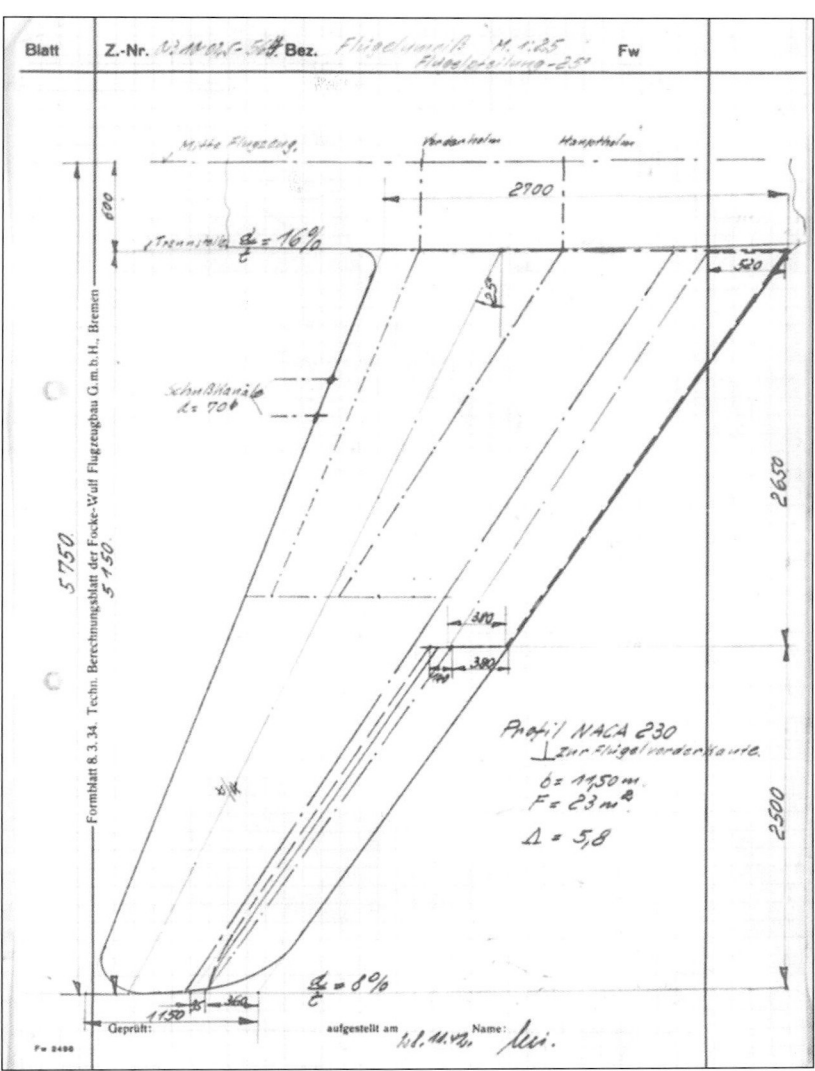

ABOVE: The 25-degree forward-swept wing design associated with the aircraft depicted in drawing 0310 025-564.

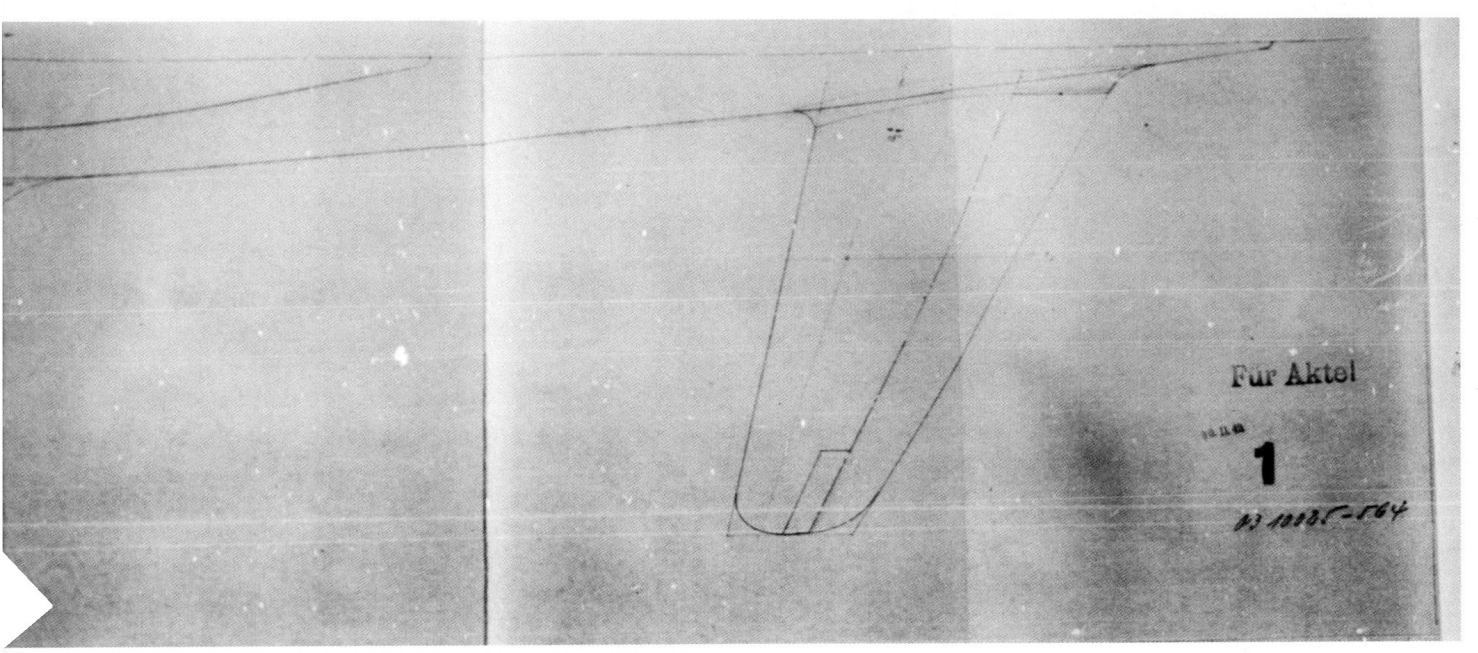

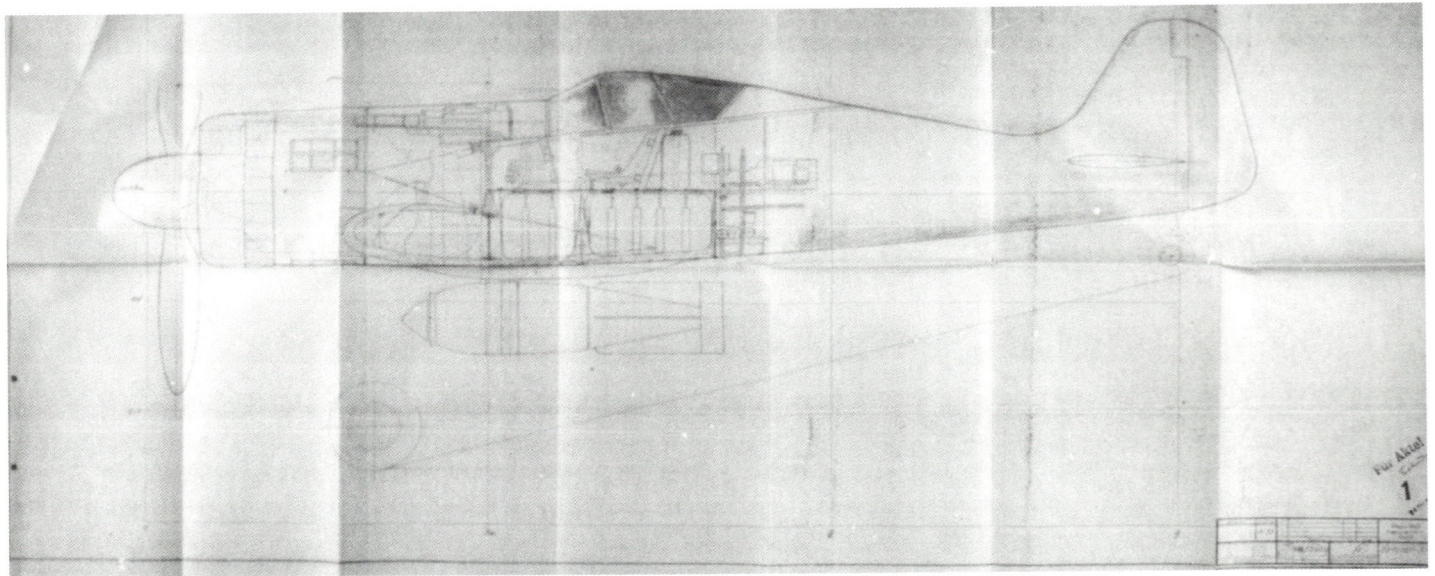

ABOVE: Unfortunately somewhat indistinct, this drawing is 0310 025-557 and was featured in Focke-Wulf's November 29, 1942 report on straight- and swept-wing Jumo 222 fighter designs.

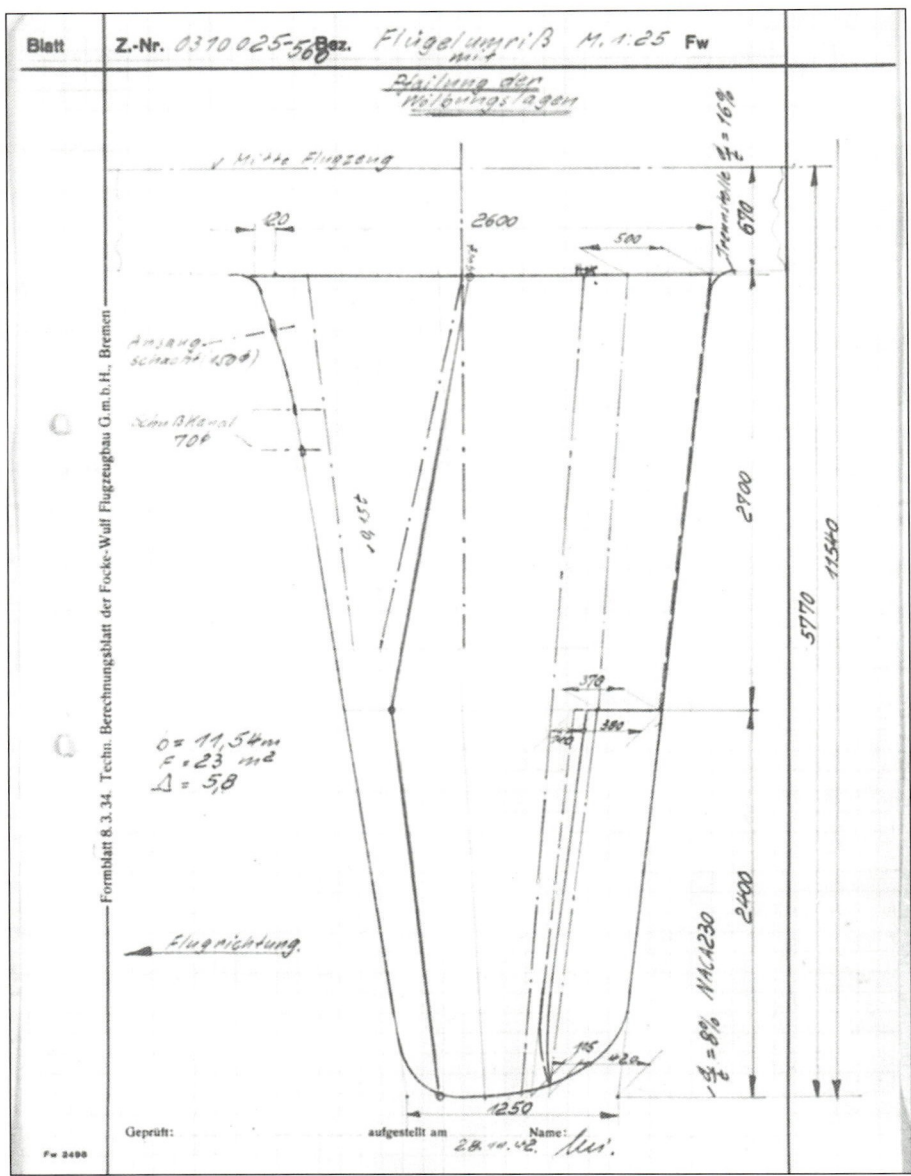

ABOVE: The straight wing design associated with the aircraft depicted in drawing 0310 025-566.

entire velocity field of the wing, causing complete detachment."

Measures outlined to increase the critical Mach number – delaying the onset of compressibility effects – included wing sweep, changing the wing thickness and changing the wing profile shape. It was noted that according to Betz and Busemann, a 45-degree forward swept wing would be almost as effective as the same degree of sweepback.

Subsequently, two different Jumo 222-powered fighters were designed; both with the same wing area (23sqm) and nearly the same wingspan, but while one had straight wings similar to those of the Fw 190 but thinner (wingspan 11.54m), the other had its wings swept forward by 25 degrees (wingspan 11.5m). The straight wing fighter appeared in drawings 0310 025-566 and -557, while the latter appeared in drawings 0310 025-564 and -563. Focke-Wulf, with its usual rather arcane and somewhat inconsistent naming convention for projects, referred to them as 'Jäger mit Jumo 222 Entwurf 0310025-566' and 'Jäger mit Jumo 222 Entwurf 0310025-564'.

The reason for sweeping the wings forward rather than back on -564 was "for reasons of centre of gravity". It was noted that the straight-wing design exceeded its critical Mach number at its peak calculated performance of 750km/h at 6.8km altitude – but it could carry a 1,000kg bomb beneath its fuselage.

With forward-swept wings, the critical Mach number was increased by 5-5.5% but the possible under-fuselage bomb load was reduced to 250-500kg "due to the clearance of the undercarriage and flight mechanics".

The report detailing these two designs was dated November 29, 1942.

JAGDFLUGZEUG MIT JUMO 222 C/D

More than three months then passed with apparently no further work being

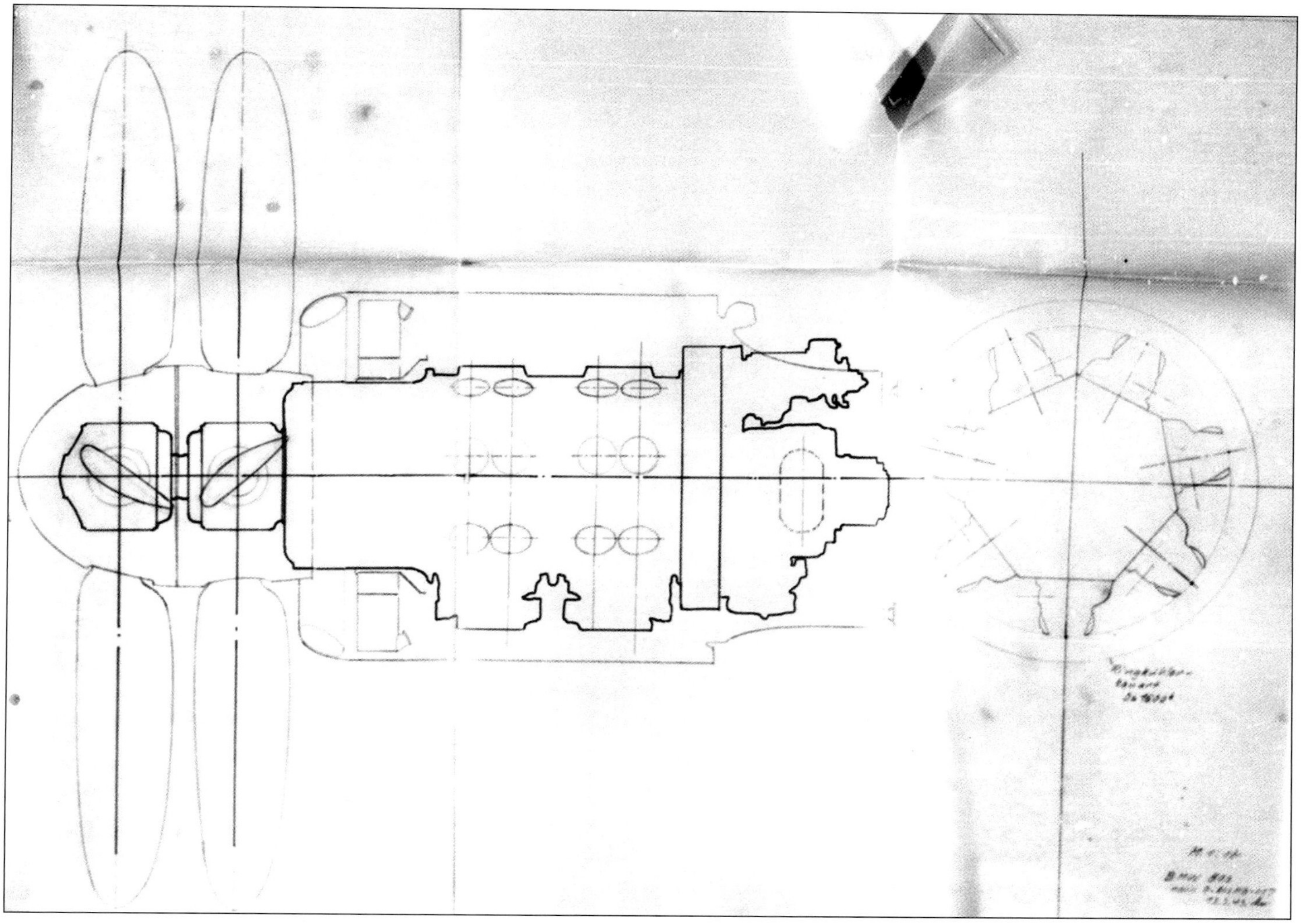

ABOVE: This Focke-Wulf drawing from March 13, 1943, illustrates the basic shape of the BMW 803 and its contra-rotating propellers when installed in a regular tractor-position engine nacelle.

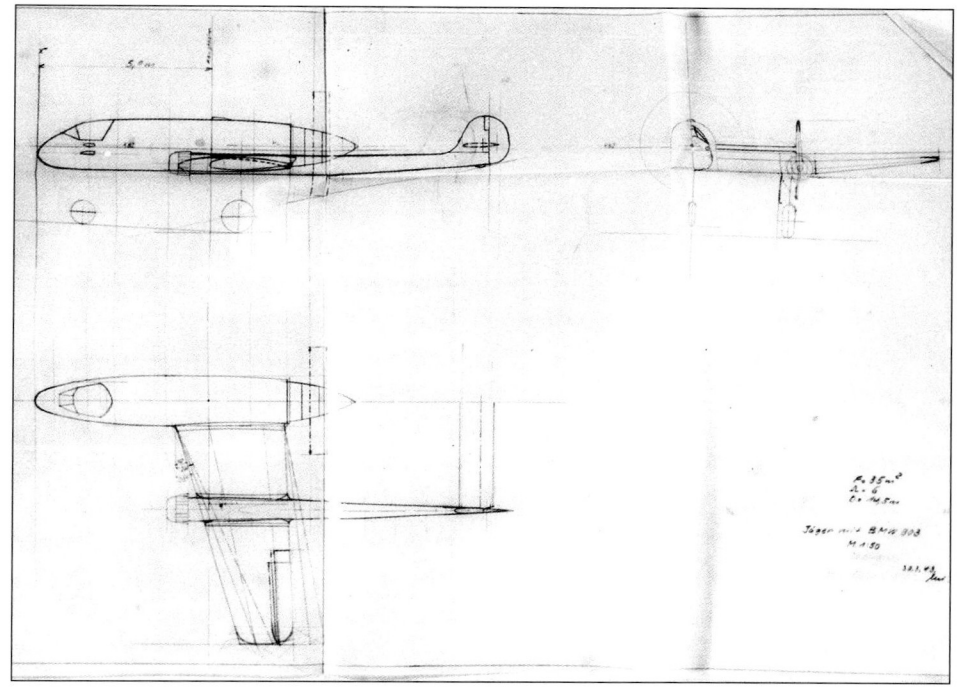

ABOVE: Preliminary design work showing the old Einsitzer mit BMW 803 modified to incorporate annular radiators at the forward tips of its booms – rather than having them positioned within the fuselage. The sketch is dated March 30, 1943.

done on any Jumo 222-powered fighter at Focke-Wulf. The German Air Ministry, however, was evidently keen to utilise the 222 as a fighter engine. A meeting was arranged between Ministry Technical Office engineers and staff from Junkers' piston engine development arm, Otto Mader Werke (OMW), on January 26, 1943, at which OMW was asked to work out how the 222 could be used as the basis of a single-engine fighter.

The resulting investigation was carried out with Focke-Wulf as consultant and a report was published on March 5, 1943, which discussed the "Jumo 222 as a fighter and destroyer engine". One key question was the propeller. OMW looked at three options: four-blade, five-blade or two counter-rotating three blade propellers. But the report noted that "from the side of the airframe manufacturer, a counter-rotating propelled is not considered absolutely necessary for this performance (2,500hp). On the propeller side, this knowledge is of great advantage, since the development of a counter-rotating propeller takes too long. Thus only the four- and five-blade propeller options remain".

It wouldn't be possible to install a motor-cannon on the 222, firing through the propeller hub, so there was then a question

Secret Projects of the Luftwaffe 13

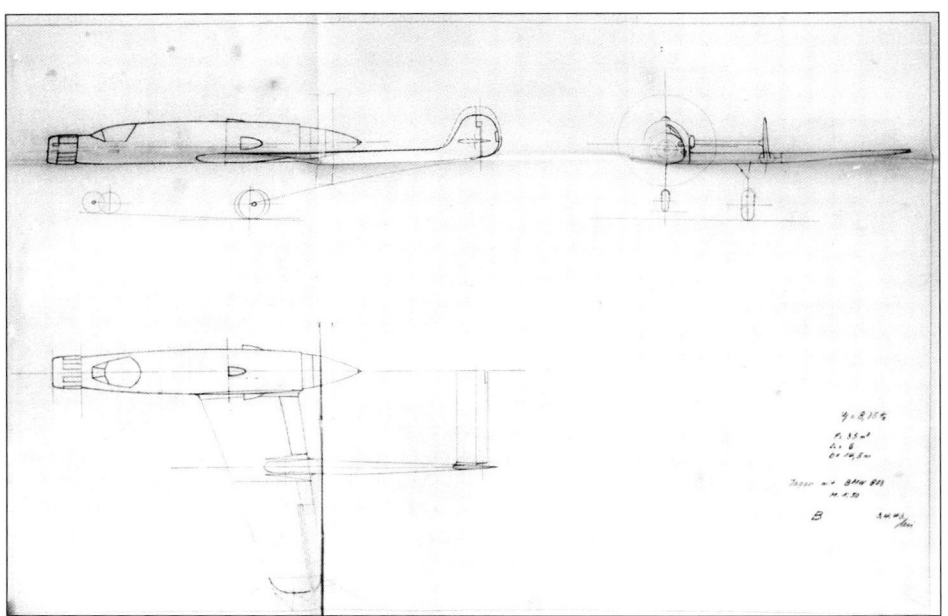

ABOVE: The alternative to using two annular radiators on the Einsitzer mit BMW 803's booms was to use a single large radiator positioned on the aircraft's nose. This resulted in a rather grotesque look for the aircraft but presumably saved on pipework. The date of this sketch is April 3, 1943.

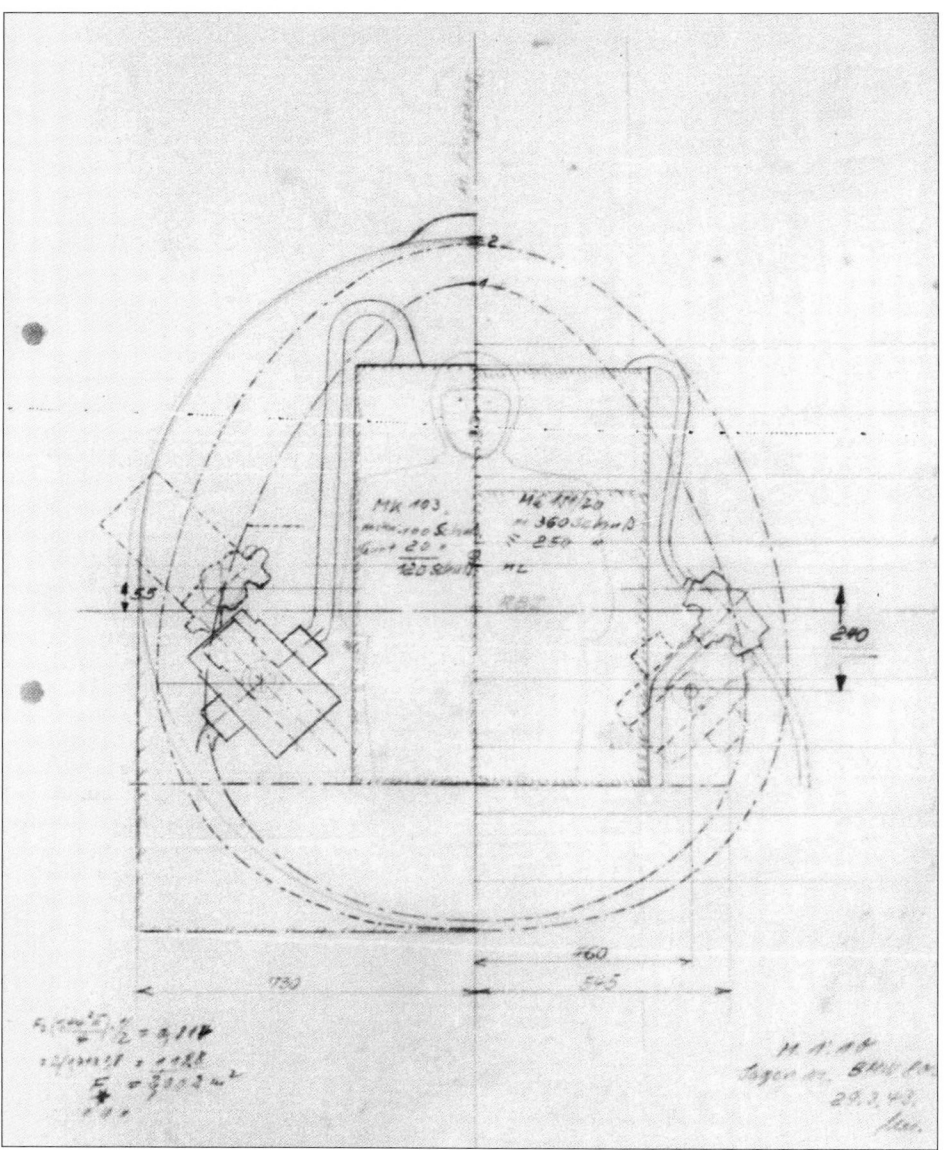

as to which and how many weapons could be synchronised to fire through the blades. Options included four MG 151s and two MG 131 or four MG 151s and two MG 17s. Perhaps surprisingly, calculations showed that it was easier to shoot through two counter-rotating three-bladed propellers than it was through a normal four- or five-bladed propeller.

Lastly, it was clear why the 222 had disappeared from Focke-Wulf's considerations. The OMW report notes: "Focke-Wulf has meanwhile commented on this project in a report dated February 23, 1943, and has come to the conclusion that the performance of the Jumo 222 A/B-1 is too unfavourable if the same is compared with the 213 B and 801 F, each with 2,000hp. By way of comparison, top speed for the Fw 190 with 801 F = 710km/h at 7km altitude. Top speed with 222 A = 700km/h at 6.5km altitude.

"With 222 A, the climb time over 10km is approx. 15% and the wing loading is approx. 12% higher than with the 801 F, although a slightly stronger armament is possible compared to the 801 F version."

That said, Focke-Wulf still produced a new report on March 8 entitled Kurzbeschreibung Nr. 05 Jagdflugzeug mit Jumo 222 C/D. This basically described the Jäger mit Jumo 222 Entwurf 0310 025-566 design again, but in more detail. Wingspan and wing area remained the same – indeed, the same two drawings were included again. The aircraft would be armed with two MG 151/20s in its fuselage and four more in its wingroots; fuel would be held in two armoured fuselage tanks of 330 and 415 litre capacity; 62kg of armour would be installed; a single 1,000kg bomb could be carried under the fuselage. It was lastly noted that the aircraft would need new 800 x 200mm wheels with a load capacity of 2,500kg each. Existing Fw 190 mainwheels were 700 x 175mm.

On March 10, four different iterations of the Jumo 222 fighter were set out. Two were based on the standard Fw 190 airframe (Fw 190 mit Jumo 222 A and Fw 190 mit Jumo 222 C) while the others were based on the Jäger mit Jumo 222 Entwurf 0310 025-566 design (Jäger mit Jumo 222 A and Jäger mit Jumo 222 C).

The Jumo 222-powered 190s were each 1m longer than the standard 190 at 9.95m but their wingspan remained the standard 10.5m. The 222's 3.4m diameter propeller would have four blades and armament was two MG 131s in the fuselage plus two MG 151s in the wing roots in both cases. The 222 C-powered Fw 190 was expected to offer the best performance – 740km/h at an altitude of 6.9km.

The Jäger mit Jumo 222 Entwurf 0310025-566-based designs were slightly different from one another. The Jäger mit Jumo 222 A had the 9.95m long fuselage while the Jäger mit Jumo 222 C was 15cm longer.

LEFT: A sketch from March 29, 1943, showing the cramped interior of the Einsitzer mit BMW 803 fighter's cockpit with cannon on either side. This was presumably to work out whether the proposed armament would actually fit.

Both aircraft retained the original design's wingspan of 11.54m. The 222's propeller would now be 3.9m in diameter but would still have four blades. The advantage of employing an entirely new airframe was that six guns could be accommodated rather than four – all of the MG 151s. This time no bomb is mentioned. Peak performance of 725km/h was achieved by the Jäger mit Jumo 222 C at 6.9km altitude.

JAGDFLUGZEUG MIT BMW 803

The Jumo 222 studies appear to have gone no further at this stage, but in March 1943, the Focke-Wulf design team instead went all the way back to the twin-boom pusher-prop Einsitzer mit BMW 803 design, shown in drawings 0310 207-02 and 0310 207-04 from June 1941 – some 21 months earlier.

Exactly why this design was revisited at this time is unclear, but Focke-Wulf nevertheless spent several weeks refining two updated variants under the slightly amended title Jagdflugzeug mit BMW 803. These appeared in drawings 0310 231-04 A and -02 A, and in 0310 231-04 B and -02 B.

Both had the same basic dimensions: wing area 40sqm, wingspan 15.5m, length 13.7m, height 4.75m and take-off weight 8,630kg. Armament was two MK 103s with 120 rounds plus two MG 151/20s with 300 rounds in the fuselage. Both had a pressure cabin with 180kg of armour.

This made them slightly bigger and significantly heavier than the Einsitzer mit BMW 803 of 1941, which as noted earlier had a wing area of 35sqm, wingspan of 13.2m, length of 13.8m, height of 3.2m and take-off weight of 7,500kg. Armament had been four MG 151/20s with 400 rounds.

There were other physical differences too – the extra height was a result of the two new designs having taller undercarriage legs. And where the Einsitzer had had its wings set slightly higher, with the tail booms correspondingly higher and with rounded tailfins high-set interconnecting tailplane, the Jagdflugzeug designs had low-set wings, lowering the tail booms, with more conventional-looking tail fins and a tailplane set much lower – so that it was directly opposite the tip of the pusher-prop's spinner, rather than being set above it.

The most striking physical difference, however, concerned the radiator arrangement. Where the Einsitzer had had a central radiator fed by air from

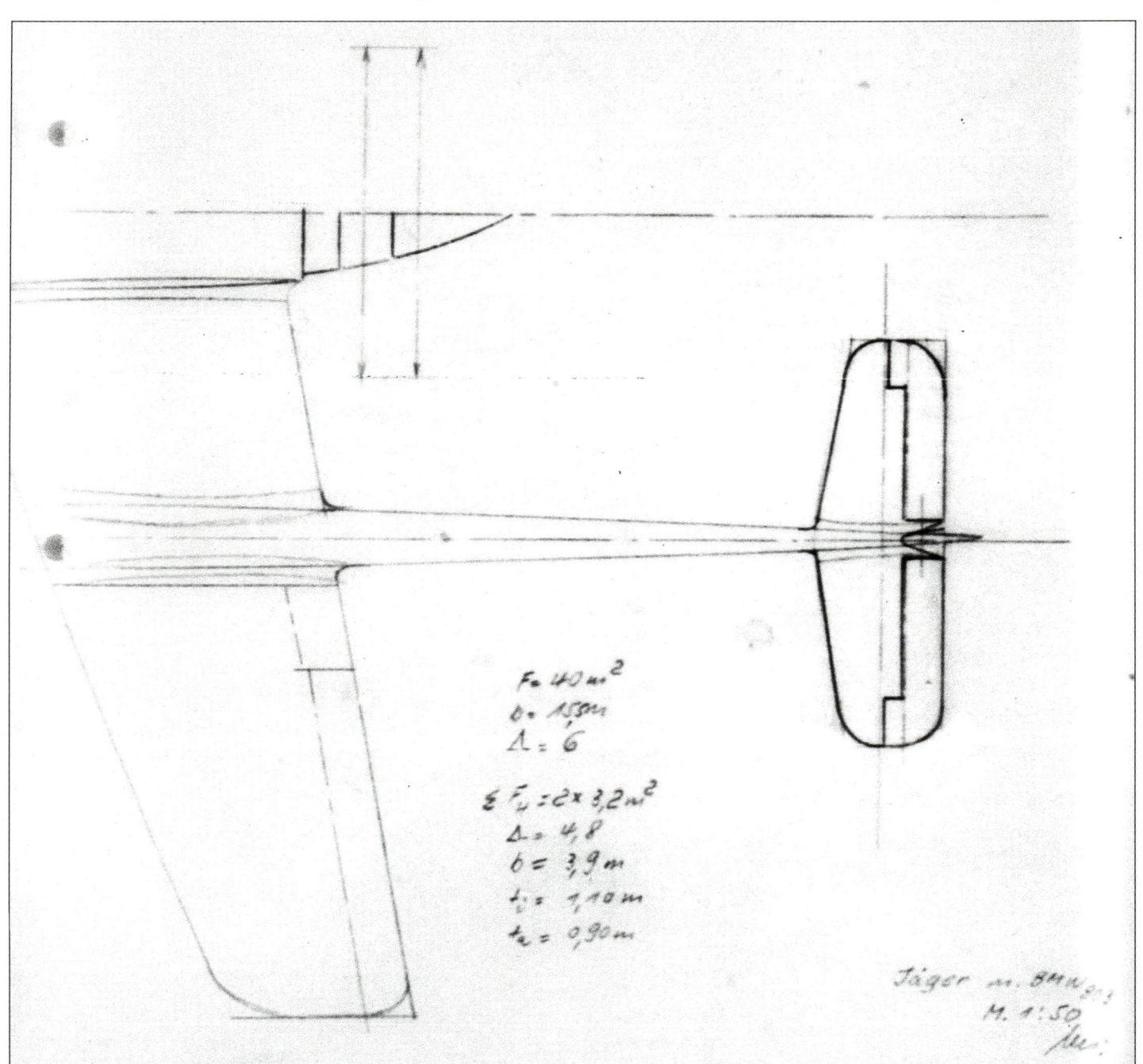

ABOVE: Undated sketch showing work on an unconnected twin boom arrangement for the BMW 803-powered fighter.

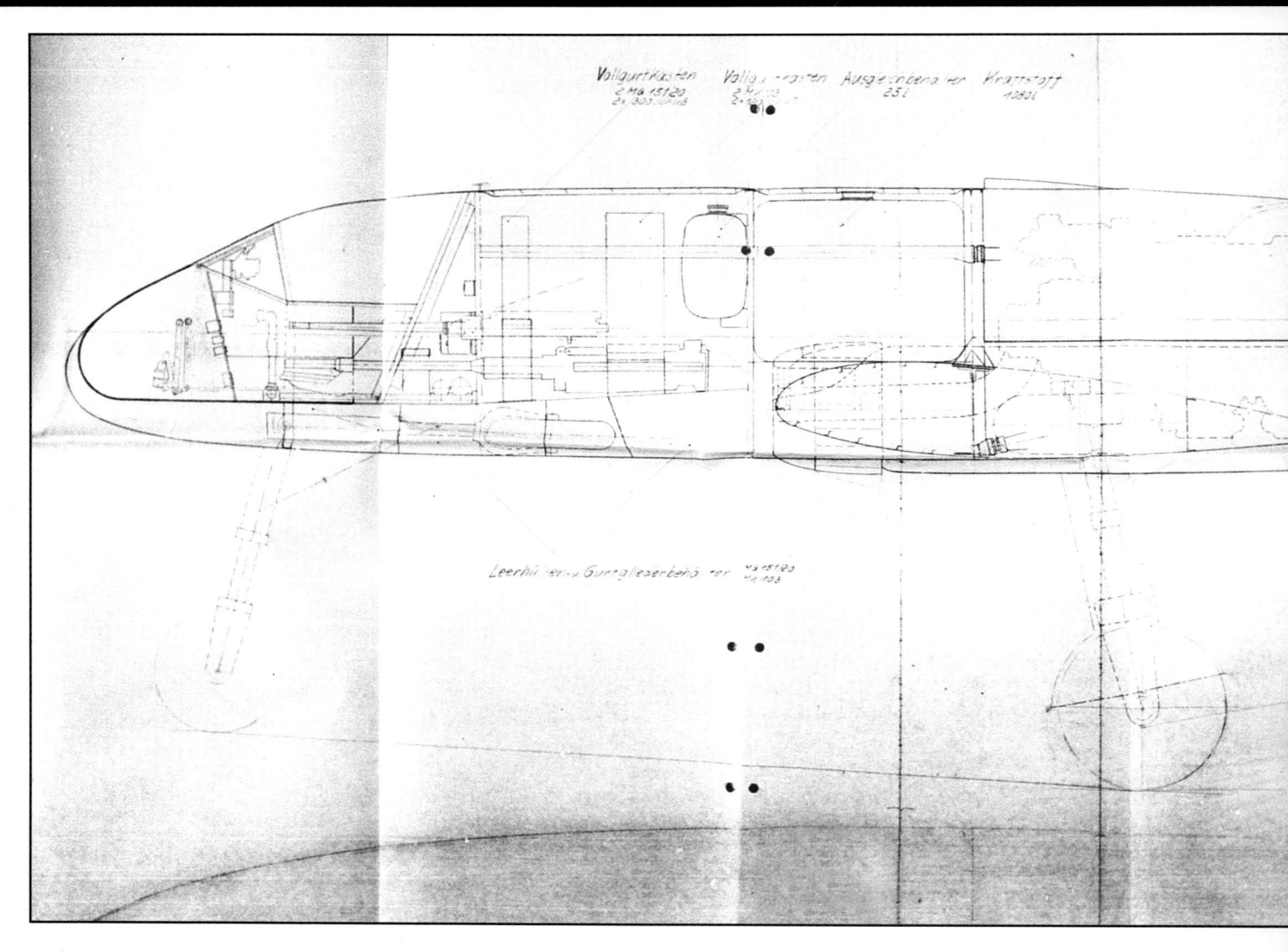

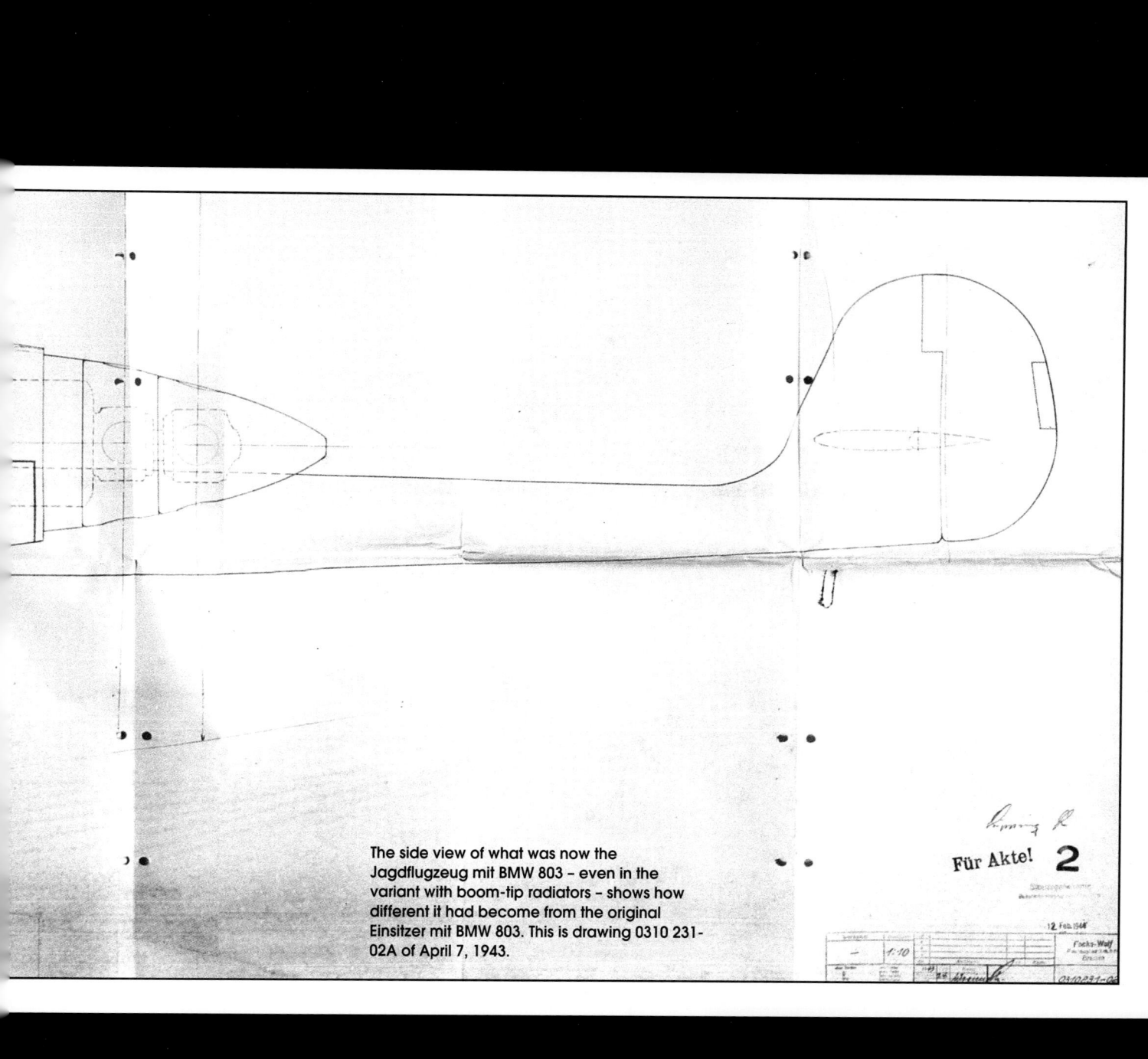

The side view of what was now the Jagdflugzeug mit BMW 803 – even in the variant with boom-tip radiators – shows how different it had become from the original Einsitzer mit BMW 803. This is drawing 0310 231-02A of April 7, 1943.

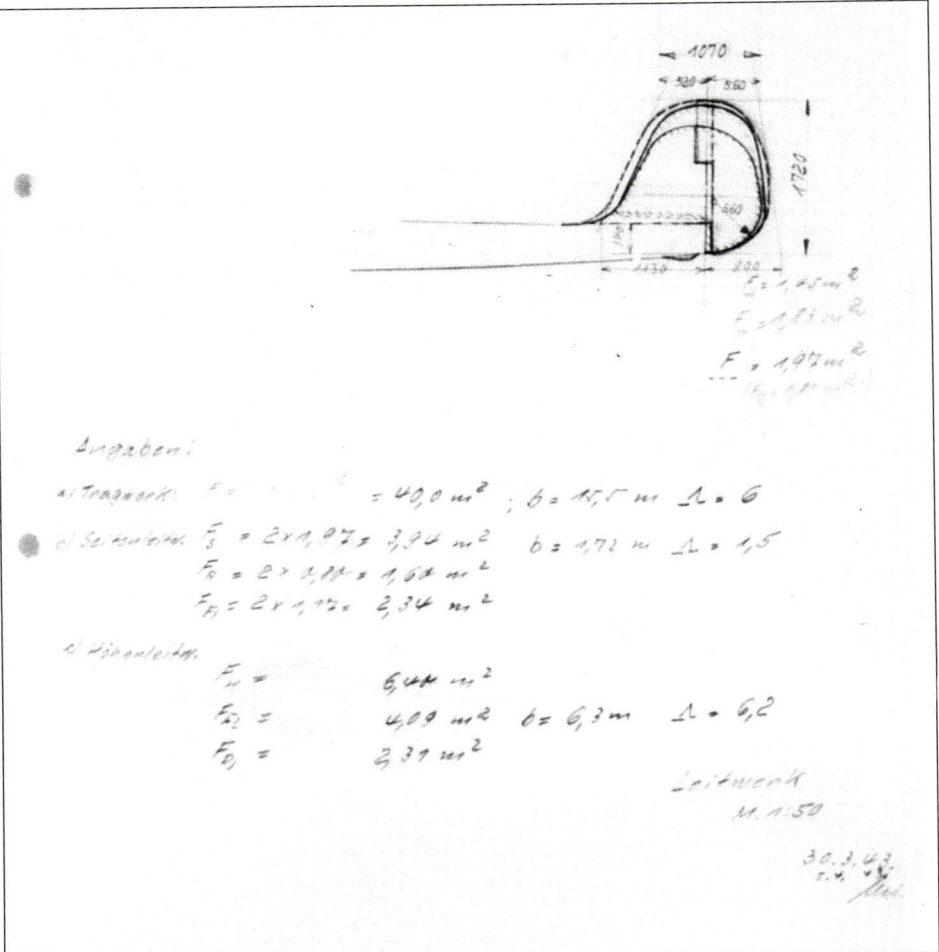

ABOVE: Now that the Einsitzer mit BMW 803 was being worked through as though it could become an actual aircraft, rather than a mere design study, considerations such as fin size came under scrutiny, as this sketch from March 30, revised on April 5, 1943, shows.

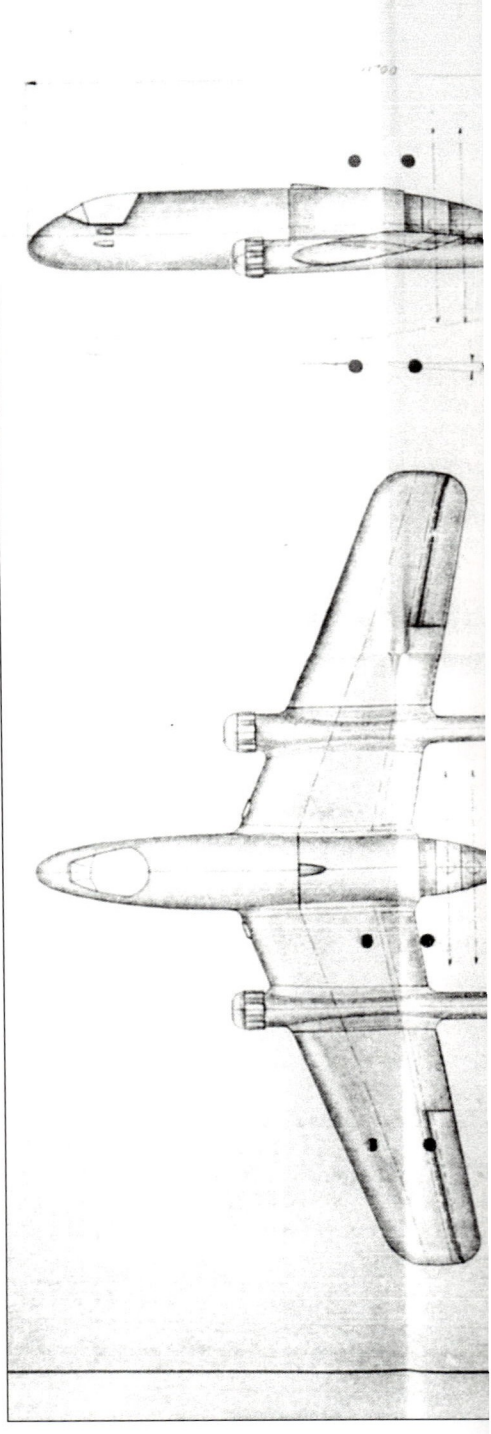

mid-fuselage upper and lower inlets, the Jagdflugzeug designs each showcased a different approach. The 0310 231-04 A and -02 A design had tail booms which extended all the way forward to the wing leading edge – and protruding from the tip of each boom was an small annular radiator. The 0310 231-04 B and -02 B design, on the other hand, featured a single large annular radiator on the nose of the central fuselage pod – a feature which certainly did nothing to enhance the aircraft's looks.

The two new designs were outlined in a report entitled Kurzbeschreibung Nr. 08 Jagdflugzeug mit BMW 803 dated April 9, 1943. Even this was not quite the end – the nose-radiator variant was revisited briefly on June 30, 1943, with a further set of diagrams and calculations being production. This, though appears to have been the last gasp of the BMW 803-powered fighter.

REWRITING THE PAST

As before, nothing seems to have come of Focke-Wulf's studies but the notion of a single-seat fighter powered by a Jumo 222 resurfaced yet again in October 1943.

Focke-Wulf produced something which purported to be a "Nachtrag zur Baubeschreibung Nr. 05 vom 22.10.43" – an addendum to the Kurzbeschreibung Nr. 05 from March 1943. The pages were still dated March 8, 1943, just like those of the original, but the title had been subtly changed from Kurzbeschreibung Nr. 05 Jagdflugzeug mit Jumo 222 C/D to Kurzbaubeschreibung Nr. 05 Fw 190 mit Jumo 222 C/D. The drawings that had originally accompanied the report (0310 025-566 and -557) were gone – replaced with the all-new 0310 228-04 and -05.

The October version of the report now also included a "statement on the installation of the Jumo 222 in the Fw 190 fighter plane" which said: "Research carried out at Fw [in referring to their own company, Focke-Wulf staff generally used 'Fw' rather than the more logical 'FW' – external agencies referring to the company using both versions interchangeably] has shown that it is possible to install the Jumo 222 engine in the Fw 190 C airframe. The required modification effort extends to undercarriage changes and reinforcements in the fuselage front section, as well as the installation of about 115kg of ballast in the rear fuselage.

"The installation of the Jumo 222 in the Fw 190 aircraft not only provides the opportunity to quickly test the airworthiness of the engine under fighter flight conditions, but also represents the final stage in the performance development of the Fw 190 as a fighter aircraft, although armament cannot be improved. The performance calculation shows that the Jumo 222 engine in fighters is only superior to the well-known BMW 801,

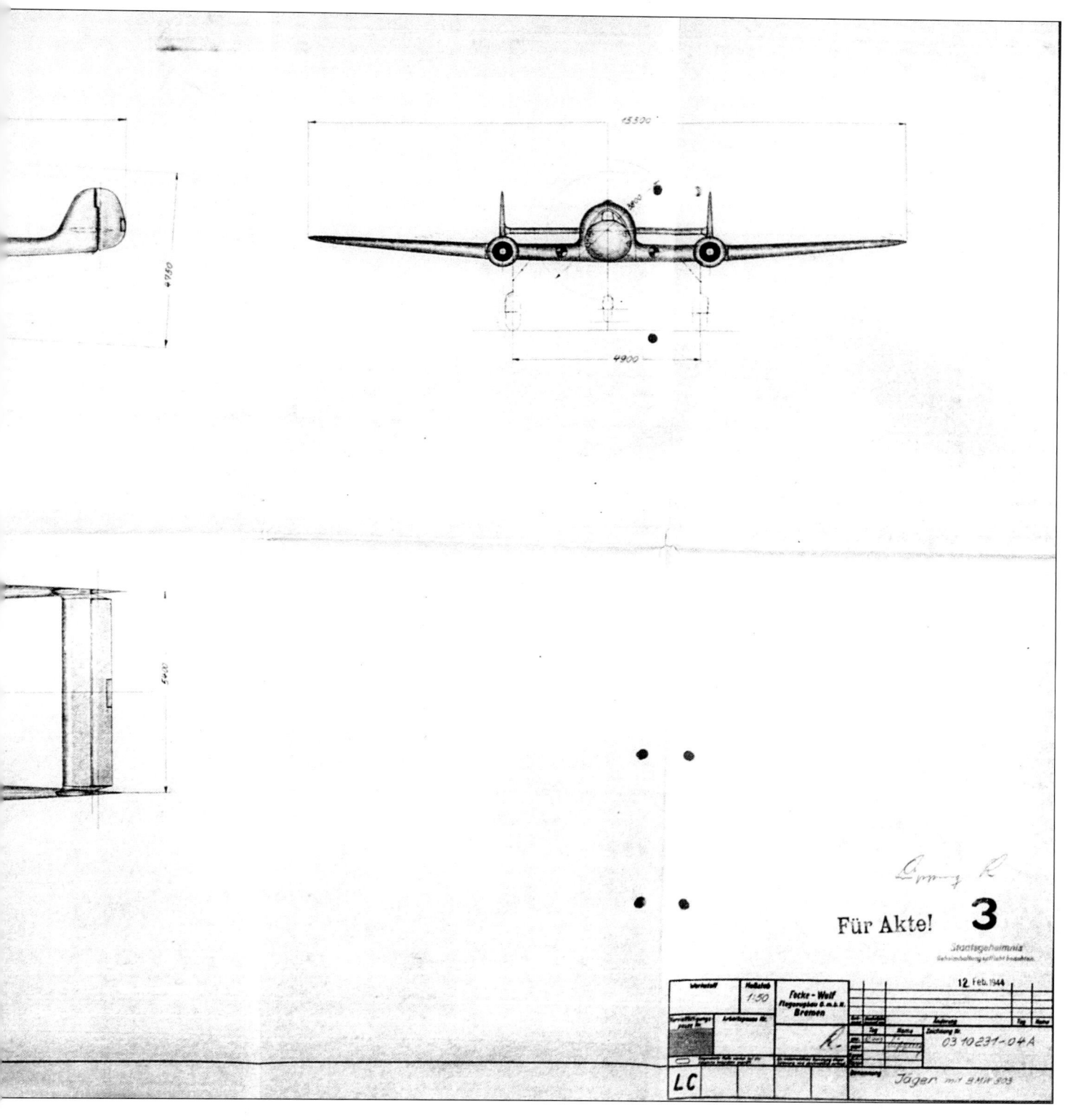

ABOVE: The final version of the revised Einsitzer mit BMW 803 design featuring boom-tip radiators. This is drawing 0310 231-04A as it appeared in the April 9, 1943, report Kurzbeschreibung Nr. 08 Jagdflugzeug mit BMW 803.

Jumo 213 and DB 603 engines if it comes with a take-off power of 3,000hp."

The Jumo 222-powered Fw 190 C was to have the standard Fw 190 A wingspan of 10.5m with wing area of 18.3sqm. Armament was two MG 131s in the fuselage with 300 rounds each plus two MG 151/20s in the wingroots with 250 rounds each. No fuselage length was given and neither of the images appears to have survived, so it is not entirely clear what this very late addition to the Fw 190 C family would have looked like. Take-off weight with the Jumo 222 engine included was 4,900kg, compared to the Fw 190 A-1's 3,770kg.

Even this additional flurry of activity seemingly had little impact and the Jumo 222-powered fighter concept would once again enter a period of dormancy lasting eight months. When it returned it would prompt a phase of even more frenetic activity and some even more outlandish aircraft designs – this time with competing designs from other companies in what would be called the Hochleistungs-Otto-Jäger competition. •

Secret Projects of the Luftwaffe 19

20 Secret Projects of the Luftwaffe

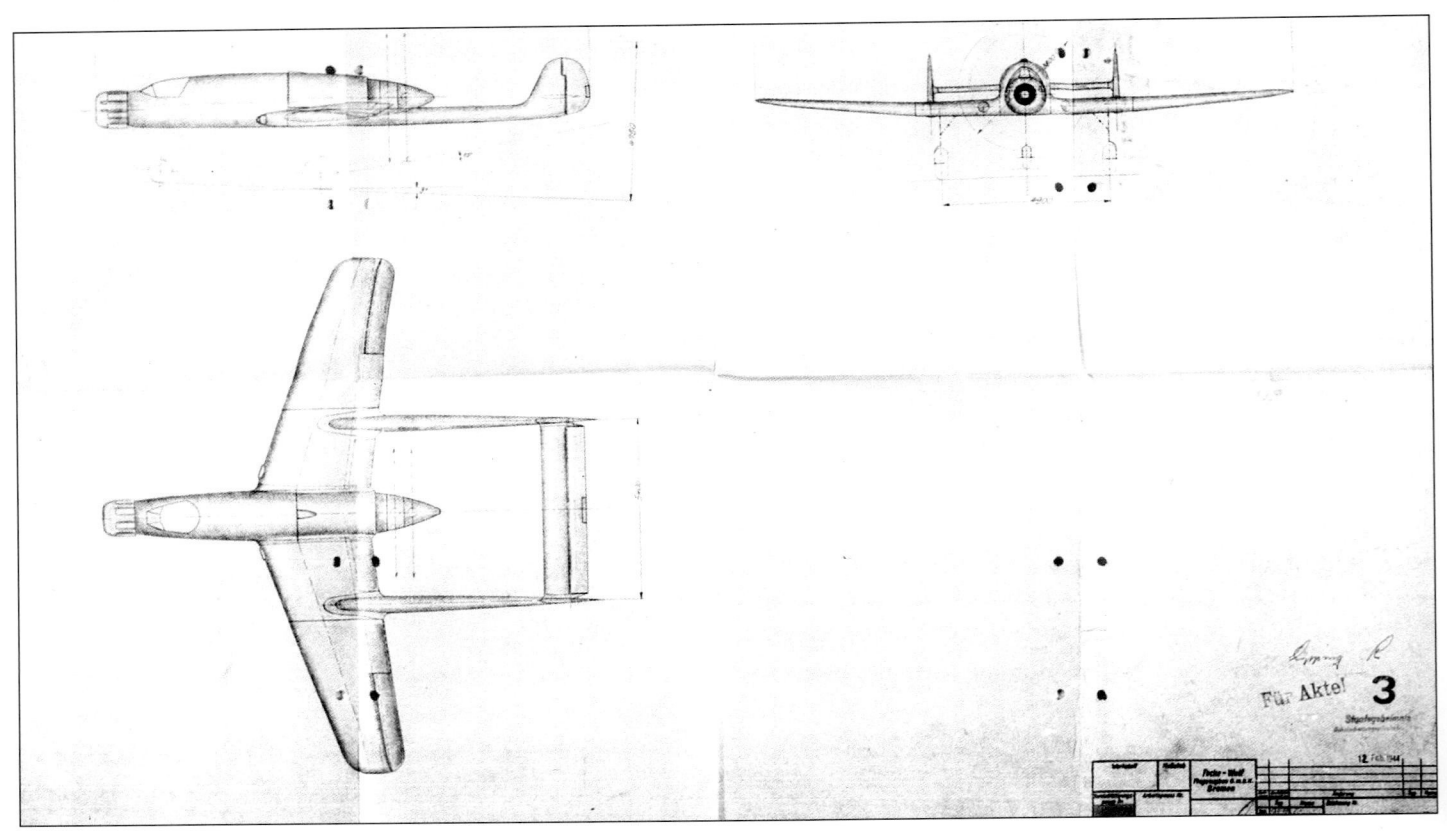

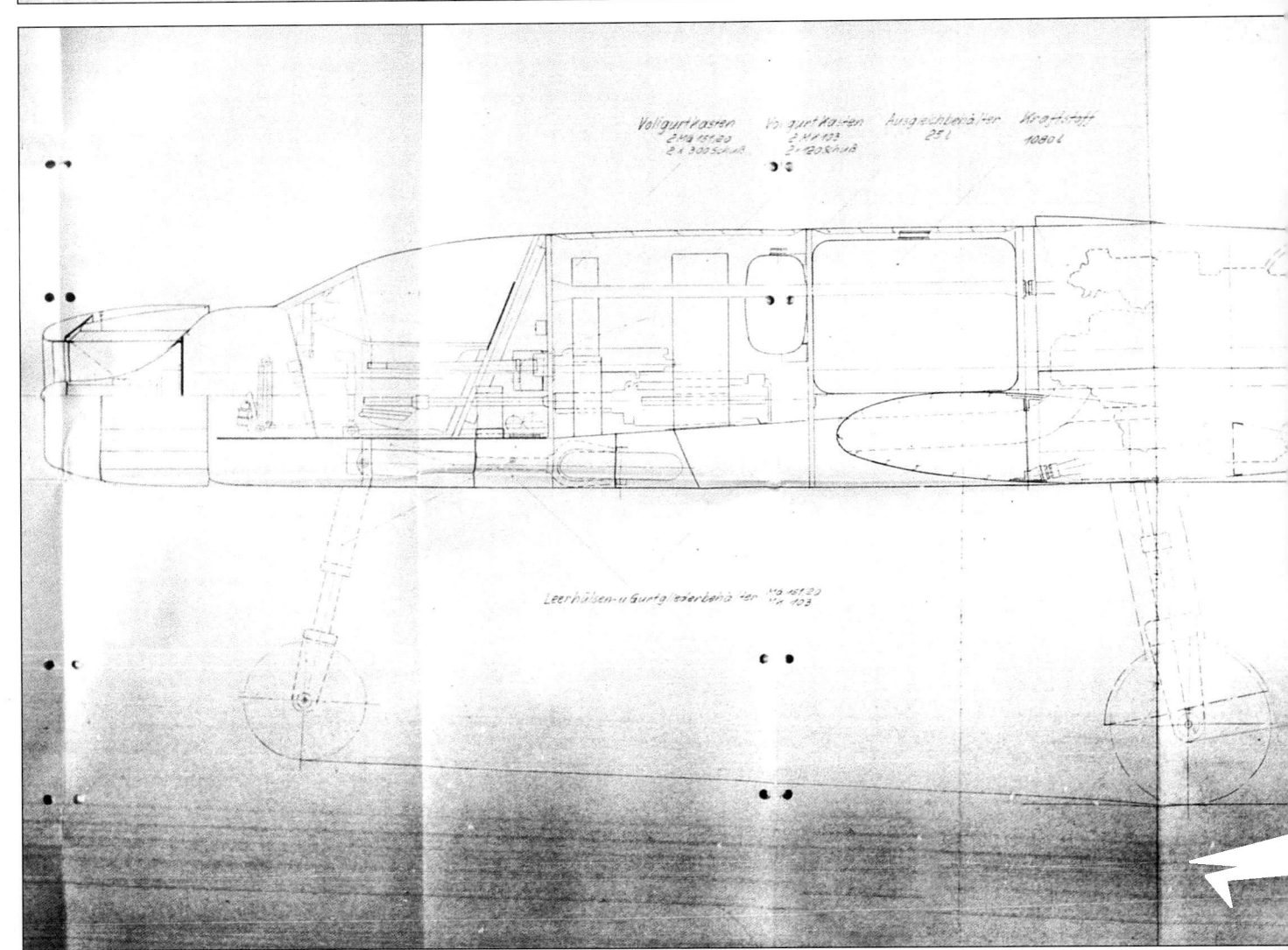

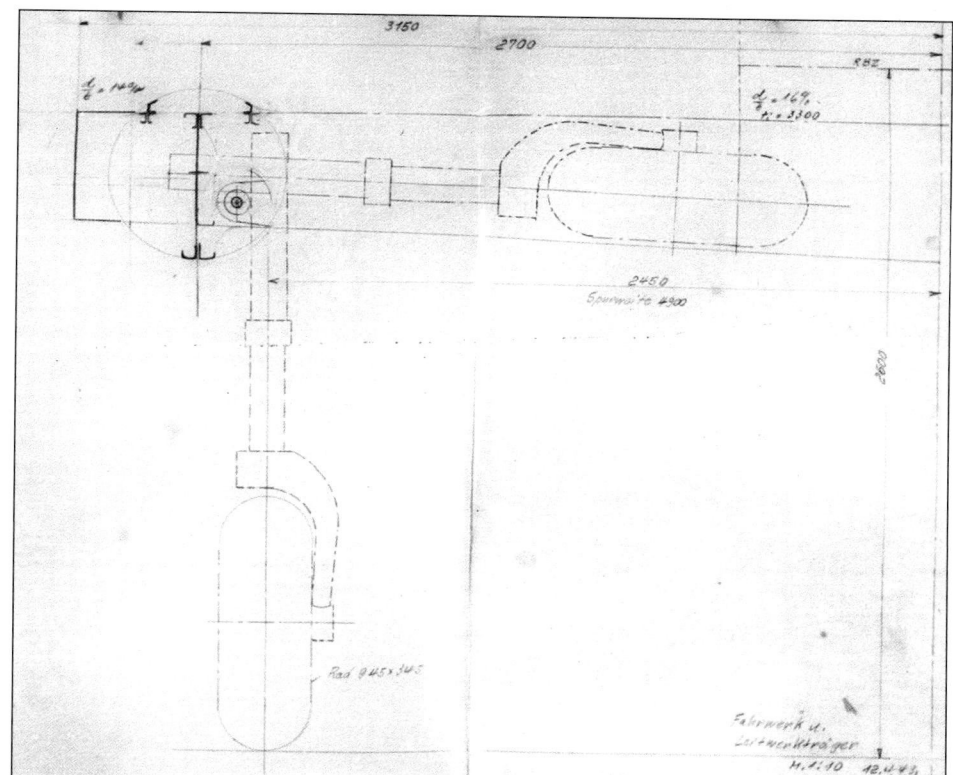

LEFT: The nose-radiator version of the BMW 803-powered fighter from Kurzbeschreibung Nr. 08, as shown in drawing number 0310 231-04B.

RIGHT: Three days after the publication of the Kurzbeschreibung Nr. 08 Jagdflugzeug mit BMW 803 report, on April 9, 1943, the Focke-Wulf was still clearing up details of the type's undercarriage retraction system as this April 12, 1943, sketch shows.

BELOW: Side view of the nose-radiator Jagdflugzeug mit BMW 803, in drawing number 0310 231-02B dated April 8, 1943.

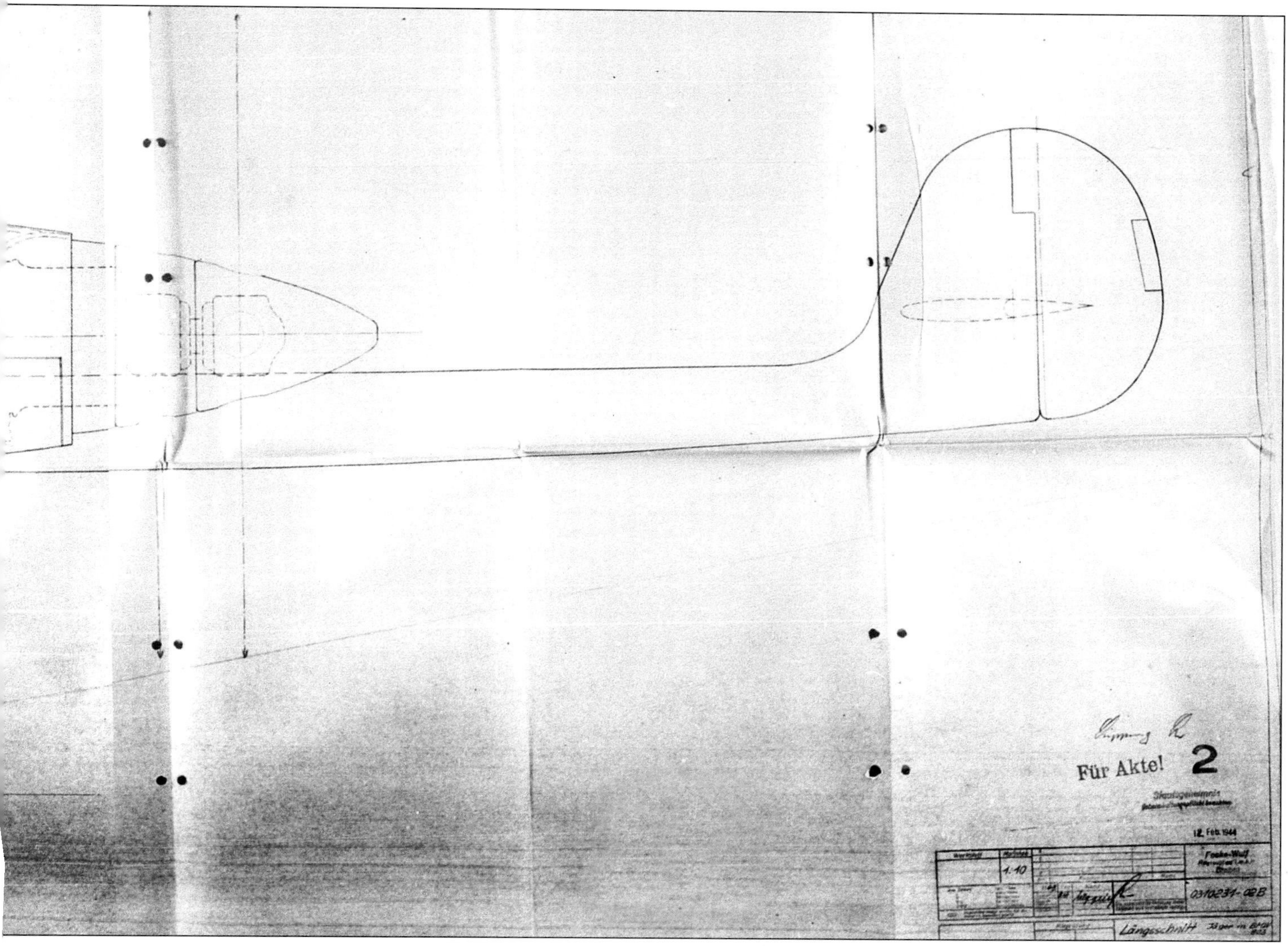

Manager's special

Focke-Wulf Fw 187 als Höhenjäger, Kampfzerstörer und Nachtjäger

Largely abandoned in 1939, the Fw 187 Falke fighter project was abruptly resuscitated three years later as a competitor for Heinkel's He 219. This unlikely revival had more to do with management machinations than good sense, however…

When it comes to chief executive officer succession planning, a strong internal candidate with the right vision and strategy for the organisation is usually best. They are already familiar with the organisation, its processes and its work and can pick up where their predecessor left off in a seamless transition.

The appointment of an external successor can create a difficult situation for both the new CEO themselves and the organisation they are now responsible for leading – particularly if they have arrived in the midst of a crisis. They may feel that they need to assert their authority as quickly and as forcefully as possible. They may also want to surround themselves with a new senior team who they themselves have hired, freezing out, reassigning or even dismissing experienced staff who may have valuable knowledge and insight concerning the organisation's situation.

Worse yet, they may feel that they know the organisation's business better than those experienced staff members and as a result may come up with – and enforce – new ideas which the experienced staff know have already been tried and have already proven unsuccessful.

First World War fighter ace and postwar airframe manufacturing company owner Ernst Udet had been head of the Air Ministry's Technical Office since February 1936 and Generalluftzeugmeister, head of procurement for the Luftwaffe, since February 1939. He had been deeply involved in the development of almost every aircraft type to see Luftwaffe service during the Second World War – in many cases being personally responsible for approving their entry into service. Highly successful types such as the Bf 109, Fw 190, Ju 88, Do 217, Ar 96, Fw 200 and Ju 90 went into mass production on his orders.

He was also responsible for overseeing the Me 210 and He 177 development programmes – both of which had gone disastrously wrong for technical and political reasons largely beyond his control, precipitating his suicide on November 17, 1941.

Erhard Milch had flown relatively briefly as an artillery observer during the First World War and had become a director at Junkers during the early 1920s, during which time he had provided financial and material support to political extremists Adolf Hitler and Hermann Göring. Consequently, he had been made Secretary of State for Aviation in May 1933 and then Luftwaffe Inspector General in February 1939. His oversight of

ABOVE: Generalfeldmarschall Erhard Milch was put in charge of procurement for the Luftwaffe in November 1941, following the suicide of his predecessor Ernst Udet. He arrived in-post at a time of crisis and with a determination to assert his authority.

ABOVE: One of just five Fw 187 A-0 two-seaters manufactured by Focke-Wulf during 1939. By 1942 standards it was grossly underpowered and far larger, heavier engines than the weedy 671hp Jumo 210 would be essential if the design was to be revived.

ABOVE: A pair of Fw 187 A-0s, Yellow 7 and Yellow 1, while in use by a Focke-Wulf 'factory protection squadron'. At least one Fw 187 was still flying by June 1942.

ABOVE: Pilot and radio operated seated in tandem, both facing forward, in an Fw 187 A-0. The type's slender fuselage lacked capacity to meet the Luftwaffe's operational demands.

German aviation, both civilian and military, was at a broad strategic level and he had no background in engineering to speak of.

On November 19, 1941, Göring appointed him as Udet's successor and plunged him into the highly complex nitty gritty of aircraft development and production.

Milch's first order of business was getting to grips with the Air Ministry and its work. As such, he took no real action before the beginning of 1942. His second task was attempting to sort out the Me 210 mess. Having begun to familiarise himself with the situation and taking advice from his supporters, he concluded that Willy Messerschmitt himself was the problem and had him removed as chairman of his own company. He simultaneously attempted to cancel the Me 210.

However, Messerschmitt had powerful friends and could not be removed entirely from the picture – and Milch's heavy-handed efforts only really succeeded in causing mayhem and discord within the Messerschmitt company which, as the manufacturer of the Bf 109 and Bf 110, was a critical component of the Luftwaffe's supply chain.

The Luftwaffe had wanted the Me 210 not only as a replacement for the aging Bf 110 heavy fighter [the German term was 'Zerstörer' – literally 'destroyer' – but the slightly more descriptive English equivalent term, heavy fighter, has been used throughout this publication] but to concurrently fulfil a variety of roles including low-level fast bomber, high-altitude fighter and night fighter. These conflicting requirements and the Luftwaffe's constant meddling, via the Air Ministry, in the Me 210's specification had been at least partly responsible for its dire problems.

And Milch's attempt to cancel it could not have come at a worse time. Willy Messerschmitt had, apparently personally, just come up with a design 'fix' which cured the worst of its problems – lengthening its rear fuselage for increased stability. The 210 also appeared eminently suitable as a platform for the new DB 603 engine, making it even more appealing from a performance perspective.

Once these factors were taken into account, Göring overturned Milch's cancellation and the Me 210 was allowed to proceed – eventually being redesignated Me 410, though it was still the same aircraft.

Milch reluctantly acknowledged that the Me 210 had been expected to fulfil too many roles and that more specialised designs might well be required to suit particular missions. Consequently, he set about commissioning designs for a new fast bomber from Me 163 designer Alexander Lippisch (technically a Messerschmitt employee, but Milch specifically gave the commission to Lippisch and his Department L team rather than the Messerschmitt company of which they were a part – causing further angst and unrest at Messerschmitt), Junkers, Blohm & Voss, Focke-Wulf, Heinkel and others in a competition known as 'Schnellstbomber' or 'Schnellbomber', more on which later.

That left the heavy fighter, high-altitude fighter and night fighter roles. Given developments in Britain and the US, it seemed by mid-1942 that the development of a high-altitude fighter was going to be a particularly tricky task in its own right and that the result might well need to be a specialised purpose-built machine.

This left the heavy fighter and night fighter roles. The primary candidates for these were the Me 210 itself, the old Bf 110 and Arado's Ar 240 – a competitor for the Me 210 which seemed to suffer from similar problems and to offer no tangible advantages over it. None of these options proved particularly appealing to the Luftwaffe, the Air Ministry or Milch himself.

However, another aircraft which had entered development under Udet was looking increasingly promising – Heinkel's He 219. This had been designed from the outset as a specialised night fighter and the question had arisen as to whether it might also cover the heavy fighter role. The Luftwaffe was so keen on the He 219, in fact, that it wanted to bypass the usual lengthy development process of prototypes and testing and rush it straight into series production instead. This was exactly what had happened with the Me 210 and the very thought of it appears to have horrified Milch.

He seems, therefore, to have come up with an alternative solution himself: bring back the Fw 187 and build that as a heavy fighter and night fighter instead. The prototyping and testing was already done and with a few quick tweaks to fit the latest engines it would be ready to mass produce in record time, or so he thought.

ABOVE: In addition to being underpowered, the Fw 187 A-0 as-built was lacking in the weapons department – its four side-mounted MG 17s being supplemented by a pair of MG FFs in the lower fuselage

BRINGING BACK THE FALKE

Focke-Wulf received a contract to develop the single-seat twin-engine Fw 187 in November 1935 and the first mock-up was inspected by the Air Ministry in January 1936. The final version of the design was described in a report dated April 1, 1936, and the first prototype made its flight debut on April 10, 1937.

By all accounts, the Fw 187 was a 'private' venture (a term which here requires some qualification – see below) commenced by Focke-Wulf as an attempt to regain some prestige following the ignominious failures of the Fw 159/259 and Fw 57. The former had competed against and been roundly defeated by the Bf 109 and He 112, while the latter had achieved a miserable third place against the Bf 110 and Henschel Hs 124.

The Fw 187, powered by two Jumo 210s, showed some promise but was too late to challenge the Bf 110. It eventually found itself in competition against the next round of single engine single-seaters – the He 100, Bf 209 and Focke-Wulf's own Fw 190 – and lost out once again despite three single-seat prototypes having been manufactured (V1-V3).

There was a glimmer of hope that the Fw 187 could be repurposed as a night fighter and three further prototypes were built as two-seaters (V4-V6) plus five Fw 187 A-0 pre-production machines (a grand total of 11 Fw 187s, with a handful more having been partially completed) but the project was dropped with the outbreak of the Second World War.

So how did Milch, seemingly out of the blue, come to select the old Fw 187 as a competitor for the Me 210, Ar 240 and He 219 as a heavy fighter or night fighter?

Milch himself explained the situation to Göring during a meeting at the Reichsjägerhof in Berlin on June 29, 1942, which rambled on from 6.45pm to 9.15pm. According to the minutes of the meeting, he first told the Reichsmarschall that "tenders for a fast bomber [the Schnellbomber competition] are underway. The following should be involved: Lippisch, Junkers, Blohm & Voss, Focke-Wulf and the rest. The problem of the fast bomber has so far only been attempted with the Me 109 as a fighter. While browsing through the existing documents, I noticed the design of the Fw 187, which has been around since 1936 but has been pushed aside. With a new engine, the Fw 187 can be built as either a single-seat high-altitude bomber or a two-seat heavy fighter."

Based on this explanation, it appears that Milch had been leafing through documents left lying around in what had been Udet's offices and had happened upon some relating to the Fw 187. Back in 1939, attempts had been underway to equip it with DB 601 engines – though no flying 601/187 testbed was ever completed. Presumably Milch reasoned that fitting the DB 605, a development of the DB 601, would not pose any particular difficulties. Later on during the same meeting, Milch "mentions that the Fw 187 could possibly be used as a replacement for the Me 110".

Another factor which would have commended the Fw 187 to Milch was its manufacturer Focke-Wulf and company leader Kurt Tank. Unlike Messerschmitt, Focke-Wulf was not a standalone privately-owned business. Rather, it was a subsidiary of manufacturing giant AEG – producer of everything from power stations to household electrical devices. AEG, at that time, was a corporate backer of the Nazi party and as such was extremely pliant in acceding to the government's demands. So while Focke-Wulf was not technically owned by the German government, it was to all intents and purposes controlled by it.

While Tank had a great deal of latitude to express his opinions, to organise his staff and direct their work as he saw fit, he held his position solely at the pleasure of the Nazi leadership and was required to do as he was told when necessary.

Milch had evidently approached Tank with his plan to revamp the Fw 187 and put it into production. Tank, for his part, appears to have promised Milch that this could be done relatively easily and that preparations would commence immediately. Milch had initially told Göring that the re-engined Fw 187 would be suitable in the high-altitude and heavy fighter roles and "as replacement for the Me 110" but at a further meeting at the Reichsmarschall's Carinhall residence on July 20, 1942, he said that "currently, the Fw 187 is being investigated for the purposes of the XII. Air Corps [the XII. Air Corps being the Luftwaffe's dedicated night fighter command created by General Josef Kammhuber in August 1940]". This was in response to Göring ordering that "the He 219 is to be accelerated in testing and to completion".

HIGH-ALTITUDE AND NIGHT FIGHTER

The earliest known evidence of Focke-Wulf working on the revised Fw 187 is a pair of graphs dated June 8, 1942, which show the Fw 187's climb time and top speed performance stats when fitted with DB 605s and two more showing the same datasets for the Fw 187 when fitted with DB 628s. These were followed by slightly amended graphs showing the same information points on June 22, 1942. Focke-Wulf also appears to have produced a brief text report with some nice drawings around this time, showing what both a single-seat high-altitude/night-fighter version of the Fw 187, and a two-seater heavy fighter version, would look like.

Two variants of a cover for the report were produced which appeared identical except for the title – one being 'Fw 187 als Höhen-und Nachtjäger' and the other being 'Fw 187 als Höhenjäger, Kampfzerstörer und Nachtjäger'. Both gave performance figures for the Fw 187 with either DB 605s or DB 628s – top speed being 725km/h with the former or 740km/h with the latter. Below that, a short block of introductory text read: "Summary: It turns out that the Fw 187, which has already been tested and is in use in some examples and which was originally developed as a heavy fighter, can meet all of today's requirements for a high-altitude and night fighter after installing a more powerful engine with very few modifications. The flight characteristics, wing loading and other design of the Fw 187 fully correspond to the new intended use. The 605 engine from the Me 109 G is used."

The main text, which only appears to have accompanied the 'Fw 187 als Höhen-und Nachtjäger' version of the report, read: "Studies on fighter planes have shown that with the engines available today, significant improvements in performance in terms of climb and maximum altitude cannot be achieved with a single-engine aircraft carrying sufficient weaponry.

"This consideration leads to a twin-engine aircraft, as the power load can be kept significantly lower. For this reason, the Fw 187 was examined for its suitability for conversion into a) high-altitude fighter, b) night fighter. It turned out that some of the Fw 187s, which were originally developed as heavy fighters, met all the requirements of a high-altitude and night fighter. The existing wing loading and the aspect ratio correspond to the new purpose in full, so that no fundamental constructive changes are to be made.

"Because of their performance characteristics, 2 x DB 605s were chosen as engines. The 605 engine from the Me 109 G is used as the engine system. The resulting conversion in the wing is minimal because the connections in the airframe are already set up for the DB 601. In contrast to the Fw 187 V1 to V5, the radiator cannot be arranged as a belly or longitudinal radiator, but only as a nozzle radiator between the fuselage and the engine nacelle in the inner wing. The position of the oil cooler remains the same. The resulting changes in the wing are also small, because the corresponding sections are already available.

"The fuel tanks previously located in the inner wing must be removed. However, since the aircraft is to be designed as a single-seater, space can be created for another fuselage container with a volume of approx. 250 liters after removal of the equipment for the radio operator, for which construction documents are already available.

"The fuselage must be extended by approx. 1m. This lengthening only affects the simple tail section between frames 15 and 27, which has few built-in components. This results in a flying weight of 6,050kg.

Since the mainwheels fitted to the [existing] Fw 187 with the dimensions 815 x 290 is no longer sufficient for the increased flying weight, the wide-rim 840 x 300 wheel must be provided. The slightly larger dimensions of the new wheel only require minor changes to the current chassis.

"Armament is: a) high-altitude fighter – 2 x MG 131 with 700 rounds of ammunition each + 2 x MG 151 with 500 rounds of ammunition each. b) night fighter – 4 x MG 151 with 500 rounds of ammunition each. The previous arrangement of weapons is retained [i.e. all four guns arranged around the sides of the cockpit].

"Since – apart from the lengthening of the fuselage – the external airframe components are retained, the well-known good flight characteristics of the Fw 187 can only continue to develop in the most favourable sense. The investigation has shown that a conversion of the Fw 187 can be carried out in a short time with little construction work."

It was noted that revised construction documents and drawings could be completed by November 1942, although "the prerequisite is that all designers etc. loaned out to external companies come back". Exactly which firms Focke-Wulf's designers had been loaned out to is unclear.

Four prototype/sample aircraft were to be constructed by mid-1943 "for the purpose of clearing the construction documents of drawing errors from the start of series production and for the purpose of repeated testing of the airframe and engine (engine taken over from Me 109, airframe already tested)".

After that, the first series production model Fw 187s could be delivered in early 1944.

MILCH THREATENS TANK

The next available document, chronologically, is an updated drawing showing the type as a two-seater 'Kampfzerstörer' dated July 15, 1942. This was a subtly revamped version of the design from June, with a different cockpit canopy, a different internal cockpit layout, heavier armament, a larger internal fuel tank, a larger bomb attached below the fuselage, revised engine nacelle profile and revised radiator arrangement.

According to historian Dietmar Hermann, writing in his 2003 book Focke-Wulf Fw 187 – An Illustrated History, "On July 20, 1942, Focke-Wulf received the official development contract to redesign the Fw 187 … to be powered by the new Daimler-Benz DB 605 engine. Focke-Wulf assumed from the development message sent on August 7 that the Fw 187 V5 would [need to] be converted and ready to fly by October 31, 1942, and the second aircraft, the Fw 187 V7 (B-0), by November 30. Focke-Wulf assigned this conversion plan Priority Level 2, behind the Fw 190 high-altitude fighter, which had top priority at that time … Focke-Wulf scheduled overtime and Sundays in order to have all the necessary drawings completed on time. The necessary drawings had to be available to the assembly facility on time … The DB 605 engines for the two conversions were [to be] procured by August 30 and September 30 at the latest."

At the end of a lengthy Air Ministry management meeting on August 4, 1942, Milch was clearly in a bad mood. He had just been discussing Allied aircraft developments, requirements for additional flak batteries and materials shortages that were crippling the Ministry's aircraft programmes. Now he waved a Focke-Wulf report at his staff. As usual it had been drawn up based on a Ministry requirement calling for enormous transport aircraft designs but evidently it was absolutely not what Milch wanted. Rather than working out how the whole aircraft could be made of steel, the company had instead presented different options based on the percentage of steel to be used.

He said: "Here I have a very bad draft regarding the iron issue from Tank giving the individual steel percentages: 20%, 35%, 50%. He wants to carry 40t [the transports being intended to carry armoured fighting vehicles] each time and always states how much fuel is needed. This calculation is of no use to us at all. He should have left that alone; I ask that the relevant personnel be withdrawn from him in good time; apparently he has too many.

"It's not yet certain which steel will be used to do this. So that's not a working basis at all. The working basis is clear: you have to bring about the same performance using the other material. The question is: can I use 100% steel or not. The goal is the use of steel, not in the question of how much fuel I use, what payload and what distance. The task is approached completely wrong – Lucht [Generalingenieur Roluf Lucht – Milch's loyal

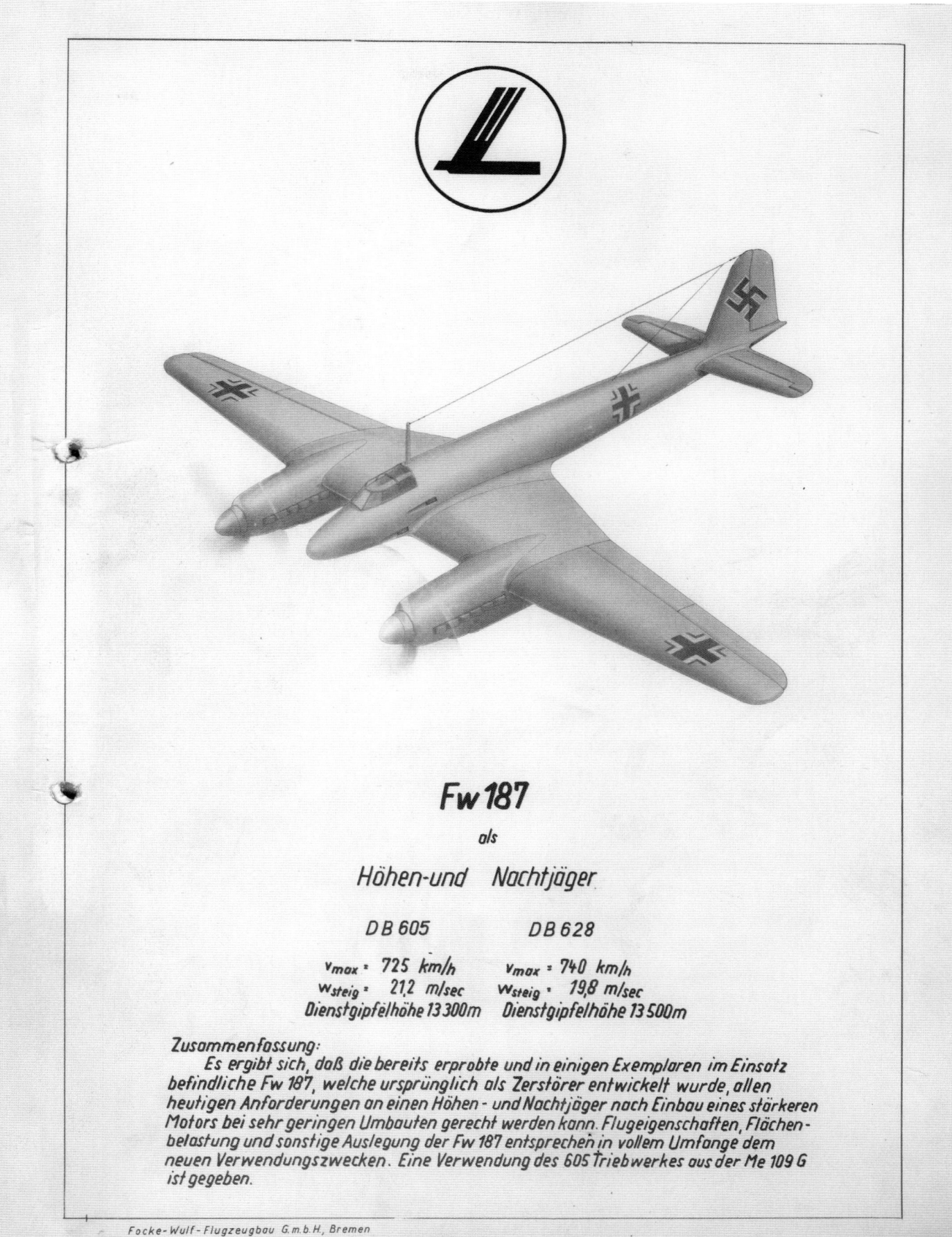

ABOVE: Cover of the first outline report on how the Fw 187 could be revived – as a high-altitude or night fighter. It is not immediately obvious from the drawing, but the 'new' Fw 187's fuselage was to be stretched by 1m compared to that of the original.

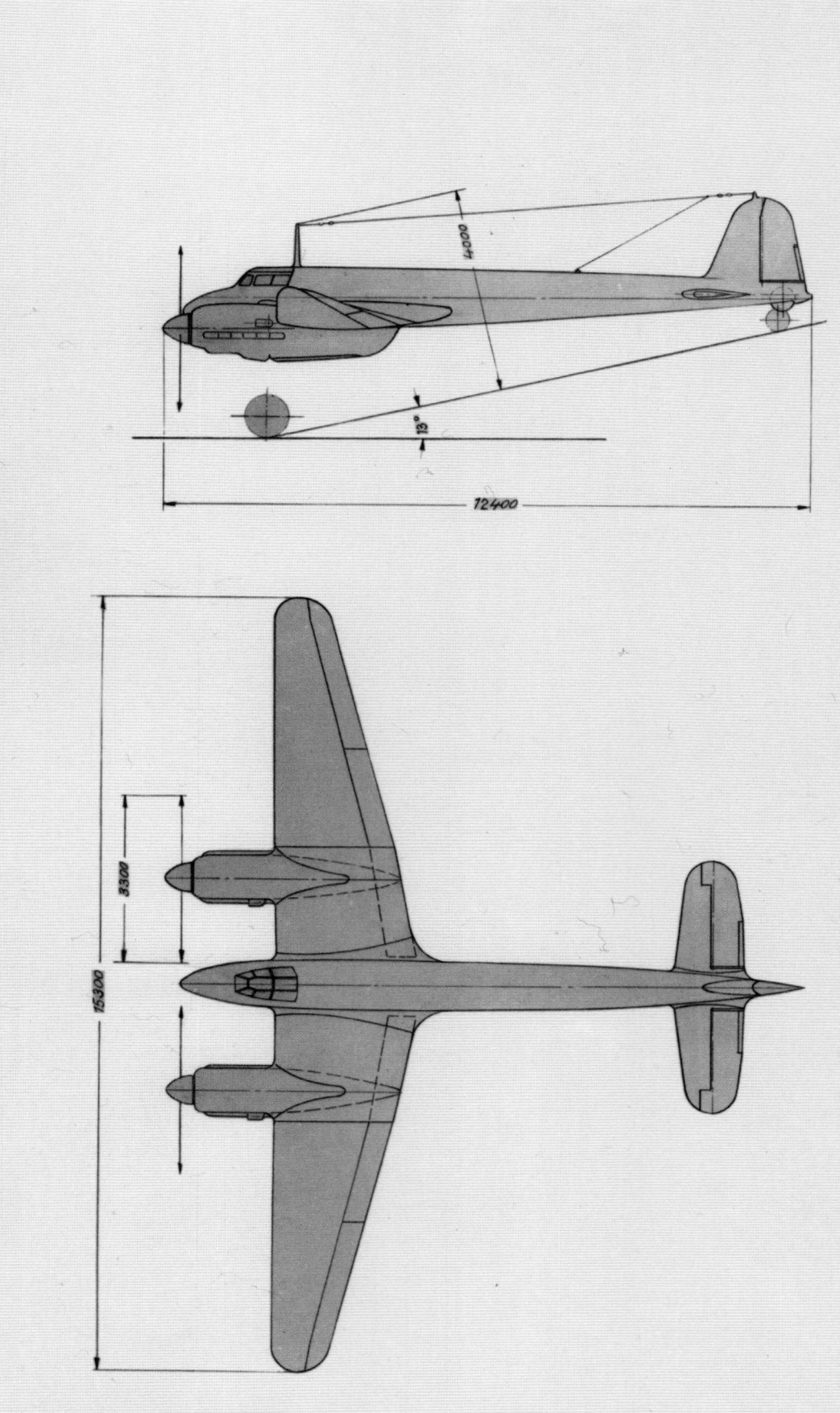

ABOVE: Focke-Wulf initially pitched the single-seat Fw 187 design as the basis for a 'new' DB 605/628-powered fighter.

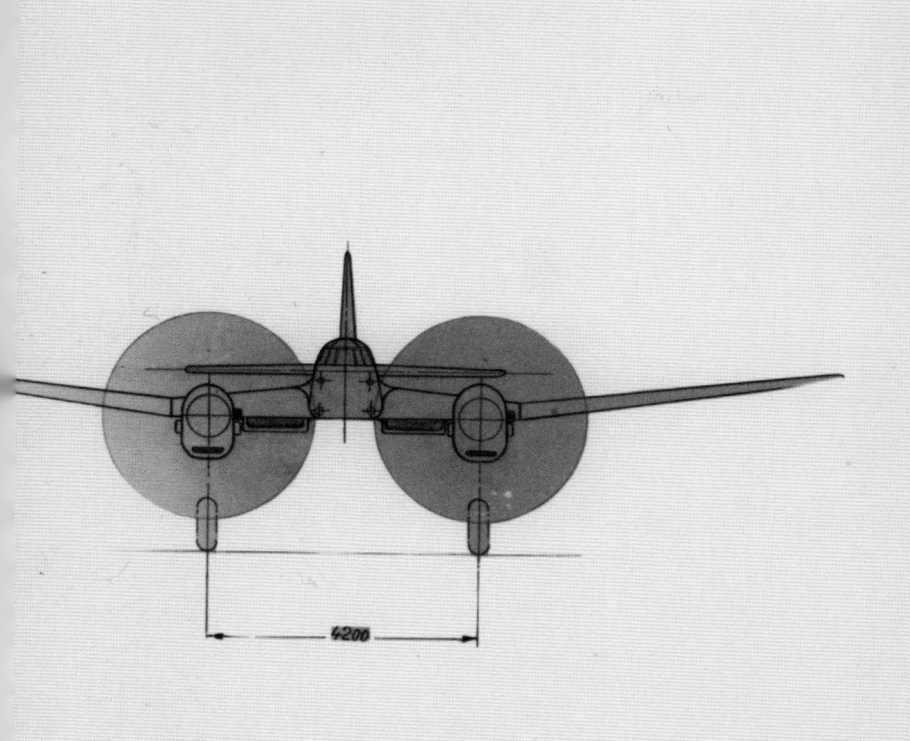

Fw. 187
als
Höhen - und Nachtjäger
Dreiseitenansicht

hatchet man, who had previously been sent to tell Messerschmitt he was being forced to resign], you can call him and tell him that I had criticised his work, if I wanted such stupid work I didn't have to employ him.

"The question of securing the design drawings still has time. I will withhold judgement until the end of the year to see if Mr Blume [Walter Blume of Arado – another company leader who had to do as he was told, since Arado was fully state-owned] can continue to design with his design office after he so bitterly disappointed me with this one bird [the Arado Ar 240]. The question with Tank also hangs in the balance; if he disappoints me with the 187, then it's pitch black with him; then I don't need him."

Having presented the notion of a revived Fw 187 to Göring as his own idea – a sure-fire solution to the critical Me 210 situation – Milch undoubtedly felt that he had invested a great deal of political capital in it. Should it fail due to some unforeseen flaw, or due to some error or inaction on Tank's part, he risked losing face. Having already punished Messerschmitt, Milch appears to have felt that punishing Tank and Blume or at least threatening them with punishment, would achieve some sort of positive outcome.

A week later, on August 11, 1942, Focke-Wulf produced a rather bare-bones report entitled '2 motoriger Kampfzerstörer Fw 187' as well as a further selection of drawings. The Fw 187 variant described was a two-seater Kampfzerstörer, a heavy fighter-bomber, but it was made plain that "the aircraft can be converted for use as a short-range night fighter, all-weather fighter or armed reconnaissance aircraft". The high-altitude fighter configuration appears to have now been dropped.

Two engine options were presented – DB 605 or BMW 801 D – and take-off weight was 7,200kg. Range was 1,200km with 880 litres of fuel in the internal fuselage tank plus 210 litres each in a pair of wing tanks. This could be extended to 2,100km using another 900 litres in drop tanks.

Armament was four MG 151s in the forward fuselage plus two fixed rearward-firing MG 131s in the rear fuselage and a single MG 81 to be operated by the rearward-facing back-seater. Provision would also be made for exchanging the lower two MG 151s up front for a pair of MK 103s. The maximum possible bomb load was 2,000kg with four possible arrangements suggested – 1 x 1,000kg bomb plus 2 x 500kg bombs, or 1 x 1,000kg bomb plus four 250kg bombs, or 10 x 50kg bombs, or 10 x AB 23/AB 24 cluster bombs. Radio equipment was Fu G X P; Peil G VI, Fu Bl 2 F, Fu NG 101 and Fu G 25a. Total armour protection amounted to 167kg.

Fitted with DB 605s, the aircraft would be 12.45m long with a wingspan of 15.3m and a wing area of 30sqm. The engines would get three-bladed 3.4m diameter props. Top speed was calculated as 682km/h at an altitude of 7,100m. Data based on the use of BMW 801 Ds was not provided.

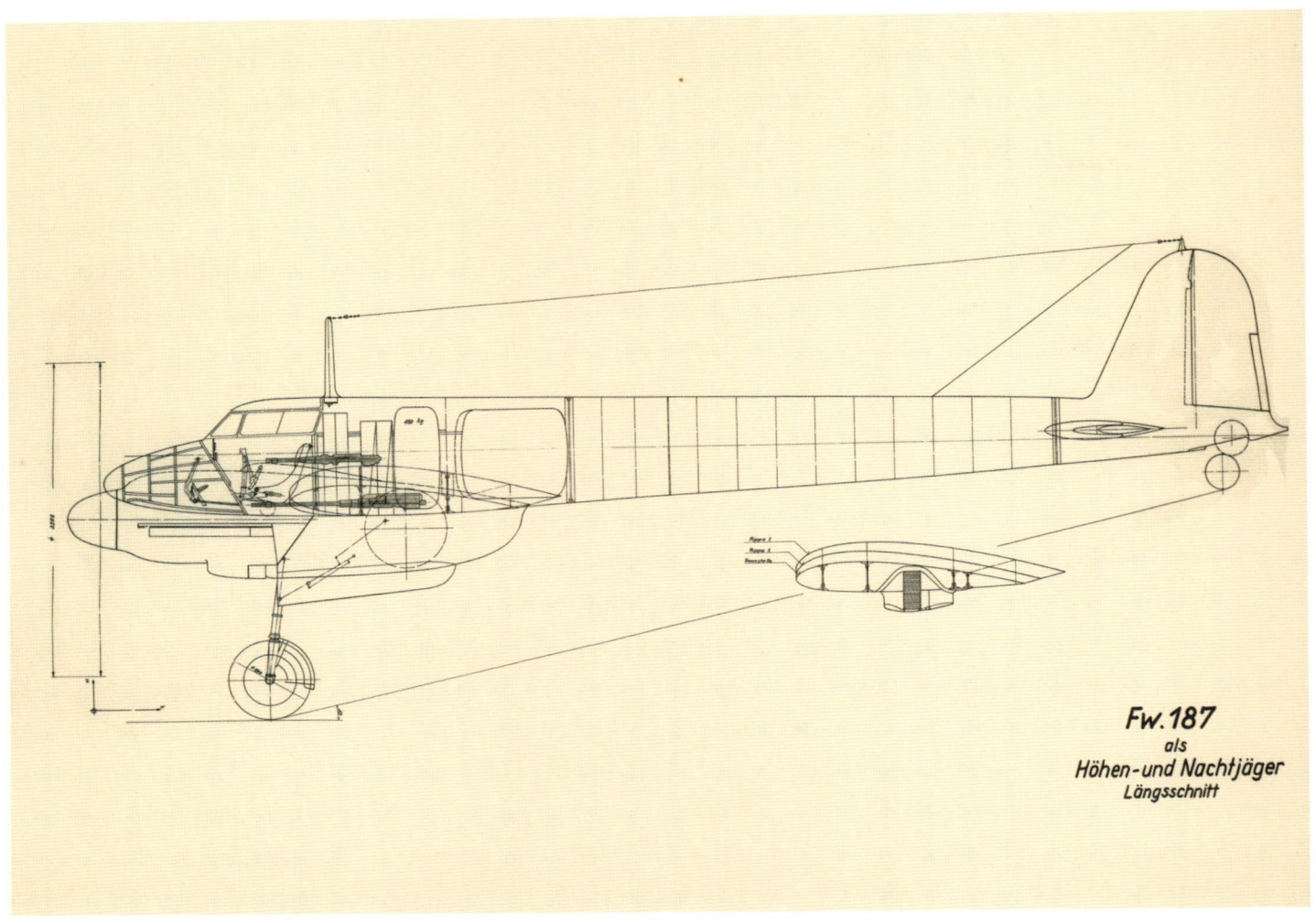

ABOVE: Side view of the single-seater with inset showing how a new feature –radiators below the inner wing sections - would be installed.

FW 187 VS HE 219

Following on immediately after the Air Ministry management meeting on August 18, 1942, a development meeting was held to work out how to proceed with the He 219, Me 210, Fw 187 and Ar 240.

It began with a presentation by Ministry staff engineer Walter Friebel: "I have once again compiled the data for the He 219s [two slightly different versions] as they are now to go into series production and have them here. The differences between the two aircraft, which I have listed in two columns, only exist with regard to the engine, namely we are now starting with the DB 603 A and then want to change over to the DB 603 G later; it is available in mid-1943. I have written the take-off power next to it for comparison; it is 1,750hp and 1,900hp.

"With the He 219, a distinction must be made between the heavy fighter version and the night fighter version. The most important aircraft that we are now concentrating on is the night fighter version. The difference between the night fighter and the heavy fighter is based only in the different armament, namely the heavy fighter has additional armament compared to the night fighter. It has twin MG 151s at the top and bottom, and the night fighter does not have those at the bottom. The two machines do not differ in terms of airframe and construction, and hardly at all in terms of performance either, only in terms of climb performance, which is caused by the 100kg difference in armament.

"The maximum speed is 485km/h at ground level and 635km/h at 8km altitude. With the old one [an earlier version of the He 219 presented previously?] it was 490km/h or 615km/h. Today it would be time to consider which of the currently existing twin-engine heavy fighters or night fighters can be eliminated little by little. I have therefore put together a speed versus altitude graph on a single sheet for the aircraft currently under review: Me 110, Arado 240, Fw 187, Me 210 and Me 210 with DB 603 G.

"The black line is the Me 110 as discussed in the delivery plan. The blue line is the Me 210. So the speed curve of the Me 210 is 540km/h at the first kink and then it goes to 630km/h and then falls again accordingly over the full pressure level. Completely parallel to this aircraft – it has the same engines and is almost exactly the same aircraft in terms of wings – is the Arado 240.

"The He 219 is compared to this – albeit with a different engine, the 603 – in its first version, with the 603 A. It is hardly different from the others near the ground and also at medium altitudes up to 3,000m. From 3,000m it gets a little better. In the lower range it is definitely not better in relation to the Me 210 and Arado 240. At higher altitudes it gets a little better, here it is on average about 10 to 15km above the range of the Arado 240 or. Me 210 today's version. It has its main advantage in the fact that it was deliberately designed and refined by all departments involved for the purpose of 'night fighter'.

"Now, in comparison, the Fw 187, which Focke-Wulf has recently unearthed and thrown into the debate again. The aircraft is actually very different in its overall design. Let's start with the wings. The Me 110, Me 210 and Arado 240 are relatively close to each other in their wings. The ones that stand out at the extremes are the Fw 187 on one side and the He 219 on the other. These are actually the two types that we have to choose between in the near future. The large wing – the large aircraft in general – of the He 219 results from the night fighter requirements, namely on the one hand the requirement for defensive and attacking armament and on the other the long flight duration, which the night fighter must reasonably possess in order to make it possible to remain on station.

"So if, in the near future, we have to discuss the question of building the He 219 as a standard aircraft, as a heavy fighter and night fighter, or the Fw 187 as a standard aircraft,

Fw 187
Einsitziger Höhenjäger

Fluggewicht	6050 kg
Flächengröße	30 m²
Flächenbelastung	202 kg/m²

Bewaffnung: 4 x MG 151
 oder
 2 x MG 151 und 2 x MG 131
 oder
 2 x MG 151 und 4 x MG 131
 oder
 1 x MK 103 und 2 x MG 151 und
 2 x MG 131

Triebwerk: 2 x DB 605 Triebwerke von der Me 109 G oder 2 x DB 628

Leistungen: mit DB 605:
 v_{max} = 725 km/h in 8100 m
 10 000 m Höhe in 11 min
 Dienstgipfelhöhe 13 300 m

 mit DB 628:
 v_{max} = 740 km/h in 10 500 m
 10 000 m Höhe in 10,6 min
 Dienstgipfelhöhe 13 500 m

Der Einsatz dieses Ausgangsmusters als Kampfzerstörer (siehe nächstes Blatt) ist nach Austausch der blau angelegten Teile (also lediglich Haube und Rumpf= mittelteil) möglich.
Alle übrigen Teile sind für beide Verwendungszwecke vollständig gleich.

ABOVE: Data sheet on the DB 605/628-powered high-altitude variant.

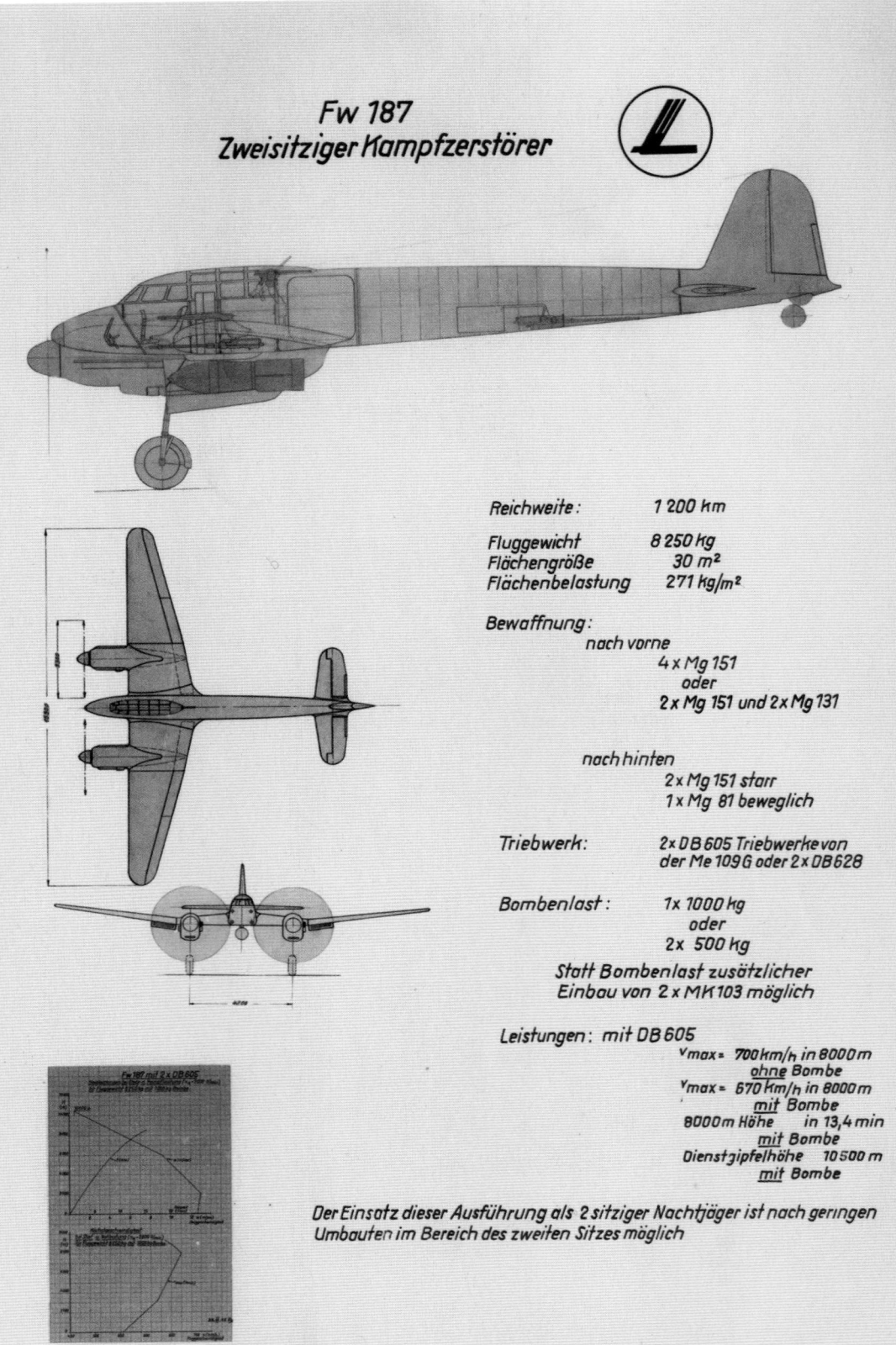

ABOVE: The two-seater Fw 187 heavy fighter arrangement with rear-facing radio-operator and radiators now under the outer wing sections. The note at the bottom says: "The use of this version as a two-seater night fighter is possible after minor modifications to the area of the second seat."

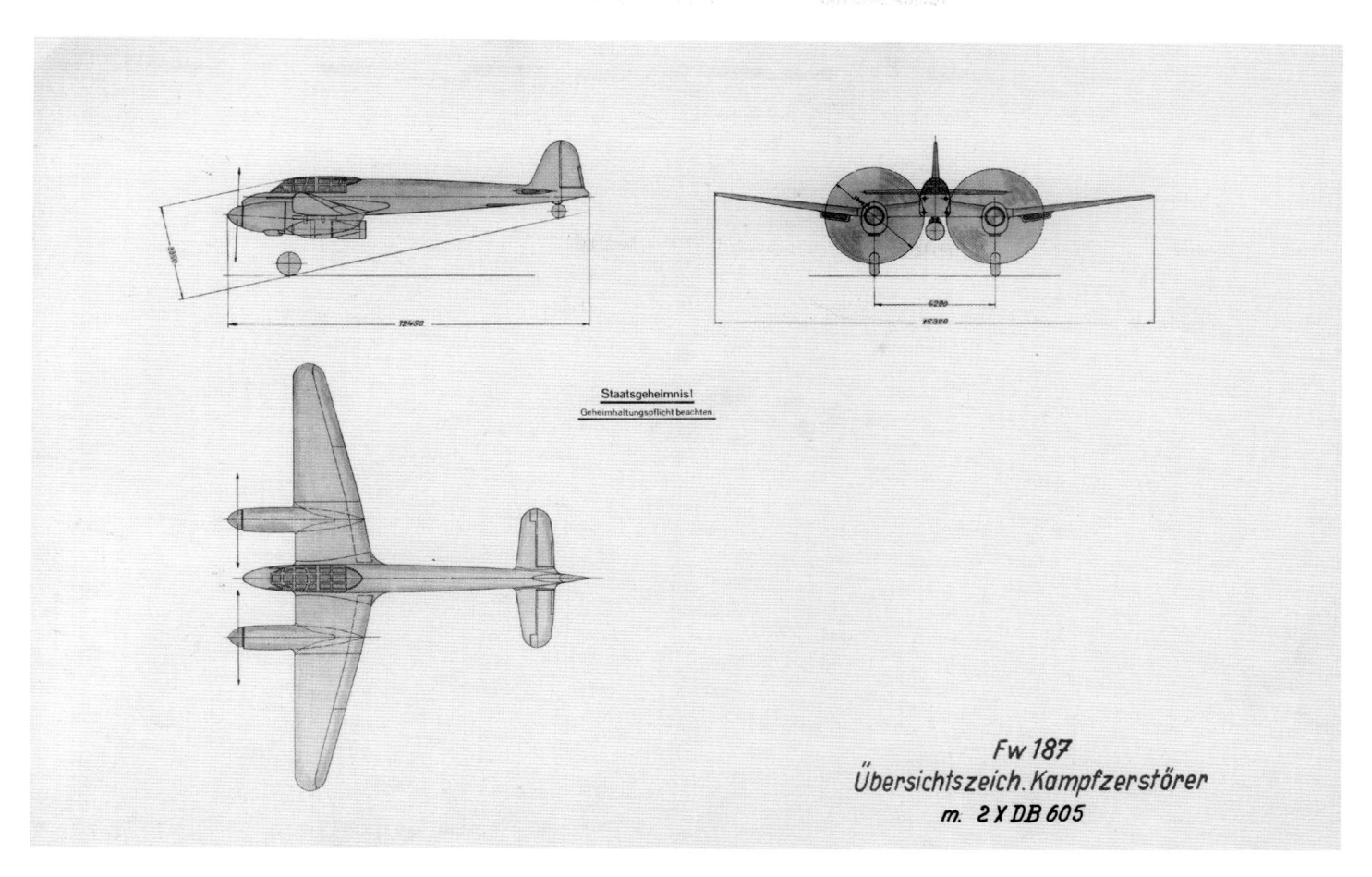

Fw 187
Übersichtszeich. Kampfzerstörer
m. 2 X DB 605

ABOVE: Revised design for the two-seater Fw 187. It was now being presented under the catch-all 'Kampfzerstörer' label, rather than specifically as a high-altitude or night fighter. The underwing radiators are now further away from the engines than they were when first presented.

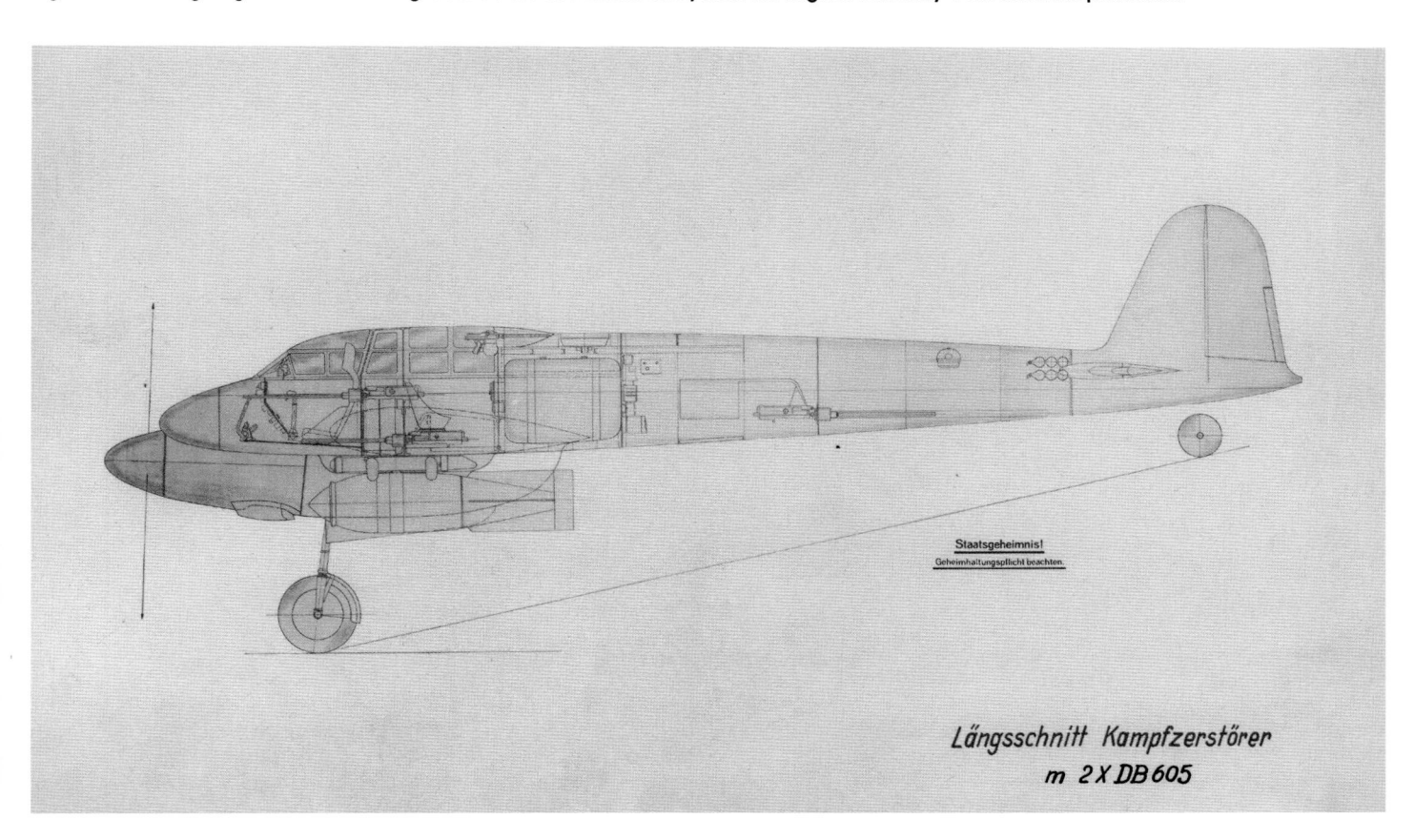

Längsschnitt Kampfzerstörer
m 2 X DB 605

ABOVE: This side view shows numerous differences between the first and second revived Fw 187 two-seater designs. This one has a completely new cockpit canopy, new engine cowlings and other detail changes.

Secret Projects of the Luftwaffe 33

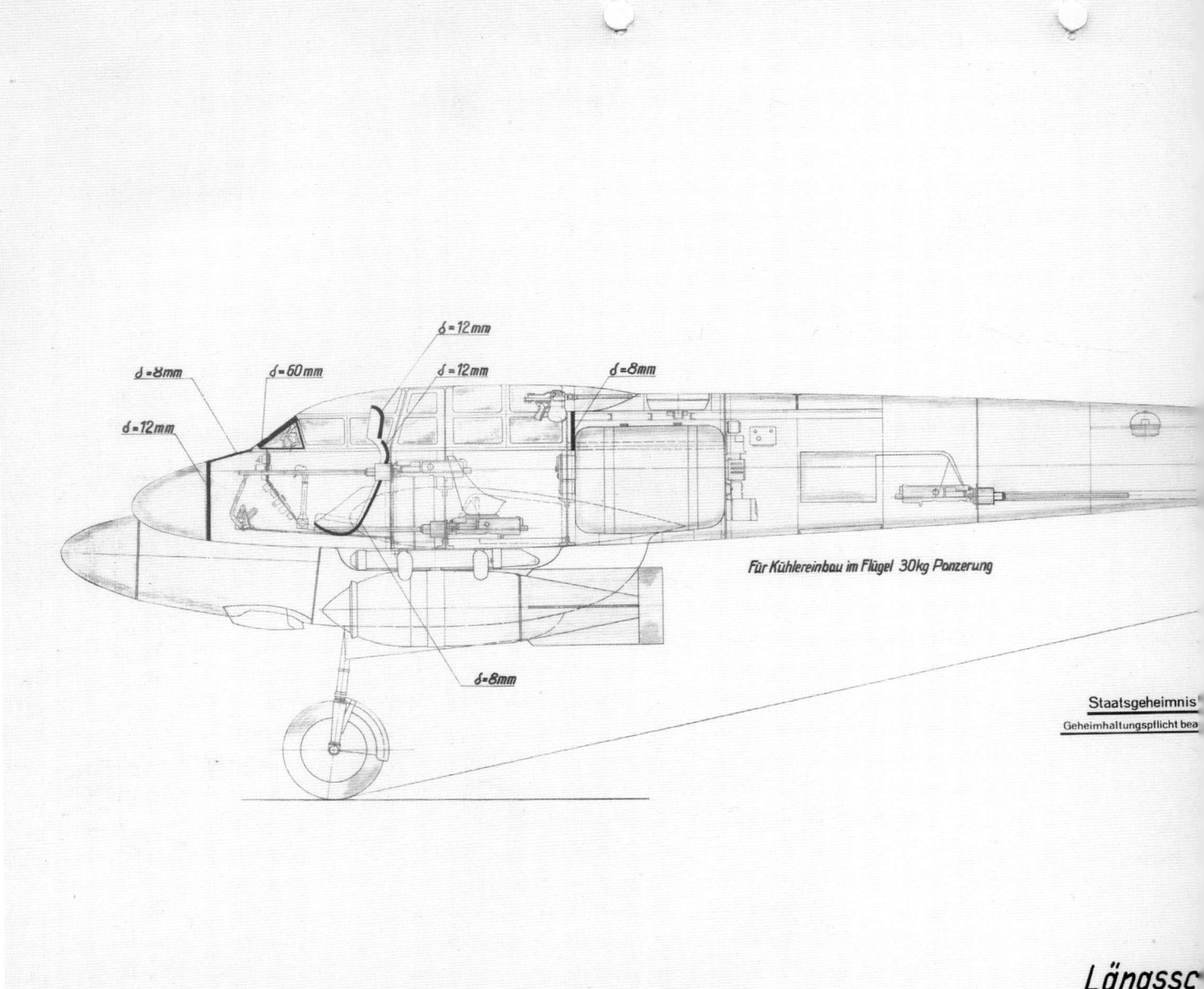

ABOVE: Armour thicknesses of the Fw 187 two-seater. The underwing radiators would also get armour protection.

as a destroyer and night fighter, the following must be considered: the He 219 is definitely a good night fighter because the entire aircraft is designed accordingly. On the other hand, as a heavy fighter it would be a little too big, especially given the current demands of the General Staff. The heavy fighter is mainly used at lower altitudes, i.e. occasionally as an attack aircraft. This machine wouldn't be much worse [than the other designs]."

Milch then responded: "With the exception of the old Me 110, the speeds of all four machines are only different on paper. In reality, they are equally fast; they are at 630-640km/h. Personally, I'm not interested in the size of the wings, but I am interested in the wing loading. The wing loading of the Fw 187 is significantly better than the He 219. That's the one thing you have to compare. The second thing you need to compare is range. One machine only has 1,200km and the other 2,600km, so exactly double."

Friebel: "The amount of fuel is the decisive factor, because one machine is

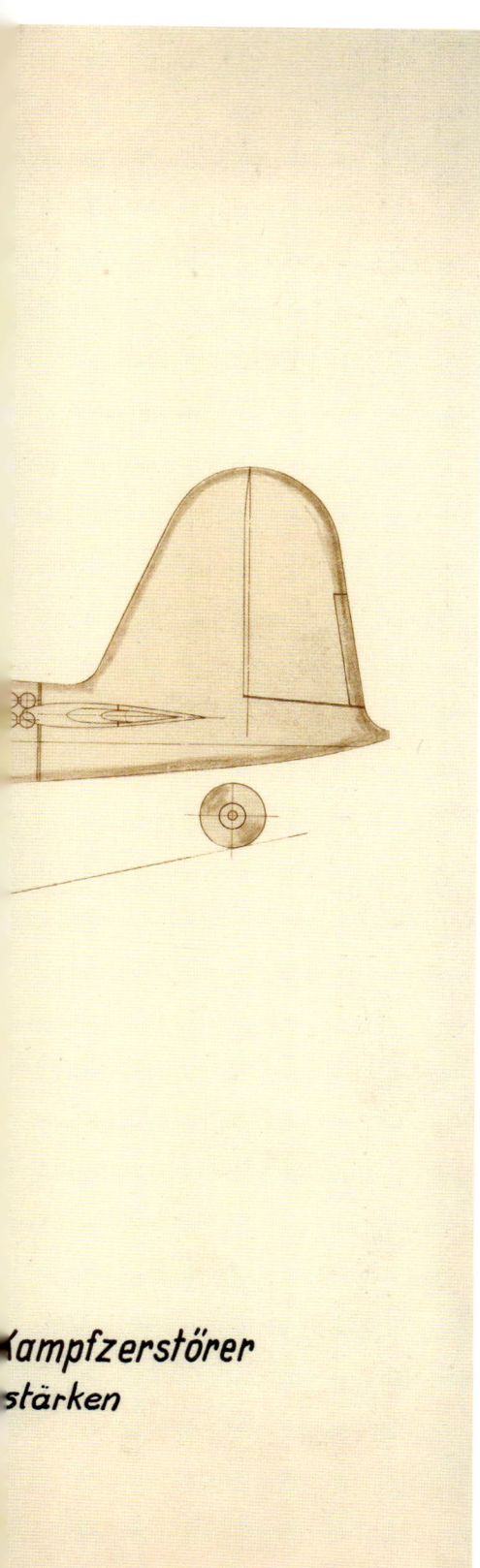

Kampfzerstörer stärken

designed for flying in a holding pattern. It has a long flight endurance, while the Fw 187 is a very short-endurance aircraft. Therefore, the following results: the He 219 certainly fulfils the requirements of the night fighter very well and those of the heavy destroyer to some extent, while the Fw 187 fulfils the requirements of the heavy fighter well, but not those of the night fighter.

"This means that if you had to make the decision on this basis, you would have to pick the He 219, because it does one thing correctly and the other to some extent; the Fw 187 does one thing well and the other certainly not at all, because its use as a night fighter is out of the question, due to equipment load, fuselage size, etc. That is quite certain. Also, the necessary investments and manpower have not yet been allocated for the Fw 187 and with the already heavy use of Focke-Wulf it would probably take some time; Focke-Wulf is now being used with all its strength on the Fw 190 – to do everything possible to increase the quality and the number of units made."

Milch: "If the Me 210 were really okay, then it would have fully met both needs, both as a heavy fighter and as a night fighter. The cheapest machine would without a doubt be the Me 210. The Arado 240 is completely out of the question. You can see that very clearly. The big question now is whether the range of the Fw 187 is sufficient. The Fw 187 has one disadvantage: the short range compared to the He 219. It has two advantages: only half the flying weight, i.e. much cheaper in terms of man-hours, and cheaper to build. Then the Fw 187 is about there, while the He 219 is still a Christmas present for us [i.e. still a long way off]."

Friebel then bluntly contradicted the Generalluftzeugmeister: "The Fw 187 is of course not there, for the following reasons: the aircraft that Focke-Wulf takes as a starting model is a 5.2 ton aircraft. But this new version is 7.2 tons. The weight without bombs is 7.2 tons. With bombs it's 8.2 tons. The aircraft therefore needs to be strengthened from 5.2 tons to 8.2 tons. This means we have to make a completely new wing; only the external form remains. The flight characteristics are of course retained within certain limits.

"What is not preserved is the fuselage and the undercarriage, which must be completely rebuilt in terms of wheel size, suspension strut, bearing connections etc. The tail unit is also new because of the greater speed when it dives, etc. We will definitely be able to adopt the external shape, perhaps not with the same fin because it may need to be made larger. But apart from the flight characteristics, the entire aircraft will have to be rebuilt. So that is the task that Focke-Wulf faces today."

Milch: "Where would the Ju 188 fit into this?"

Friebel: "It's roughly on the same lines as the old Me 210, a little bit slower."

Milch: "Why do we even want to build an He 219 and a Fw 187? Does 20km matter? Is it really so important that you build a completely new type or maybe even two new types?"

Edgar Petersen, head of the Luftwaffe test centres, said: "From our perspective, the Me 210 with 603 is expected to drop bombs at 670 to 680km/h. That would be a machine that would be significantly faster than the Ju 188, namely about 80km/h."

Friebel: "The difference is that big. Based on these graphs, the suggestion would be to use the He 219 as a night fighter, and, according to the demands of the General Staff, it would be advisable to try to get the Me 210 as a heavy fighter."

Milch: "Why don't we want to make the Me 210 a night fighter? Isn't that possible? It has at least 2,000km range and that would be enough."

Friebel: "That would be enough. What would have to be redesigned for the Me 210 night fighter is the entire interior layout, since the Me 210 is already fully developed and used for certain tasks as a bomber or heavy fighter and is an aircraft that is complete in its interior design. A completely new cockpit would have to be built."

Ministry Technical Office chief Wolfgang Vorwald said: "It had already been investigated whether the currently in production [Me 210] series could be converted into a night fighter. But that resulted in an enormous effort, which was rejected at the time by the field marshal [Milch himself]."

Milch: "We always think about it back and forth. We have now heard that the Fw 187 would have to be completely remade. The second thing is that the He 219 has a very specific date when it is supposed to come. I don't like the He 219 for purposes outside of the night fighter because of its extraordinarily heavy weight and the associated clumsiness."

Luftwaffe General Staff representative Franz-Dietrich von Ditfurth said: "Above all, the He 219 does not have the option of carrying bombs."

Milch: "I would even consider that secondary; you could still do this or that. But first of all it's the basics. I want a machine – barring night fighting – that is fabulous for diving. It is clear that a nine ton machine can be dived much more easily than a 13 ton machine. I can also turn it faster and better on the target. I see practically no difference at all between the He 219 and the Ju 188, because what little extra I have in terms of speed is so small that it is within the margin of error. I am also convinced that one or two things can perhaps be achieved with the Ju 188."

von Ditfurth: "General Kammhuber, who was very committed to the He 219, focused mainly on the altitude performance, which is significantly better than that of the Ju 188."

Friebel: "The service ceiling of the current He 219 machine is 10.5km and the other 10km."

Milch: "So it's the same for both. In terms of climbing time, the Me 210 is significantly superior. How does the Ju 188 compare?"

Friebel: "That is not stated here. But I think it is probably worse than the He 219, i.e. over 20 minutes, because the Ju 188 is a much heavier aircraft."

Milch: "With the Ju 188, when it goes as a night fighter, you have to say: without bombs. It's a shame that we don't have the Ju 188 on the table too. I would ask that we include that next time. Let's look at the tables straight away so that we have them in front of us and not just on the wall. You can also take them home with you to check them more closely in the evening."

Petersen: "May I also point out the defensive armament of the Fw 187. It is looking malnourished with two MG 131s and an MG 81."

Secret Projects of the Luftwaffe

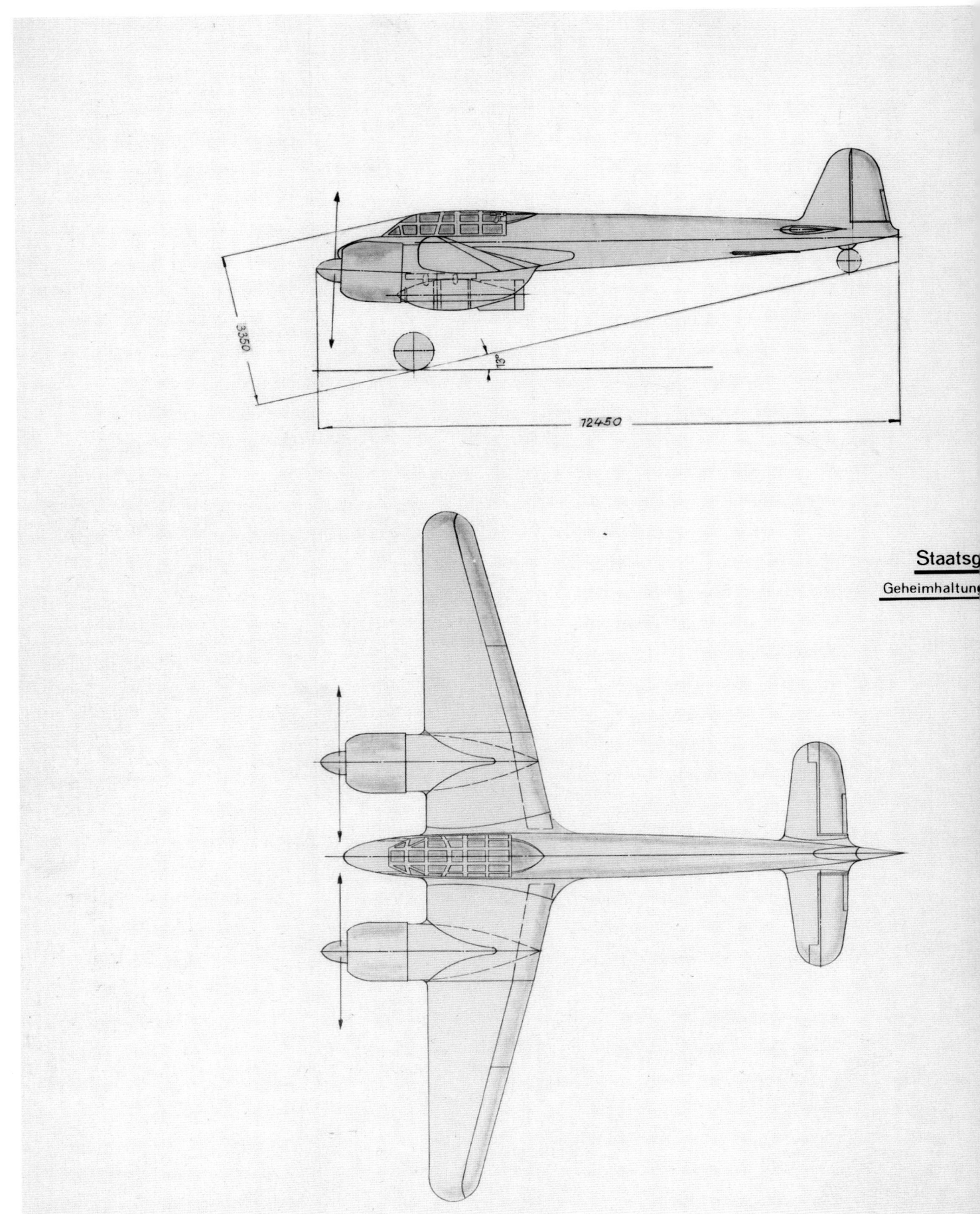

ABOVE: The two-seater Fw 187 Kampfzerstörer as it would look with BMW 801 engines and their associated annular radiators.

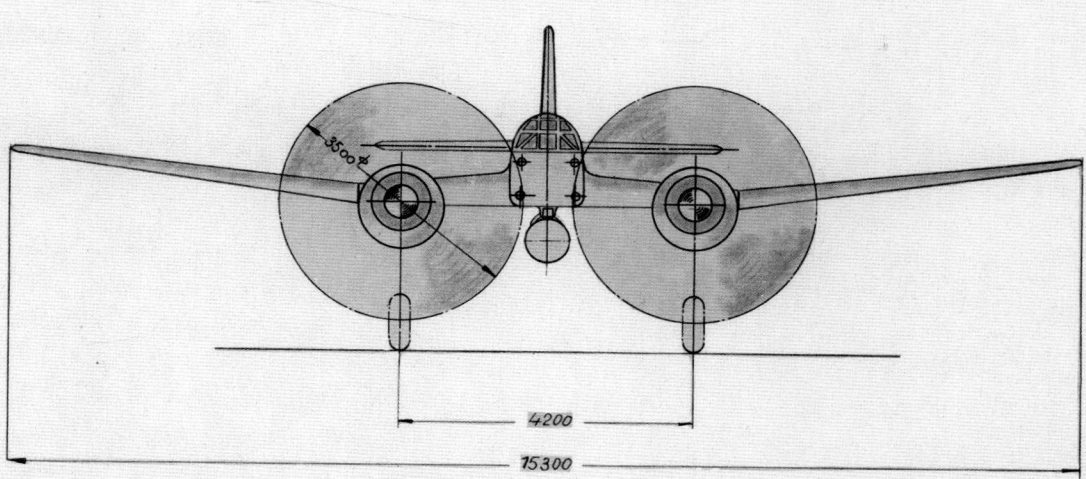

Kampfzerstörer mit 2 X BMW 801 D

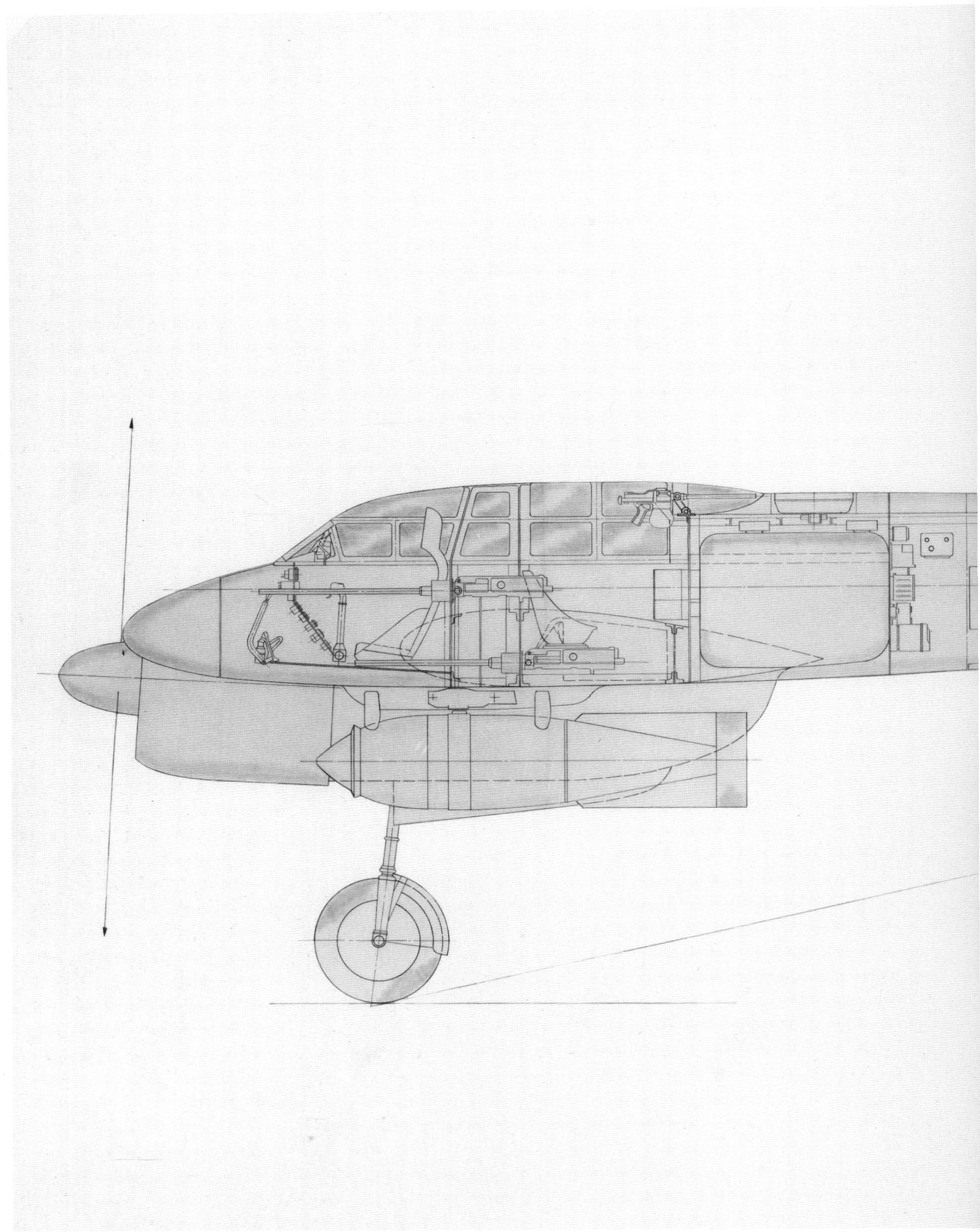

ABOVE: Side view of the 801-powered Fw 187 Kampfzerstörer.

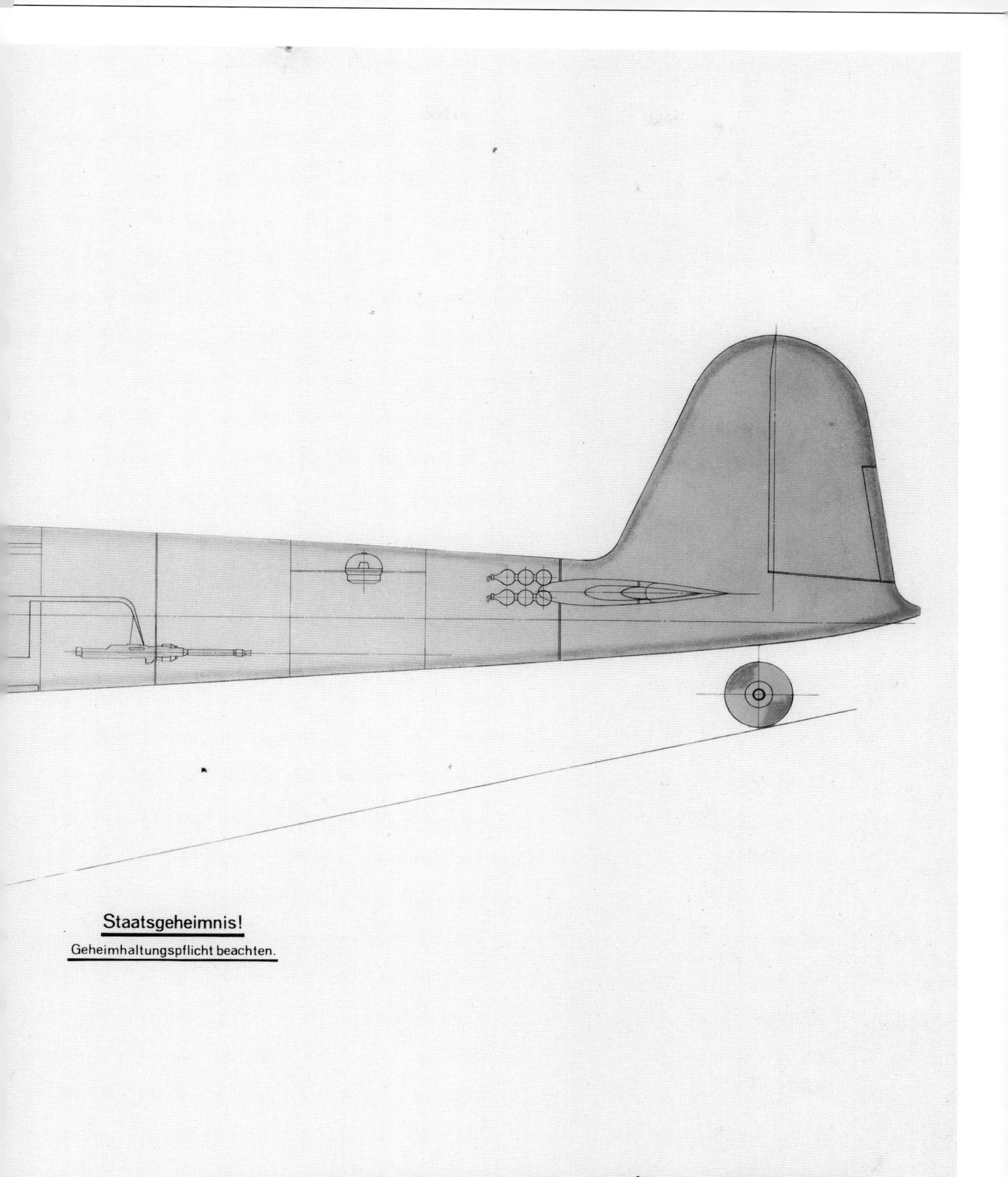

Staatsgeheimnis!
Geheimhaltungspflicht beachten.

Längsschnitt Kampfzerstörer BMW 801

| Focke-Wulf Flugzeugbau G.m.b.H. Bremen | Fw 187 | Blatt: |

Fw 187 m. 2 x DB 605   Fw 187 m. 2 x BMW 801 D

| Fluggewicht 8 200 kg | 1 000 kg | Fluggewicht 8 730 kg |
| Fluggewicht 9 200 kg | 2 000 kg | Fluggewicht 9 730 kg |

| Fluggewicht 8840 kg | 500 kg   500 kg   500 kg | Fluggewicht 9370 kg |

| Fluggewicht 8960 kg | 2x250   2x250   2x250 | Fluggewicht 9490 kg |

| Fluggewicht 7940 kg | 5 x 50 kg / 5 x AB 24 / 5 x AB 23 — 5 x 50 kg / 5 x AB 24 / 5 x AB 23 | Fluggewicht 8470 kg |

Focke-Wulf Flugzeugbau G.m.b.H. Nr. 26 a

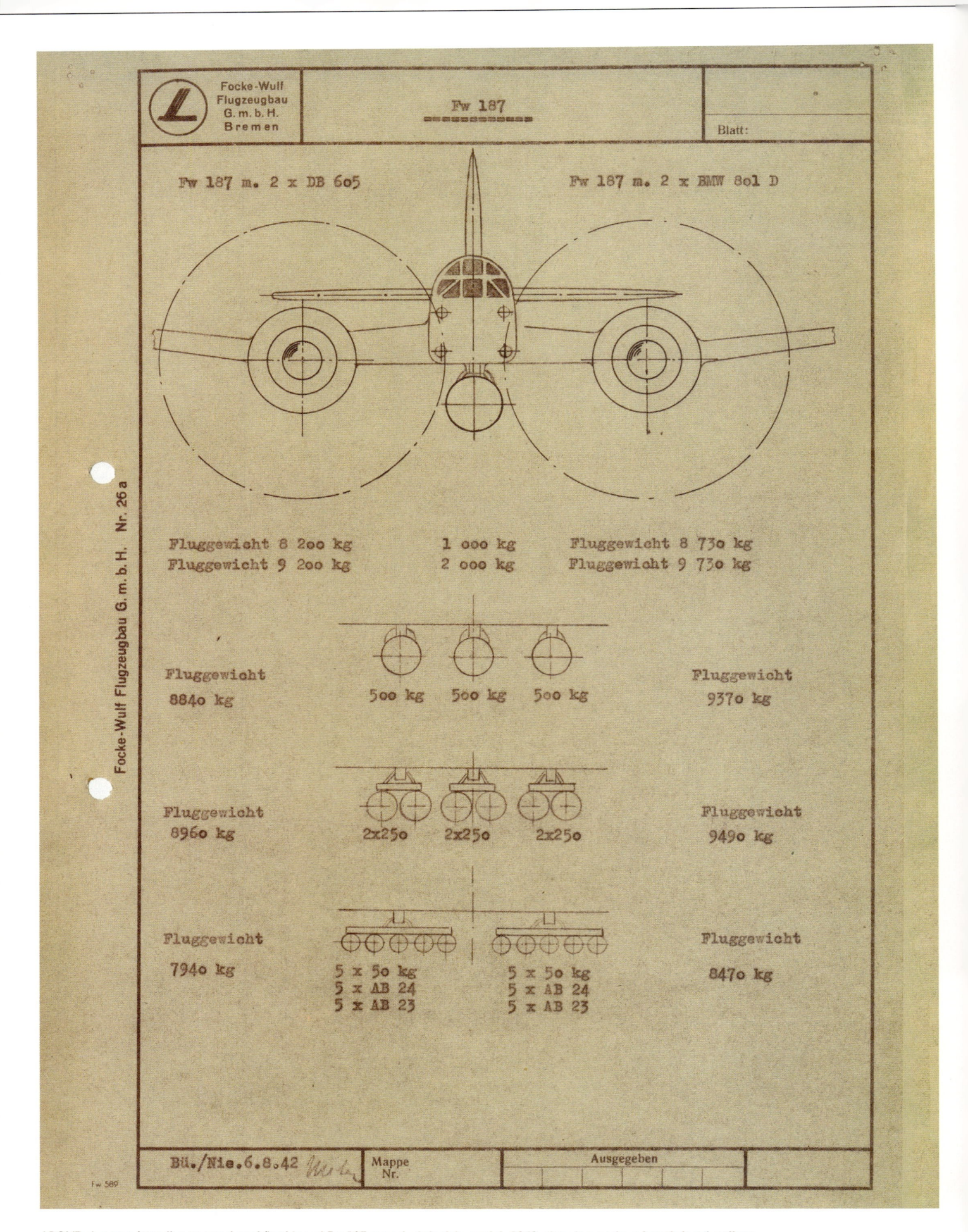

Bü./Nie.6.8.42   Mappe Nr.   Ausgegeben

Fw 589

ABOVE: A page from the second and final 'new' Fw 187 report, dated August 6, 1942, showing various bomb load options.

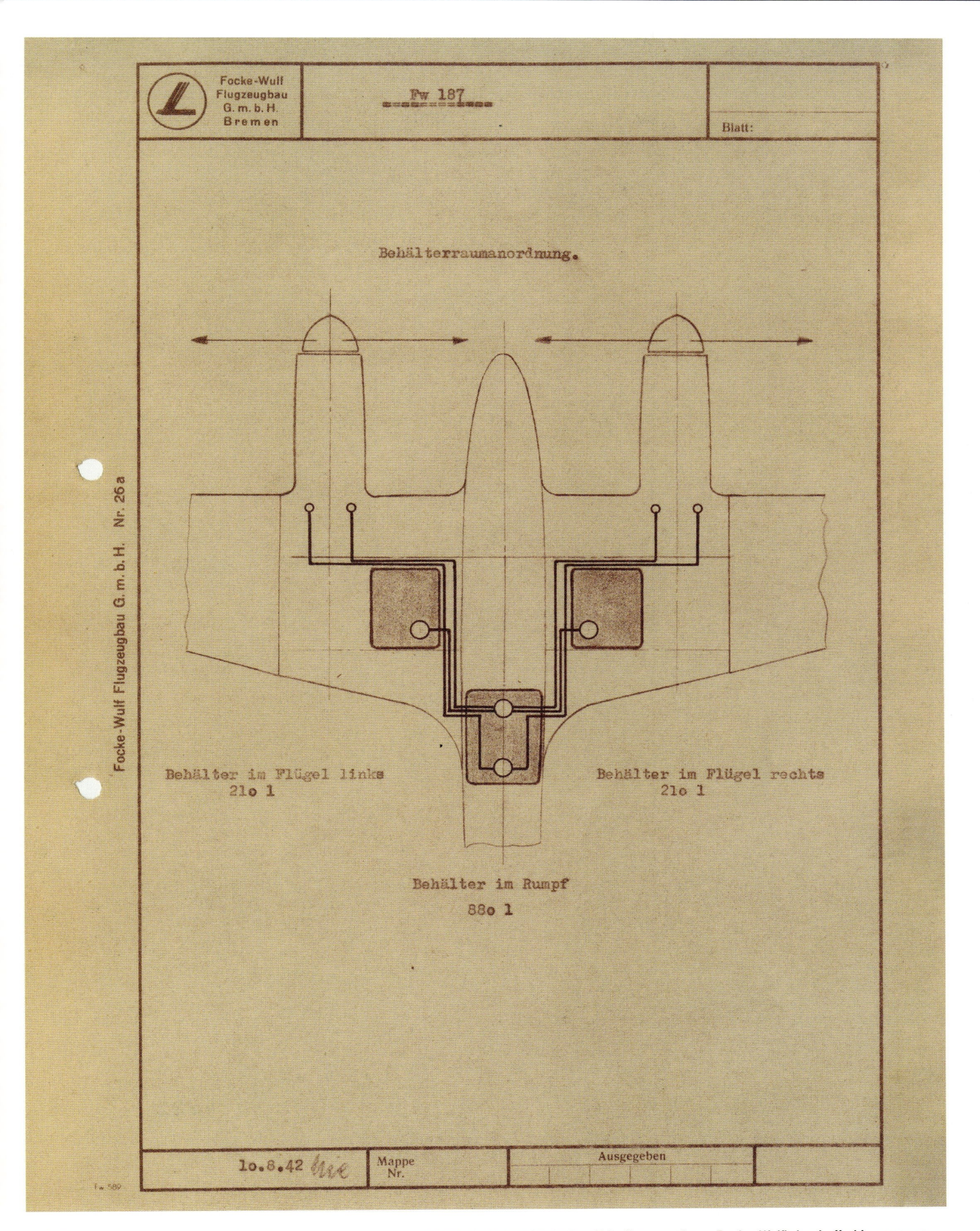

ABOVE: Lack of fuel capacity and therefore range was a major criticism of the Fw 187 design. This diagram shows Focke-Wulf's best effort to squeeze in as much fuel as possible – an 880 litre fuselage tank plus two 210 litre inner wing tanks.

Milch: "I don't think we really need to pursue the Fw 187 any further based on what we've seen here. It doesn't have much of an advantage as a heavy fighter of any kind."

The stenographer recording the meeting noted that, at this point, someone shouted out: "It can't be improved either!"

Milch: "On the contrary, it is already highly enhanced. But it lacks speed and has no real weaponry. The bomb thing is just a stopgap measure. In any case, there are other aircraft that are already there that are just as good. It needs to be redeveloped and is therefore still behind the He 219. The big advantage it has – the only one that would convince me – would be its low weight of 7.2 tons. The only thing that bothers me about the He 219 is its heavy weight."

Friebel: "This table shows the influence of weight again. The Fw 187, as a heavy fighter, was once a competitor to the Me 110. But even back then it was an extremely small aircraft. You can see: version one would look like this: 8.2 tons. If you were to take it as a heavy fighter, then it would come to 11.5 tons."

Milch: "Galland opposes the use of the word 'Kampfzerstörer'. He definitely doesn't want it."

Another anonymous shout: "It has already been killed!"

Milch: "So let's call it something else. So the weight question again! I have to disagree with you, the Fw 187 and the Me 110 are completely the same; it is 7.2 tons. The Me 110 didn't start with 7.3 tons either, but has already increased."

Friebel: "I was misunderstood. I meant: the starting point was 6.2 tons on one machine and 5.2 tons on the other machine."

Milch: "I don't see the He 219 having the highest performance that could be achieved due to its weight. That bothers me about the He 219 compared to the Me 210. I completely ignore the fact that the Me 210 didn't make it for other reasons. But if we had the Me 210 and it was suitable for night fighting, then we wouldn't have to worry any more. So we have to add the Ju 188 for comparison, not as a bomber, but as a night fighter and heavy fighter. We would have to make this comparison and we would also have to bring them to the same range."

Petersen: "Even more! Above all, they would have to be powered by the 213 or 603."

Milch: "We want to be clear about this: if we could use the Ju 188 for one of the two purposes, even with a small change, modification, etc… You also have to consider the number of crew; The He 219 has two and the Ju 188 has four, and if you ask the night fighters whether they can get by with two men or whether they would prefer to have a third or even a fourth man, then of course you get one other comparison into this matter."

Friebel: "I can report that the He 219 originally started with three men. Then it was in the same size class as the Ju 188. But it was then determined, in collaboration with the command staff and the night fighter division, that it would also work with two men. This made the aircraft smaller. Even if you were to use the Ju 188 as a night fighter, then we would still need a heavy fighter class aircraft next to it, i.e. a twin-engine aircraft. It then doesn't matter whether you put the heavy fighter and the night fighter together or combine the heavy fighter with the night fighter at the same time."

Milch: "Right. The question that needs to be asked here – which lies outside the scope of performance, which I would assume would be satisfactory – is which type can be produced in large numbers? Where can I focus on success? The second question is: which can I get fastest? Finally, a third question is: where do I have the lowest construction effort in terms of the lower weight?

"We have to put these three questions very much in the foreground in terms of production. Of course, we shouldn't let these questions get us into a performance comparison. So we have to make two comparisons: first the performance comparison and then the production and schedule comparison. The He 219 is coming anyway. What we can influence is the number made and the question of their configuration. The Ju 188 is coming anyway. The Fw 187 would have to be completely rebuilt, as would the Arado 240. The Me 110 has been phased out. I think we can put these three guys in the background for performance reasons. The question remains open as to whether the Me 210 can still be made into one aircraft or the aircraft for both purposes – heavy fighter and night fighter."

Friebel: "It would be useful if it were possible to have one aircraft for both. Then the question for the Me 210 would have to be answered positively."

Milch: "Based on the 603 graph, the Me 210 is already somewhat superior to the He 219. I see Heinkel falling behind the next design possibilities. The Heinkel machine is not as high as the others."

Friebel: "Firstly, it is a little earlier, and secondly, sacrifices were made in favour of [specialisation for] night fighting operations; the people haven't spared anything for the sake of making a real night hunter, they've included everything you need for night fighting, whereas with the Me 210 it will be quite a struggle and with a considerable loss of performance."

Milch: "We want to march undeterred towards the night fighter area with the He 219 and be clear that this will cover everything that lies in this area. The question is whether the machine will fly as expected in theory today. Here we are approaching full series production again without any practical testing. We hope to save one-and-a-half to one-and-three-quarters of a year. We don't know what turns fate may take. I am fully aware that I am making a big mess here."

von Gablenz: "If the Ju 188 were to be configured as an ordinary fighter with a performance compared to the He 219 – not the Me 210 – it can't be that far away."

Milch: "Why don't you want to put everything in the cabin of the Ju 188?"

Friebel: "It's been a terrible monster so far. We now have to attach a giant armour plate to the front of the night fighter, which is now twice as wide due to the cockpit, and the machine suffers much more from this than the He 219, where I only have a very small, optimal cross-section to protect."

Milch: "If you say: I'll make the Ju 188 as it is, just with a different cockpit for night fighting, then that would still be significantly cheaper than a completely new aircraft, and you could do a lot with it. We don't want to come to a decision very quickly in our development meetings, but rather we want to think the whole thing through carefully, taking all the data into account. I have resolved never to make a decision in one meeting, but rather to wait.

"You wouldn't believe how much it burdens me inside that I have made the decision to give in to the request of the night fighter division and the General Staff to have the He 219 arrive earlier, because I know that I am doing the greatest nonsense that I have always fought against. But it is the only way to bring the He 219 to a point in time where it is still interesting. If it came in 1944, as it was supposed to, it would be completely uninteresting."

FW 187 RULED OUT

Some time after the August 18 meeting, as usual, a brief report was published which summarised the discussion and the decisions that had arisen from it.

This had the headline 'Comparison He 219/Fw 187 for night fighter and heavy fighter use' and it reported: "He 219 certainly fulfils the requirements of the night fighter. For use as a heavy fighter, however, the effort is too high. Fw 187 would be a good heavy fighter. Due to its small size, it does not seem suitable as a night fighter. In addition, it would practically mean a new development, since not much more than the external form can be taken over from the old Fw 187.

"The Field Marshal sees a great risk in the accelerated start of series production of the He 219, which must take place without any testing, which makes it necessary to provide alternatives. For this, the Fw 187 is ruled out due to scheduling reasons. The Me 210 and Ju 188 would primarily come into question, namely the Me 210 could be used as a short-range night fighter in addition to being used as a heavy fighter, and the Ju 188 especially could be used as a for long-range night fighter.

"Accordingly, at the next development meeting, lists are to be submitted in which the following questions are examined from the point of view of performance comparison, the schedule and the production possibilities: I. He 219 as a night fighter and heavy fighter; II. Me 210 as a heavy fighter; III. Me 210 as a heavy fighter and night fighter; IV. Ju 188 as (bomber and) night fighter."

It must have been galling for Milch to see his Fw 187 proposal shot down so easily – and his true reaction to Friebel's assertion that the aircraft would have to be completely redesigned to suit an overall increase in weight is unknown. Certainly, he did not decide to have Kurt Tank removed as Focke-Wulf Betriebsführer. For the Fw 187 this was, finally, the end. But it was certainly not the end of Tank's own ambition to build a twin-engine fighter. •

Bewaffnungsmöglichkeiten

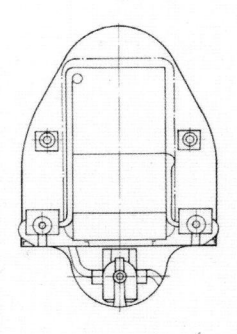

MG 131   2 MG 131 mit je 500 Schuß
MG 151   2 MG 151 mit je 250 Schuß
MG 103   1 MK 103 mit je 180 Schuß

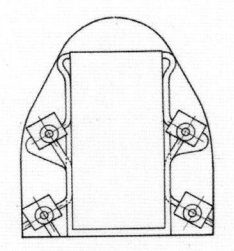

4 MG 151 mit je 500 Schuß

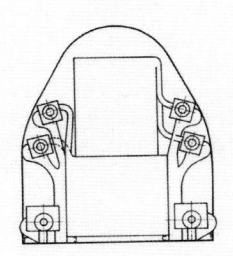

4 MG 131 mit je 500 Schuß
2 MG 151 mit je 500 Schuß

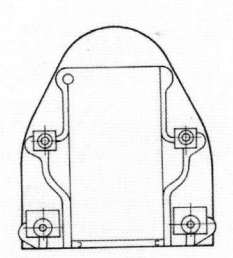

2 MG 131 mit je 700 Schuß
2 MG 151 mit je 500 Schuß

ABOVE: Focke-Wulf's attempt to address the Fw 187's armament shortcomings with four options, all including 1942-era cannon.

Rise of the Falkskito

Focke-Wulf Jäger mit 2 x BMW 801 F

From mid-1942 into the first half of 1943, Focke-Wulf's designers worked on numerous development strands – some separate and in parallel, others closely interwoven. One loose thread was an Fw 187 successor based on the Ta 154…

The second cancellation of the Fw 187 on August 18, 1942, no doubt came as a blow to Kurt Tank, who had felt it was a winning design since its earliest beginnings in 1935. However, it did allow his company to forge ahead with other projects.

Less than a month later, at another Air Ministry management meeting on September 16, 1942, Milch and his senior team were still agonising over which airframe should be built for the Luftwaffe's night fighter units.

There was a plan to build 250 Daimler-Benz DB 628 engines – essentially DB 605s with two-stage superchargers – and use them to power night fighters from mid-1944 onwards, but it was pointed out that only the old Bf 110 could accommodate them. The He 219 was being built to take the DB 603, a physically larger engine than the 605 that the 628 was based on. And the Me 210, now being called the Me 410 (and also now in the running as a night fighter airframe despite what had been said during the August 18 meeting – see previous chapter), had been redesigned to take the 603 – so it couldn't take the 628 either.

Milch pointed out that the He 219 would not become available in quantity until the end of 1944, so "with which aircraft is the night fighting actually done in 1943 and 1944?"

There was an anonymous should of, "Only 110!" and Vorwald shouted: "And some Ju 88s!"

Milch: "The [Ju] 188?"

Vorwald: "No, the 188 doesn't come until 1944."

Milch: "The main thing is that the 188 is provided."

Vorwald: "The N [presumably a projected dedicated night fighter variant of the Ju 188] doesn't come until July '44. We can try to bring it forward to April '44. It has the [Jumo] 213 and perfect night equipment."

After a brief discussion between Milch and Oberstingenieur Franz Mahnke, representing the Ministry's engine section, William Werner spoke up. Werner was the technical director of Auto Union, which built Junkers aero engines in huge quantities under licence, and the industry liaison for aero engines.

He said: "Couldn't you think of significantly increasing the 1,500hp version of the [Jumo] 211 and using it for a light night bomber, so doing some magic here? The 211 is the only base that is really realistic because it is a well-worn engine that has been running for years. The facilities for it are the best at any engine plant. All remaining engines are new starts and must first be largely rationalised. The question is whether one should not try to create something for the very near future, for 1943."

Designed as a competitor for Daimler-Benz's DB 601, Jumo's 211 was a liquid-cooled inverted V12 that had been powering Ju 87 dive-bombers and He 111 bombers since 1937. It was also, as Werner pointed out, a very mature and refined design already being manufactured in vast quantities. Indeed, it would end up being the most-produced German aero engine of the war. In its 'F' form, it could generate 1,320hp – not earth-shattering performance but perhaps sufficient for a night fighter.

Milch was naturally sceptical about the possibility of designing and building a night fighter, or bomber, powered by the 211 in time for it to enter service in 1943. He responded to Werner: "We can't get a machine ready that quickly."

Werner: "I just mean that we might take it even further. I see the easiest way [forward is] to pull up on the 211. We can get 1,000 units out in three quarters [of a year,] to a year."

Mahnke: "With the 211, it doesn't matter whether we make 1,000 more units."

Werner: "This possibility needs to be clarified at some point. It's terrible when you think about waiting until 1944."

Milch: "The question is whether you can get an airframe together so quickly."

Mahnke: "We could even maintain capacity on the 211 … for a longer period of time without disrupting the 213."

Werner: "The basis we have there is not even remotely used. We could pull it off completely differently because we have all the resources. It's just a question of rationalisation. If we ramp it up properly, we'll get to 1,000 engines, I'm not worried about that. I'm not that pessimistic about people. We just have to bring in more special machines to save money on people."

Milch: "You think that the machine [the Jumo 211-powered night fighter] has value if it comes quickly. Who would be suitable in this area, who could do quick work here?"

Pasewaldt: "Only Focke-Wulf would come into question."

Someone shouted: "They're not fast enough!"

Generalingenieur Walter Hertel said: "In my opinion the only possibility would be Heinkel."

Milch: "We have now slowed down Heinkel. We told him to sort things out now. He has enough to do with his machines. I'm also not convinced he could put a wooden machine down fast enough. He doesn't even have the people to do it."

Werner: "What other furniture factories, chair factories, etc. do we have that are not being utilised at all?"

Milch: "The Americans are now sending their furniture manufacturers to England so that they can see how the English do it. It's probably due to the Mosquito. We don't have a Mosquito motor. How much horsepower does the Mosquito motor have?"

Werner: "1,200hp [NB: the Mosquito's Merlin 21 actually generated 1,280hp at take-off, rising to 1,490hp at 12,500ft (3,810m)]! Since the meeting on Sunday I've only had one thought: how to do it differently. We have to do it here and we can do it if this path is taken."

Milch: "What does Dornier actually have to do in his design office?"

Pasewaldt: "Dornier is currently underutilised."

Milch: "He fumbles around with all sorts of tasks that don't interest him. In his stubbornness he continues to do all sorts of things. I would like to take that away from him."

Werner: "Wouldn't it be useful to give it to the entire aircraft industry? You would say to the industry: it will not be one brand, but a joint effort of the industry; the industry should prove what it can do; I demand that it be in the spring of next year."

Milch: "You have to think about that. But first we have to see who else comes into question from a purely construction office perspective. Junkers is fully utilised and well founded; you can't take anything away from them and you can't give anything either. Heinkel needs what he has today, while combining his strengths for the tasks he still has. Focke-Wulf is not stressed at the moment. Arado is not stressed either, he is also fiddling with all sorts of things. Dornier is also not burdened, he will definitely continue with his big flying boats. All three companies have good design offices. Siebel is also free."

Gotha was also briefly mentioned as having some capacity.

Milch: "So we would have designers free for a new task. It's just a question of which man we give the job to. We also have the new bomber, the 700km bomber [Schnellbomber competition]. We don't want to be complacent about this task; we absolutely need it as soon as possible. The question is whether we can achieve something like this with such wooden construction."

Another anonymous shouter: "Don't we want to give the task to Dr Dornier?"

Milch: "No, he's way too slow. You can ask [him] once in 20 years."

Werner: "One of the most lively in society is [Kurt] Tank. Hertel [Heinrich Hertel of Junkers, rather than Walter Hertel who was present at the meeting] is also enthusiastic. It has to be someone who really puts their heart and soul into it and sees it as their most sacred task."

Hertel: "Tank is not suitable for mixed construction and not for timber construction, he has no experience in this."

Werner: "But he has the initiative, and the initiative is the primary thing. We need initiative because there is no time. We would already be working on the crankshaft issues. A blacksmith's line would have to be set up immediately, the legs would have to be welded on, etc. We would then set up a shop."

Milch: "Who made the He 70?"

Hertel: "Especially Schwärzler [Karl Schwärzler, chief designer at Heinkel], he has the most experience."

Milch: "Is Schwärzler a man who can do something quickly?"

Hertel: "Schwärzler must have a strong leader."

Milch: "Is Schwärzler absolutely necessary at Heinkel right now?"

Alpers: "Yes, he is the leading engineer in the construction field."

Milch: "Who would be considered for the task? Personally, I still think Tank is the right man."

Pasewaldt: "I would also advocate for Tank, I think he is the fastest."

Werner: "You should put the three together."

Milch: "But someone has to lead! You would have to tell the companies: it is not the work of a single company, but the work of German industry."

Sellschopp: "I would take Tank, and Tank could bring in all the people."

Milch: "We want to tell Tank to be here tomorrow at noon for the meeting and then [he can] tell us what other designers he might need for the task."

Some discussion followed of whether to involve Arado, Messerschmitt and factories making wooden furniture.

Werner: "Something really needs to be done here with the magic wand if we want to get ahead of the others here. In 1944 it comes too late. The thing has to be as primitive as possible. Only the primitive can do it."

Pasewaldt: "Look at the English aircraft, how primitively they are put together! But our people can't do that."

Werner: "That's how we have to do it too. We can't get by with thorough precision work."

Milch: "What do you think, Vorwald?"
Vorwald: "You definitely have to try it."
Milch: "Are you also for Tank?"
Vorwald: "I'm very fond of Tank."

Werner: "We can give Cambeis [Walter Cambeis, Junkers director] – Vorwald and Mahnke will be with him tomorrow – a study assignment: 1,500 more [Jumo 211] engines by mid-1943, starting in January, through rationalisation, not through [more] people."

Milch: "You can do that easily."

Werner: "You have to think about what we spend on resources for 603, 801, etc. and what pathetic numbers come out of it. Here I have real numbers. I can do the 1,000 engines much more easily. The Daimler-Benz Ring is the weakest thing you can imagine. People are losing their nerve; why should we hand over our many workers and our most valuable material to get 100 engines [presumably a reference to the DB 628], when here we can have 1,000 engines!"

Sellschopp: "But… for the fighters!"

After another brief discussion, Milch said: "I am grateful to Mr Werner for initiating the matter. It's absolutely in line with what we want. What's new to me is that you can get even more engines from Junkers."

Werner: "Yes, that can be done."

Milch: "So I would like us – Pasewaldt and Alpers are here – to have a preliminary meeting with Tank tomorrow at 1pm. Motto: Think about this whole task, do the planning, start series production as quickly as possible."

Werner: "And as primitive as possible!"

Milch: "When do you think the series can come on schedule? If the machine can come quickly, then this can be done purely in terms of performance. But if it comes late, then it has no purpose, then it is surpassed by other things."

Werner: "My stance is: either the machine will be there in nine months, or…"

Alpers: "If the first series machine doesn't arrive in July, it has no value. We are not allowed to make prototypes at all."

Vorwald: "But the machine has to fly and be tested first. I think it is impossible that it will fly before July/August next year."

Milch: "You mean the prototype?"

Vorwald: "The first aircraft you can judge. You could just let the series run and take the risk."

Milch said he thought the first series production model "could arrive on July 1, 1944, if everything happens very quickly, unless the man comes to terms with the problem so much that he says: I'll put out the first three test machines in the first three months. But there is too much in the box for that."

Alpers: "The question of whether the machine should be Mosquito-like, whether it has three or four crew, that's all crucial."

Milch: "Three people would be enough."

Vorwald: "The cockpit could be taken over from an aircraft that is already there."

Milch: "Then everything would be fine. If we had the Mosquito, we could recreate it straight away. Then I would immediately take the 188 cockpit."

Werner: "Do you even know how much effort the Mosquito requires?"

Milch: "We have finished [shot down] a few; but they were all completely destroyed. In any case, this will be a cheap machine. I'll speak to Tank tomorrow at 1pm."

Werner: "In the meantime, Cambeis can think about the matter of the 1,000 engines. He then has to consider his other tasks as completed."

FROM FW 191 TO MOSKITO

William Werner's suggestion that a night bomber could be created using readily available Jumo 211 engines, along with Milch's suggestion that it should be made of

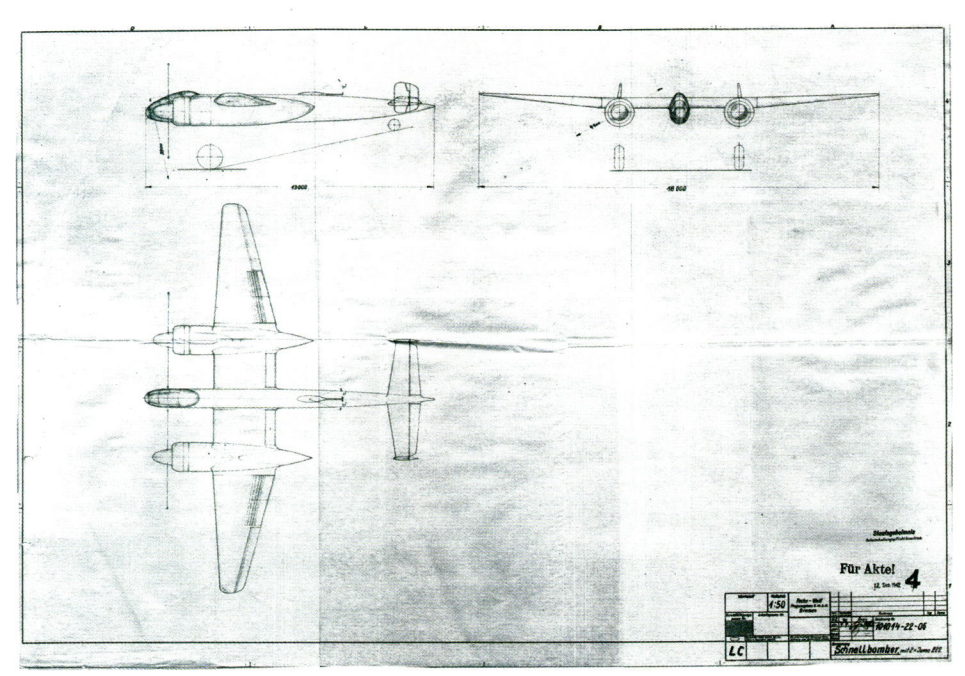

ABOVE: The less adventurous of Focke-Wulf's two Schnellbomber designs was this conventional-looking high-wing machine. The drawing is dated September 9, 1942.

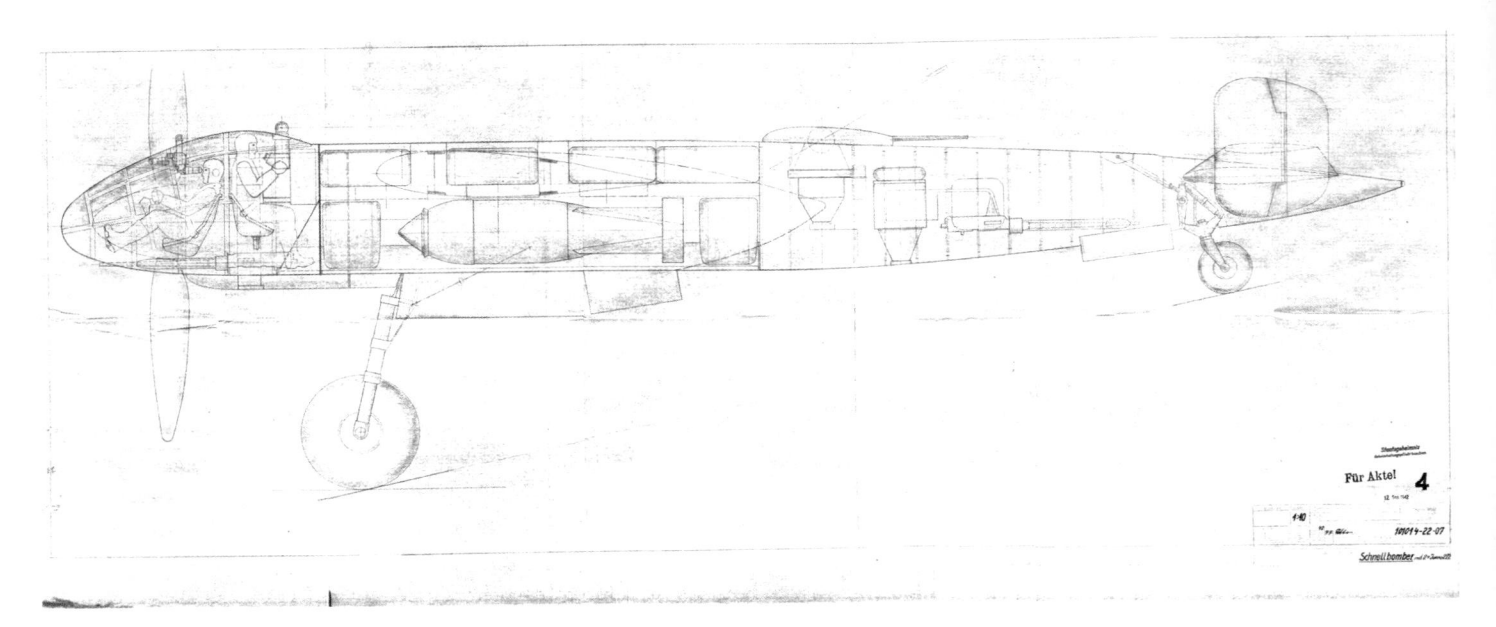

ABOVE: Side view of the more conventional Schnellbomber, showcasing its capacious bomb bay. The design is reminiscent of the company's Fw 191 Bomber B.

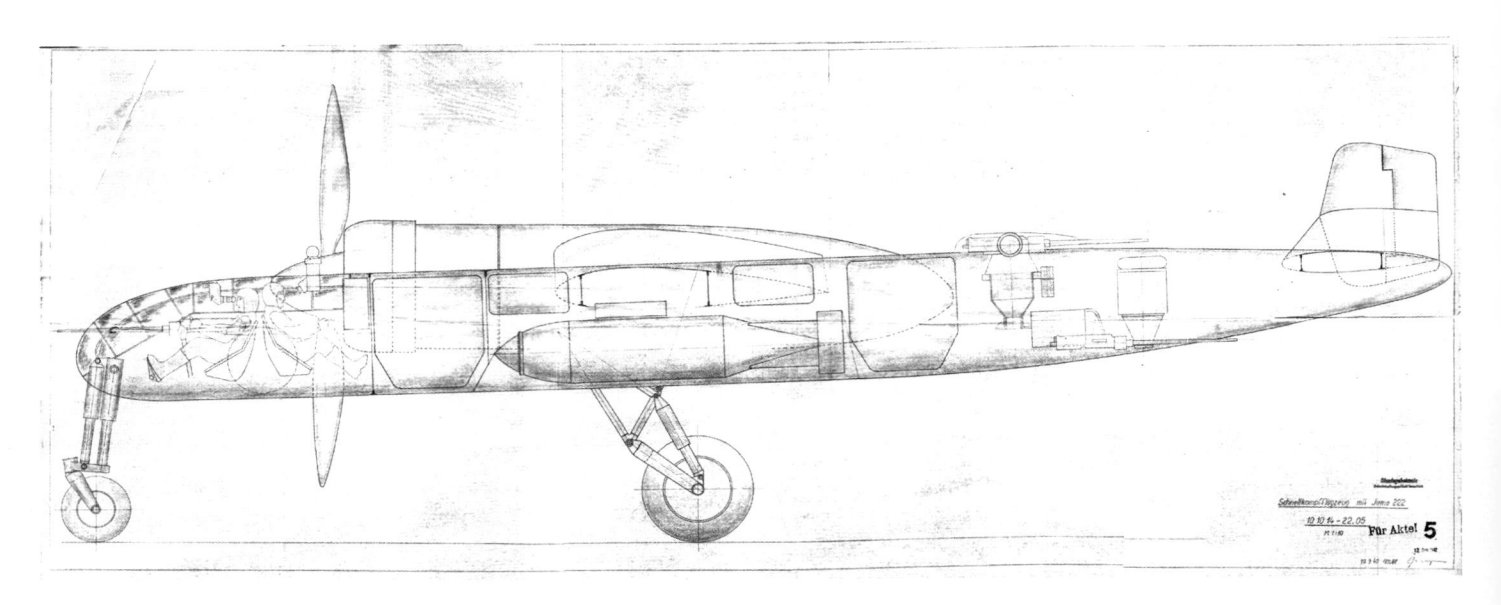

ABOVE: The tricycle undercarriage Schnellbomber in side view. It is not clear where the nosewheel was supposed to go when retracted!

wood, was the genesis of the Focke-Wulf Ta 154. Kurt Tank was given the "most sacred task" of first designing and then building an aerodynamically straightforward wooden Jumo 211-powered night fighter, and in record time to boot, on September 17, 1942. Tank's reward for taking on this seemingly impossible task was, evidently, permission to stamp his name on his company's aircraft going forward. This would be the first aircraft to use the code 'Ta' for 'Tank' rather than 'Fw' for Focke-Wulf'.

Clearly the Fw 187 was not going to be an adequate basis from which to develop this new aircraft since its fuselage had already been deemed too slender to accommodate all the equipment, weapons and fuel that would be essential for a night fighter expected to enter service in 1944. It was, after all, a design rooted in the mid-1930s.

Fortunately, Focke-Wulf had been among the multitude of companies and design groups invited to tender for Milch's Schnellbomber competition, starting in May 1942 (see previous chapter). The initial Schnellbomber specification had set out a number of performance goals: 2,000km range, 500kg payload and maximum speed of 800km/h – or no less than 750km/h without the use of GM1 or water-methanol injection. But it did not specify what engines should be used nor how many, nor did it stipulate the aircraft's configuration.

The result was an incredible diversity of designs from the manufacturers, eventually whittled down to two contenders in January 1943: Messerschmitt's twin-fuselage Me 109 Zw and Dornier's push-pull P 231 design. The latter won and received the designation Do 335, eventually becoming a fighter rather than a bomber. Focke-Wulf, like the others, had drawn up several designs which varied considerably in their adventurousness.

Two of these had been presented in separate reports entitled Schnellbomber mit zwei Jumo 222 C/D and Schnellbomber mit zwei Jumo 222 C/D mit Bugradfahrwerk (tricycle undercarriage), published on September 9 and September 10, 1942, respectively – just a week before Tank was summoned to receive his latest marching orders.

The two Schnellbomber designs were 13m and 14.1m in length respectively and had an identical wingspan of 18m. Looking at Focke-Wulf's long-running Bomber B design, the Fw 191 (which had a fuselage 19m long and a wingspan of 25m), the lineage is clear. These were Fw 191 derivatives but shrunk by 30% – retaining the upper turret but replacing the lower one with fixed rearward-firing cannon.

The second of the two Schnellbombers, featuring a nosewheel, differed the most from the Fw 191 – with an unusual

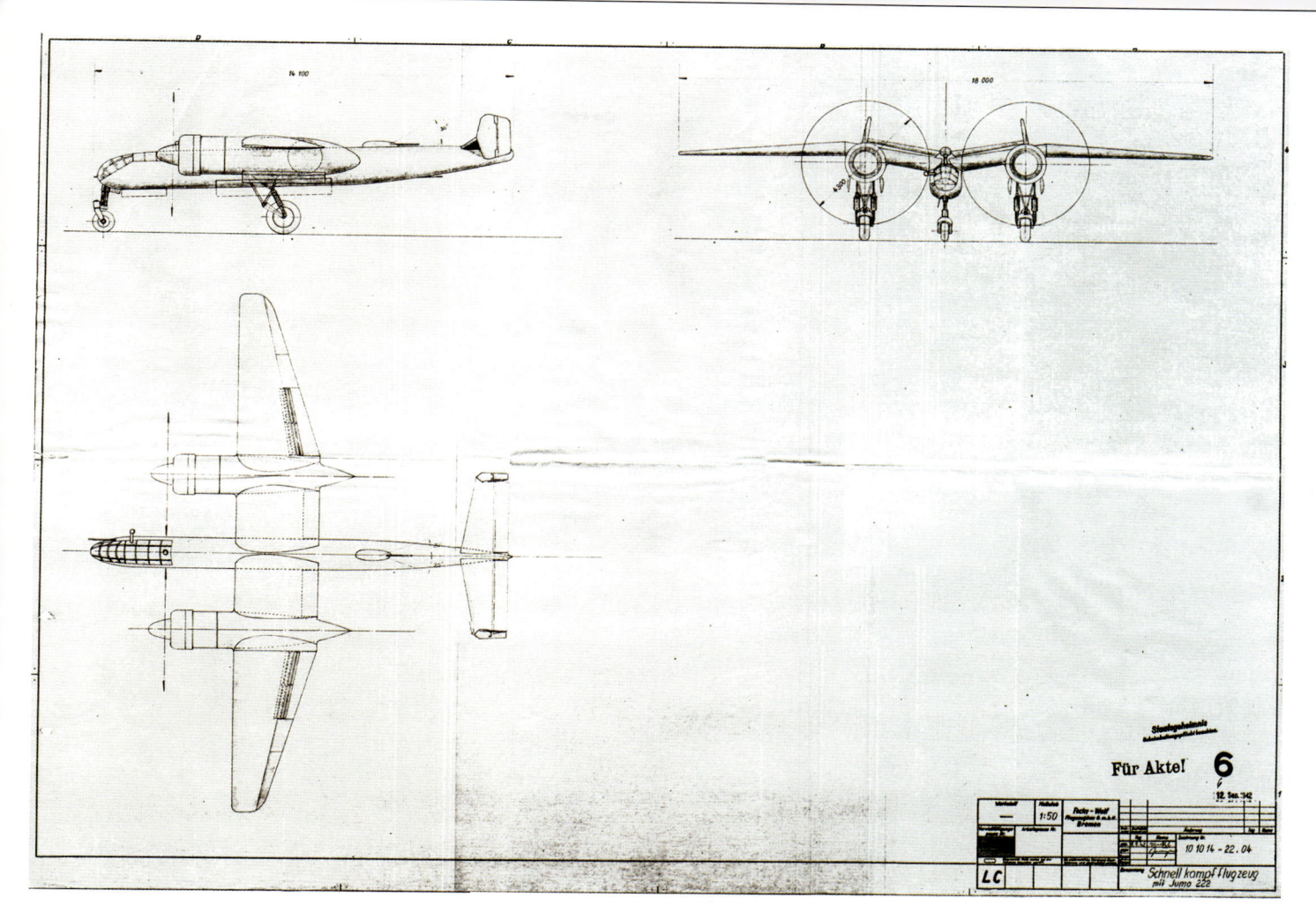

ABOVE: Focke-Wulf's other Schnellbomber design took a slightly more radical approach, with a tricycle undercarriage. The high-set gullwing positioned the engine nacelles higher than the fuselage, allowing the nosewheel leg to be kept short.

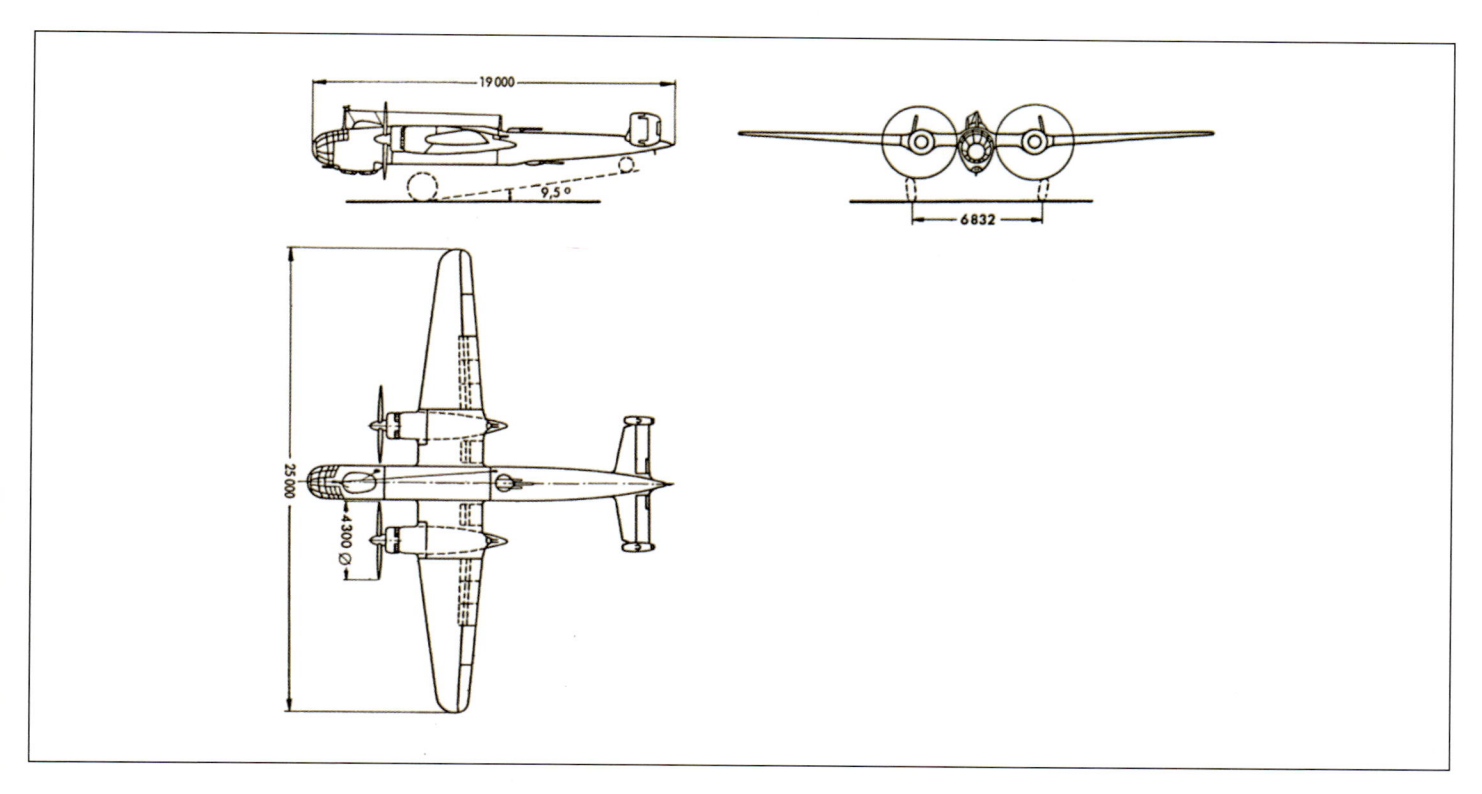

ABOVE: Focke-Wulf's Schnellbomber designs owed much to the company's earlier experiences in designing the Fw 191 bomber. The three views in this drawing are from a January 1, 1942, type sheet but rearranged to allow easier comparison with the other drawings shown here.

Secret Projects of the Luftwaffe 47

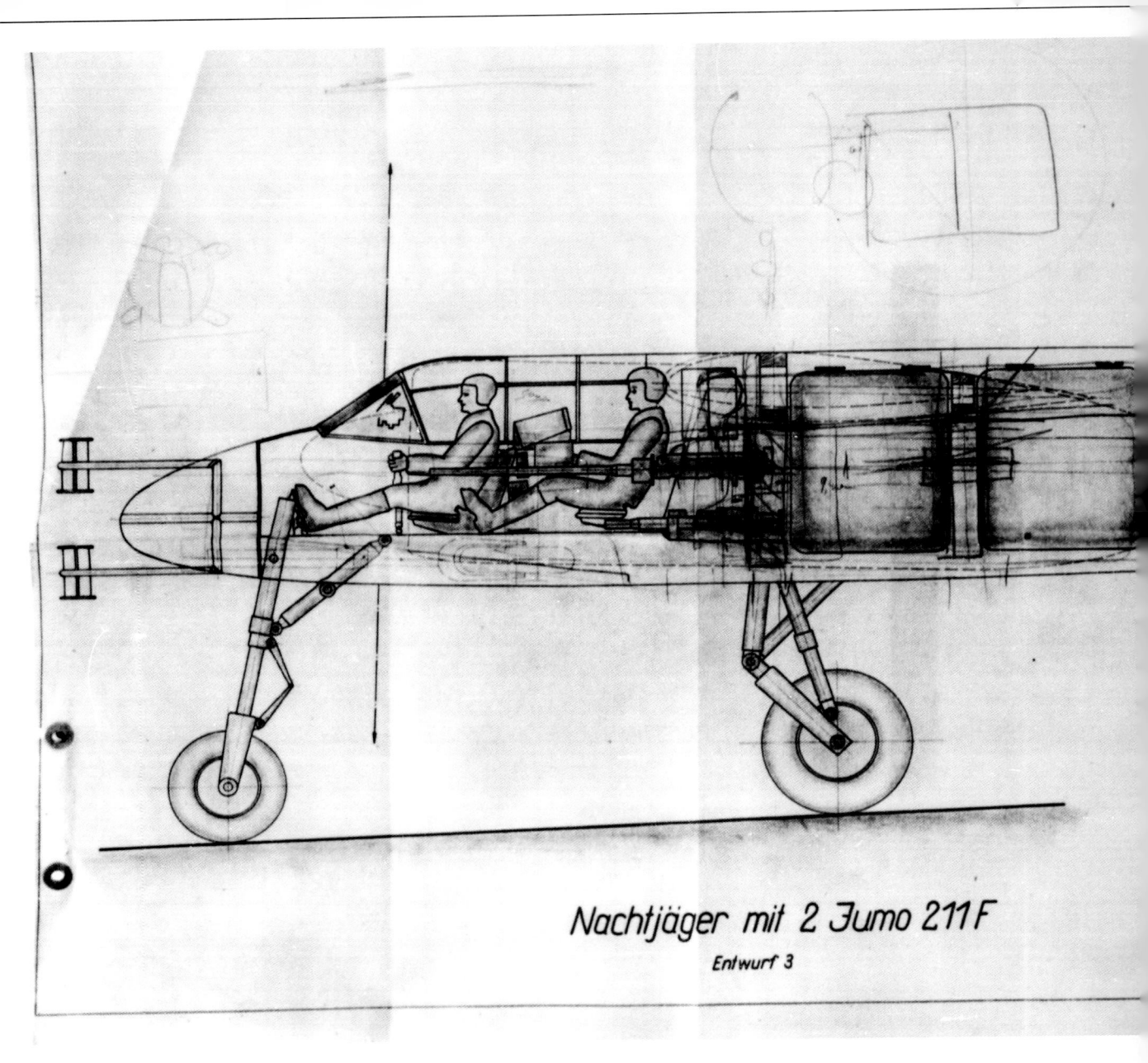

ABOVE: Nachtjäger mit 2 Jumo 211F Entwurf 3, the tricycle undercarriage design which evidently provided the basis for the Ta 154.

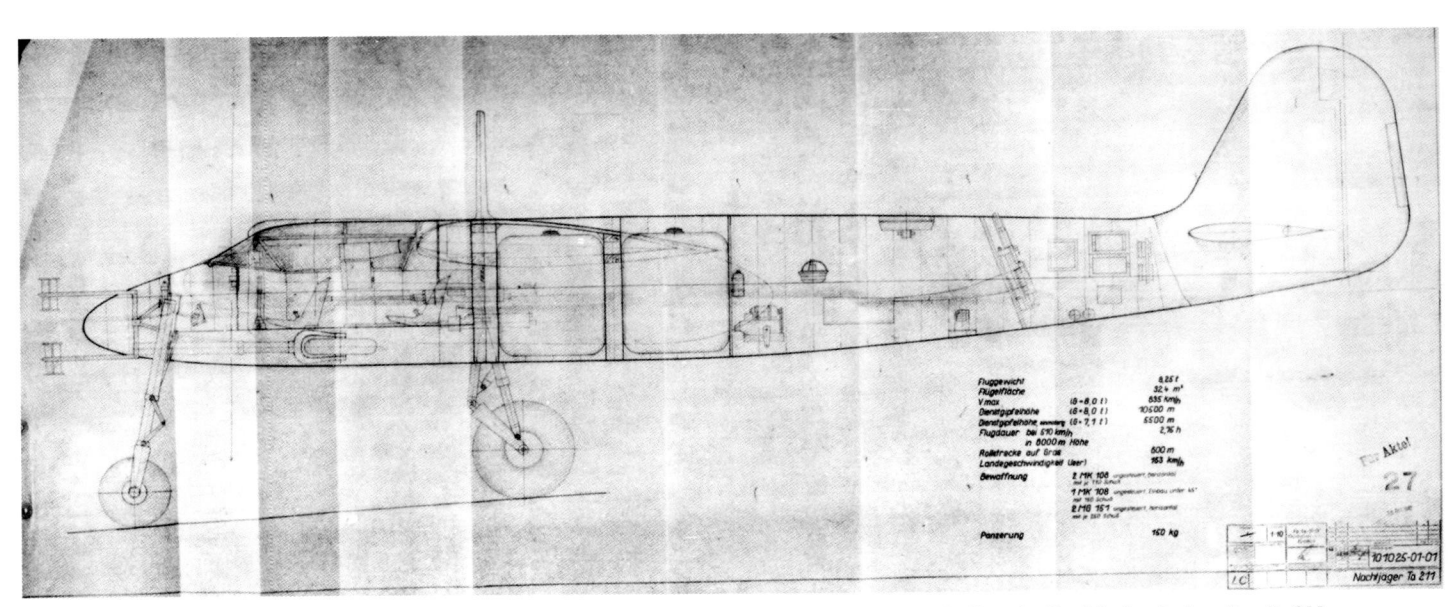

ABOVE: This drawing, dated October 23, 1942, shows the layout of the Ta 154 almost fully formed, albeit under the interim designation Ta 211.

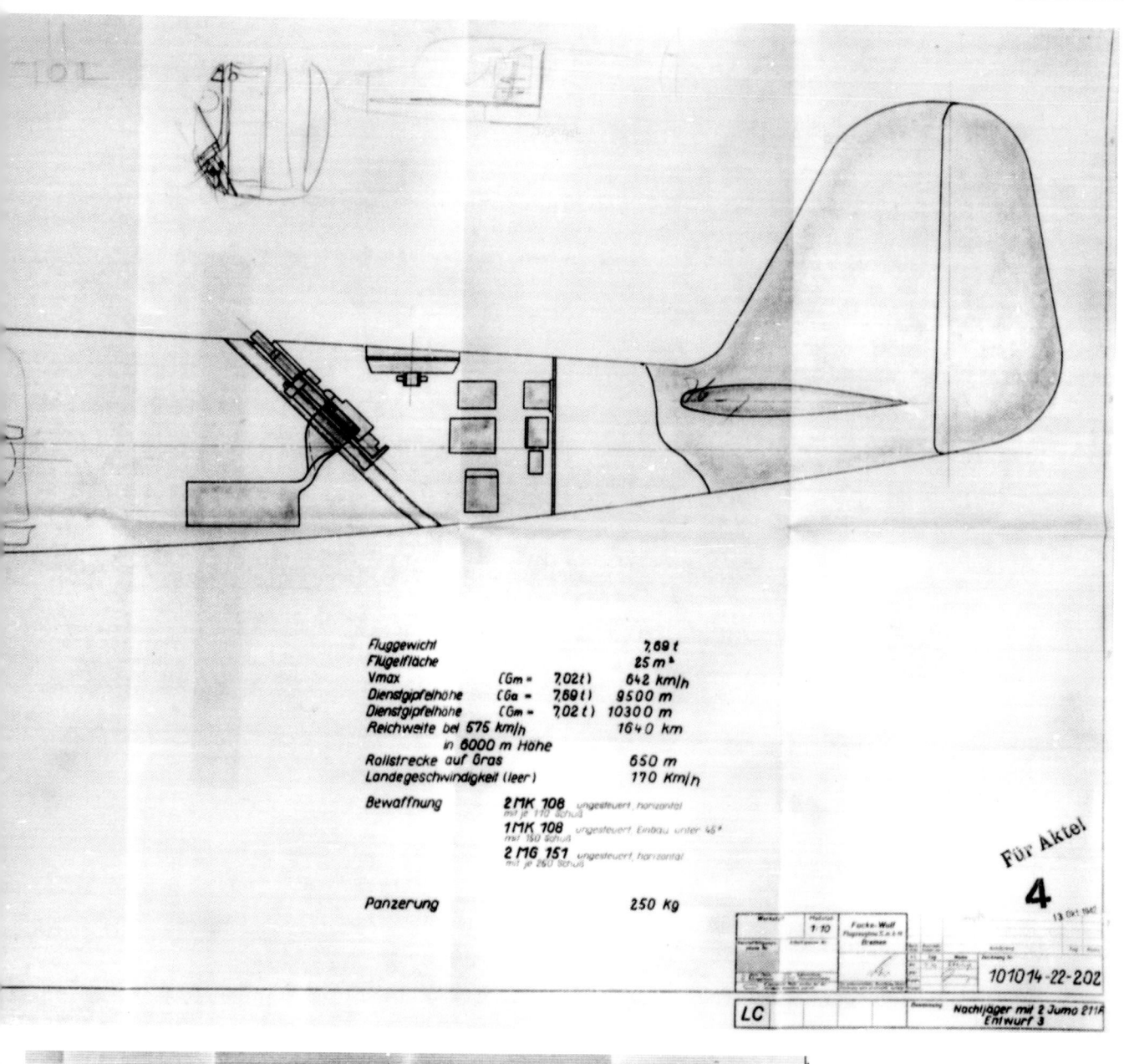

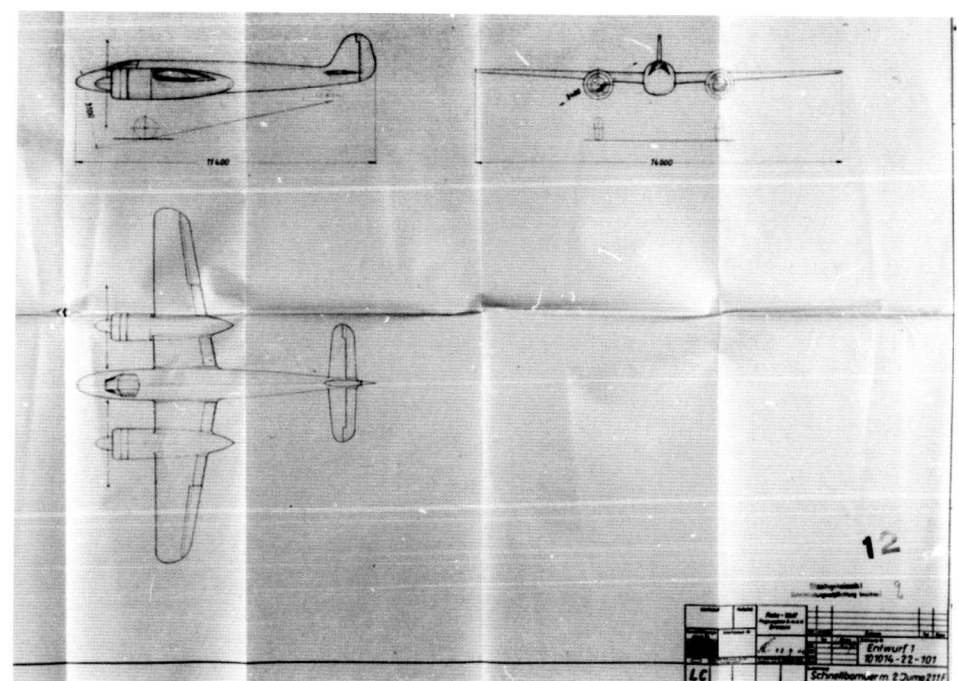

Fluggewicht		7,69 t
Flügelfläche		25 m²
Vmax	(Gm = 7,02 t)	642 km/h
Dienstgipfelhöhe	(Ga = 7,69 t)	9500 m
Dienstgipfelhöhe	(Gm = 7,02 t)	10300 m
Reichweite bei 575 km/h in 6000 m Höhe		1640 km
Rollstrecke auf Gras		650 m
Landegeschwindigkeit (leer)		170 Km/h
Bewaffnung	2 MK 108 ungesteuert, horizontal mit je 110 Schuß	
	1 MK 108 ungesteuert, Einbau unter 45° mit 150 Schuß	
	2 MG 151 ungesteuert, horizontal mit je 260 Schuß	
Panzerung		250 Kg

LEFT: The Jumo 211-powered Schnellbomber. In plan view, the line of descent from the Fw 191 is clear.

Secret Projects of the Luftwaffe

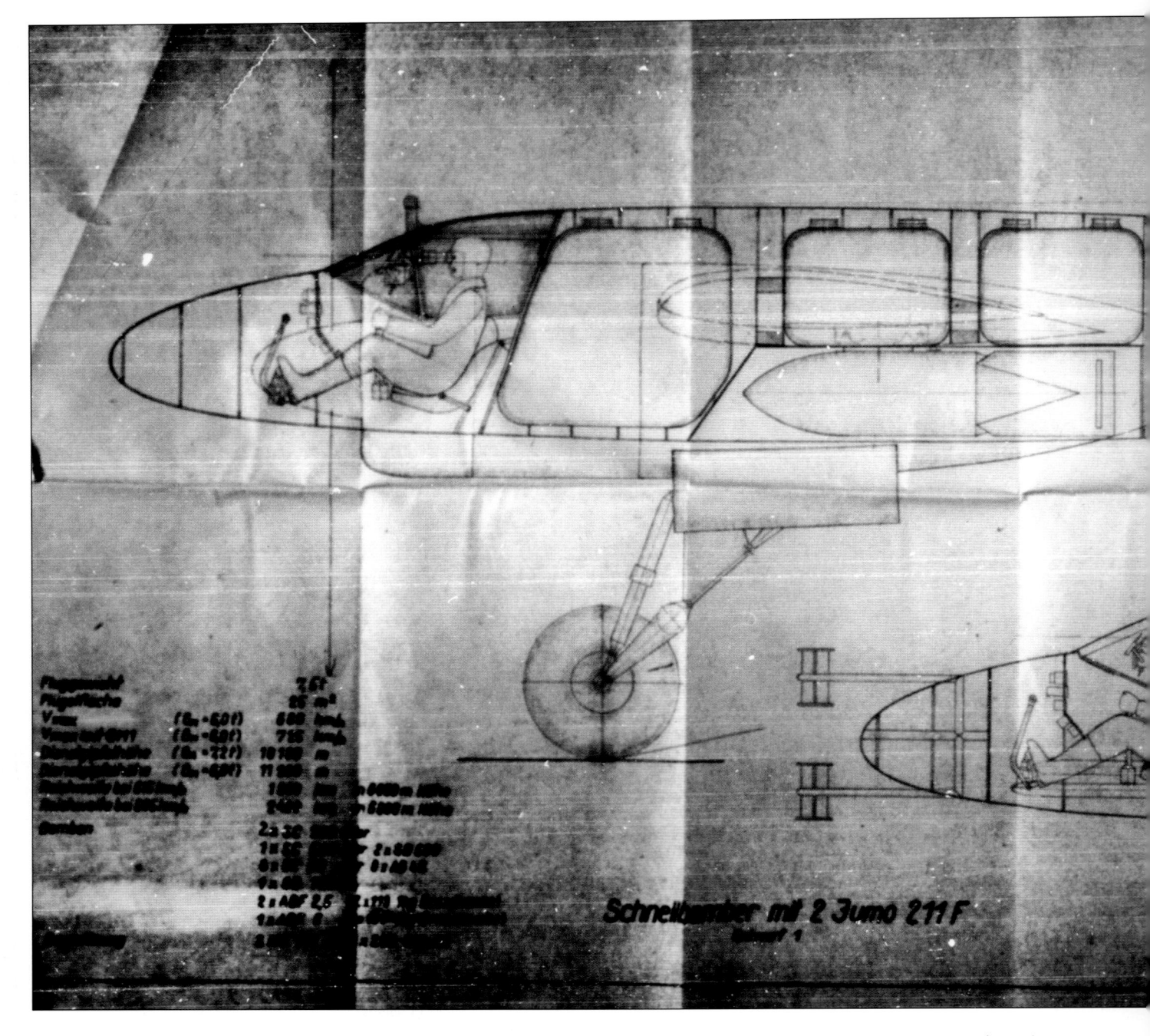

ABOVE: Here the second Jumo 211-powered design, a two-seat night fighter variant, is presented alongside the first – which was configured as a bomber. The third design, not pictured, evidently featured a high wing/nosewheel arrangement.

gullwing arrangement and tailplanes given a strong dihedral. Focke-Wulf was clearly experimenting with an alternative to the standard tail-dragger arrangement but the drawings accompanying the Schnellbomber mit zwei Jumo 222 C/D mit Bugradfahrwerk give little indication of how the nosewheel retraction was supposed to function, since the enormous wheel is depicted occupying the same position as the two crew. The drawing numbers of the two Schnellbomber designs range from 101014-22-04 to 101014-22-07.

From this starting point, Focke-Wulf's designers appear to have shrunk the design once again, this time by 12% in length from 13m to 11.4m, and by 22% in wingspan from 18m to 14m, to create another even smaller aircraft under the designation Schnellbomber mit 2 Jumo 211 F. The drawings are dated September 28, 1942, and are numbered 101014-22-100 and 101014-22-101. It is unlikely that there were 92 drawings between 101014-22-07 and 101014-22-100, particularly given the timescale. Far more likely that Focke-Wulf simply added a digit and restarted the sequence from -100 for these related projects.

Drawing 101014-22-100 depicted the Schnellbomber mit 2 Jumo 211 as an 'Entwurf 1' or 'Design 1' in the main portion of the image but supplemented by an 'Entwurf 2' Nachtjäger mit 2 Jumo 211 F below. The former had a single crewman in the nose, with a fighter-type cockpit. Behind him was a large fuel tank and behind that were two smaller tanks above a bomb bay. To the rear were a pair of fixed rearward-firing cannon. The aircraft is a conventional tail dragger.

The Nachtjäger mit 2 Jumo 211 F featured a two-seater cockpit covered by a much longer canopy. Behind the backseater were large ammo boxes for a quartet of cannon mounted in the sides of the fuselage. With the bomb bay deleted, it was possible to carry two very large fuel tanks in the centre fuselage. A third drawing apparently showed the same design but with a tricycle undercarriage – and it was this that would receive, initially, the designation Ta 211.

But Focke-Wulf evidently did not stop at that third design. By October 7, 1942, the company's designers had reached what was described as 'Entwurf 6, 2 motoriger Jäger mit 7x3cm Kanonen' (Design 6 twin-engine fighter with 7x3cm cannon) or just '2 motoriger Jäger' for short.

wurf 1

Entwurf 2

Fluggewicht		7,5 t
Flugelfläche		25 m²
Vmax	(G_n=6,3t)	650 km/h
Dienstgipfelhöhe	(G_A=7,5t)	9 700 m
Dienstgipfelhöhe	(G_n=6,3t)	10 800 m
Reichweite bei 470 km/h		2 250 km
Rollstrecke auf Gras		600 m
Landegeschwindigkeit (leer)		167 km/h

Nachtjäger mit 2 Jumo 211 F
Entwurf 2

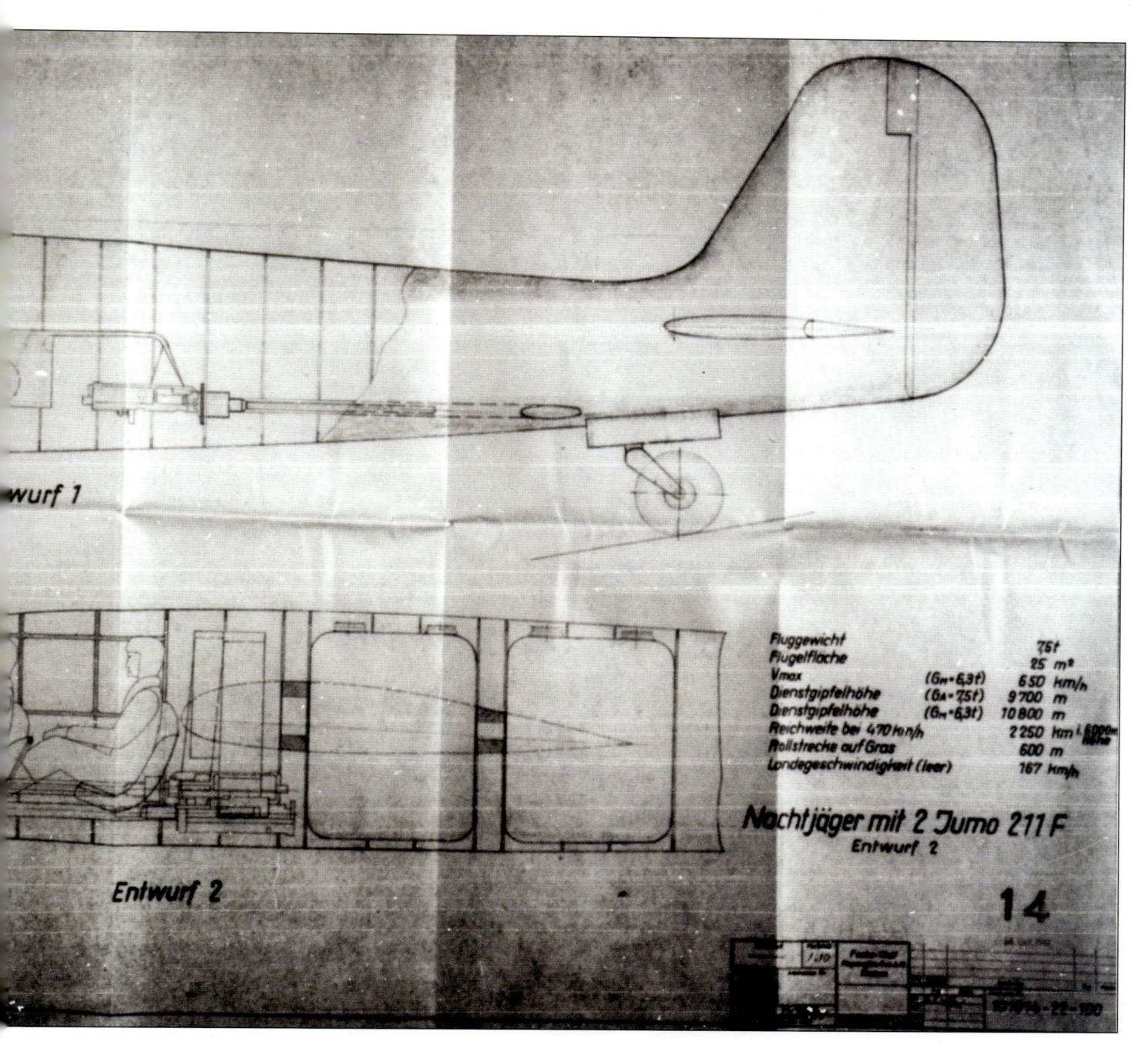

14

This aircraft, no known drawing of which survives, was described as having "rear fuselage, fuselage tail unit, wing structure and landing gear like high-speed bomber in wooden construction. The cockpit structure and equipment arrangement was adopted from the Fw 190 and the engine side was expanded to include two engines".

This presumably meant that the aircraft was to look more like the tail-dragger Schnellbomber depicted in Entwurf 1 than the tricycle undercarriage night fighter apparently shown as Entwurf 3. The wingspan is given as 14m and the wing area as 25sqm, which fits this description.

Exactly how the Fw 190's cockpit, including its canopy, would be grafted onto this, is unclear. Equally unclear is what would happen at the front end of the cockpit since the engines would be in the wings. Perhaps it was simply to have been given a rounded aerodynamic fairing.

The engines themselves would be a pair of BMW 801 Ds – exactly as used in the Fw 190 – and take-off weight would be 7,850kg. The aircraft's armour plating and its positioning, just like the structure of its cockpit and its engines, would be lifted directly from the Fw 190 design.

Armament was remarkably heavy as the aircraft's name suggests: two MK 103s with 150 rounds each and no fewer than five MK 108s, also with 150 rounds each.

Although the report states that the 2 motoriger Jäger was to be made of wood, the actual materials percentage breakdown was 45% wood, 42% steel and 13% other.

The 2 motoriger Jäger went no further at this stage but it would be making something of a reappearance later.

A brief report on the Nachtjäger Ta 211 mit 2 x Jumo 211 F was produced on October 23, 1942. The type was still known as the Ta 211 as of November 12, 1942, but shortly thereafter it was redesignated Ta 154 and a full description, Baubeschreibung Nr. 256 Nachtjäger Ta 154 was published on December 20, 1942. Focke-Wulf was, by this time, seemingly already far advanced in its work on the new night fighter.

FROM MOSKITO TO FALKSKITO

Starting on or before February 20, 1943, while the Ta 154 was still in its infancy, Focke-Wulf designer Voigtsberger, under the direction of chief designer Ludwig Mittelhuber, commenced work on a new 'Jäger mit 2 BMW 801 F' – a fighter powered by two BMW 801 F engines.

The impetus for the project was, perhaps, the receipt of new data sheets on the 801 F, dated January 15, 1943, from BMW. The 'F' was essentially a BMW 801 E (see the first chapter of this publication) now specifically adapted to suit a fighter application. It measured 1.31m high, 1.31m wide, 2.43m

Nachtjäger Ta 211 mit 2x Jumo 211F

ABOVE: Artwork from a Focke-Wulf Ta 211 description report dated October 23, 1942. Just over a month after Kurt Tank was tasked with creating a new wooden night fighter using Jumo 211 engines, its design was already recognisably that of what would become the Ta 154.

Nachtjäger Ta 211 mit 2x Jumo 211F

ABOVE: The same Ta 211 artwork design also appeared in the report set against a 'night' background.

52 Secret Projects of the Luftwaffe

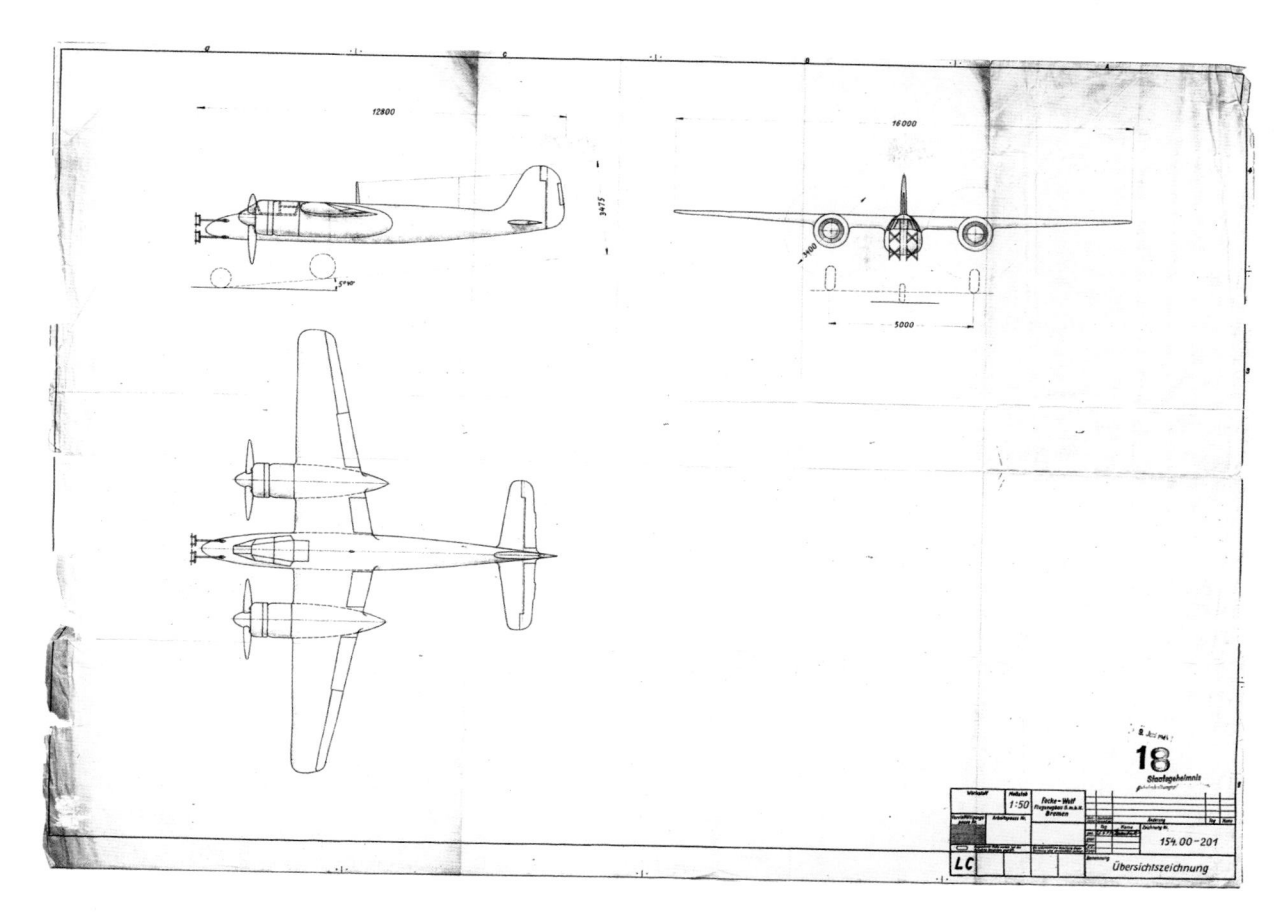

ABOVE: The Focke-Wulf Ta 211 had been redesignated Ta 154 by December 20, 1942, and this drawing dated April 25, 1943, shows its design had changed little during the preceding six months.

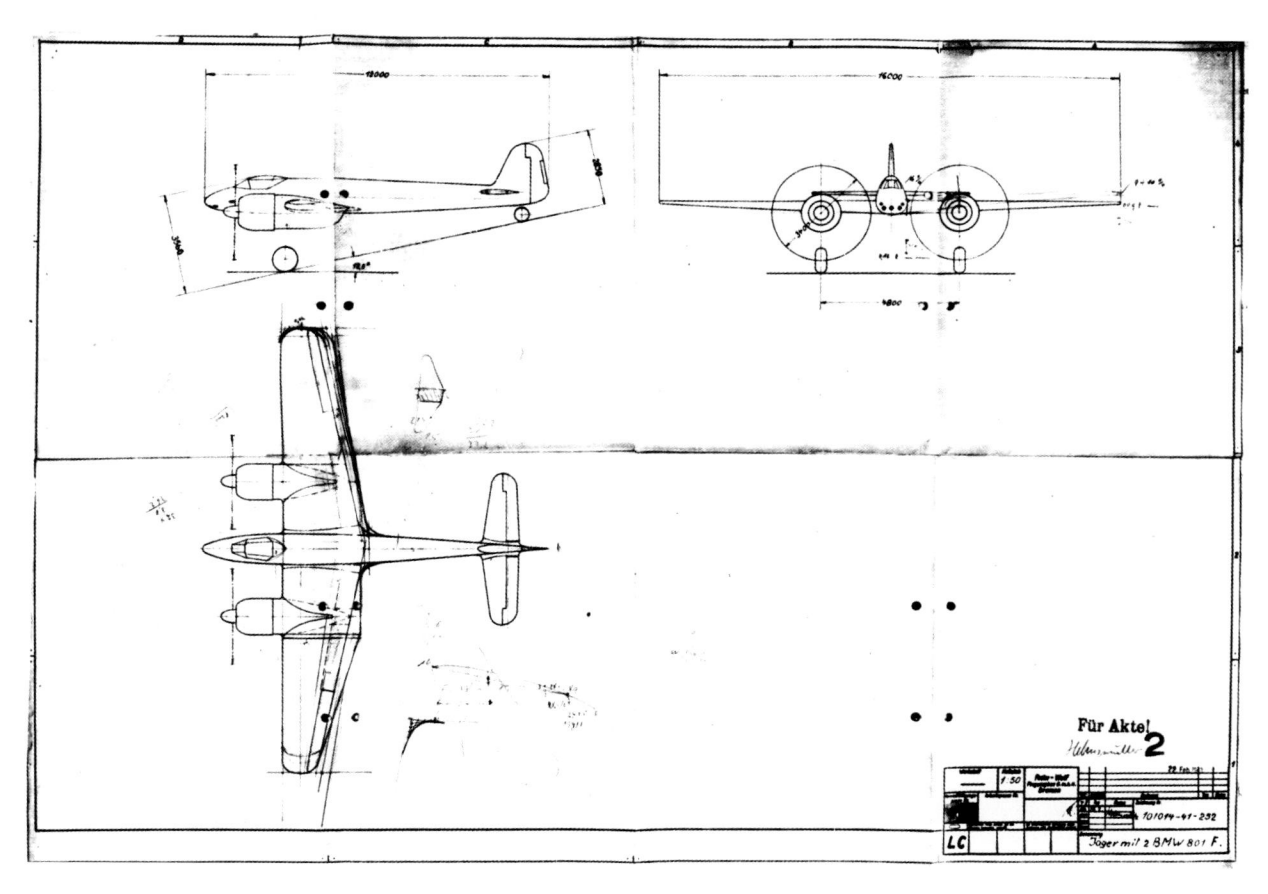

ABOVE: Focke-Wulf's Jäger mit BMW 801 F, shown in drawing number 101014-41-252. The overall configuration is similar to that of the Fw 187 but the component parts are much closer in design to those of the Ta 154.

Secret Projects of the Luftwaffe   53

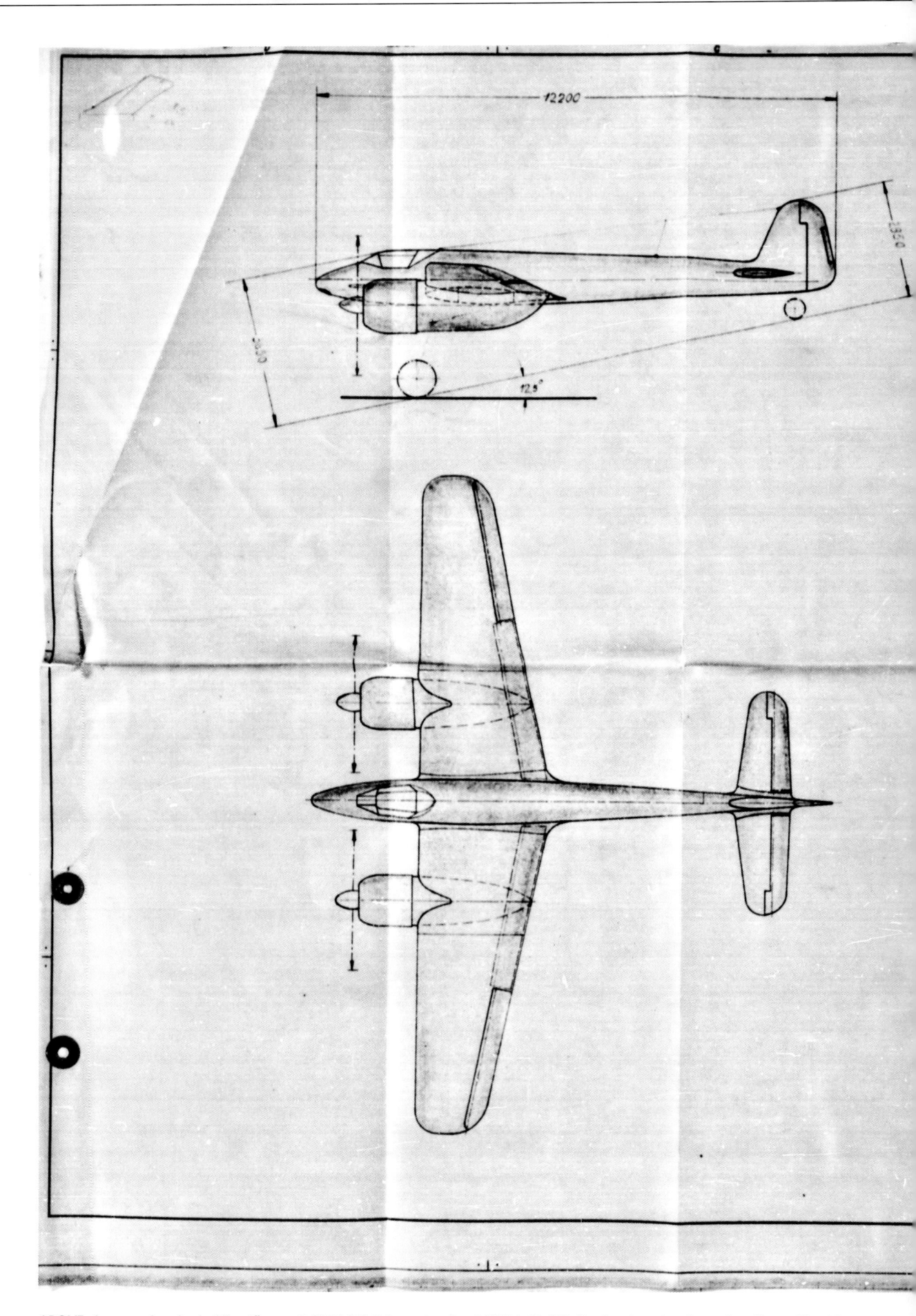

ABOVE: A second variant of the Jäger mit BMW 801 F, from drawing 101014-41-253. The fuselage has been lengthened by 20cm and the wings – previously straight – have been given dihedral.

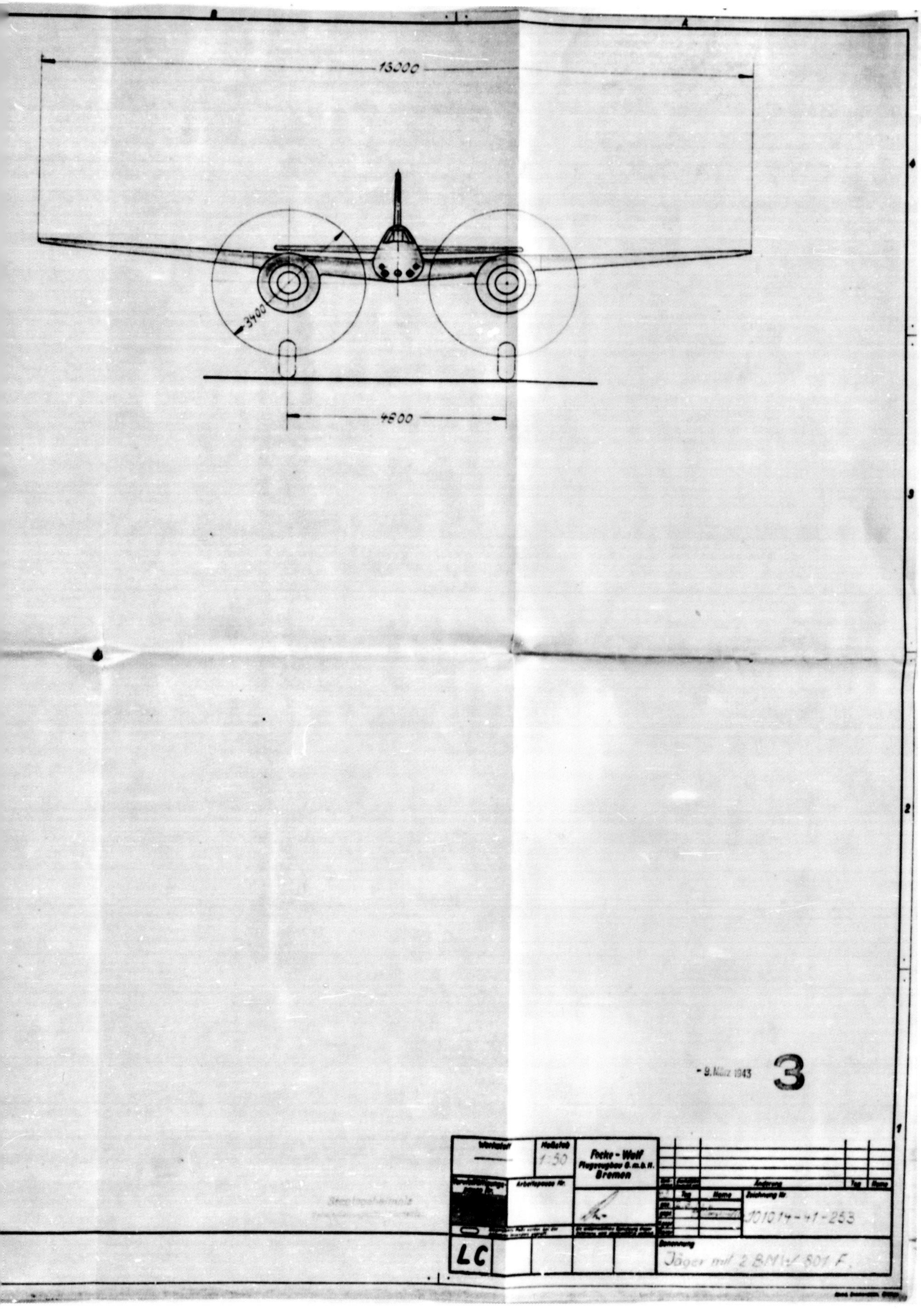
15000
3400
4800
9. März 1943
3
Maßstab
1:50
Focke-Wulf
Flugzeugbau G.m.b.H.
Bremen
Arbeitspause Nr.
Änderung
Tag
Name
Zeichnung Nr.
J01014-41-253
Benennung
Jäger mit 2 BMW 801 F.
LC

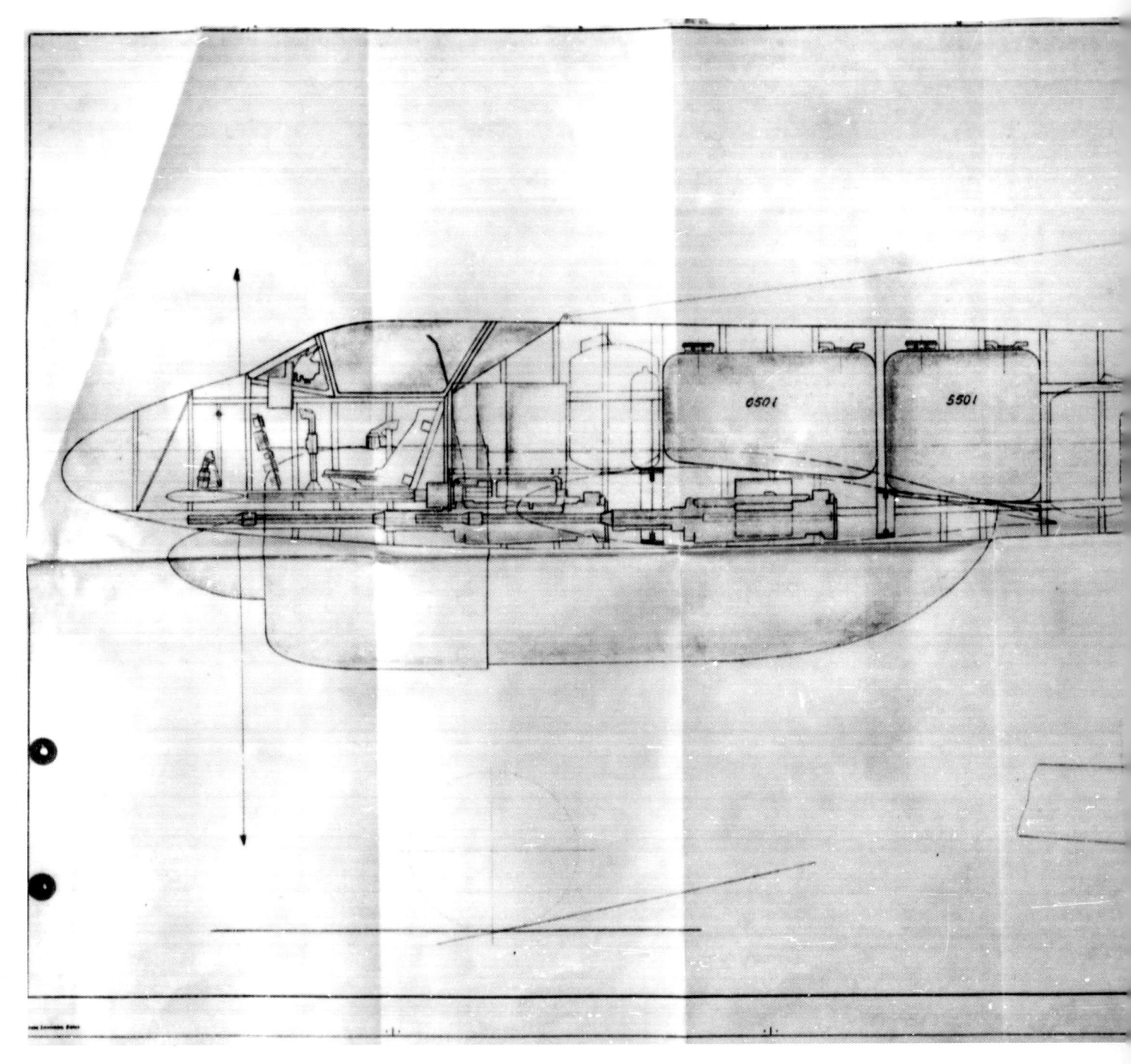

ABOVE: This interior view shows the straightforward and economical layout of the Jäger mit 2 BMW 801 F. It would presumably have been quicker and easier to build than the Ta 154 – and far more powerful as a fighter, though less adaptable to other roles.

long and with a frontal area of 1.35sqm. By way of comparison, this made it 2cm taller than the BMW 801 D, 2cm wider, 42cm longer and 0.04sqm larger in frontal area. The 801 F weighed 1,675kg compared to the 801 D's 1,558kg and would, incidentally, be renamed BMW 801 TH (with the BMW 801 E being renamed 801 TG) within a few months. Confusingly, a later project developed from the original 1942-43 BMW 801 E/F would then be designated BMW 801 F circa mid-1944.

Where the Ta 211/154 drawings produced towards the end of 1942 had been numbered 101025.01-XX – a whole new sequence – Focke-Wulf returned to the 101014 line for the Jäger mit 2 BMW 801 F.

The first two drawings in the series, 101014-41-251 and 101014-41-252, show an aircraft very similar in planform to the Ta 154. But where the 154 famously had high-set wings, placing the engine nacelles parallel to the fuselage on either side to facilitate the inclusion of a tricycle undercarriage, the Jäger mit 2 BMW 801 F had a low-wing layout. This put the engines below the fuselage, allowing the use of the simpler tail-dragger configuration.

The single-seater Jäger mit 2 BMW 801 F was 12m long in this version – about the same length as the Fw 187 not counting the prop spinners or the Ta 154 not counting the radar antennas – and had a wingspan of 16m, which was exactly the same as the Ta 154. Wing area was 36sqm however, compared to the 154's 32.4sqm. The next drawing in the sequence, 101014-41-253 dated March 2, 1943, shows the aircraft as 12.2m long and with a pronounced wing dihedral but otherwise unchanged.

The Jäger mit 2 BMW 801 F was heavily armed with five cannon clustered together

56 Secret Projects of the Luftwaffe

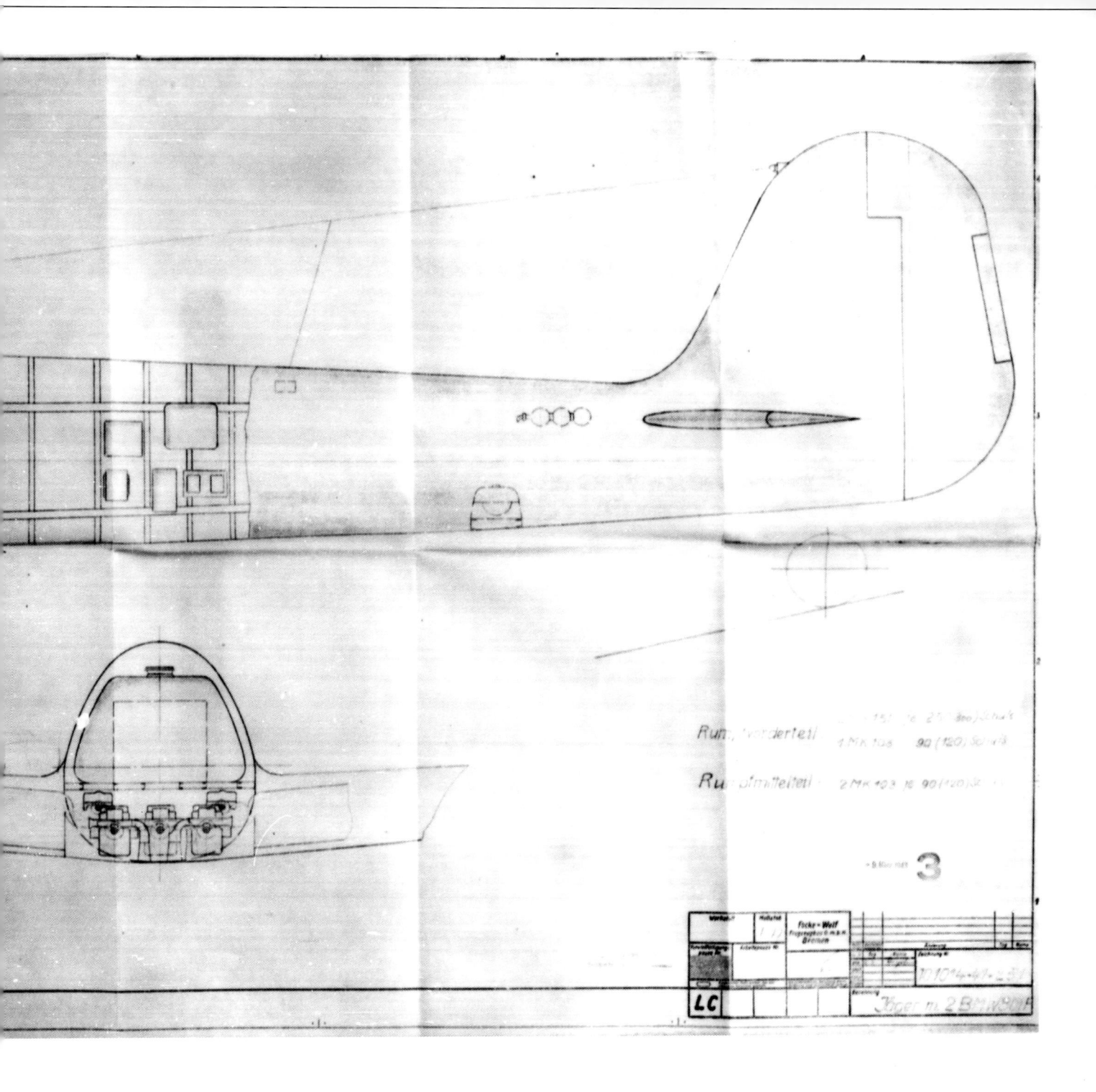

up front, echoing the basic principal that had underpinned the earlier Entwurf 6, 2 motoriger Jäger mit 7x3cm Kanonen. These consisted of a pair of MG 151s on either side, slightly elevated, with three MK 103s next to one another in the centre, sitting at the bottom of the fuselage. The central 103 was set forward while the other two were positioned further back, below the forward fuel tank. No provision was made for carrying bombs.

The aircraft would be equipped with standard fighter radio gear – Fu G 16 ZY and Fu G 25a, with a Revi 16 B gunsight – and would provide 220kg worth of armour protection for the pilot.

Perhaps the biggest difference, apart from the fact that the Jäger mit 2 BMW 801 F was to be made of aluminium alloy, rather than wood, was in performance. The Ta 154's Jumo 211 Fs each offered 1,340 PS starting power against a take-off weight of 8,250kg, resulting in a top speed of 625km/h at 6.1km altitude.

The Jäger mit 2 BMW 801 F's engines each generated 2,000 PS and it had a take-off weight of 8,200kg – giving a calculated top speed of 695km/h at 6.9km altitude. In fact, it was overwhelmingly quicker than the Ta 154 at any given altitude.

Like the 2 motoriger Jäger, nothing appears to have come of the Jäger mit 2 BMW 801 F and Focke-Wulf concentrated on designs based much more firmly on the Ta 154 going forward. With jet engines on the horizon by mid-1943, one could be forgiven for thinking that the age of the clean-sheet piston-engine fighter project was over. Indeed, Focke-Wulf designers were already working their way through a succession of single-jet fighter projects, but arguably the company's most outlandish and impressive piston-engine fighter designs were still to come. •

Secret Projects of the Luftwaffe 57

Parts bin bomber

Messerschmitt Schnellbomber „Do"

When it was clear that what would become the Dornier Do 335 had defeated his competing design, Willy Messerschmitt hatched a plan to get the Do 335 made using existing components from his production lines.

The Schnellbomber competition of May 1942, mentioned in both preceding chapters, was intended to produce an unarmed and unarmoured light bomber fast enough to outrun any potential interceptors. The designs solicited by the Air Ministry from Alexander Lippisch, Junkers, Blohm & Voss, Focke-Wulf, the Messerschmitt company, Heinkel and later Dornier varied wildly in their layout and equipment.

Eventually however, the choice came down to just two designs – Messerschmitt's Me 109 Z and Dornier's Do P 231. The former consisted of two Bf 109 fuselages positioned side by side and joined together using constant-chord centre wing and tailplane sections in the manner of the later North American F-82 Twin Mustang. The result was a twin-engine aircraft without a centre fuselage; the crew, fuel, payload and weapons being housed in what amounted to the engine nacelles. This reduced frontal area, lowered drag and increased speed.

The Do P 231, on the other hand, was a twin-engine aircraft with nothing but a centre fuselage. One engine was up front pulling while the other was pushing from the rear – an arrangement Dornier had previously used for flying boat engine nacelles. During the final Schnellbomber meeting on January 19, 1943, it was decided that Dornier's design, though more expensive, was simply faster. The Me 109 Z was defeated and the Do P 231 was ordered into production as the Do 335.

Willy Messerschmitt was reportedly horrified, believing that the difference in performance between the two types would be negligible in reality and that the Me 109 Z could be ready to enter full production within a year.

Even so, Messerschmitt still tried to retain some influence on the project. During the meeting, when it was clear that Dornier had won, he said: "If the aircraft industry works together, it will be able to offer Dornier a lot of parts and make the work much easier, especially the start of the series [production]; Because every tool that has to be made now means expenditure of valuable manpower."

Pasewaldt noted that plans had already been made to use engines developed for the Me 209 as the front engine of the production model P 231 (Do 335).

Messerschmitt went on to say that Dornier's aircraft might include other Messerschmitt parts too – such as wing components.

Claude Dornier, also present at the meeting, replied: "I would really welcome it if a collaborative effort came about ... we would very much welcome it if there is experience in other companies dealing with high-speed aircraft if we could receive and take this experience into account."

According to a memo signed by Messerschmitt Project Office chief Woldemar Voigt dated January 21, 1943, and headed 'Me 109 Z', immediately after the meeting Willy Messerschmitt met with Voigt and "announced the results of the discussions [at the Ministry] on January 18 and 19, 1943 as follows: Heinkel and Junkers recognise the Me 109 Z as the better solution. Dornier offers a different design (pull and push propeller) which is intended to reach speeds of 800 to 850km/h with a wing area of 36sqm. Mach influence is not to be included in this 'since we don't know anything about it'. Prof Messerschmitt orders that the Project Office prepare a design according to Dornier's suggestions and determine the performance using our calculation method. In addition, an attempt should be made to achieve the same construction using the modular principle".

In other words, Messerschmitt wanted his men to design their own version of the Do P 231/Do 335, ideally using existing Messerschmitt components. Whether this was the help Dornier had nominally welcomed or an attempt to 'take over' the project from Dornier, which was entirely lacking in experience of high-speed aircraft, is unclear.

The Project Office duly came up with something they referred to internally as Schnellbomber „Do". Four different wing areas were tried, 27, 30, 33 and 36sqm, and the engines were both DB 603 Gs with annular radiators – the type specific for the Me 209 at that time. Armament was two MK 108s and the internal bomb bay

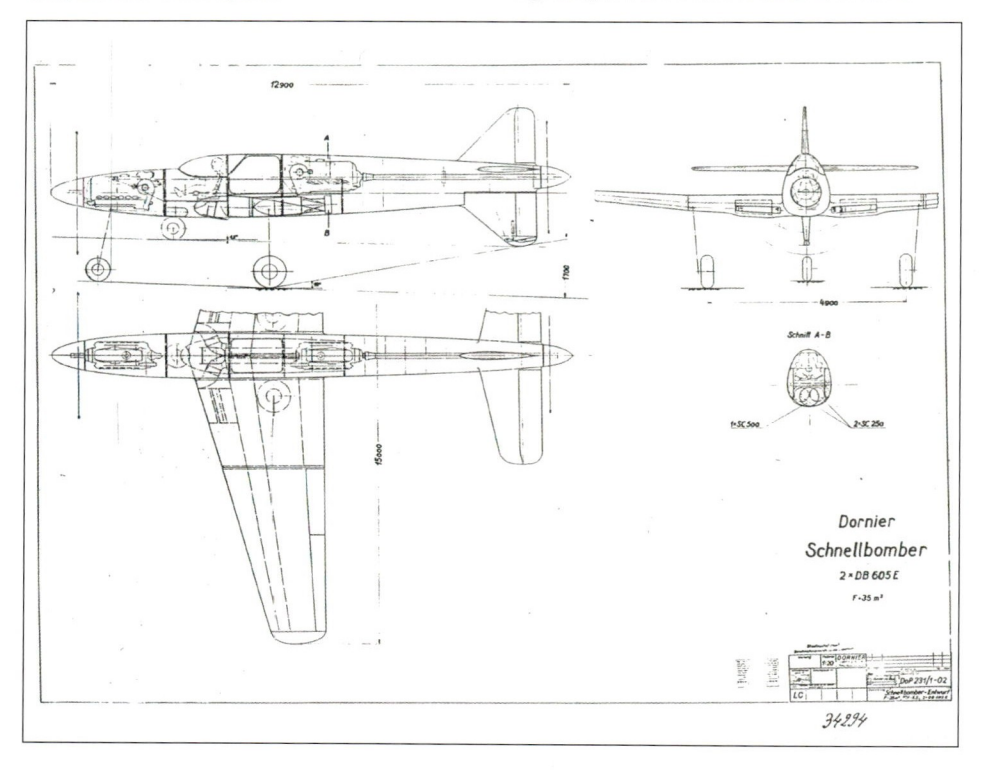

ABOVE: The Dornier Do P 231 Schnellbomber, in DB 605 E-powered form, as it was pitched to the German Air Ministry's decision-makers on January 19, 1943. Overall length is 12.9m, wingspan 15m and wing area 35sqm.

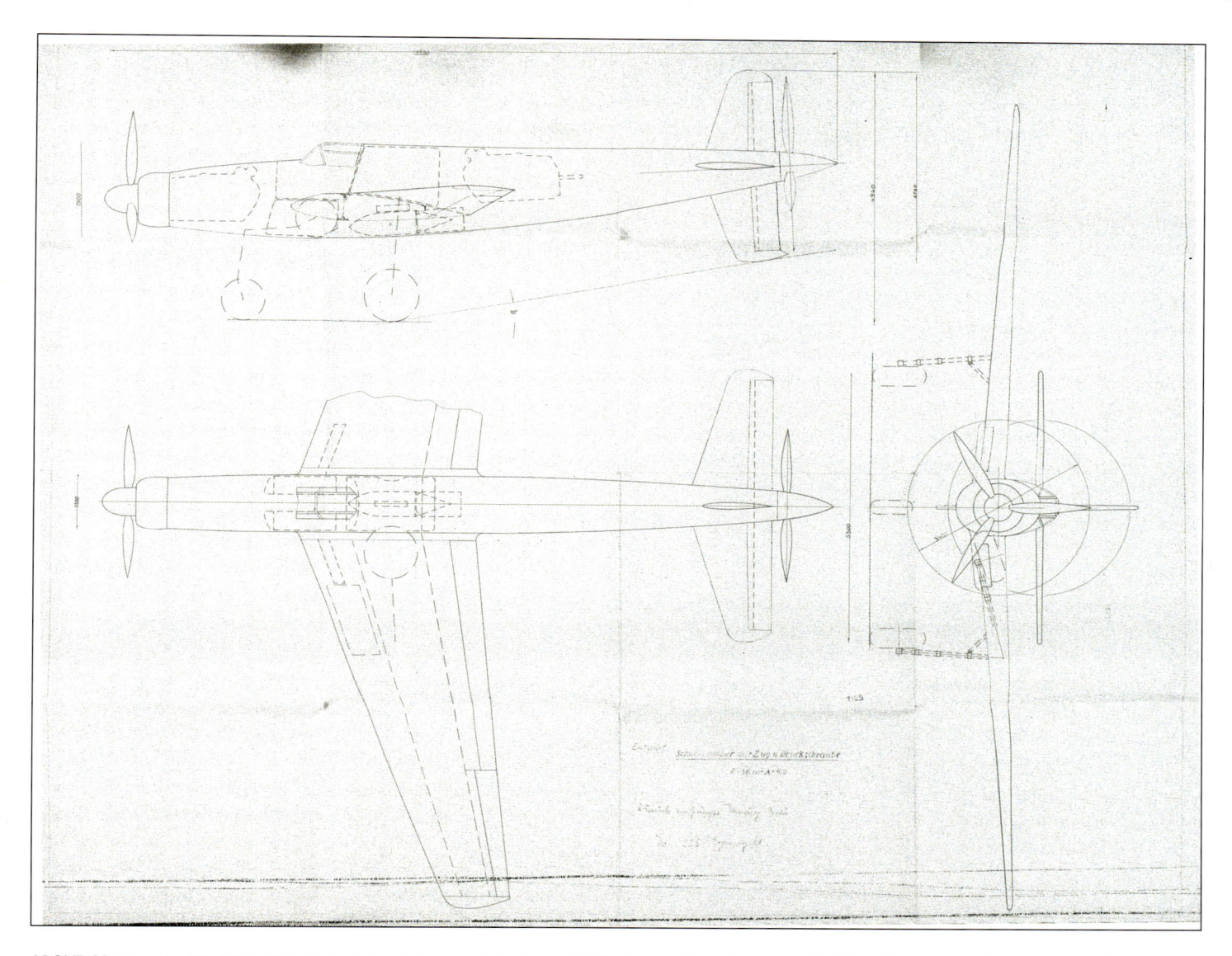

ABOVE: Messerschmitt's Schnellbomber „Do" of February 1943. It was 13.53m long with a wingspan of 15.75m. Wing area in this version was 36sqm.

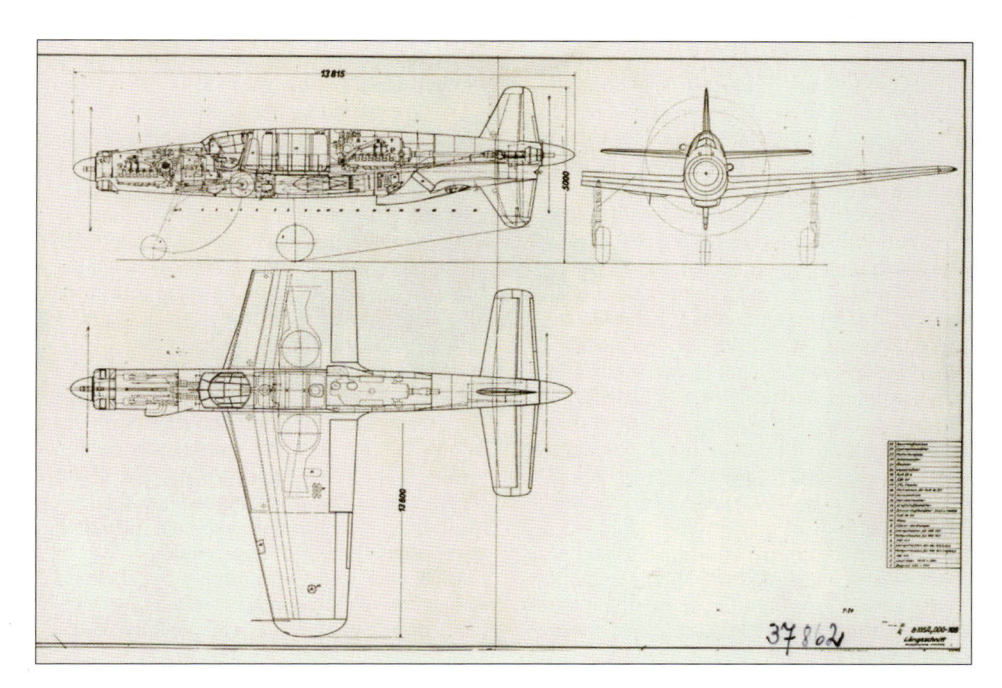

ABOVE: The final form of the Dornier Do 335 A fast bomber variant for comparison, measuring 13.815m long and with a wingspan of 13.8m.

could accommodate a load of 500kg. Oddly enough, it looked more like the final form of the Do 335 than the P 231 as it had been presented at the January 19 meeting.

A couple of meetings were held between Messerschmitt, Dornier and Air Ministry staff, at which it was determined that the performance calculation formulas being used by the two companies were different and it was difficult to determine which was correct. Back at the Project Office, work on this was still ongoing by April 29, 1943. Ultimately however, little further 'aid' from Messerschmitt appears to have been forthcoming. Even so, given that the war ended before the Do 335 could enter full series production let alone Luftwaffe service, and given that the F-82 continued to serve successfully into the early 1950s, it appears that the Me 109 Z may have been the better choice all along. •

Secret Projects of the Luftwaffe

End of the Line

Blohm & Voss BV 40

Originally designed to shoot down bombers, the BV 40 armoured glider was almost cancelled before the first prototype had flown – only to be rescued and repurposed as a weapon for suicide attacks on Allied shipping.

Operation Gomorrah saw large formations of heavy bombers from the RAF and USAAF hit Hamburg in northern Germany repeatedly over the course of eight days, starting on July 24, 1943. The night of July 27 would prove to be the most devastating – with 353 Avro Lancasters, 244 Handley Page Halifaxes, 116 Short Stirlings and 74 Vickers Wellingtons deliberately hitting densely populated housing estates in the city centre with high explosive and incendiary bombs.

A combination of warm dry weather, high explosive bombs with delayed action fuses to suppress firefighting efforts and the sheer concentration of the attack created an unprecedented firestorm – a shrieking tornado of flames – with winds reaching up to 240km/h and temperatures above 800°C. This was hot enough to melt roads above ground and sucked the oxygen out of basements and air raid shelters below, replacing it with suffocating carbon monoxide and smoke.

The death toll for that night has been estimated at more than 18,000 people and the overall toll for Gomorrah is thought to have been around 37,000. An estimated 800,000 people were left homeless. During the whole operation, RAF losses amounted to 57 aircraft: just 2.4% of the total number involved.

The attack on July 27 was by far the single deadliest air raid in history up to that point. By way of comparison, the deadliest an attack on London during the Blitz, on May 10, 1941, killed 1,436 people. In the aftermath, Germany was stunned and horrified. The Luftwaffe had proven entirely ineffective in preventing the attacks on Hamburg – despite the repetitive and therefore predictable nature of the attacks. Hamburg's own anti-aircraft defences had proven equally impotent.

Unbeknownst to the Germans at the time, Gomorrah had seen the RAF using Window anti-radar countermeasures for the first time, making it almost impossible for Germany's radar systems to pick out individual aircraft and direct fighters or defensive fire onto the bombers.

While the most destructive attacks had hit civilian housing, the aircraft design and manufacturing facilities of Blohm & Voss, situated on the eastern side of Hamburg, on an island in the River Elbe, had also been targeted – albeit ineffectually.

In the immediate aftermath of Operation Gomorrah, Bohm & Voss's creative chief designer Richard Vogt and his team came up with a concept for a new aircraft, designated P 186, that was intended specifically to target and destroy enemy bombers.

It was to be a small, heavily armoured, glider that would be towed aloft by a conventional fighter aircraft before being released to swoop down on the bomber formation with the goal of ramming their fragile tail fins, inflicting enough damage to knock them out of the sky.

Meanwhile, just over three months earlier on April 17, 1943, a new unit had been established specifically to develop and test experimental weapons and equipment for bringing down the Allies' heavy bombers – Erprobungskommando 25 (E.Kdo 25).

According to former unit commander Horst Geyer, "We tried many things, but the ideas did not always originate from within. We received many letters and proposals from civilians, from companies and manufacturers, from other branches of the armed services and also from the Luftwaffe testing centre at Rechlin; 'Why don't you try this, or that?' – and so on. All suggestions were investigated, and if something looked hopeful, then we proceeded with trials. We were basically free to do what we liked, buy what we liked, design what we liked and test what we liked. But it fell to me to report everything to Oberst [Adolf] Galland, the General der Jagdflieger [Inspector of Fighter Pilots], and the test centre at Rechlin."

Exactly when Vogt presented the P 186 concept to the German Air Ministry is unclear but evidently it received a favourable response and attracted the attention of E.Kdo 25. That unit's Major Hans-Günther von Kornatzki evidently wrote to Galland at around this time with a proposal "to have enemy four-engined bombers rammed by volunteers, [who have been] little used in this war and due to age, suitability and agility [and who] even in the future [are] hardly to be used as full-fledged fighter pilots". Kornatzki thought that "enough old fighter pilots have volunteered to set up a strong squadron. Young aviators, who are located in the west of the empire and who lost property and, in some cases, their relatives due to bombing, also came forward. The aim of the ramming of the enemy aircraft is to decisively impact the morale of the enemy pilot crews and to blow up the enemy organisation sustainably, so that shooting down is made much easier for the fighters immediately following".

The P 186 had already been presented and discussed by August 19, 1943, when the ministry wrote a letter to Vogt headed 'Regarding: Glide-fighter'. It said: "You are asked to continue to work seriously on the proposal you have submitted for the 'Glide-fighter' [Gleitjäger] and to comment immediately on the possibilities of the design work you will carry out.

"For the execution of the P 186 project, as already discussed with you, the idea of ramming the aircraft against the enemy's vertical stabiliser is to be given special consideration. Under these circumstances, installing just one MK 108 is sufficient to pin down the enemy rear gunner."

GOING PRONE

More than five years earlier, on March 21, 1938, an unusual glider constructed by students of Akademische Fliegergruppe (Akaflieg) Stuttgart made its first flight at Teck airfield near Dettingen/Teck. Known as the fs17, its most novel feature was the position of its pilot – lying almost prone, head forward, on a specially constructed couch within the nose of the vehicle.

Work on building the glider had begun in 1937, based on the theory that a pilot lying down would be able to withstand higher g-forces than one sitting down. Fully loaded it weighed just 230kg, wingspan was 10m and wing area was 12 square metres. A total of 98 flights were made with the fs17 by 15 pilots, amounting to a total of 56 hours in the air.

The concept was then revived in 1942 by the Deutsche Versuchsanstalt für Luftfahrt (DVL), who commissioned the Flugtechnische Fachgruppe Berlin (FFG-Berlin, aka Akaflieg Berlin) to start work on a powered aircraft which would allow further testing of the prone pilot position. The result was the B 9, a tiny machine with a fuselage made from steel tubes and wooden formers covered in fabric. The trapezoidal fuselage cross section had a maximum area of just 0.67 square metres, tapering down to a fin at the tail end. The pilot lay in the nose beneath a jettisonable 1.5m-long canopy.

The wings were made entirely of wood, each fitted with a Hirth HM 500 four-cylinder air-cooled inverted inline engine driving a

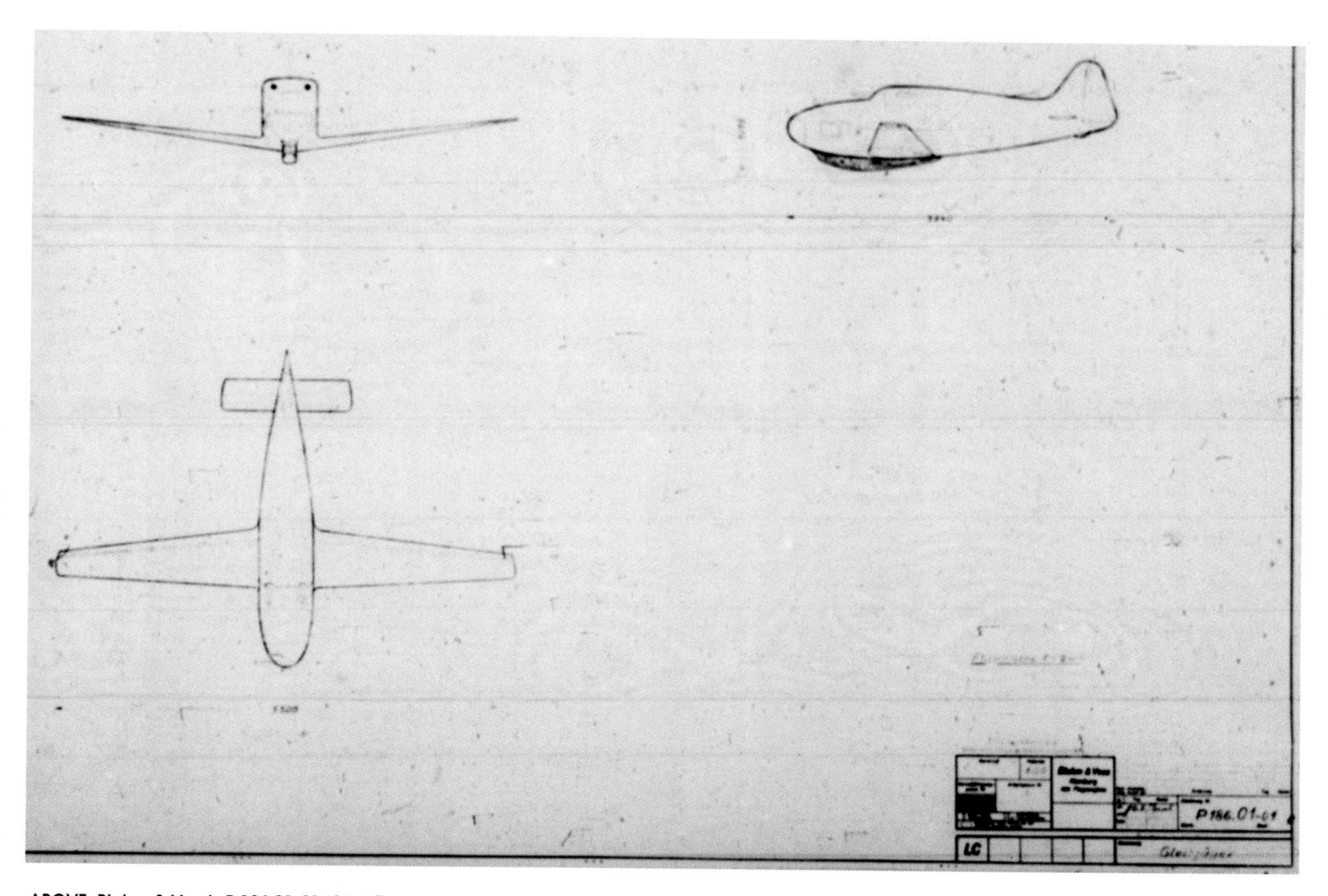

ABOVE: Blohm & Voss's P 186.01-01 'Gleitjäger' design – less than 4m in length and with a wingspan of 5.5m. Two cannon are positioned in a 'hump' above the prone pilot's tiny cockpit and the undercarriage is a thick skid.

2m diameter Schäfer propeller. Each wing contained two fuel tanks and total fuel capacity was 95 litres. On wing the trailing edge were ailerons and split-flaps. The struts and mainwheels, which retracted rearwards into the engine nacelles, were Messerschmitt Bf 108 components.

The B 9 weighed 1,115kg fully loaded, had a wingspan of 9.4m, wing area was 11.9 square metres and was 6.09m long. The introduction to a DVL report on the B 9 dated May 1944 outlined the reasons for continuing work on the prone pilot configuration: "It is customary for the pilot of an aircraft to have a seated position, taken over from vehicles designed for two-dimensional movement on the ground. This provides him with a comfortable position with which he is familiar, suitable for long duration piloting and in which he possesses the freedom of movement necessary for flying the aircraft, together with a good view forward and upward.

"[However,] the conditions originating from movement in space – flying – and the associated increased physical demands on the human being necessitate the investigation of other positions for the pilot: 1. Prone, prostrate or kneeling, 2. Lying on the back, 3. In backward-tilting seat. Lying on the back is, in spite of being suitable for high accelerations, impracticable on account of poor vision forward and downward and the general feeling of helplessness when in this position.

"The backward-tilting seat would combine the advantages of the normal seated position (good view) with those of lying back (for high accelerations). It requires much space, additional mechanism and causes considerable difficulties in shifting the controls and switches. The weight, bulk and complication are not justified when compared with the possibilities of the prone position.

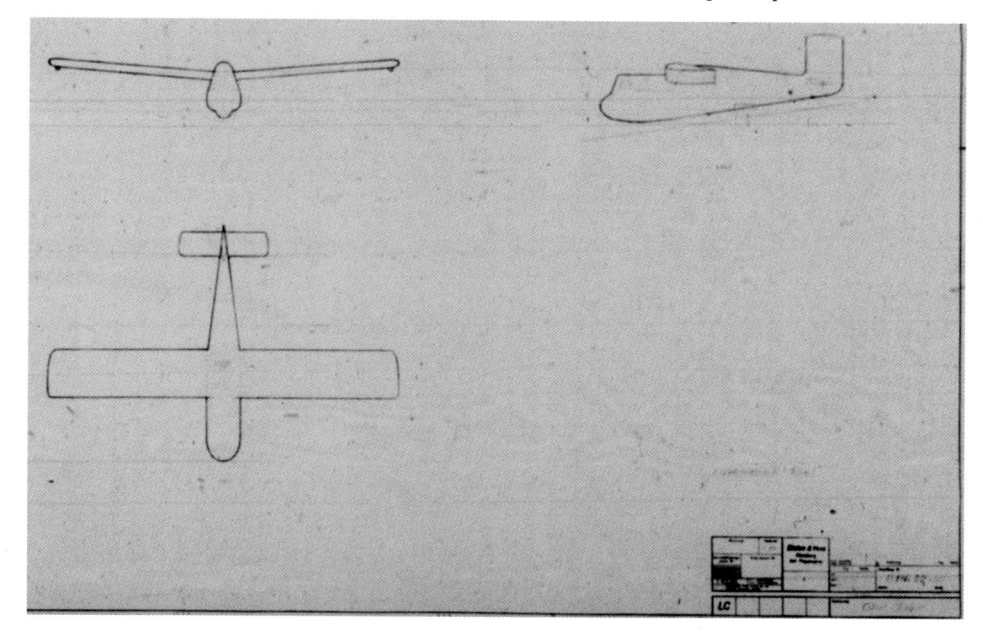

ABOVE: The only other known drawing of the 'Gleitjäger' before it became the BV 40 is this depiction of the P 186.02-02. Armament has apparently been reduced to a single cannon while both the wings and fin have been simplified. The forward fuselage is now recognisably that of the BV 40.

Secret Projects of the Luftwaffe 61

ABOVE: The Akaflieg fs17 glider. This experimental vehicle, constructed in 1937, pioneered the concept of a prone position cockpit – which allowed the pilot to withstand greater g-forces.

"The idea of the prone arrangement of the pilot is not new. It was used by the Wright brothers in their first flights. The psychological advantage of the prone position lies in the fact that the position of the body is adapted to movement in space, comparable to movement under water or to that of a high diver … the shift of the direction of view from forward-upward to forward-downward to observe the ground also counts … in favour of the prone position.

"The tradition of flying aircraft from a seated position counts against the prone position. This is particularly emphasised since it is undesirable to shift the position of the horizon from its customary place in the field of view. A judgement on the advantages and disadvantages of the new arrangement and on the resulting difficulties can only be given after flight investigations."

It was further noted under a heading of 'tactical applications' that "the increase of the tolerable acceleration from approx. 5g in the seated position to 12g in the prone position [based on data presented in a 1940 report by Dr Siegfried Ruff, who had studied the effect of high acceleration on the human body in laboratory tests using a centrifuge] renders possible a reduction in the radius of turn, or in the radius of a pull-out, even from an increased diving speed".

In other words, a prone pilot would be able to safely perform extreme manoeuvres which might render a seated pilot unconscious.

Although, "in bombing or gun-aiming allowance has to be made for the human reaction time lag, e.g. between bomb release [during a dive] and control application [to pull out of the dive]". The report also stated that "the potentialities of forward armour protection for the prone pilot are extremely favourable as this position gives the smallest cross section to be protected. Protection against shelling from below and from the rear is also favourable, [although] larger areas have to be protected against attack from above and from the side.

"The favourable conditions of visibility and the potentialities of armour protection make the aircraft with a prone pilot position particularly suited for use as an attack weapon."

ON THE COUCH

A key aspect of the B 9's testing regime was establishing the fundamentals of prone pilot cockpit design. The report stated: "The pilot is best placed in the fuselage nose … space requirements are 220cm in length, 90cm maximum height and 80cm maximum width, measured in the shoulder region. The cross section is narrowed near the head to reduce the cross section area and improve the pilot's view. Controls and switches can be situated in long instrument banks at armrest level on both sides of the fuselage. The emergency exit can be provided either rearwards-upwards or rearwards-downwards. Access from above, underneath or from the side.

"The couch must provide a comfortable position for all pilots of service height (1.65m to 1.90m) in which the flying time required for tactical reasons can be endured by the pilot on fighter or ground support duty without inconvenience. Relaxed muscles and wide, even support on good padding are essential. Special care has to be directed towards the lower ribs, which are particularly stressed, being in the transition region between the rigid chest and the soft parts of the abdomen. Arms and legs must have the necessary freedom to operate the controls and switches.

"Fore and aft adjustment [to suit the pilot's height] is made only by moving the pedals; the head should – for reasons of visibility – be kept in the same position, independent of the pilot's height. In order not to strain the nape of the neck excessively the upper part of the torso is slightly raised. When holding the head relaxed the centre of the field of view is declined by 30-degrees; the horizon is in the upper part of the field of view. A chin rest, adjustable in height and fore and aft, serves as support for the head at higher accelerations. Experience has shown that it is usually not used in normal flight.

"The forearms rest on a support so as to distribute the weight equally on the chest and elbows. To achieve this equal distribution a height adjustment of the parachute box or the chest rest is provided for adjustment on the ground. The leg is slightly bent."

ABOVE: The Akaflieg B 9 took the prone pilot concept one step further by adding engines, allowing for extended periods of testing.

ABOVE: B 9 in flight.

Secret Projects of the Luftwaffe 63

ABOVE: The pilot's chin rest from the B 9, a white oval on the end of a rod in the cockpit, would be replicated in the BV 40, as would other aspects of the cockpit layout.

Fitting a parachute into the prone pilot cockpit proved to be a major difficulty initially. According to the report: "At the time of the construction of the mock-up for the B 9, existing German parachutes did not comply with the requirements of a prone position. These requirements are: i) no locks or other mountings on chest or abdomen, ii) freedom of movement for legs and arms in the prone position.

"As the back parachute puts additional load on the pilot, a chest type parachute was required. Schroeder & Co. developed such a chest parachute [designated] BH6, according to data supplied by the FFG-Berlin. It has two strap catches at hip height and is packed so as to give maximum possible freedom of movement to the arms. The parachute with padding serves simultaneously as chest support. A chest parachute has, however, the disadvantage that during the opening process face injuries may occur."

Later, Schroeder developed a back parachute, designated RH28 for use with prone pilot cockpits. It featured a similar harness to the BH6 but did place additional weight on the pilot as well as slightly restricting freedom of movement and being more difficult to fasten. Nevertheless, it was adopted for the B 9. According to the report, "when using a back parachute the layout of the couch has to be modified by abandoning the parachute case and the chinrest. The couch is a complete unit, terminating at the front in a fixed rounded end which serves as a chinrest. One object of frequent pilots' complaints, the extra chinrest, is removed".

PRONE CONTROLS
Designing the B 9's controls presented the DVL with a dilemma. It would be very difficult for the pilot to reach controls on the left side with his right hand and vice-versa, since he was effectively resting on his elbows throughout the flight. As such the controls were strictly separated into right and left-hand side sections.

The "right hand is fixed for aileron and elevator control and the left for all secondary controls and switches. Rudder control and brake application are, as in the seated position, by the feet. The right hand additionally operates emergency handles for harness release and hood jettisoning. In accordance with the purpose – single pilot fighter or ground support aircraft – the left hand will, particularly at the moment of highest concentration (in the attack), stay at the throttle and only the right hand will be free for the primary controls. Wheel control, however, is not justified for continued single handed operation. Experience with present day fighter and intruder aircraft weighs also in favour of stick control.

"The central arrangement of the stick in the fs17 glider and in the earlier mock-ups was changed to an asymmetric one which is particularly adapted for right hand operation … in spite of the asymmetry the left hand is still able to take the control grip in the case of an emergency. On the other hand, this stick arrangement frees an additional field of view vertically down which is important for the observation of ground targets."

BLOHM & VOSS AND THE B 9
First to fly the B 9 was test pilot Hauptingenieur Hans-Werner Lerche at Rechlin on April 10, 1943, followed by one of the aircraft's designers, Leo Schmidt, on April 14. Several DVL engineers clambered into the small machine's cramped cockpit and flew it throughout June and July. Then, on July 30, Focke-Wulf Betriebsführer Kurt Tank flew the B 9, followed the next day by two of his test pilots – Werner Bartsch and Kurt Mehlhorn. Heinz Scheidhauer, test pilot for the Horten brothers' Sonderkommando Horten, flew it on August 29.

Back at Hamburg, Vogt wrote a memo on September 8, 1943, saying "I found out from Mr Schmidt, Akaflieg Berlin, that Mr Malz wants to fly the machine with another pilot tomorrow. Schmidt wants to come to Wenzendorf at the beginning of next week. Check with Malz and Czolbe that this deadline will be met and that we will have the aircraft for at least one to two weeks."

Otto Malz and Helmut Czolbe were Air Ministry staff engineers working in the airframe division of the Technical Office. Malz in particular specialised in advanced and unorthodox aircraft design for much of his career – from the pre-war precursors of the Messerschmitt Me 163 rocket-propelled interceptor to the Heinkel He 162 jet fighter right at the war's end.

Vogt was evidently attempting to book the B 9 so his engineers and test pilots could spend time examining its layout and systems – Wenzendorf being the Blohm & Voss factory airfield. The P 186 glide-fighter/rammer was designed with a prone pilot position in mind from the outset, so having access to the B 9 for a week or more would be crucial in gaining practical experience of that configuration.

Malz and Czolbe would both be heavily involved in the development of the P 186 later but it is unclear whether, at this stage, their interest in flying the B 9 was directly linked to that project. Nevertheless, they both first flew the prone cockpit prototype on September 9, 1943.

Blohm & Voss chief test pilot Flugkapitän Helmut Rodig flew the B 9 on September 15, followed by his colleagues Rautenhaus and Hilleke on the same day. They would continue to fly it until September 23, when it was delivered to the Luftwaffe's Rechlin test centre.

GALLAND'S VIEW
A day earlier, Galland had written a letter to Reichsmarschall Hermann Göring which outlined Kortnatzki's rammer proposal and presented his view on the most viable solution for countering the enemy bomber fleets: "The Inspector of the Fighter Pilots takes the position that every enemy four-engine bomber has to go down if you shoot at it from close range with a specially armoured aircraft and makes the following suggestions: 1) Establishment of a special unit, which is called Sturmstaffel. 2) Attacking enemy four-engine bombers with specially armoured fighters with strong weapons up to the closest distance. 3) Secondary ramming if the gunfire does not lead to the target's destruction.

"This proposal is based on the consideration that a) every fighter that has rammed must be regarded as completely lost … and b) not every ramming impact leads to the complete destruction of the enemy aircraft, so ramming can be very uneconomical under certain circumstances. The Inspector of Fighter Pilots intends to accelerate [the establishment of] a reinforced squadron (16 aircraft) after a successful test."

On September 25, Blohm & Voss's Berlin representative Wolfgang Bürkner wrote a memo noting that "independent of Dr Vogt's suggestions, the [Egon] Scheibe group came up with similar ideas [for the] creation of a ramming aircraft, which is to be towed into the air by combat aircraft".

Scheibe, formerly a glider designer and now an aircraft development engineer working for the DVL, had initially come up with a rocket-propelled attacker – which "was to be used to tow some 100kg bombs on a relatively short rope. The aircraft would then have to fly low over the enemy bombers and automatically release the bombs at the appropriate moment".

This one-man aircraft, no drawings of which are known to have survived, would be heavily armoured and would have a take-off weight of 2,500kg with a wing area of 10 square metres. Bürkner noted that "in order to give the aircraft a little more manoeuvrability, it is proposed to install a rocket motor with 500kg thrust … available for five minutes".

However, Bürkner wrote, "this seems to me to be very complicated and will certainly require a long series of developments. The gentlemen now primarily think of ramming. This thought had already occurred to us [Blohm & Voss]. They didn't plan to install weapons … I explained our ongoing work on the glider to the gentlemen and suggested that the gentlemen [presumably Bürkner means Scheibe's group at the DVL and the Air Ministry] coordinate internally first.

"The installation of a Walter rocket motor seems to me to be a good thing, even if it also makes the aircraft considerably larger. The pulsejet tube will always have the disadvantage that it has little effect at higher altitudes and will probably not start at all. If possible, I will have a meeting with Mr Scheibe and Mr Malz at the beginning of the week in order to coordinate the two proposals [Scheibe's design and Blohm & Voss's P 186], if possible."

SHOOTING, NOT RAMMING
Vogt wrote to the Air Ministry's Technical Office on October 30, 1943, to say that "following our suggestion to use a glider towed by the normal fighter as an offensive weapon against enemy bomber formations, we have made some considerations and calculations".

It had been worked out that attacking an enemy bomber formation from behind was unlikely to be a viable option, since it would require the fighter/glider combination to be extremely high above the formation before the attack could begin. Adding a rocket motor to the glider would mean the attack altitude could be reduced but would also mean adding 200kg and considerable complexity.

Therefore, "on the occasion of a visit from your men Malz and Czolbe, the attack from the front was discussed and judged to be the only promising procedure. Of course, it made sense to consider ramming the tail fin of the enemy machines in addition to firing [at them] from very close range.

"In view of the psychological difficulties [of a ramming attack] and the need to put considerable weight into [providing] ram-proof wings, we would like to propose … refraining from intentional ramming for the time being and sticking to close range shooting attacks as the task".

He had enclosed a drawing showing the field of vision available to the P 186's prone pilot "who is lying down due to weight reasons" as well as the thicknesses of armour plate protecting the cockpit against fire incoming from different directions.

He added: "We want to make the overall structure as simple as possible, to above all to save on construction and equipment costs." The aircraft would have constant-chord rectangular wings and a regular cruciform tail structure.

Since both the towing and attack procedures for the glide-fighter were unknown quantities, he recommended that the Ministry should order a small number of prototypes so that testing could begin. However, a mock-up had already been built and "an immediate inspection by the Inspector of Fighter Pilots would still be up for discussion [so that we could] use our extremely small amount of available construction capacity immediately".

The P 186's 'customer' at this stage was clearly Adolf Galland's office – with a view to the glider being used as exactly the sort of weapon E.Kdo 25 was looking for. Indeed, Galland himself (or rather, his secretary based on his dictation) wrote to the Air Ministry on November 13 to say: "The Inspector of Fighter Pilots asks that Blohm & Voss continue to develop a so-called ramming aircraft. If the losses in climbing performance due to attachments to fighter and destroyer aircraft are within acceptable limits, the ramming aircraft in conjunction with cut-rope devices [presumably the Schlinge device] could be used as a valuable support for home defence.

"The Inspector of Fighter Pilots asks for documents about the Blohm & Voss glider fighter and, after inspection, will make appropriate proposals for the development."

A document on P 186 design load assumptions produced on November 29, 1943, stated that "The type is used as a pure glider without propulsion. Using the Me 109 G as a tow plane results in a maximum initial altitude of 11km. The modification of the fighter [the P 186] as a ramming aircraft is not being investigated for the time being. Armament 1 x MK 108, 1 man crew. Skids for landing and jettisonable wheelset for take-off".

Wingspan was given as 7.1m and wing area was seven square metres, with take-off weight of around 750kg. Terminal dive speed was given as 970km/h but "for tactical reasons flying at this speed is out of the question".

On the same day, Vogt wrote to the Air Ministry's Technical Office requesting an urgent decision to approve construction of the first P 186 prototypes since "it takes about 10,000 hours to complete the design drawings and calculations … if production could be started immediately, the possible flight-ready date would fall at the turn of the month of March/April".

PROTOTYPE ORDER
Vogt attended a meeting on December 8, along with Rodig and Hamel from Blohm & Voss's flight test division, to discuss an order for 12 P 186 prototypes with Galland's representative Hauptingenieur Knorr, along with Heinrich Beauvais and Julius Klein from the Rechlin test centre.

According to the meeting summary report: "Both for operational reasons and for work planning at Blohm + Voss, it is necessary to order a sufficient number of about 12 units of the P 186 glider immediately and at the same time to make a decision about the final number over the next few days."

Now the armament would be increased to two MK 108s with 35 rounds each with "wing area increased accordingly while maintaining wing loading (max. 110kg/square metre). Armour had to be sufficient to resist .50 cal enemy bullets at a distance of 200m and it was suggested that "the two existing hinged windows on the side are designed as fixed 5cm thick armoured glass panes".

It was further suggested that part of the detachable canopy – much of the glider's 'roof' above the pilot was designed to come off as a single piece – should be "slidable to the left and right". Consideration would be given to installing a long-range compass and "in addition to the armament, the 'Schlinge' [Sling] device is to be installed. The Inspector of Fighter Pilots will arrange for a sample device to be sent".

The Luftwaffe apparently also considered "it very important that the wing can be assembled extremely quickly with just a few movements" and "since it is planned to be towed behind the single-engine fighter for reasons of performance, the chassis has to be modified. In order to get the aircraft through the propeller wash as quickly as possible during take-off, it must first be held on the ground. This is only possible if the main landing gear is close to the centre of gravity".

Schlinge was essentially a cable-towed aerial bomb, the development of which had begun at the Rechlin test centre at around the same time that the original P 186 proposal was being submitted in August.

After some experimentation, by November 1943 Schlinge consisted of a cylindrical metal container housing a cable of between 100m and 400m in length. This could be attached to any aircraft via an ETC 50 bomb rack. The 10kg bomb itself was positioned outside the container as a weight on the end of the cable.

For an attack, the bomb and its attached cable would be spooled out from the container, which remained attached to the host fighter. At this stage the fighter was effectively towing the bomb along in the air on the end of the cable, which was extremely sharp 2-3mm thick steel wire.

The fighter would then be flown over the target bomber in the hope that the bomb would hit it and explode or the wire would snag on it, potentially also causing the bomb to whip around the bomber and blow up. Either way, the cable had a weak section which would cause it to snap off on impact. The fighter pilot could then jettison the empty Schlinge container.

The Technical Office wrote to Vogt on December 14, proposing that during take-off the P 186 should be positioned on the left side of the towing aircraft in order to keep it out of the propeller wash, necessitating an asymmetrical tow rope attachment point.

On the same day at Blohm & Voss, however, a design meeting was held to discuss the 'Gleitjäger BV 40'. It was recorded that "the order for the delivery of 12 aircraft has been received. New designation: 'BV 40'. The work is being accelerated so that the first aircraft can be ready by the end of February/beginning of March".

Evidently Knorr was behind the "demand" for a second MK 108 cannon, which had resulted in a weight increase of 82kg including ammunition. He had also required that the pilot's armour protection be extended further to the rear, adding another 40kg. Keeping the wing loading at 110kg per square metre meant increasing wing area to 8.2 square metres, with wingspan rising to 7.5m. Take-off weight was now around 880-900kg.

Up to this point, the P 186/BV 40 was designed with its weapons positioned on top of the fuselage – firing over the pilot's position – but "in another meeting on December 15, 1943, the previous weapon installation was fundamentally changed". It was feared that recoil from the cannon in this 'top-heavy' position would cause inaccuracy so, "to be on the safe side here, it was decided to arrange the weapons on the right and left of the fuselage directly under the wing. This creates additional protrusions, causing drag, but it also means that the entire back of the fuselage above the wing is smooth. A further advantage is the simple accommodation of the ammunition in the wing".

Shifting the cannon from a 'hump' above the fuselage to underwing nacelles also meant they had to move a little further forward but "the resulting shift in the centre of gravity is partly compensated for by the installation of the 'Schlinge' device (approx. 30kg, calculated as an overload!), but this still has to be checked".

A memo dated December 15 confirmed the BV 40 designation and noted that the project had only been given the 'SS' level of priority for allocation of resources but that an application had been made for 'DE' priority – the highest priority.

PRODUCTION BEGINS

Work on preparing the BV 40 prototype's workshop drawings began immediately. A production meeting held at Blohm & Voss on December 17 noted that "the project work is completed" but "the planned 'ready to fly' date at the end of February seems to be very short under the given conditions".

The company's construction department proposed to deliver the "raw mass" of the armoured cockpit within just five days – by December 22. The wings would be ready by January 8, 1944, and the rear fuselage with tail would be completed by late January.

It was noted that delivery of controls and equipment would be ongoing throughout this period, starting with the pilot's control column and the rudder on December 18. The workshop staff had apparently agreed to work using "drawings of the most primitive kind" to save time but even so, "the planned date at the end of February seems untenable". More realistically, "a completion date at the end of March is possible".

A design meeting took place the next day and it was stated that the number of structural engineers working on the project "is now increased to 6-7" and "at the expense of the BV 155 [high-altitude fighter project], two good designers (Kaminski and Strauss) are also assigned to the BV 40. Desirable date: publication of all documents by mid-January".

It was further stated that the Technical Office had required the BV 40's side armour to be increased in thickness from 5mm to 8mm, adding another 20kg and necessitating another increase in wing surface area. The new take-off weight was given as 930kg. Equipment now included two compressed air bottles and two oxygen bottles, with space for three.

The question of a towing aircraft was raised and it was thought that a BV 141 could do the job, at least initially.

Blohm & Voss then received a memo on December 22, 1943, to say that Knorr had lost all documents relating to the P 186 in a fire, and could the latest drawings be sent to the offices of the Inspector of Fighter Pilots immediately. They were duly sent out the following day, with a note explaining the reason for moving the guns to their new positions and the increase in both side armour and wing area.

A memo dated Christmas Eve 1943 stated that Blohm & Voss had been attempting to order the necessary wood for the BV 40 prototypes from a company called Wächter at Neustadt but had been told that without a DE priority level, the earliest date that the wood could be made available for collection by courier was January 15. And the requested beech plywood could not be supplied – only birch. And the delivery of laminated timber was proving even more difficult to arrange.

Blohm & Voss statics department representative Fahlbusch wrote a memo on December 27, stating that Wächter were continuing to refuse the supply of beech plywood. He wrote: "The Wächter company informed us that, according to the RLM [Air Ministry] circular, they were entitled to deliver birch plywood instead of beech plywood. [But] since birch plywood is weaker than beech plywood, our delivery order is therefore for beech plywood; it is essential to ensure that beech plywood is delivered".

Attempts to get the BV 40 regraded to the DE priority level had gone nowhere since, it was reported on December 28, Czolbe at the Air Ministry had gone away on holiday and would not be back until January 3.

A letter was written to Schroeder & Co on December 30, urgently requesting "the dimensions of your quick release 10-7U-218 [harness fittings] as well as the corresponding buckles and snap hooks. We also need the dimensions and weight of the BH6 special design chest parachute. We ask that you provide us with the relevant drawing documents". A second letter was sent to Berlin firm Kehler & Son requesting the dimensions of their safety harness back buckle.

Another letter, written by Vogt himself, was sent to Galland's office on the same day. He wrote: "The 'Schlinge' device was handed over to us yesterday by courier. We ask for clarification as to whether the entire sheet metal container is jettisoned and the free end of the cable remains attached to the fuselage, or whether the container remains attached and the cable is fitted with an unknown weight and jettisoned. Only in the second case would installation inside the fuselage be possible. The first case would result in an external suspension in exchange for one of the two MK 108. Since we are working flat out on the construction, we would ask for your immediate response, preferably through a technician who understands the device."

In other words, 'Schlinge' consisted of a metal container – presumably containing explosives – attached to a cable. The question was whether the explosives container was jettisoned and then dangled free as the BV 40 towed it onto its target, or whether the explosives container remained aboard the BV 40 and the cable was dangled out instead, with a weight on the end, which would then snag on the target and yank the explosives container free of the glider.

Vogt also attempted, again, to get DE priority for the glider: "Since the purchase of building materials is causing difficulties in view of the tightness of the desired construction deadline, we have submitted a DE application. We ask for support in this regard from your office because we fear that the process of the application will take so long that there will no longer be any corresponding advantage. We hope to be able to send you a detailed description of the prototype by the end of the first week of January."

A fourth letter of December 30 was fired off to both the Kronprinz company – seemingly the go-to undercarriage manufacturer of the Third Reich – with a copy going to another firm, Fluggeräte Elma of Stuttgart-Bad Cannstatt. The Kronprinz version said: "For our new BV 40 model, a small glider with a take-off weight of approx. 900kg, we need a spring strut according to the attached drawing ALSK 314. The spring strut is used to cushion a skid. The space [available to house it] is somewhat limited; the outer diameter of the spring should not exceed 75mm if possible.

"The BV 40 should be ready to fly by the end of February. We are aware that you will not be able to develop a new spring strut for us before this date; but perhaps it would be possible for you to take a spring strut with similar dimensions from an existing series or from other stocks. All in all, we would need about 15 spring struts, for which we would send you a corresponding order."

The Elma version had a supplementary note attached: "For your information, we have attached a carbon copy of a letter that we sent to the Kronprinz company. From the attached drawing you can see the arrangement of the desired spring strut. If a similar spring strut is already being made by your company, we would like to ask you to send us documents and to support us in the procurement."

SHIPBUILDING STEEL

A meeting was held at Blohm & Voss on January 3, 1944, to discuss measures now being taken to circumvent the usual supply chain and obtain the plywood and steel needed for the BV 40 by other means.

It was noted that "an attempt is being made to procure suitable plywood from the shipyard for the frame production of the first and second machines machine". Blohm & Voss Flugzeugbau was a division of the much larger Blohm & Voss shipbuilding company, founded in 1877 to construct steel-hulled vessels and later responsible for building warships such as the battleship *Bismarck* and the U-boats mentioned earlier.

Naturally the shipyards had access to huge quantities of material – which could conceivably include aircraft-grade plywood. And "if the armour steel, which is procured from the construction office, is not available at the time, four pieces [airframes] can be made of shipbuilding steel. The electrodes required for armoured steel welding must be specified and ordered in good time".

It was stated that the fifth BV 40 off the line would be completed without internal fittings or equipment for use as a stress-testing mule.

Kronprinz wrote back on January 4 regarding the spring strut to say that "we can give you two suggestions on how to make spring struts from existing spring units by simply converting them, which should roughly correspond to your wishes. A letter with drawings could go out tomorrow. However, in view of the urgency you emphasised, we recommend that you send a courier to pick up the letter and the drawings here, since post can take a very long time these days".

The second BV 40 production meeting was held on January 6, 1944, and this being the depths of winter it was emphasised

ABOVE: The cover of Blohm & Voss's January 1944 description of the BV 40 Gleitjäger.

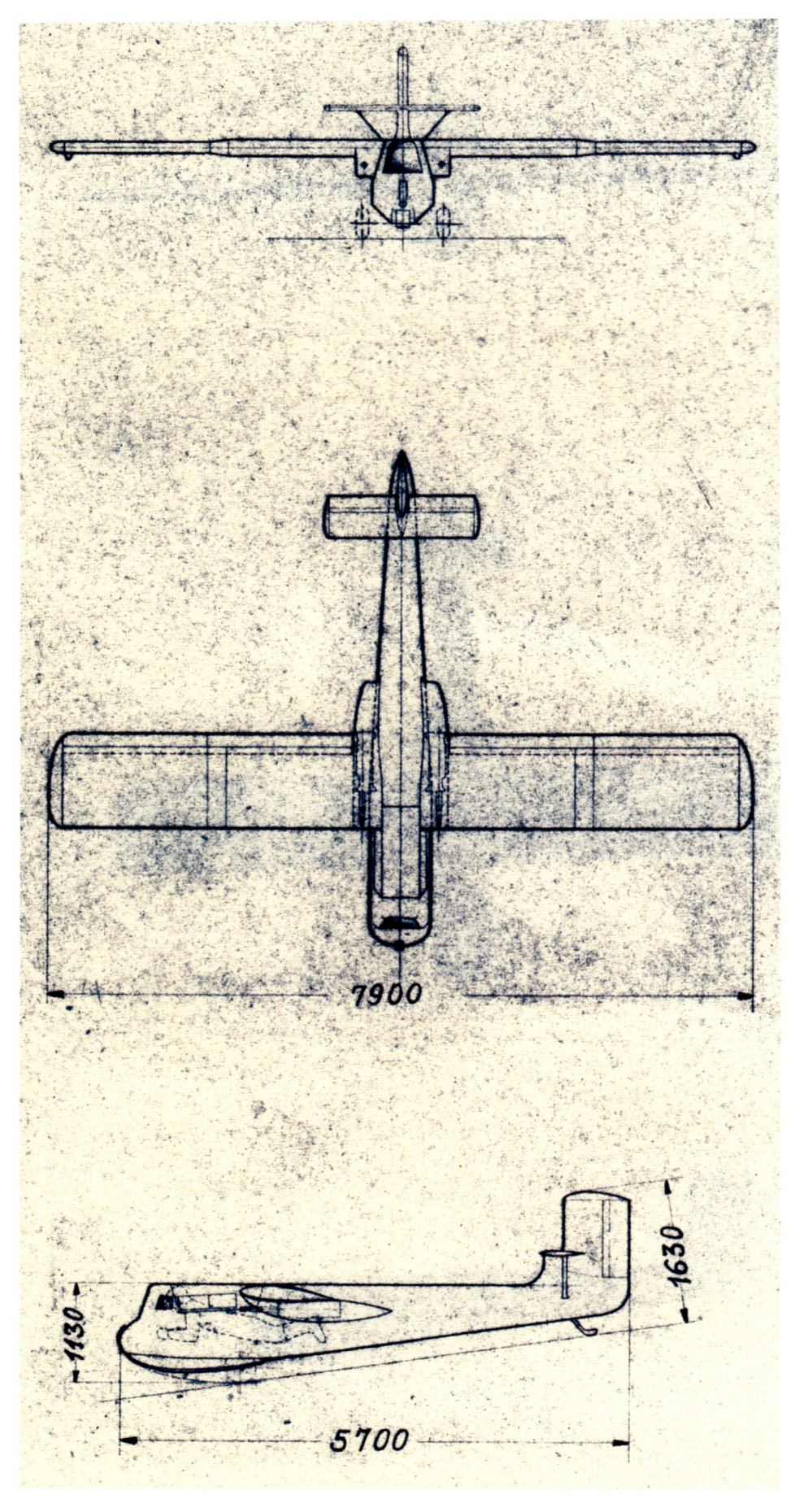

ABOVE: This illustration from the type sheet within the January 1944 description shows the BV 40's final layout as a 'glide-fighter', with twin MK 108 cannon in wingroot nacelles.

that where woodworking was concerned, "maintaining the correct temperature and humidity levels is very important. A suitable space is available for the end of the fuselage, tail unit and wing spar". Wing assembly was likely to take place in a former construction office room. The glue to be used was referred to as 'WHK' and "the wood parts are preserved in accordance with Air Ministry regulations … the surface smoothness does not need to be overly good".

The necessary laminated wood and plywood was still missing and "can be brought in by January 20 at the earliest, and even then only if there is a DE order. The armour plates can only be delivered six weeks after ordering; the necessary drawings will not be available before the end of January. The first four aircraft will therefore be built from normal shipbuilding steel".

A set of BV 141 tail wheels was tentatively specified for the BV 40's jettisonable take-off undercarriage as an interim measure and delivery dates were set for the various collections of construction blueprints. Finally, it was noted that "contrary to an earlier decision, not the fifth, but the third aircraft is to be built as a stress testing mule".

BV 40 ADVANTAGES

The first full description of the BV 40 had been completed by January 7, 1944, when two copies were sent to Galland's office.

The introduction explained what Blohm & Voss perceived to be the BV 40's greatest virtue – it's small frontal area which made it very difficult to hit when faced head-on. It said: "The chances of success in attacking an enemy bomber depend primarily on two factors: 'combat distance' and 'weapon strength'.

"The shorter the combat distance, the more the accuracy of the enemy's defensive fire increases, so this path [shooting at an enemy bomber from close range] can only be taken if the chances of being hit by the enemy's projectiles are reduced by the use of suitable means.

"It only takes a simple comparison to show that if the attacking aircraft's structural dimensions are reduced in proportion to the reduction in the attack distance, the enemy's chances of hitting will not increase as the attacking aircraft closes in.

"So if the enemy has a certain chance of hitting an attacking fighter with a frontal area of 1.6 square metres at 1,000m, for example, then the chance of hitting a fighter with half that frontal area are only half as large."

The report pointed out that reducing the frontal area of a conventional fighter was unlikely to ever be possible "because the combat conditions categorically require ever greater flight performance and thus always more powerful, i.e. larger engines, so that there is no prospect of reducing the frontal areas. However, it [a reduced frontal area] can be successfully used for a variant of the fighter, that is the glide-fighter.

"By putting the pilot in a horizontal position, the endangered frontal area can be reduced to about 0.5 square metres, which is only a third of that of a fighter with an air-cooled engine, so that in the context of the above comparison, the 1,000m starting distance only corresponds to about 580m.

"If you now combine that with strong frontal armour, in terms of reducing the hit effect [of the enemy's weapons] – and that is possible with such small cross-sectional dimensions without great sacrifices in weight – then you have created an extraordinarily effective weapon for the very close combat distance".

The glide-fighter was by no means invulnerable though, since "although the wing and tail units are correspondingly reduced [in size] in such a glider, hits on these components must be expected. Since full protection is hopeless, so the pilot must be able to safely exit".

Nevertheless, "in terms of value, the glider represents a minimum of effort: without engine, propeller or landing gear and without large equipment, with about a third of the wing and fuselage dimensions, and built with the cheapest material, primitively without reducing operational effectiveness, its use is justified even if the possible uses are limited.

"One must not make the mistake of trying to compare the naturally limited deployment options [of the glide-fighter] with those of a conventional fighter. You have to compare these more appropriately with the possible uses of glide bombs, compared to which the glider will be a weapon with extraordinarily increased accuracy. But just as the gliding bomb requires a well-chosen attack position when dropped, the use of a gliding fighter also requires a well-considered attack approach".

The report stated that the BV 40 operational flight had two phases: tow and attack. It was only worthwhile beginning the operation, it was noted, if sufficient advance warning could be given. Assuming this condition was fulfilled, the fighter and its towed BV 40 would take-off and climb to an altitude of 8.5km, with both fighter and glider travelling at 475km/h. For the glider pilot, determining the proper point of release would be a case of correctly lining up a 'notch' on the bulletproof glass visor. Once released, he would then have to keep the bomber correctly positioned in his visor in order to line up the attack, which could then commence at a distance of 1,200m from the target.

All this would be easier said than done as the report acknowledges: "One can see that there is little prospect of success if the glider pilot is not instructed about the possible attack positions and trained on them and then sticks to them in an emergency. If he fulfils this requirement, then he deserves a good share of the success of the kill."

For the towing phase, it was pointed out that the performance of the towing fighter would be unavoidably hampered before release but "it is even possible to tow two gliders at the same time with a normal fighter and thus still reach considerable altitudes". For the second phase, "theoretical investigations have shown that a glider attack from behind is inadvisable … The only promising attack direction is therefore from the front or to a certain extent from the side".

A head-on attack meant the glider pilot would only have a brief window of opportunity to open fire so "we have therefore taken up the suggestion of the Inspector of Fighter Pilots … to fire the planned amount of ammunition in two weapons. Likewise, the Schlinge device seems to us to be largely suitable for use".

The report's introduction concluded with the following rather colourful passage: "The glider is a weapon for the level-headed and for the intrepid; the pilot of the towing fighter [presumably the 'level-headed'] must be prudent, they have to bring the gliding fighter into the attack position with reason and deliberation; the glider pilot, on the other hand [the 'intrepid'], must be a cold-blooded daredevil who has the opportunity to look the enemy in the eye from behind a protective armour plate and hit him devastatingly. If these requirements are practiced and maintained, this new weapon will find its rightful place alongside the existing ones."

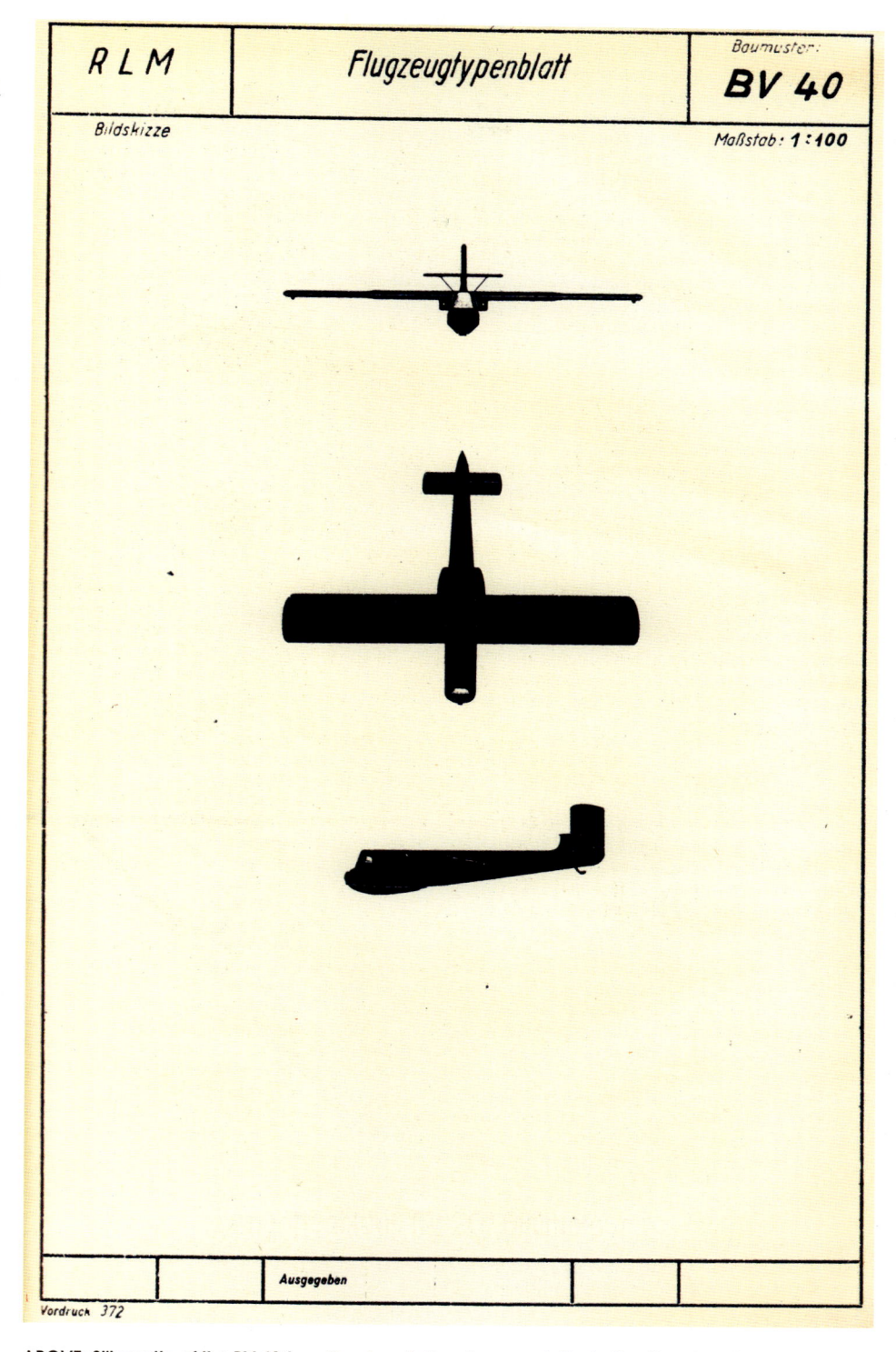

ABOVE: Silhouette of the BV 40 from the description document, illustrating the aircraft's remarkably small frontal area.

BUILD DESCRIPTION

The same report described in detail how the BV 40 was constructed. The constant-chord wing was a single assembly made entirely out of wood without dihedral or anhedral. There was a leading edge box spar and an auxiliary spar at the wing trailing edge, plus plywood ribs, covered with a 5mm thick laminated beech plywood skin. Control surfaces consisted of ailerons and flaps – all made of wood. The flaps had three positions: 0 degrees for flight, 50 degrees for landing and 80 degrees for glide angle control or when an air brake was required.

The fuselage consisted of three sections: the front section "fitted with an in-flight quick disconnect", a centre section and tail section. The cockpit shell was made entirely out of flat armour plates with aerodynamic fairings attached. The front consisted of two 20mm thick plates, a vertical lower one and an upper one which sloped backwards slightly. The former was the point at which the tow cable attached and the latter was fitted with a pane of bulletproof glass, giving the pilot a viewing angle of 35 degrees up and down and 20 degrees from side to side. Incredibly, the pilot's 'gunsight' was "applied to the front and back of the 120mm thick bulletproof glass pane using paint".

The side walls consisted of sloped armour plates 8mm thick, each including an irregularly shape glass window measuring about 150 x 150mm slightly in front of and above the pilot's head. These could each be covered by a steel plate during the attack run.

The removeable canopy above the pilot was 8mm thick at the front and 5mm further back. This included side sections with sliding windows measuring 350 x 180mm. The flat cockpit base plate was 5mm thick for its whole length and below that was the spring-loaded landing skid. The jettisonable take-off undercarriage, consisting of an axle tube with a 350 x 135mm BV 141 tailwheel on either side, and was connected to the skid by welded brackets with wire bracing holding it in place. All that was required to release it was the pulling-out of a pin, releasing the wire.

The fuselage centre section, with a cut-out for the continuous wing spar between two frames, was made of 0.8mm thick sheet steel but with 8mm thick armour plates strategically placed to protect the pilot's legs. According to the description document, the entire front section could be separated from the centre section, together with the wing, "in flight by means of an emergency lever".

The rear fuselage section was made entirely of wood and was "firmly screwed" to the centre section. The elevators, fin and rudder were also wooden and were designed to be as simple both in terms of their construction and their operation. Fitted to the tail end underside was a small spring-loaded skid.

When it came to the controls, clearly some effort had been made to study and improve upon those of the B 9 since those initial test flights by Blohm & Voss engineers four months earlier: "The control column is slightly to the right of centre, so it can be comfortably operated with just the right hand. However, if necessary, an attack with the left hand is still possible.

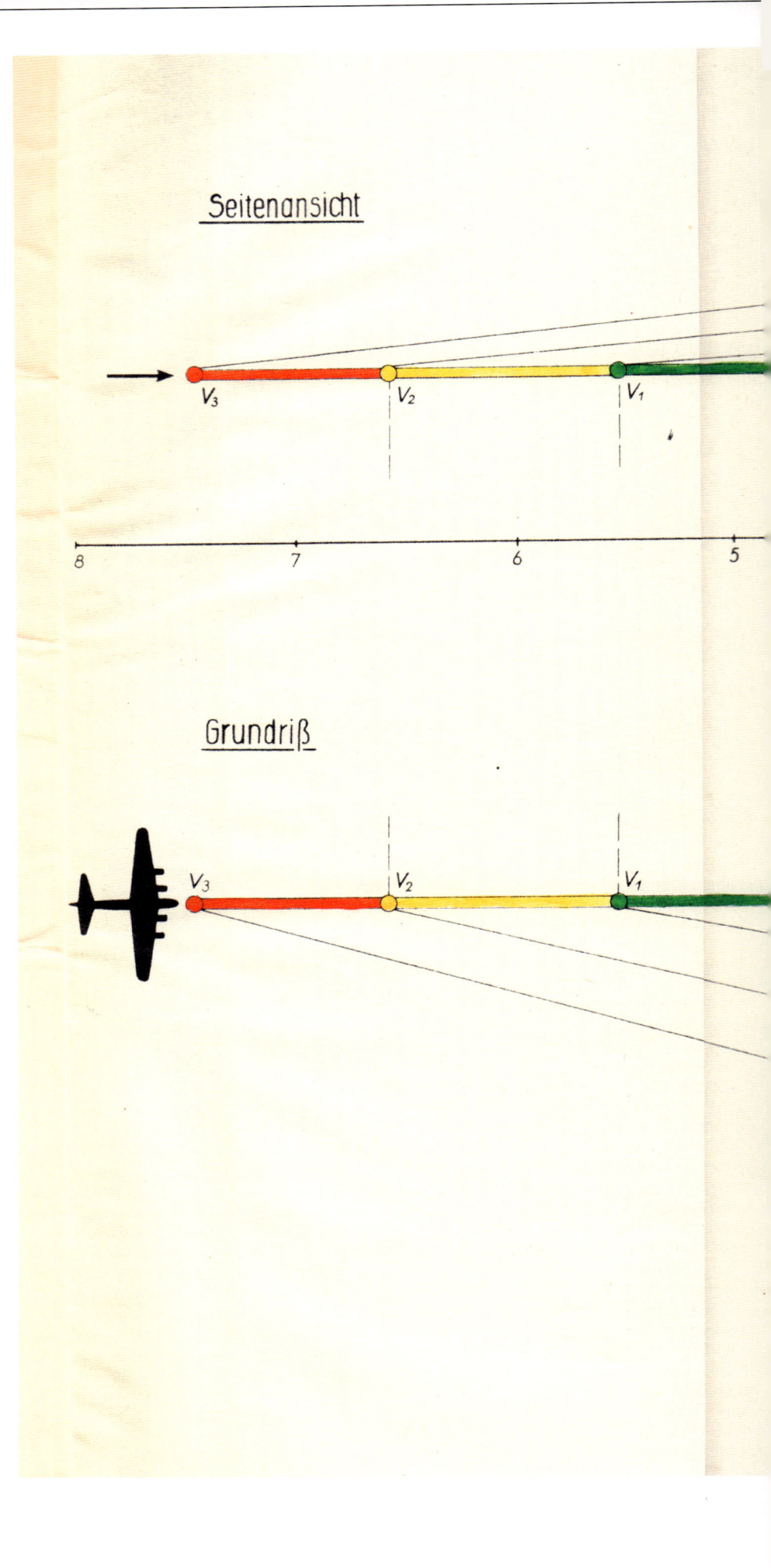

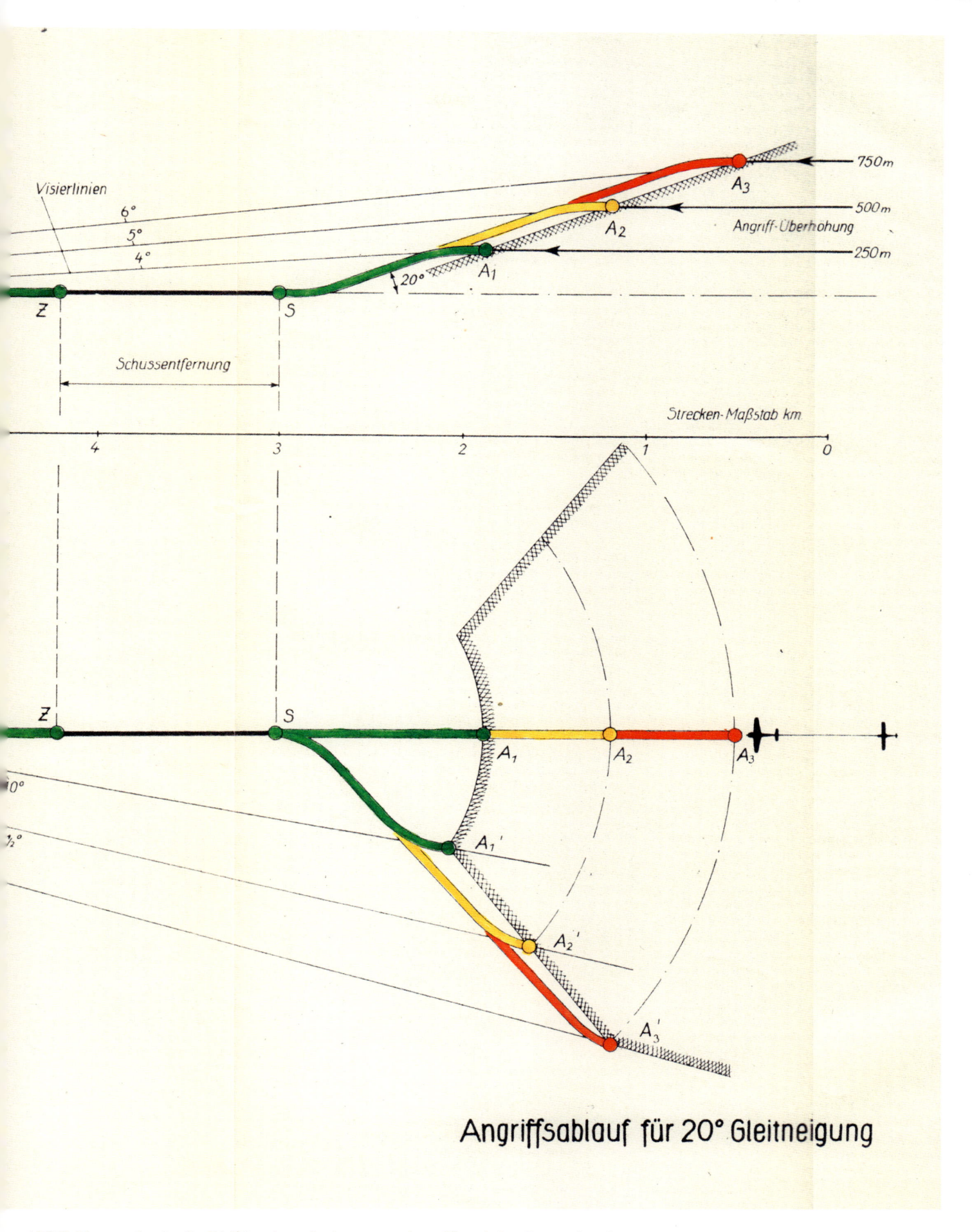

ABOVE: Diagram showing the BV 40 head-on attack sequence from different elevations and angles.

"The stick movements are transmitted to cables to operate the elevator and ailerons. The rudder is operated with the tips of the toes. The toe caps rest in pockets, so the movement comes from the ankle." The pedals were adjustable to suit the pilot's height.

The pilot would lie on a Schroeder BH6 chest parachute and on his back would be a back cushion with an FE5/2a back seat belt buckle from Kehler & Sohn, holding his six-point harness together. This buckle could be unfastened, in an emergency, via a Bowden cable.

Back up front, a ratchet lever on the left operated the flaps, a handle behind the pilot's left elbow released the jettisonable wheels on take-off, a cable-pull handle at the front left of the bulkhead actuated the tow line release, the 'emergency lever' for separating the cockpit from the rest of the glider was on the right and the canopy could be opened using handles on the left and right. The latter could also be opened externally from the left-hand side.

The pilot's compass was "stored in the fuselage panelling outside the lower front armour plate and can be viewed through two mirrors". This rather odd positioning of the compass – effectively on the glider's nose – was "a result of the relatively large proximity of the steel parts [and even then] the accuracy of the compass display must be expected to be lower than is otherwise required".

The aircraft's electrical system also included a communication link with the towing aircraft, heating clothing connection, lighting for the compass, pitot tube heating and power for the MK 108 cannon. The cockpit instrument panel included an airspeed indicator, altimeter, emergency turn pointer, oxygen monitor and pressure gauge. It also included a pitot tube heating indicator and one switch each for pitot tube heating, lighting and armament. The pitot tube itself was located on top of a small mast on the upper fuselage behind the wing.

Under tow, the electrical system received power from the towing aircraft via the tow line but once released the glider was powered by a 7.5 Ah battery installed, with insulation to protect it from the cold, in the wooden part of the fuselage.

The two MK 108 30mm cannon were carried in aerodynamic underwing nacelles to the left and right of the fuselage. Each had 35 rounds of ammunition and since the cannon were installed on their sides, the ammo was fed from above – having been loaded through hatches in the upper wing – and the spent cartridges would be ejected from below. The gap between the main and auxiliary wing spars where the ammo was stored before being fired was protected by a narrow strip of 8mm thick armour plate.

It was uncertain at the time of the report's publication whether the Schlinge device could be carried as an overload or whether it would be necessary to remove one of the MK 108s in order to install it.

BV 40 DISADVANTAGES

The description report pulls few punches when it comes to outlining the disadvantages of the system. Take-off would be "the most difficult part of the operation in terms of flying", and that was saying something, given how difficult every other aspect of the operation was likely to be.

This was because "the strong concentration of power in the propeller is expressed in a very pronounced twist of the turbulent air behind the fighter, especially [immediately] after take-off and during climb. Hence the need to find a take-off method that would allow the glider's pilot to stay out of that area, or at least to pass through it quickly.

"The simplest procedure would be to start with a very long tow line. It would have the disadvantage that in bad weather flight, e.g. when climbing through high layers of cloud, the line of sight of the towing vehicle would be lost. The possible solution to this – a retractable tow line – is not recommended for the time being because of the winch that would have to be developed for it".

Once in the air, "the prone position of the pilot naturally impedes his ability to operate the rudders. This can only be compensated for by the fact that all rudders, despite small control paths, are designed for small but steadily increasing operating forces. We also tried to give the aircraft as good-natured a character as possible". So keeping the BV 40 fully under control was likely to be a challenge.

And then, once the mission was complete, the pilot would have to try and bring the glider with its heavyweight frontal armour in for a skid landing – most probably without access to an airfield. The report acknowledges that "personal experience [of this sort of landing] is not available" but states that "a landing speed of less than 120km/h could be achieved". Consideration had been given to providing the pilot with "special means of increasing lift, such as slats and Fowler landing flaps" but these had all been "dispensed with in view of providing the most primitive and robust aircraft possible".

Assuming that the pilot had somehow managed to bring his glider down undamaged, perhaps in a farmer's field, there remained the tricky task of getting both pilot and aircraft back to base.

According to the report: "The frontal use of the gliders will mean that only a small percentage of the deployed machines will glide back to their operational base. In the majority of cases you have to reckon with a rough field landing.

"Since transport in an unassembled state is not possible, given the existing dimensions, attention will be paid to easy dismantling during construction. After removing the canopy roof and the wing panelling [skin] on the fuselage, there should be no difficulties in removing the 170kg wooden wing by undoing the two pairs of screw bolts and lifting it free of the cut-out in the centre section of the fuselage.

"Only the aileron and landing flap cables have to be separated [presumably this means 'cut'] and the ammunition belts that may not yet have been fired can be pulled out of the wing channel. With its sturdy construction, the wing can be loaded onto a farmer's wagon without being damaged if handled with some care. Appropriate lettering and painting are used to identify the places suitable for storage.

"The fuselage without wings weighs about 580kg. The simplest method of transport is obtained when using the original starter gear [by refitting the axle tube and two BV 141 tailwheels]. In most cases it will therefore be worthwhile to obtain this landing gear from the nearest base and [use it to] tow [the BV 40] down the country road. For cases where this is impossible, precautions have been taken to ensure further disassembly.

"You can activate the quick-release point of the cockpit and then transport the armoured section, which weighs about 300kg, by on its own. Two suitable through-openings are provided above the skid for this purpose."

CAMOUFLAGE COLOURS

A Blohm & Voss 'production instruction' was issued on February 5, 1944, to provide the recommended camouflage colours for the BV 40. All of the aircraft's metal parts "must be preserved with K paint TL 6316 B.99 (grey) before installation. The preservation of the parts mentioned [all metal parts including the armour structure] may only be carried out after careful cleaning of rust film, dirt, grease etc. Use P 3, Siliron WL or the cleaning agent 'Z'". It would appear that "K paint TL 6316 B" was what today is commonly referred to as the 'RLM' colour palette. 'B.99' is therefore RLM 99 and the document explicitly states that this colour is (grau) – grey.

Over the grey, the inner and outer surfaces of the steel cockpit area were to be given one coat of RLM 66, described elsewhere as Schwarzgrau or 'black-grey', with the addition, to the outer surfaces, of RLM 65 'light grey' for the underside and RLM 71 'dark green' for the top.

The outer surfaces of the plywood fuselage, wings and tail unit were supposed to get one coat of "Fg 7/560 (colourless)", one coat of "Fg 7/565.99 (grey)" – listed separately from "K paint TL 6316 B.99 (grey)" – and one coat of RLM 65 for the underside and RLM 71 for the upper areas.

The inner surfaces were also to be painted, but only with a single coat each of Fg 7/560 (colourless) and Fg 7/565.99 (grey). This seems to have meant that every component was to be painted, even though it might not be visible externally – including all frames, ribs, belts and strips made from plywood, laminated wood or solid pine.

Under a heading of "remarks", the document noted that "if plywood glued with imprenal is processed, preservation with Fg 7/560 is omitted". Also, the paint applied by spraying or dipping must be removed from the surfaces to be glued". And finally, "as a boundary line for the camouflage in tones 65 for below and 71 for above, use the largest frame width". The "imprenal" referred to may in fact have been Impranal – a thick-layer glazing varnish for wooden surfaces that is still commercially available today.

WEIGHT CREEP

The Air Ministry wrote to Blohm & Voss on February 15, 1944, stating that "it is intended, after checking and accepting the bid you have yet to submit, to place a corresponding order with you for: prototype construction of another 14 BV 40/V7-V20 type aircraft. A total of 20 BV 40/V1-V20 type aircraft are to be delivered".

The mention of "another 14" with the designations BV 40 V7 to V20 suggests that at some point the previously mooted order for 12 prototypes had in fact been reduced to just six airframes – BV 40 V1 to V6. Now, however, Blohm & Voss was expected to build 20 airworthy gliders. A subsequent note, also dated February 15, shows that the stress-test mule was now to be regarded as separate; a 21st airframe. The project's priority status, however, remained resolutely set at SS rather than the long-hoped-for DE.

Given all the unaccounted-for paint weights and other somewhat optimistic weight estimates strewn throughout the project documentation, it comes as little surprise to learn that attendees of the third BV 40 production meeting on February 16, 1944, were told "a new weight estimate has shown that the aircraft will be prohibitively heavy. It is therefore necessary to save weight on all components under all circumstances".

In order to get testing underway, "the first six aircraft will be completed with the following changes: 1) The front bulletproof glass is omitted [saving] 35kg. 2) The upper canopy and the side steel windows are made of wood 42kg. 3) The side foot armour is omitted 8kg. 4) On the left side of the wing the ammunition bay is armoured and on the right the ammunition armour is left out 13kg. 5) One gun and ammunition accounts for 79kg. 6) The bearing arms of all rudder and landing flaps are drilled out 2kg. 7) The wing leading edge spar is milled out 3kg. Total saving 182kg".

The mention of "the first six aircraft" supports the idea that either the initial order for 12 examples was never officially approved or it was approved but subsequently halved at some point between December 14, 1943, and February 15, 1944.

A host of changes to the specification of the production model BV 40 were then outlined: dropping all 8mm armour plate thicknesses down to 6mm (27.5kg saving), deletion of armour for the ammo (8kg), the mid-fuselage to be made of wood rather than sheet steel (30kg), fuselage end skin reduced to 2mm thickness and tail bulkheads lightened (10kg), skin thicknesses reduced to 1.5mm on the ailerons and elevators, and 1mm on the flaps (5kg).

Another 6kg was saved from the frame for the bulletproof glass, the wing spar was lightened (20kg), the ribs were lightened (15kg), the wing skin was thinned out from 5mm to 4mm or from 4mm to 3mm (10kg), the wing leading edge spar was milled out (3kg), the rear spar was made to taper as extended towards the wingtip (3kg), the bearer arms of all rudder and landing flaps were drilled out (2kg) and the landing skid was made slightly taller then drilled through (5kg). All these measures combined saved 144.5kg.

Thinning the aircraft's skin all over and weakening its spars and ribs meant its safe dive speed was reduced to 650km/h but "as a result of these measures, there will be no particular delay in the production of the first two aircraft. The third machine is still used as a stress-test airframe and, in order to save money, is immediately fitted with the thinner plywood skins at the end of the fuselage and on the wings; in addition, the glued strips on the frames in the fuselage are left out."

SUICIDE ATTACKER

Vogt wrote to the Air Ministry on February 23 to express his concerns about the BV 40's ballooning weight – necessitated by the conflicting demands of the Air Ministry. He wrote: "[It] has now been shown that the increased demands during development for the greatest structural strength, high dive speed, reinforced armour and dual armament has led to a total weight of about 1,150kg. We are of the opinion that you should do everything you can to reduce this back to a tolerable level.

"Since only a small proportion of the total weight can be influenced by the high quality of the through construction, we ask you to check all points of the requirements again in the interest of the speed of the entire aircraft.

"Limiting the structural strength to the usual fighter level seems all the more appropriate to us, since only a single attack can be flown. With regard to the armour, we recommend reducing the arbitrary impact angle on the side, deck and floor walls, so that 6mm of armour steel is sufficient.

"By overhauling the construction, we ourselves want to shave off some structural weight, so that a take-off weight of around 1,000kg could be achieved. We ask for a decision to be made as soon as possible.

"In order to retain the testing schedule for the first six aircraft, which are only armoured with normal steel and are not suitable for active use, we made some components in wood and only equipped them with a single cannon, in order to approach a test weight which will correspond with the later series machines. We ask for your approval of the project."

Vogt and two of his engineers – Hermann Pohlmann and Schaudt – met with Czolbe,

ABOVE: A BV 40 prototype under construction.

The first BV 40 prototype looking somewhat incomplete without its underwing nacelles. A hatch panel is missing from its side and it would appear that the windscreen has not been fitted or has been removed.

Malz and Klein to discuss this on February 26, 1944. Evidently the Blohm & Voss team were reassured that "taking into account the [combat] experience of close attacks" only the front of the BV 40 needed to be heavily armoured. The sides and underside could go completely unarmoured. Based on new calculations, it was estimated that the BV 40's safe dive speed was 850km/h above 4km altitude and 700km/h nearer the ground.

The Air Ministry arranged, on March 2, to have a Messerschmitt Bf 110 G-0, WNr. 5188, transferred to Blohm & Voss specifically for the purpose of towing BV 40 prototypes. Meanwhile, Vogt had been investigating the possibility of fitting the BV 40 with the liquid-fuelled HWK 109-507 rocket motor from an Hs 293 anti-shipping missile. This would give the glider pilot nearly two minutes of thrust, with the promise of four minutes from a "later device".

He noted in a memo dated March 16, which he passed to Bürkner for the attention of Malz, that "with a deployment path of 15-30km after the [glider's] release, a new tactical situation has arisen that needs to be considered seriously".

Blohm & Voss's fuselage construction group sent out a memo of their own on March 30, stating that the removable canopies of BV 40 V2-V6 would be made of wood, like that of V1, and "in order to prevent destruction by air pressure, the sliding flaps are to be made of steel and the side walls are to be reinforced with 2mm sheet steel".

Czolbe wrote to Bürkner on April 15 with an unusual request for Vogt. He "asks for the following study: BV 40 loaded with bombs but without firearms; determination of the maximum possible payload for take-off, climb and approach in Mistel configuration with He 177. What is the best gliding angle and speed with the maximum payload?"

Bürkner then wrote to Vogt five days later outlining Czolbe's request but adding: "additional Walter [rocket] drive not desired. The matter comes into question for all machines for special purpose. The Inspector of Fighter Pilots is no longer interested, but another department is".

Without the backing of Galland's office the BV 40 might have been cancelled immediately had it not been for the interest of the unnamed 'other department'. And this 'department' appears to have been none other than the Luftwaffe's notorious special operations unit Kampfgeschwader 200 (KG 200). Fliegerstabsingenieur Hans Christian Tilenius, KG 200's technical officer, was now liaising with Blohm & Voss on preparing the BV 40 for a new mission. Tilenius attended a conference on precisely this mission on April 17 with former glider pilot Oberleutnant Karl-Heinz Lange of I. Luftlandegeschwader (Glider Assault Wing) who, in late 1943, had put forward the view that, to quote author Robert Forsyth, "a small unit of ideologically radicalised pilots could inflict great damage against an anticipated Allied invasion fleet by flying Totaleinsatz ('total commitment' operations) in manned glide bombs. Put another way, these would be Selbstopfer (self-sacrifice) missions. Lange put his idea forward to the OKL as a serious proposal.

"It was, obviously, an extreme and contentious suggestion that ran against the fundamental creed of the German officer corps. But these were extreme times, and there was an adequate number of young pilots within the ranks of the Luftwaffe who were sufficiently imbued with National Socialist fervour to execute Lange's radical measure as a way of defending both their principles and their homeland.

"But there was one problem: in early 1944, no such manned glide bomb existed to carry out the task."

In fact, exactly such a manned glide bomb very nearly did exist in early 1944: the BV 40. By mid-April, Blohm & Voss had already done most of the design work and the first prototype was almost completed. And now that Galland's men no longer wanted the glider for their bomber-killing mission, it was available for other customers.

From this point on, the BV 40 was effectively repurposed as a manned glide-bomb. Blohm & Voss's initial response on how to modify the design to suit this new mission was simply to remove the two underwing MK 108s and replace them with attachment points for two BT700 anti-shipping torpedoes. So-armed, a pair of BV 40s would be carried aloft beneath the wings of an He 177 bomber before being released over the target.

The chances of the BV 40 pilot surviving such an attack would have been very slim indeed. Even if they managed to drop their torpedoes and pull up in time, there would be nowhere to land out at sea – and the armoured fuselage of the BV 40 would ensure that it sank like a stone. It was a suicide mission.

FIRST TEST FLIGHT

The results of flutter tests on the BV 40 V1 prototype were published on April 27 and it

ABOVE: The BV 40 V1's tail is lifted for the photographer, showcasing the somewhat unusual design of the fin and tailplane arrangement.

was concluded that there were no concerns in this area. However, it was recommended that the glider only be flown at speeds above 300km/h at altitudes greater than 2km.

Vogt sent a memo to Bürkner on May 2, 1944, asking him to "contact the DVL's flight mechanics management [department] immediately and ask Mr Schmidt to bring the prone position aircraft [B 9] to Wenzendorf in the next few days. After an unsuccessful take-off with the BV 40, Mr Rautenhaus wishes to fly the said aircraft again immediately before the next take-off".

Clearly, Blohm & Voss test pilot Rautenhaus had attempted a take-off in BV 40 V1 but had failed to become airborne – presumably some time between April 27 and May 2. Why this take-off failed and whether he did indeed get to fly the B 9 again before his next try at a prone position glider take-off is unclear.

However, the glider apparently suffered no damage in the attempt and Rautenhaus was ready to go again on May 6. Vogt sent a brief telex to the head of the Air Ministry's Technical Office in Berlin shortly afterwards to "share the successful first towed flight with the BV 40. Landing at the edge of the field over the fence caused minor wing damage. Flight characteristics seem to correspond well to the calculations".

Rautenhaus's report on the BV 40 V1's first flight, particularly the section dealing with the take-off, provides some clues as to what might have gone wrong during his abortive late April/early May take-off attempt.

He wrote: "The overall impression of the first factory flight is quite positive. Difficulties are to be expected on take-off, which requires some flying experience as it tends to get choppy, largely due, I believe, to the layout of the controls. Thorough preliminary training in the novel arrangement of the controls will be essential.

"After just one take-off, it is difficult to judge to what extent propeller wash from the towing machine or the lack of rudder effectiveness or the unevenness in the aerodrome [runway] are involved [in causing the choppy behaviour of the aircraft on the ground]. In flight the effectiveness of all three control surfaces is good, the forces are almost too small if they do not increase with increasing speed."

Once airborne, "the tow does not cause any difficulties, tow line movements can be compensated for quickly and easily. Flight once released was also flawless up to 250km/h and there is stability around all three axes. The setting of the elevator damper is very top-heavy".

Rautenhaus decided "for safety reasons and in order to lose altitude" that he would touch down at 200km/h – the recommended landing speed being 120km/h – using the 80-degree landing flap setting to brake before reaching the edge of the airfield. However, at the point of touching down he discovered that "the ratchet for the landing flaps did not work properly [and] it was impossible to extend [them] beyond the take-off position".

The only source of information on what happened next is Vogt's telex and the true extent of damage to the BV 40 V1's wing was not detailed either by Vogt or Rautenhaus.

Rautenhaus's report detailed a number of further issues with the prototype: "the glide angle is too steep; the machine hangs moderately to the right; the intercom system was unclear; the canopy is very leaky, resulting in loud whistling and unpleasant draughts; the landing gear cable has snapped (cause?); the skid appears to be too weak at the pivot point; turn indicator was not working (was on)".

Blohm & Voss received a memo from the Technical Office on May 10 stating that "Henschel equipment", presumably the rocket motor from the Hs 293, was not to be procured for the BV 40 – confirming that a rocket-boosted variant was off the table.

Vogt then sent a memo to Bürkner on May 16, saying that a Major Zimmermann from Galland's office had called, demanding that the BV 40 should be armed. He wrote: "Since the Air Ministry turned down armament, I referred it to Malz. We also have to call Zimmermann and clarify, because otherwise everything will go wrong."

TEST FLIGHTS TWO TO SIX

Rautenhaus climbed back aboard the BV 40 V1 on June 2, 1944, for its second test flight. This time the landing gear wheelbase had been increased and the tyre pressure decreased significantly from 4.5 atmospheres to just 1.5. Rautenhaus noted: "The start

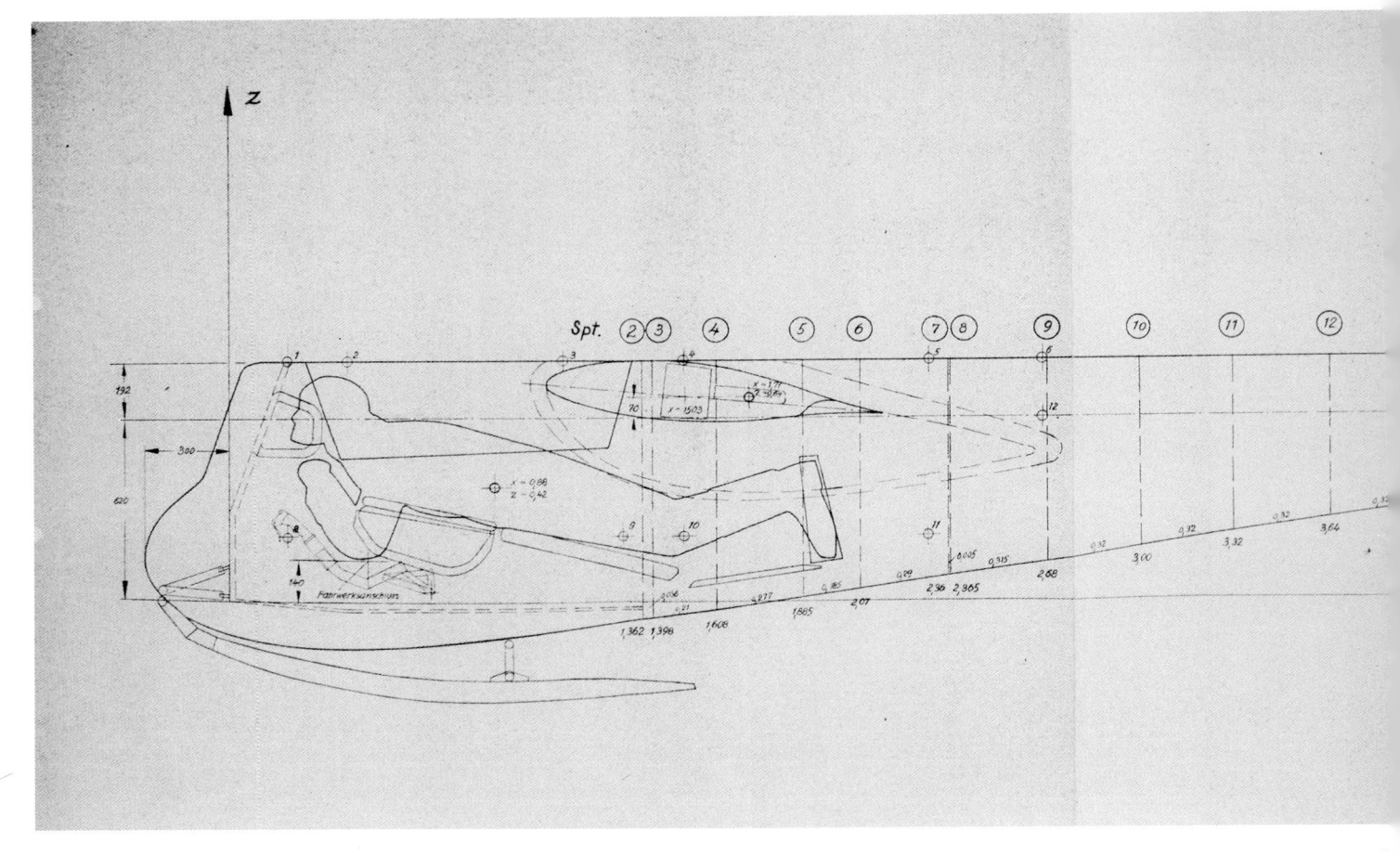

ABOVE: Side view showing the BV 40's extremely simple internal layout as well as the two 20mm armour plates between the pilot and the aerodynamic nose fairing. The drawing is dated March 16, 1944, the same day that consideration of a "new tactical situation" for the glider began.

process was much more pleasant in the first stage, i.e. the shocks were considerably softer, so that premature take-off could be prevented for longer. The BV 40 wobbled back and forth after take-off, but could be corrected more quickly when the rudder began to work sooner than on the first flight."

The flight was "flawless". The report said: "The towing was very pleasant due to the greater elevation of the BV 40 than usual. Rope fluctuations no longer occurred compared to the first flight. The release was made at a speed of 240km/h at 800m altitude; the speed with and without flaps was reduced to 150km/h on an experimental basis and everything went smoothly, i.e. the sink rate remained normal and the rudder was fully effective at this speed."

Everything went wrong during the landing, however. Rautenhaus wrote: "The landing was due to occur at 150km/h, curving close to the edge of the field. This gave the impression of having sufficient flight reserves [at 150km/h, the aircraft still seemed to be flying well], so that there was not the slightest doubt that the landing would go well. At a speed of 140km/h, however, the rate of descent increased very suddenly, so that the machine touched down about 20-30m before the edge of the field and broke through the [perimeter] fence, which damaged the fuselage, the canopy and the right landing flap.

"The oncoming stall 140km/h could be judged purely by feeling, [but was] not expected, and it set in suddenly. There was no tendency to tip over, which is a positive feature compared to the relatively high landing speed. The remaining effectiveness of the elevators to reduce the landing shock was only very weak, but a more precise assessment will only be possible after further flights.

"The effectiveness of the elevator trim is hardly noticeable, and the sluggishness when activated is too great. This position also requires the control stick to be released, which is felt to be uncomfortable. A left-hand trim is desirable, which is sufficient for a top gliding speed of up to about 350km/h. Extending the landing flaps creates a slightly top-heavy moment. The flight lasted three and a half minutes following the release at 800m.

"The unsuccessful landing is not a matter of misjudgement, but of a sudden increase in the rate of descent starting at 140km/h, without any significant change in the position around the transverse axis. Since the machine is considerably top-heavy, which is reinforced by extending the landing flaps, we propose giving the horizontal stabilizer more negative adjustment."

By now, the BV 40 V2 was ready to make its first two flights – both of them piloted by Rautenhaus at Wenzendorf on June 5, 1944.

According to the rather brief post-flight report: "Due to the low level of cloud, these flights could only be released again at an altitude of 800m, so that they could only be used to assess take-off and landing. Overall, the flights were flawless. The tyre pressure of 1.0 atmosphere at the start proved its worth. The landing flaps are overbalanced at 240-250km/h by about 4-5kg compared to the V1, where the forces remained positive even at this relatively high speed.

"During the first flight, the landing gear cable tore again, caused by the sharp edges of the patented process used instead of a splice. After the repairs were carried out, the same phenomenon [damage to the cable] was already evident on the second flight. The landing speed was 125km/h, with the skid absorbing the landing momentum excellently. The elevator effect is good enough. The braking effect of the landing flaps set at 80 degrees can also be described as good." The cable-rubbing 'patented process' appears to have involved a turnbuckle-type wire tensioner.

Three days later, on June 8, the BV 40 V2 was back in the air again for its third and fourth test flights – the fifth and sixth BV 40 test flights overall. On both occasions the take-off proceeded without incident and this time better weather meant the glider could be released at 2,200m. Rautenhaus reported that "during the subsequent flight, the maximum permitted circling speed of 350km/h was almost reached, at 330km/h, without any special incidents".

Landing also proved straightforward since "the previously overbalanced landing flaps now show pleasant forces after adjusting the auxiliary flaps. Landing still presents no difficulties. There is no tendency to jump due to the good properties of the skid. The elevator effect is sufficient until shortly before touchdown".

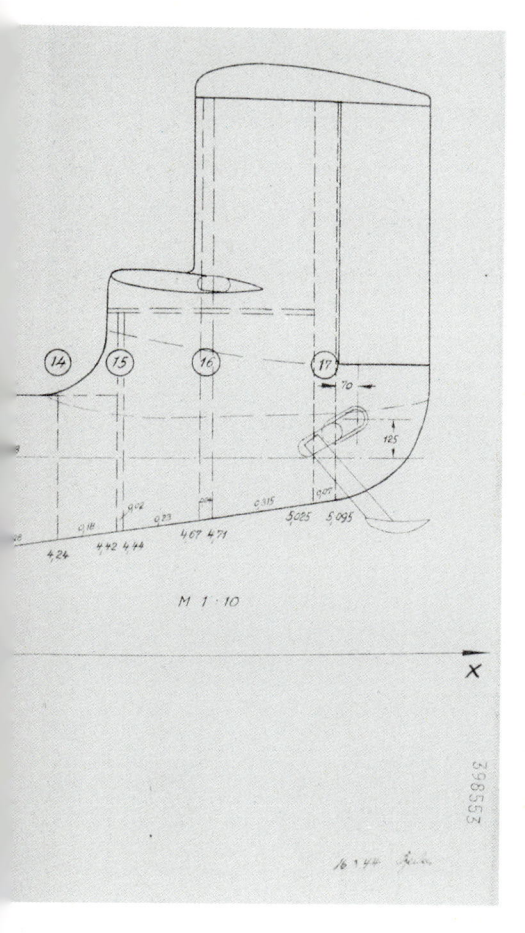

HE 177 CARRIER AIRCRAFT

While the flight tests continued, Blohm & Voss had sent a representative named Wegner from their 'Special Tasks' department to Heinkel's Zwölfaxing facility near Vienna in Austria. Wegner's mission was to liaise with Heinkel's engineers and work out the detail of how BV 40s could be attached to the underside of He 177 wings. Both the twin-prop He 177 A-5 and the as-yet unbuilt He 177 B-5 with four separate engines had been identified as suitable carriers.

In his 'Report on the installation of the BV 40 under He 177 B-5', dated June 28, 1944, Wegner wrote: "In terms of weight, the BV 40 [the report refers to the aircraft by a code name – B 4] can be accommodated under the wings of the He 177, even if it is hung further outwards than indicated in the sketch. However, the statics department of the Heinkel company has concerns about the drag that may occur, because such forces apparently cause the wing to twist, which it cannot absorb.

"The greatest difficulty, however, is to get the BV 40 free from the ground with the bomb attached. The ETC [bomb rack – to which the BV 40 would presumably have been attached] is fitted beneath the outer engine [of the He 177 B-5, with four separate engines] and for this reason had to be built far out on the wing, since we only have 500mm of ground clearance with the maximum load of 1.2 tons under the BV 40 without a bomb. We will have it a bit easier with the He 177 A-5, since this

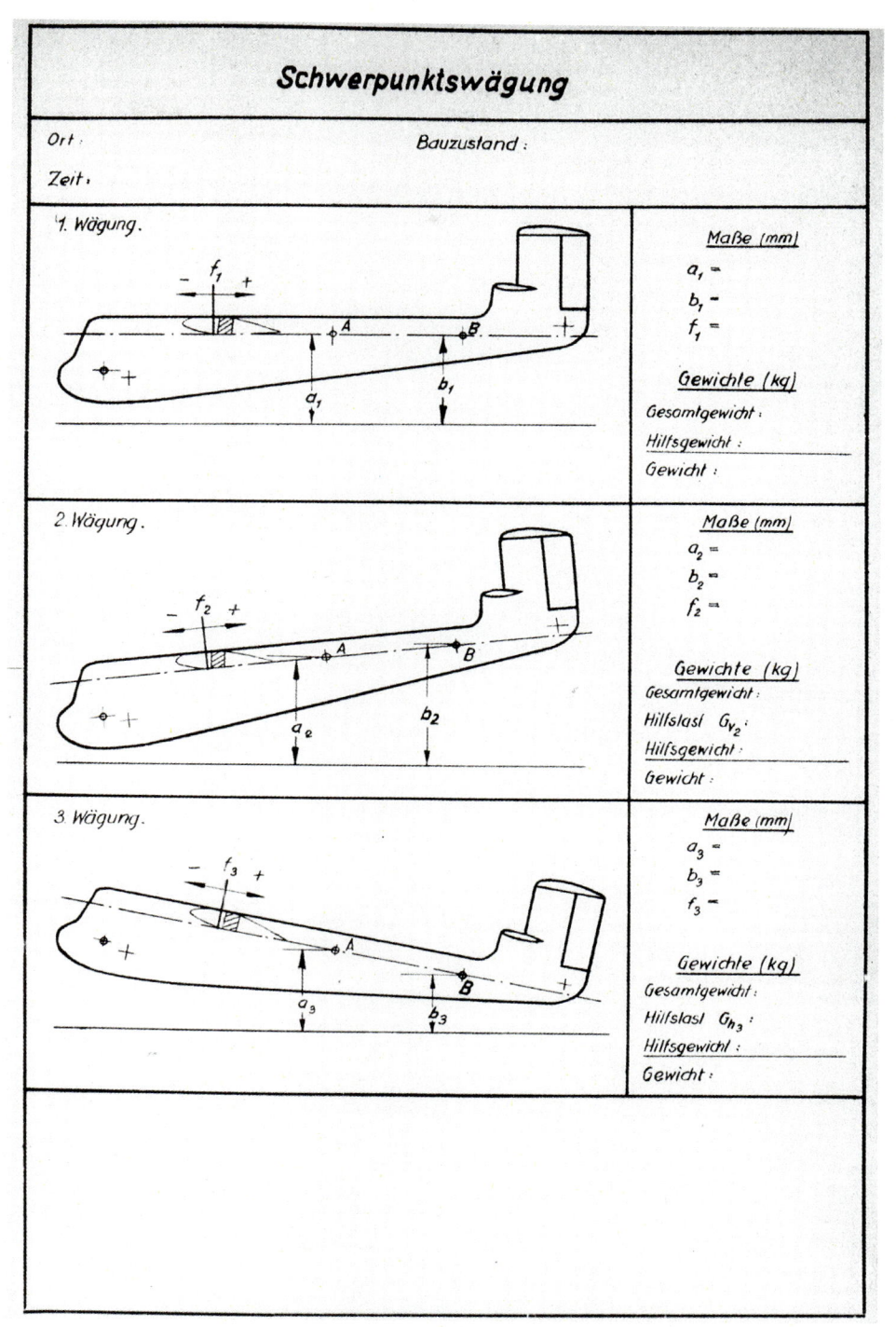

RIGHT: A diagram illustrating static centre of gravity tests on a BV 40 airframe.

machine has only two propellers and the ETC is correspondingly higher under the wing [i.e. it was attached to the wing itself, rather than the underside of an engine nacelle].

"However, production of the He 177 A-5 ended in April 1944 [Wegner wrote 1945, but presumably this was a typo], and it is very questionable whether we can obtain a corresponding number of machines of this series for our purposes."

AS OF JUNE 1944

A status update on the BV 40 flight test programme's progress to date was prepared at the end of June 1944, though it would not be published for another three months.

The introduction stated, somewhat mysteriously, that "essentially the structural condition of the V1, V2, V3 and V6 is the same. Structural differences occur on the rudders and the controls. It is therefore important to pay attention to these deviations before the flight.

"The information given for flight operations only relates to the construction status of the V2, the testing of which has not been completed. Therefore, nothing definitive can be said about the flying characteristics.

"Hanging the BV 40 under a carrier aircraft is not permitted with the current suspension fitting at the wing transition."

ABOVE: Three-quarter view of the BV 40 V1, coded PN+UA. An attempt to tow it aloft with Blohm & Voss test pilot Rautenhaus at the controls at some point between April 27 and May 2, 1944, resulted in an aborted take-off.

ABOVE: Another view of the BV 40 V1. It appears at the port side of the aerodynamic fairing on the front of the aircraft is sporting a dent from some mishap, perhaps when attempting to land or during an aborted take-off.

ABOVE: The undented starboard side of the BV 40 V1.

RIGHT: A demonstration of how easy the BV 40 was to manoeuvre on the ground – a small team could handle it.

Secret Projects of the Luftwaffe 79

ABOVE: The BV 40 V1 prototype as viewed from the front. By this time, the 'glide-fighter' concept had already been dropped because "the Inspector of Fighter Pilots is no longer interested".

A vertical black line appears next to that final paragraph for emphasis. Presumably someone had suggested – or was pressing for – practical experimentation with one or more of the existing BV 40 prototypes, which had not been designed or built with such operations in mind.

The report then provides full instructions for preparing the glider for a towed test flight, explaining the operation of the canopy, pre-flight checks and other details. This includes some useful information which does not appear to have been made available elsewhere previously. For example, the proper altitude for dropping the glider's wheelset was 5-10m and the tow line was about 80m long.

The instructions for making a parachute exit from the BV 40 are also worth recounting: "Reduce speed as much as possible. Pull the aircraft up, pull the emergency lever for fuselage separation backwards to the 'go' position. Tighten your legs! The rear part of fuselage falls off. Do not loosen the seat belts until you have separated them from the rear part of the fuselage! The seat belts are released by pulling the Bowden cable on the left in the cockpit. Open the parachute only after leaving the cockpit!"

It would appear that the BV 40 V7 prototype was intended as a test vehicle for the type's high-altitude oxygen system, since Blohm & Voss wrote to the Air Ministry on July 4 with a diagram explaining how it would work.

A SECOND PILOT

The only pilot known to have flown a BV 40 other than Rautenhaus was Wilhelm Ziegler – a Luftwaffe test pilot stationed at the Rechlin test centre. He flew the V2 up to three times at Wenzendorf over the course of two days, July 3-4.

His report states: "The plane is harmless and pleasant to fly. Tow launch on [a] grass runway becomes more difficult … as take-off speed increases, while on [a] concrete runway it is flawless.

"Due to too much rudder friction and overly sensitive rudders, a clean target approach is difficult. Landing is greatly simplified by the very effective landing flap and its excellent operation. The prone pilot

ABOVE: BV 40's wooden landing flaps had three positions: 0 degrees for flight, 50 degrees for landing and 80 degrees for glide angle control or when an air brake was required. Getting them right mechanically seems to have been one of the aircraft's most significant developmental challenges.

80 Secret Projects of the Luftwaffe

ABOVE: The interior of the BV 40 cockpit. In the foreground is the tray for the pilot's chest parachute and in front of that is the rounded white chin rest. To the right is an arm-rest cushion.

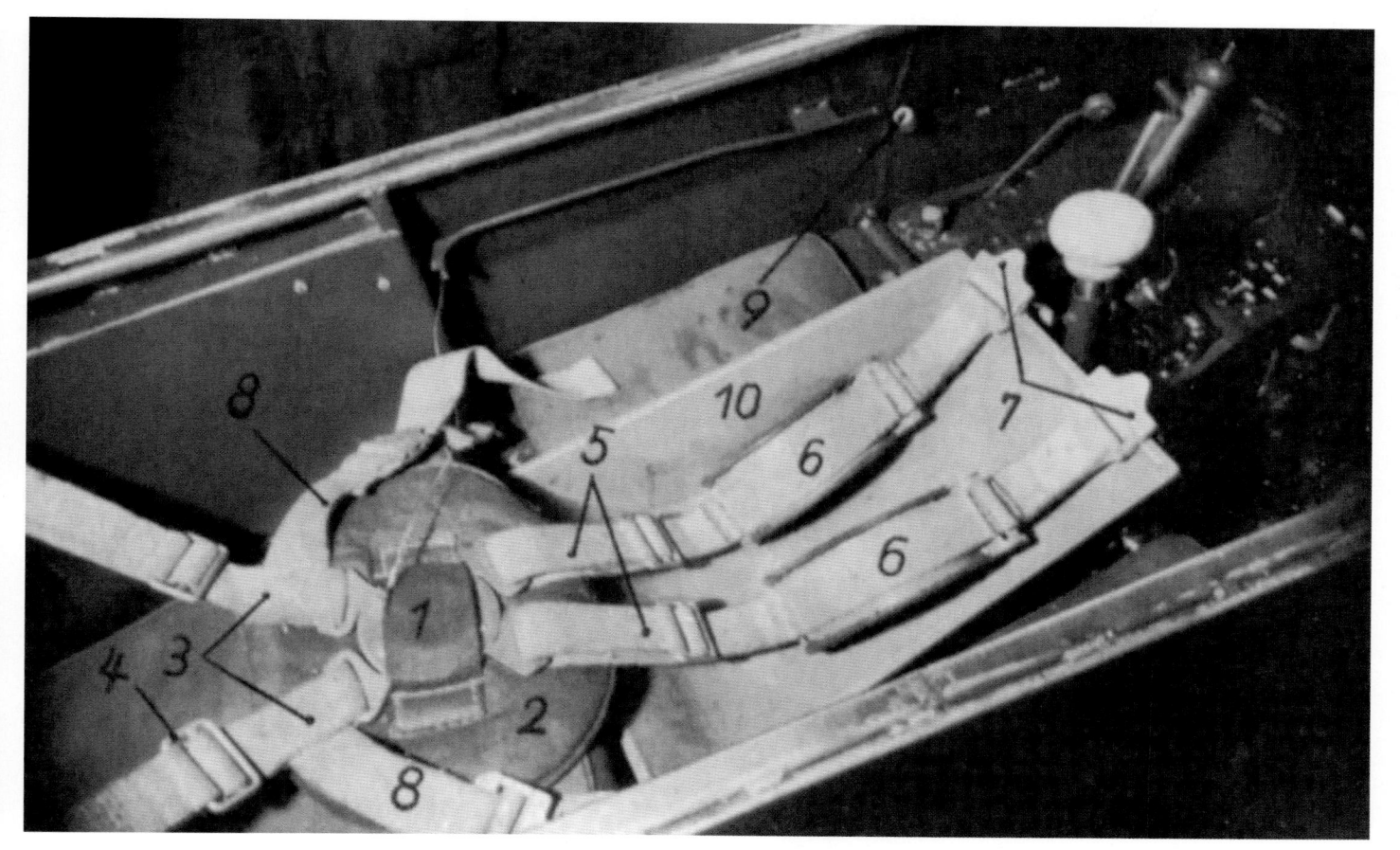

ABOVE: Looking down into the pilot's cockpit with harnesses in place.

Secret Projects of the Luftwaffe 81

ABOVE: A closer view of the area below the chin rest. The annotations are: 1 Landing skid lever. 2 Lever lock. 3 Controls for heated clothing. 4 Connection point for heating clothing. 5 Oxygen supply tube.

ABOVE: Close-up. Point 5 is the compass housing which had to be attached externally to keep it away from the steel armour plates. The pilot viewed it using mirrors inside the aircraft. Point 4 is a regular windscreen, since the planned bulletproof glass wasn't installed on the V1 prototype.

Secret Projects of the Luftwaffe   83

ABOVE: The external canopy latch – 'Zu' is closed, 'Auf' is open.

ABOVE: Inside the cockpit looking towards the rear with the canopy off. The foot pedals for the rudder are visible.

84 Secret Projects of the Luftwaffe

ABOVE: The BV 40 canopy detached.

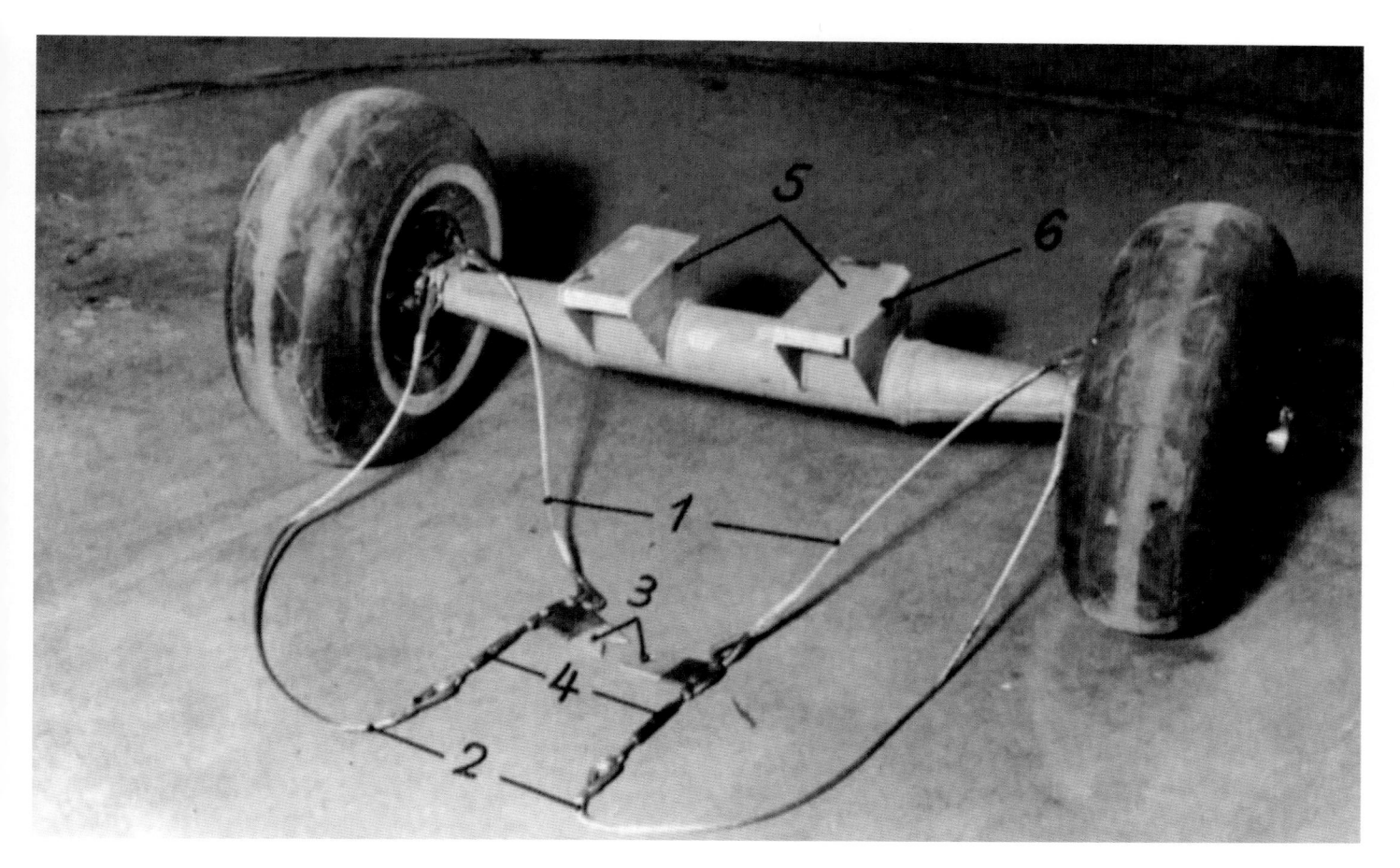

ABOVE: Consisting of two BV 141 tailwheels, the BV 40's wheelset was jettisoned shortly after take-off at an altitude of 5-10m. The pilot simply pulled a lever releasing the cables holding it in place.

Secret Projects of the Luftwaffe   85

ABOVE: The cable arrangement used to hold the BV 40's wheelset in position prior to take-off.

arrangement is good except for the right armrest, which must be softer and better shaped, otherwise the arm will tire too quickly if the [period under] tow is too long."

After explaining the aircraft's stall behaviour and controls, he made a point about how flying the BV 40 differed from flying a normal aircraft: "When the pilot is lying down, the pilot no longer steers with his elbow and upper arm, but with his much weaker wrist, so other standards must also be applied with regard to the control forces. The friction in the rudder is so great that it stops in any position."

In other words, the controls of the glider needed to be light since the pilot was unable to apply as much force to them as he might otherwise be able to.

Rautenhaus made two flights of his own in BV 40 V2 during this period and reported that gusty weather had prevent release above 1,000m altitude. He reported that the landing gear cable rubbing problem had been resolved by moving the turnbuckle and that elevator zeroing was "bad", so the control assembly needed to be checked – but the landing once again "presented no difficulties" and touchdown was gentle with the flaps at the 80-degree position and with an indicated speed of 125km/h.

On July 6, 1944, Rautenhaus reported that up to this point the BV 40 V2 had made 12 flights, with the BV 40 programme overall having made 14 (12 plus the two flights made by the BV 40 V1). Presumably Zieger's flights had been Nos. 7-9, with Rautenhaus then

BELOW: The first BV 40 prototype as viewed from the rear.

completing and reporting on flights 10-11. In the same report he noted that "for the first time a speed of 470km/h at an altitude of 2,200m was reached without any particular complaints". Since this feat is not mentioned in any of the preceding test reports, it was most likely achieved during the 12th flight.

The BV 40 programme's 15th test flight overall was made by neither the V1 nor the V2, but rather by the BV 40 V5 – the detail of which is also included in Rautenhaus's July 6 report. He wrote: "The machine is very top-heavy, so the fin is adjusted by minus two degrees. Despite this top-heaviness, the new elevator trim for towing at 250 km/h is fully sufficient and is perceived as an extremely pleasant relief for the right hand [holding the control column]. At higher speeds and larger aileron deflections, the increase in power is considerable, but bearable.

"The landing flaps were overbalanced so that they went straight to the 80-degree position and didn't need to be retracted again. Since this phenomenon is extremely unpleasant for the landing, we ask that the Finkenwärder factory be instructed to open the auxiliary flaps more on new machines.

"For the elevator we ask you to procure a spring that is half as strong, ordered three weeks ago, in order to reduce the forces. A change in the transmission ratio for the elevator does not seem necessary to me."

The 16th and 17th flights were made by Rautenhaus in the V6 prototype on July 26 – the former its first test flight and the latter a transfer flight from Stade, west of Hamburg, to Wenzendorf just south of the city. Towed starts had been carried out at Stade to test the aircraft's control surfaces, with the V6 having both a rudder and elevators of increased depth. Rautenhaus's conclusion was that trim tabs were urgently needed, "because contrary to Mr Ziegler's opinion, there is always enough time to operate a trim".

By this time, repairs to the BV 40 V1 had nearly been completed and the still-airworthy V2 was based at Wenzendorf. The V3 was being used for static tests, and the V4 had been "badly damaged; the possibility of repair has not yet been clarified". The precise circumstances of how the V4 came to be damaged are unknown. There is no known record of a flight attempt, though this seems to most likely cause.

The V5 and V6 were also airworthy, with the V7 expected to join them in August. The V8 was due for delivery in September, the V9 in October, V10 and V11 in November, V12 and V13 in December, V14 and V15 in January 1945, V16 and V17 in February 1945 and V18 and V19 in March 1945. Work had evidently not yet begun on anything after V14.

KG 200'S DEMANDS

During the preceding weeks or possibly months Tilenius of KG 200 had apparently been bombarding Blohm & Voss with requests and requirements for the BV 40. According to a company project status report of late July 1944, "the large number of different bombs demanded by Fl. Stabsing. Tilenius cannot be installed by us for design reasons. The work situation in our office

makes it necessary to limit oneself under all circumstances. That's why we decided to just hang a BT700 [anti-shipping torpedo] on the left and right under the wings. The main advantage of this arrangement is that the landing skid is not affected and [the torpedo] can be supplied with all aircraft. Furthermore, it is possible without difficulty to hang the device [BV 40 with BT 700 torpedoes] under both two- and four-engine He 177 series aircraft without additional conversion kit.

"A development of the machine [BV 40] for other special purposes, with automatic controls, with rocket boosters and as a towed fuel tank, is completely impossible for us, both for reasons of construction shortage and workshop overload. This also eliminates the production run of 200 suggested by Mr Tilenius. We are only able to deliver the ordered 20 examples."

Further details of Tilenius's demands for a BV 40 with automatic controls – perhaps a guided missile of sorts – with rocket boosters and as a flying fuel tank are not known to have survived. Similarly, nothing more is known about the proposed production variant of which he wanted 200 examples.

By now there appear to have been concerns about whether the ongoing towed flight tests were necessary. A Blohm & Voss memo of July 25, 1944, noted that "a decision on the BV 40 towing tests will be made shortly. Mr Malz has promised telephone notification of this".

Two days later, Bürkner in the Berlin office wrote to Vogt: "Today I spoke to Mr Czolbe about the BV 40 and informed him of our decision to shut down the remaining 14 machines for the time being. He fully understands this and a few days ago applied to the General Staff, 6. Dept., [for permission] to not finish building the remaining machines, since he does not believe that Mr Tilenius' office will be able to use the machine properly given the lack of clarity about the task . As soon as he has an answer from the 6. Dept., he will order the work on the BV 40 to be stopped."

Evidently Blohm & Voss had grown frustrated with Tilenius's demands, since the company was already overburdened with other work – particularly on carrying out Me 262-related work for Messerschmitt and designing the new BV 155 high-altitude fighter – and was unable to meet them.

Consequently, the company had itself requested permission to cancel the project. Czolbe rang on August 5 to say that "a decision on the BV 40 from the General Staff is still pending, but is expected shortly. It is expected that further construction of the aircraft type will be discontinued". Towed flights with the BV 40 were to be stopped immediately, though there is no known record of any further flights after Rautenhaus's second flight in BV 40 V6 on July 26 – the 17th flight of the BV 40 programme overall.

CANCELLED

Back in May, Malz had sent a requirement for a two-seater jet-propelled high-speed research aircraft to Messerschmitt, Heinkel, Arado, Focke-Wulf, Siebel, Blohm & Voss

ABOVE: While testing still required the BV 40 prototypes to be towed aloft, in operation they were to be suspended beneath the wings of He 177s and dropped onto high-value targets – particularly Allied shipping.

and the Deutsche Forschungsanstalt für Segelflug (DFS). The companies had been invited to submit designs for this aircraft and once a 'winner' had been chosen it would be constructed at Siebel's Halle facility.

The deadline for submissions was July 20, 1944, and Arado, Messerschmitt and the DFS are known to have submitted designs and certainly Siebel had a keen interest in the project.

As a result, on August 5, a Blohm & Voss memo noted that Czolbe had been in touch, asking that a wingless BV 40 fuselage be sent to Siebel at Halle because "Siebel deals with a project that also includes the prone pilot. The work we have done can undoubtedly be put to good use in such projects in the common interest. Apparently even more projects with prone pilots have been unter way lately. It would be necessary to install the control stick … Mr Czolbe asks that a fuselage be dispatched as soon as possible. I assume you have no objection to this".

Luftwaffe High Command wrote a very nice letter to Blohm & Voss on August 13, 1944, to formally cancel the BV 40. Headed 'BV 40 work', it said: "Changed operational and tactical conditions and the need to concentrate forces and save on war material have led to the decision to stop further work on your BV 40 model.

"You will be asked to submit a bill for the costs incurred. You will receive further instructions on how to use the completed prototypes; first you will be asked to send a complete fuselage to the Siebel company in Halle as an example for study.

"We would like to express our full appreciation for your initiative and the development work you have done in this task. At the same time, we regret that the contribution you intended to make to weapon development has not achieved the success it deserves for reasons beyond your control."

This letter was evidently received on August 18, with Vogt then issuing the order to cease work on the BV 40 immediately.

WIPED OUT

Two formations of 8th Air Force Consolidated B-24 Liberators from the 458th Bomb Group, consisting of nine and eight aircraft respectively, bombed Blohm & Voss's Wenzendorf facility unopposed on October 6, 1944; the hangar containing all 14 mothballed BV 40 airframes was hit and everything in it was evidently wrecked beyond repair.

Vogt sent a curt memo to Siebel on October 11 stating: "All BV 40 machines destroyed in an air raid. Therefore we can only send drawings of a fuselage longitudinal section." A formal company letter followed which said: "With reference to a call from your senior engineer Horn, we regret that we cannot keep the promise made by director Dr Vogt. It turned out that during the last air raid on our Wenzendorf plant, the BV 40 type machines that were still there were destroyed. So there is nothing left but to send you the enclosed drawing of the longitudinal section of the fuselage. You will also be able to take the most important things from it."

Siebel replied: "With your letter mentioned above, we got your drawing 8-40, which is completely sufficient for our purposes. We would like to thank you for your kind efforts."

Finally, Gothaer Waggonfabrik aerodynamicist Dr Rudolf Göthert contacted Blohm & Voss in early November 1944 to ask for information on the BV 40's prone cockpit layout, having planned a prone cockpit for his P-60 jet fighter/fighter-bomber series. The company responded on November 9 to say that engineers Scherer and Hagel were available to meet with Göthert in a hotel on Monday, November 13. Göthert contacted the company again following this meeting to ask for details of the BV 40's wing and tail construction but this appears to have been the glider project's very last gasp. •

The Big Push

Hochleistungs-Otto-Jäger

The last great piston engine fighter competition of the war resulted in some of unique proposals as designers toiled at the bleeding edge of what was mechanically and aerodynamically possible…

The entire German aviation industry stood at a crossroads– or perhaps at the edge of a precipice – at the beginning of 1944.

Milch, supported by Inspector of Fighters Adolf Galland and even Göring, had attempted a radical switch from piston engine to jet fighters in May 1943 but had failed due to fierce resistance from Willy Messerschmitt, whose business was heavily invested in piston engines and the Bf 109 airframe. Adolf Hitler himself had sided with Messerschmitt, being apparently unaware of exactly what advantages jet engines could bring.

However, the situation at the beginning of 1944 was very different. Hitler was now convinced of the jet engine's supremacy; Messerschmitt had firmly committed himself to a jet-only future, following the final cancellation of his 109-component-sharing Me 209 fighter; Milch was considering a ground-up reshaping of the aviation industry in conjunction with Albert Speer's Ministry of Armaments and War Production; and Göring – who had previously taken a hands-off approach – was now involving himself personally in the minutiae of aircraft development and production.

The question now, where fighters were concerned, was whether to go all-in on jets and gradually phase out piston engine types, or to aim for a mixed force of piston engine and jet types. Either option would take a considerable amount of time and effort to implement and would require numerous tough decisions to be made along the way.

Answering this question was deferred during the first half of 1944 while attention was focused on getting the Me 262 and its Jumo 004 engines into production. Once this process was well underway, the question of piston engines versus jets was brought back to the fore. Doubts lingered about the ability of jet fighters to cover every mission, with performance at high altitude being a particular concern. Jumo's 004 turbojet rapidly lost power above 11,000m and it was known that the Allies were working on bombers – particularly the B-29 – that were expected to operate at significantly greater altitudes. If all production was switched to jet fighters, how would such bombers be intercepted?

Endurance was also a worry; the Me 262 had two jet engines and together they consumed fuel at an alarming rate. This made it a less-than-optimal choice for long-range escort missions or loitering night fighter operations.

A requirement for a single-jet fighter, commonly referred to as Ein-TL-Jäger, with which to replace the twin-jet Me 262 was issued in early July (on or before July 11, 1944) and a parallel requirement for a new Hochleistungs-Otto-Jäger, literally high-performance piston-engine fighter ('Otto' being the generic German name for piston engines), followed on July 21, 1944. Two powerplant options were offered, the Jumo 222 E/F or 213 H, to be fitted in a pusher-prop configuration.

As mentioned earlier, the Jumo 222 had 24 cylinders arranged in six inline banks with four cylinders per bank arranged around a central crankcase. The E/F variants added a new two-stage supercharger and three aftercoolers – one per pair of neighbouring cylinder banks. The Jumo 213 H also had 24 cylinders – four banks of six cylinders lifted from the regular V12 Jumo 213 – arranged in an 'H' configuration.

Putting the engine in the fuselage to drive a propeller at the rear, an arrangement akin to that of the Dornier Do 335's back end, would leave room up front for 750kg worth of weaponry in a "central arrangement" i.e. probably in the aircraft's nose.

It had to be possible to carry up to 500kg of bombs and fuel for two hours' flying at maximum power, plus the option of another 600 litres in one or two drop tanks. Once bombs and/or tanks had been dropped, the aircraft's wing surfaces had to be smooth – no protruding fixed bomb racks or pylons.

Radio equipment and instrumentation for fighter operations, including bad weather operations, was also specified.

Listed under 'general requirements' were: "cheap and simple construction for mass production; easy maintenance possibility in front line use; extensive use of wood and steel; part of series [production run] with pressurised cabin; pusher prop [second mention, presumably for emphasis]; tricycle undercarriage; laminar wing profile". Required performance was 650km/h top speed at ground level and 850km/h at 10km altitude. Peak climb rate at low altitude needed to be 20 metres per second.

Five companies were invited to submit designs: Blohm & Voss, Dornier, Focke-Wulf, Heinkel and Messerschmitt.

THE ENGINES

The Hochleistungs-Otto-Jäger concept was underpinned by Junkers' promises that the Jumo 222 would be ready for mass production in 1945, with the Jumo 213 H expected to follow shortly thereafter. The 222 at this point was expected to provide 2,500hp and the 213 H an incredible 3,750hp, though this output was tempered by the engines' substantial bulk and considerable weight.

As previously discussed, Focke-Wulf already had quite a history with the Jumo 222. The company's most recent work with it had been a half-hearted attempt to propose fitting one to the Fw 190 C airframe in October 1943. Eight months later, the Ministry's Technical Office apparently tried to get work on the Jumo 222 speeded up, with the engine manufacturer reaching out to Focke-Wulf as before.

Junkers representative Herr Lange met up with Focke-Wulf technical director Willy Kaether, Otto Pabst, designer Voigtsberger and Lüpping at their Bad Eilsen offices on June 16, 1944.

According to the post-meeting report: "Due to official requests, the Junkers company has been commissioned to expedite the further development of the Jumo 222 (fighter programme requirement). Focke-Wulf was informed about the development status and future series."

Lange told his hosts that Jumo 222 E/F series production was expected to commence in spring 1945 and pledged to deliver drawings and performance data to them "as soon as possible in the coming days".

The history of the Jumo 213 H is less easily traced and exactly how it came to be specified for Hochleistungs-Otto-Jäger is unclear. The earliest known mention of it is in an Air Ministry development meeting on January 28, 1944, the stenographic account of which states: "The Jumo 213 H project is a 24-cylinder H engine using as many components as possible from the normal Jumo 213 and is distinguished from the DB 613 and BMW 803 by an aerodynamically more favourable installation form. V1 [first prototype] early 1945 and series early 1946 have been promised as dates."

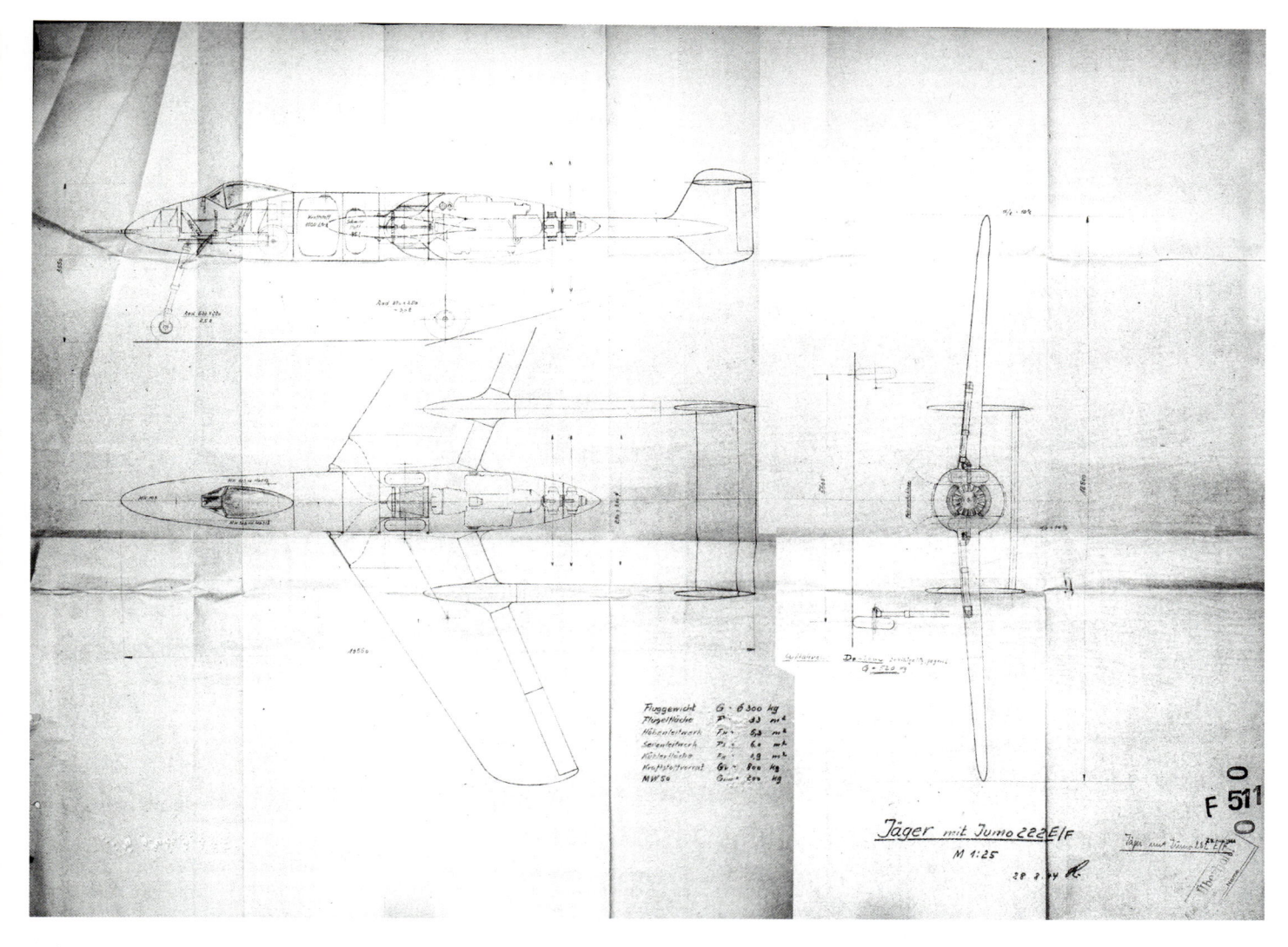

ABOVE: Focke-Wulf's earliest known attempt to meet the Hochleistungs-Otto-Jäger specification was this twin-boom fighter design, labelled Jäger mit Jumo 222 E/F.

The engine then appears alongside the 222 in the minutes of meetings held by Hermann Göring on May 23-25 to determine the Air Ministry's future development priorities.

FOCKE-WULF TWIN-BOOM FIGHTER

The earliest known Hochleistungs-Otto-Jäger design was produced by Focke-Wulf and dated August 28, 1944; following the usual highly literal naming convention of the company it was simply labelled 'Jäger mit Jumo 222 E/F'.

The company's designers had previously worked on a fighter powered by the even larger BMW 803 in August 1941, which they had revived and revised in March 1943 (see earlier in this publication). They now took this design and scaled it down slightly to suit the 222.

Where the 'Entwurf mit BMW 803' had been 13.8m long with a wingspan of 13.2m, the Jäger mit Jumo 222 E/F was 13.55m long and had a wingspan of 12.8m. Wing area was also slightly reduced, from 35sqm to 33sqm.

The unnumbered Jäger mit Jumo 222 E/F drawing shows a central fuselage housing the cockpit up front, with the nosewheel tucking up behind the pilot's seat, a 1,000 litre fuel tank, an 85 litre oil tank, then the main undercarriage wheels – which would tuck up to sit vertically in either side of the fuselage.

Then the big 222, driving 3m diameter four-bladed contra-rotating pusher props, was at the rear between the tail booms.

The booms themselves, attached to the wing trailing edges, stretched back to a pair of fins with a high-set horizontal tail surface suspended between them. The wings, swept back by 45 degrees, featured wingroot inlets for the engine's radiator, which was positioned between the landing gear mainwheels in the fuselage. Armament was to be either three MK 103s or one MK 103 and two MG 213s – with the long barrel of on MK 103 protruding from the tip of the aircraft's nose in both instances. Mauser's MG 213 was a 20mm rotary cannon which never entered service. However its 30mm form, the MK 213, would be developed by the British, French and Americans after the war as the incredibly successful ADEN, DEFA and M39 cannon respectively.

Take-off weight was 6,300kg.

FOCKE-WULF CRUCIFORM-TAIL FIGHTER PT.1

Just two days after the first unnumbered Jäger mit Jumo 222 E/F drawing was committed to paper, a dramatically different design under almost the same name was produced to meet the same specification.

This aircraft appeared at first glance to be very different – the twin booms were gone, replaced with a slender conventional fuselage ending in a cruciform tail and a single 3.4m diameter pusher prop. The wings were more sharply swept too.

But in many other respects the designs had much in common. They were a similar physical size with the cruciform-tail fighter being 13.7m long compared to the twin-boom fighter's 13.55m and with a wingspan of 12.5m compared to 12.8m. Wing area was identical at 33sqm and wing sweepback was 30 degrees.

The structure of its nose, including the nosewheel, appears to have been identical and both designs featured the same wingroot inlets for a centrally-mounted fuselage radiator. Both had the same mainwheel track of 5.6m and in both cases the wheels seem to have retracted to sit vertically within the fuselage.

Take-off weight for the cruciform-tail fighter was actually 430kg higher at 6,730kg. The design had a drawing number, 0310 025-501, putting it at the beginning of a new numerical sequence.

Secret Projects of the Luftwaffe

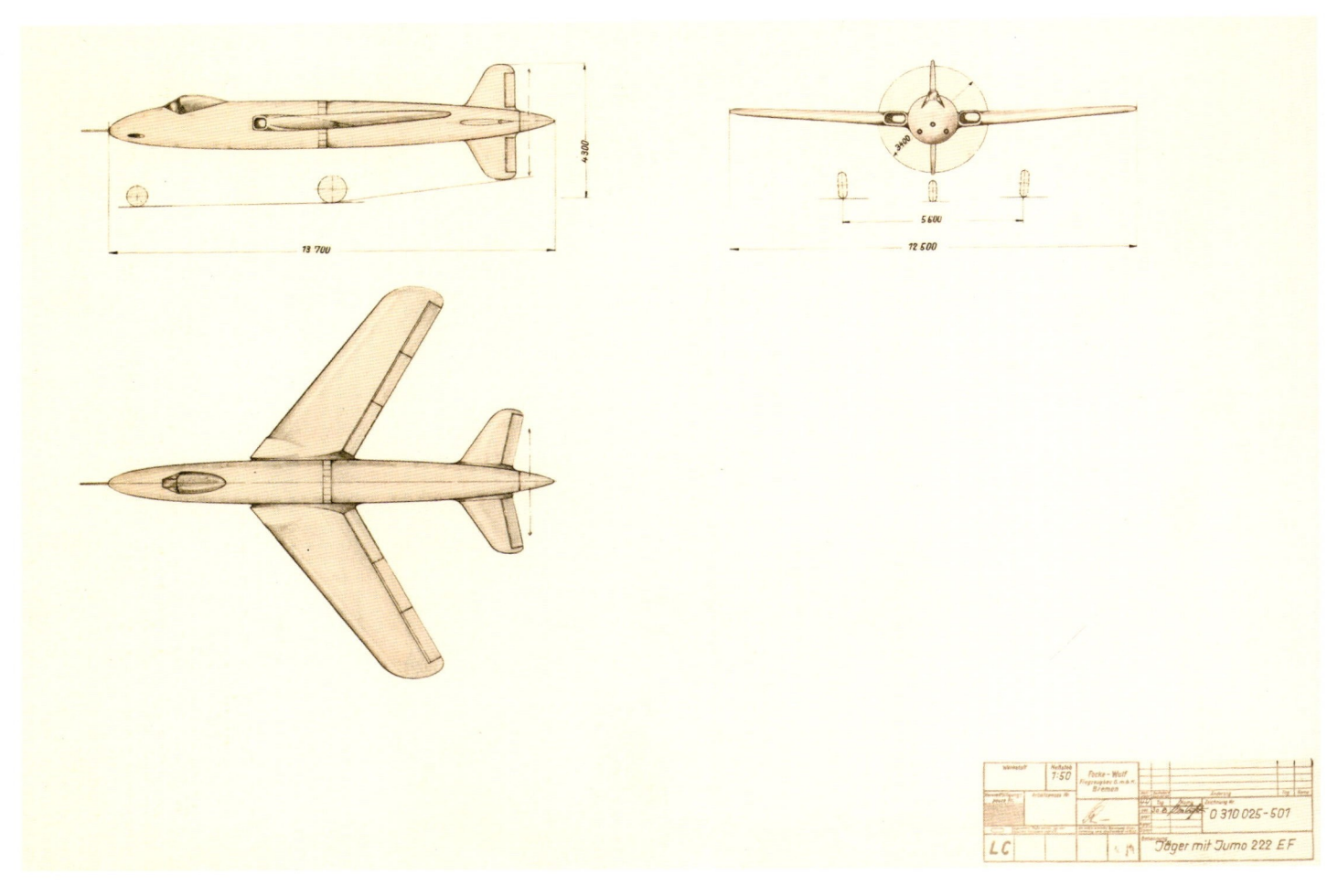

ABOVE: Focke-Wulf's second Hochleistungs-Otto-Jäger design was a cruciform-tail fighter of drawing 0310 025-501 which, while it appeared quite different at first glance, had much in common with the first Jäger mit Jumo 222 E/F.

FOCKE-WULF VIKTORIA-TAIL FIGHTER PT. 1

Having come up with two different configurations aimed at meeting the same requirement, Focke-Wulf then came up with a third which borrowed elements from both of its predecessors, as well as elements from one of the Jagdflugzeug mit BMW 803 designs from April 1943 and a highly unusual feature briefly considered for a ramjet-powered bomber design a little over two months earlier.

The Hochleistungsjäger mit As 9-413 was a weird-looking fighter. It appeared in two drawings – 0310 025-1005 and -1006, dated September 13, 1944, and a very brief text report entitled Kurzbaubeschreibung Nr. 16 Hochleistungsjäger mit As 9-413, dated September 14, 1944. It was physically larger than both of its predecessors at 14.2m long with a wingspan of 16.4m and a relatively massive wing area of 55sqm. Take-off weight was correspondingly greater at 9,800kg.

Rather than retaining the smoothly rounded nose form, it had a nose-mounted annular radiator, behind which were the pressurised cockpit, nosewheel bay and armament of two MG 213s and two MK 103s.

There then followed a single 1,300 litre internal fuel tank and a pair of 65 litre oil tanks which had the undercarriage mainwheels, positioned vertically, tucked up next to them during flight. Behind that was the engine. Where the previous two Focke-Wulf Hochleistungsjäger designs had both been powered by the Jumo 222 E/F, this design utilised the second engine option offered in the original requirement – the Jumo 213 H; except that, between May and September 1944, the Jumo 213 H project had evidently been handed to Argus and renamed as the As 413. Exactly when and how this came to pass is unclear, but there can be little doubt that the Jumo 213 H became the Argus As 413.

A relatively short driveshaft connected the As 413 to a set of 3.1m diameter contra-rotating pusher props. The tail featured both upper and lower fins, like the cruciform-tail fighter, with the lower fin having a tiny bumper-type wheel to prevent damage in the event of the tail touching the ground during take-off or landing.

The aircraft's most unusual feature was its tailplanes, which were forward-swept and connected to the trailing edges of the wings. Focke-Wulf referred to this arrangement as the 'Viktoria-leitwerk' or 'Viktoria tail', presumably due to the 'V' shape they formed when viewed from above. The wings themselves were similar to those of twin-boom fighter – quite as sharply swept as those of the cruciform tail fighter – and retained the leading edge inlets of the two earlier designs.

On the same day that the Viktoria-tail fighter's cutaway side view was drawn, Focke-Wulf also created a similar side view of the cruciform-tail fighter, drawing number 0310 025-505. This showcased a more detailed view of the nose cannon position – higher up than it had appeared on the twin-boom fighter and on the original drawing of the cruciform-tail fighter. An even more detailed drawing followed on September 15, 1944, which appeared to indicate that a mechanism allowing the nose cannon to be swung from side to side was being considered.

BLOHM & VOSS P 207

Five companies were invited to tender for the Hochleistungs-Otto-Jäger requirement but Messerschmitt and Heinkel do not appear to have submitted designs in time for the first round of comparisons. Whether they worked on designs at all is unclear – which left Blohm & Voss and Dornier as Focke-Wulf's competitors for any potential prototyping and production contract.

Blohm & Voss appears to have approached the specification with two distinct airframe layouts, working out how the required engines would suit each.

Very little documentation seems to have survived relating to the first layout – a conventional fuselage; straight wings able to rotate along their length like those of the BV 144 transport; engine directly behind the pilot and between the wings, powering a pusher prop via a lengthy drive shaft; nose-mounted armament of two MK 103s and two

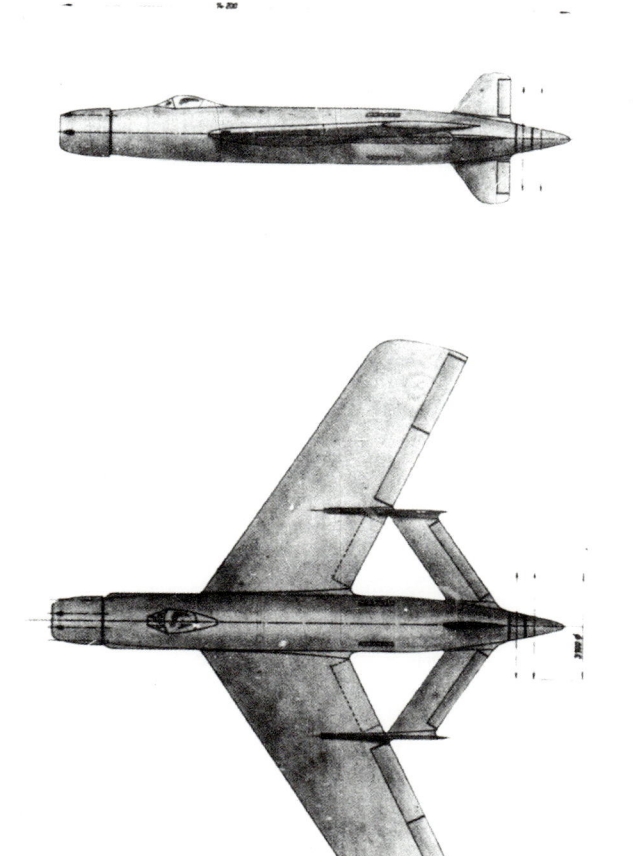

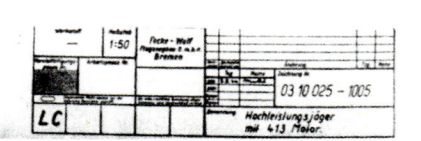

ABOVE: The third Focke-Wulf Hochleistungs-Otto-Jäger design had what the company's designers referred to as a 'Viktoria-tail' and a nose-mounted annular radiator. It appears here in drawing 0310 025-1005.

MG 151/20s; tricycle undercarriage with forwards-retracting nosewheel and cruciform tail. This was given the project name P 207.

The first design in the series, P 207.01-01, was as described above with a radiator positioned below the cockpit – resulting in an odd side profile. It was powered by a Jumo 222 E and had an 11m wingspan with a wing area of 20sqm. Fuselage length was 10.8m – making the P 207.01-01 an incredibly compact design compared to Focke-Wulf's efforts. According to a British report on the type, the design also featured variable incidence wings, perhaps similar to those of the BV 144 transport. Take-off weight was 6,200kg and top speed was calculated as 775-780km/h.

While the date on the drawing itself is difficult to determine, separate data sheets on the P 207.01-01 suggest that it dates from August 8, 1944.

The second design in the series was P 207.02-01, dated August 15, 1944, and it took the same basic layout and squeezed an As 413 into it. The result was a cigar-shaped fuselage – bulging in a rather unsightly fashion thanks to the bulky engine. Wingspan had to be enlarged up to 12m and the fuselage was stretched to 11.34m. Wing area was 24sqm while take-off weight rose to 7,750kg. Top speed was calculated at 815-820km/h.

Lastly, there was P 207.03-01, oddly dated August 12, 1944 – before P 207.02-01. This time Blohm & Voss worked out what would happen if they put the much smaller DB 603 G into a similar airframe. The answer turned out to be an even smaller aircraft, with a wingspan of just 10m and wing area of 16sqm. Fuselage length was 9.95m. The upper fin and rudder were deleted and the radiator was buried within the fuselage, being fed air from an under-fuselage inlet.

Take-off weight was just 4,995kg but performance was nevertheless somewhat lacklustre, with a top speed calculated at 635km/h. Work on the P 207.03-01 continued up to at least September 2, 1944.

BLOHM & VOSS P 208

The second airframe layout tried by Blohm & Voss for its Hochleistungs-Otto-Jäger contender was a novel departure from anything the company had tried before. P 208.01-01 took the central pod with swept wings approach but rather than utilising the familiar twin booms stretching back to fins connected by a tailplane, it had short unconnected wingtip booms and the only tail surfaces were a pair of near horizontal 'fins' featuring a slight anhedral. Wingspan, including the wingtip fins, was 13m.

Without the fins it was 10m, while wing area was 20sqm.

The front end of the 6m long fuselage pod was not entirely dissimilar from that used on the P 207 designs – the nosewheel retracted forward into the nose tip, while a radiator was positioned below and behind the pilot. The Jumo 222 E engine was set a little further back from the pilot than had been the case with P 207, but now there was no need for a long drive shaft – the pusher propeller being attached to the engine. Take-off weight was 5,500kg.

The only known P 208.01-01 drawing was dated August 30, 1944, but data sheets suggest that it was first committed to paper as early as August 8, the same day as the P 207.01-01. This shows that P 207 and P 208 were, at least initially, worked on in parallel. Curiously, the first drawing of the P 208.01-01 must have been slightly different from the one we know today, since some data sheets show a wingspan of 10.4m and a wing area of 18.2sqm.

The second design in the series, P 208.02-01, showed the same basic configuration but fitted with an As 413. Consequently, as with the equivalent P 207, the whole aircraft was a little bigger. Wingspan, including the wingtip fins, was 15.5m. Without the fins it was 12m,

Hochleistungs-Otto-Jäger

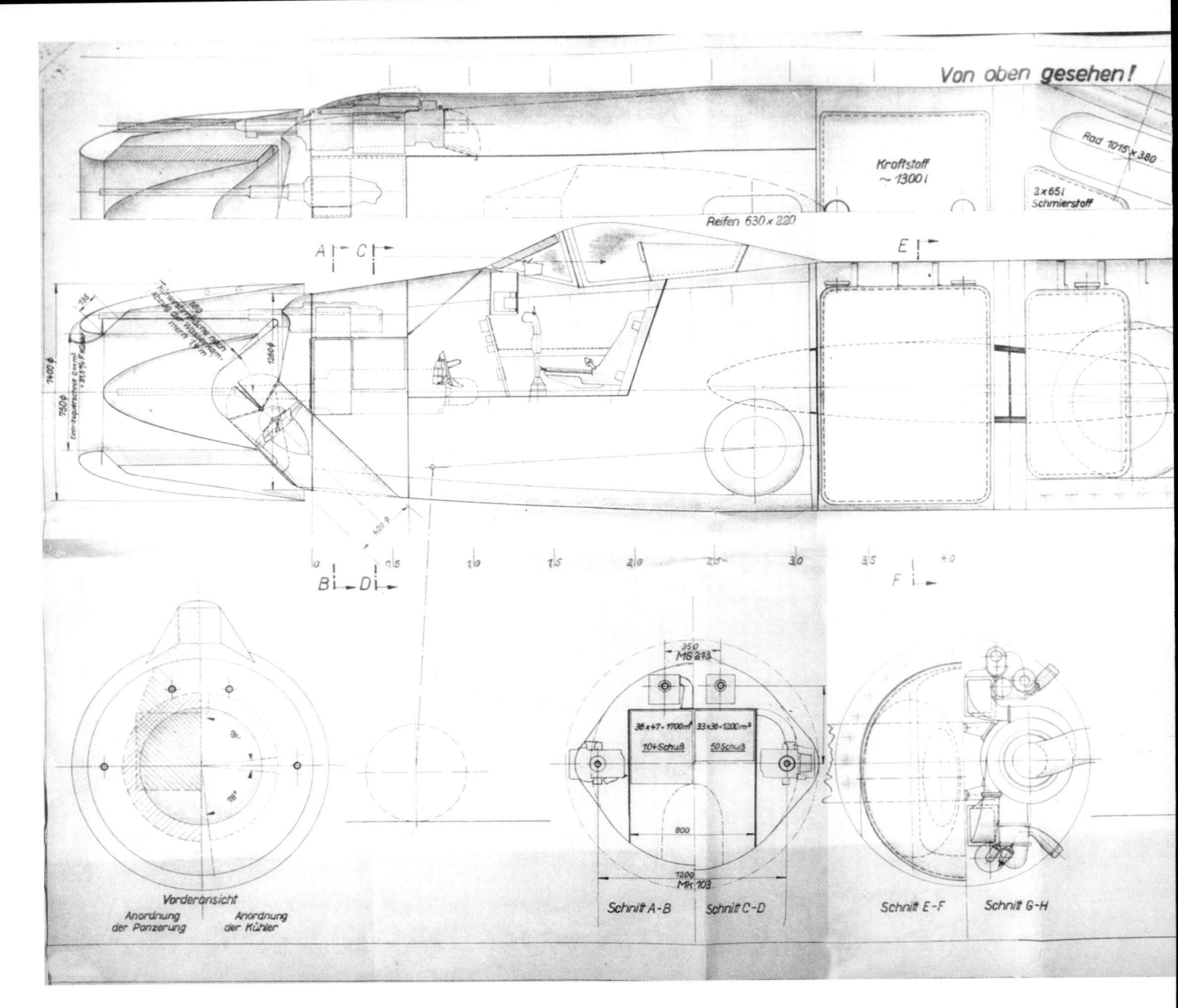

ABOVE: Cutaway showing the internal layout of Focke-Wulf's Viktoria-tail fighter, including its enormous As 413 engine. This is drawing number 0310 025-1006 of September 13, 1944.

Rumpfvorderteil   Rumpfhinterteil

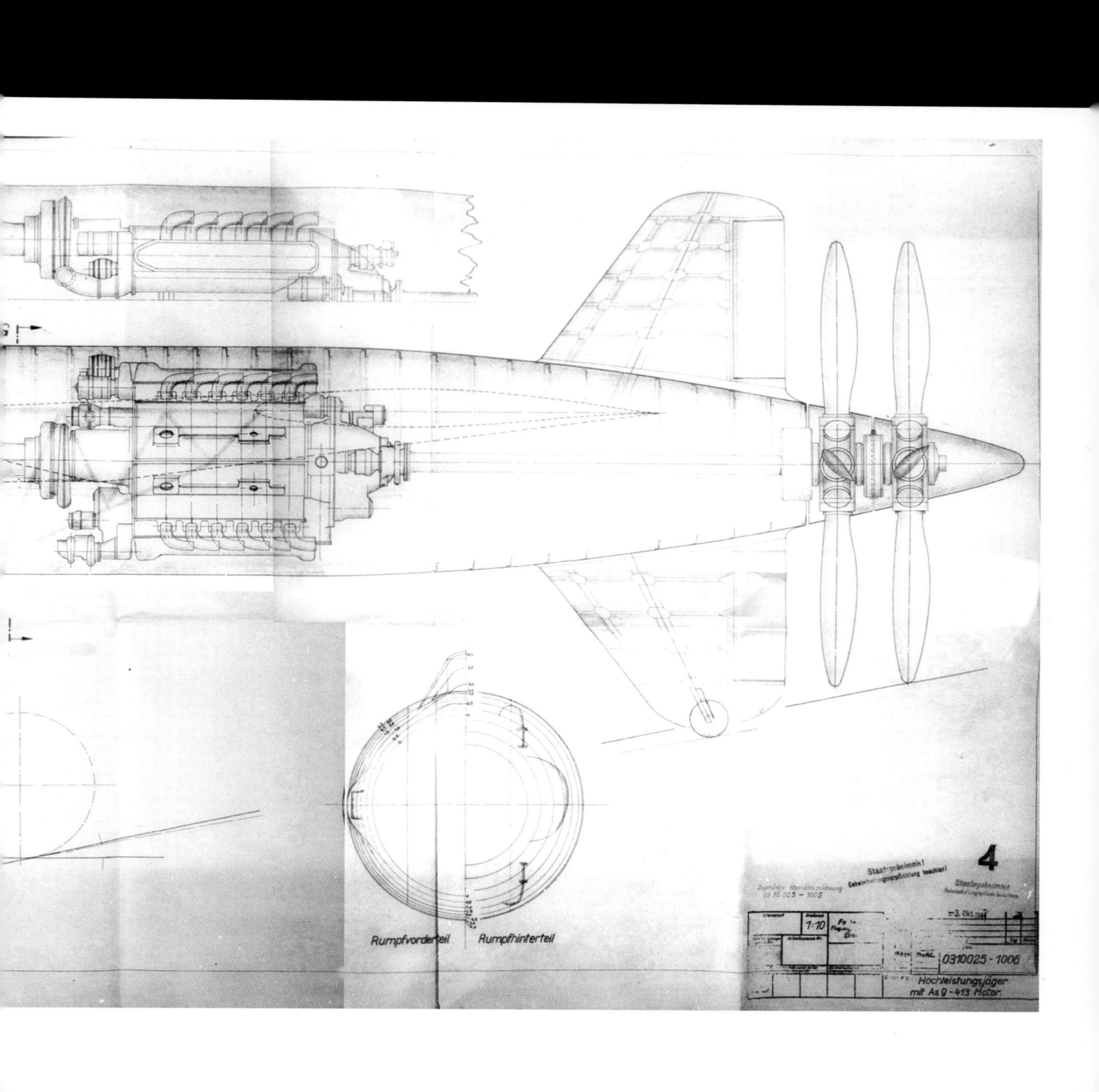

0310025-1006

Hochleistungsjäger mit As 9-413 Motor.

Secret Projects of the Luftwaffe

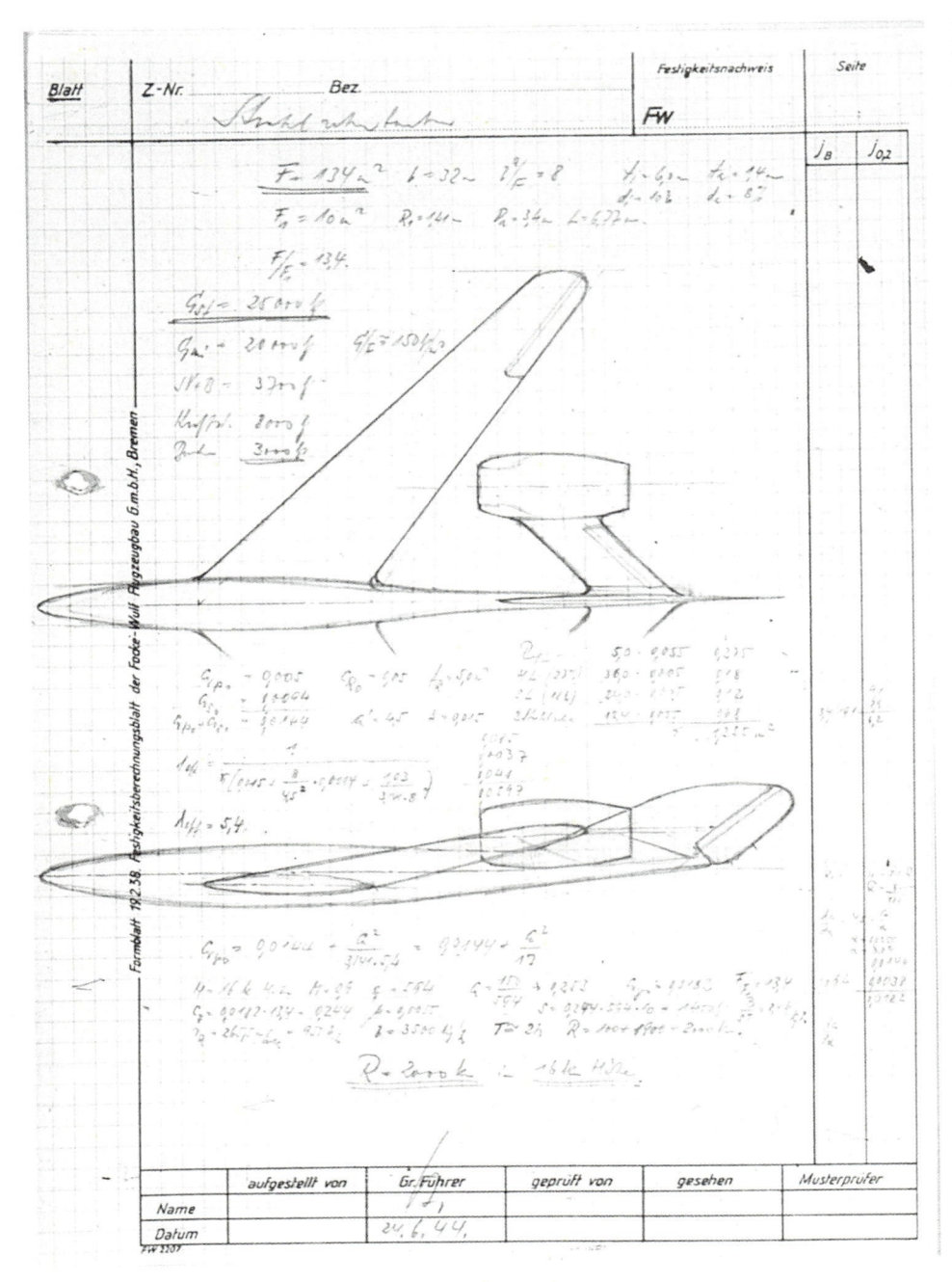

ABOVE: The earliest known appearance of Focke-Wulf's Viktoria-tail, on a sketch for a ramjet powered bomber made in June 1944.

with wing area being 24sqm. The fuselage pod was 8.4m long. The first drawing of the P 208.02-01 was dated 21.8.44 and this again appears to have been slightly different from the final version. In fact, four variants of the P 208.02-01 appear to have been designed: one with an 11.5m wingspan, 22sqm wing area; the 'final' version with 12m and 24sqm, a third version with 13.4m wingspan and 30sqm area and finally a 14.5m wingspan/35sqm wing area variant.

The P 208.02's layout differed slightly from that of the P 208.01 since it had vertical as well as horizontal control surfaces at the tips of its stubby booms.

Work on these designs continued throughout August, with comparisons being drawn up to show the features of the P 207.01-01, P 207.02-01 and P 207.03-01 against the P 208.01. By September 13, the P 207 designs had apparently fallen by the wayside and the company's designers were concentrating on P 208 – which had been submitted to the Air Ministry as the company's official Hochleistungs-Otto-Jäger contender.

On that day, Ministry official Otto Malz wrote to Blohm & Voss chief designer Richard Vogt about it, saying: "The project you have submitted encompasses new aerodynamic forms which require wind tunnel investigations and vibration studies. Irrespective of whether your project involves the implementation of a Hochleistungs-Otto-Jäger, these investigations should be carried out, since the form you propose would also offer significant advantages when applied to the 1-TL-Jäger [the single-jet fighter competition being run in parallel to Hochleistungs-Otto-Jäger]. You are asked to make arrangements for the necessary examinations."

A table produced on that date shows the P 208.01 being compared against the HeS 011-powered P 209 and the BMW 003-powered P 210, one of the company's two Volksjäger competitors. There would eventually be a DB 603-powered P 208.03, but not yet.

DORNIER DESIGN

The third contender for the Hochleistungs-Otto-Jäger competition was Dornier. It would appear, however, that no company drawings or data on this design have survived. The only known information about it comes from the September 18-20 design comparison meeting report outlined below. It had a wingspan of 13.8m and a wing area of 32sqm. Take-off weight was 6,825kg, fuel capacity was 850 litres and its armament was one MK 103 and two MG 213s. Its mainwheels measured 935x345mm while its nosewheel was 740x210mm.

The only known Dornier design which comes anywhere close to the basic layout and specification required for Hochleistungs-Otto-Jäger is the Do P 247, of which only the sixth variant has ever been discovered – and then only as a poorly reproduced out-of-context drawing shown in a British postwar summary of German wartime projects.

Dornier Do P 247/6 has a wingspan of 12.5m and a wing area of 25.8sqm, making it somewhat smaller than the September 18-20 design. It was also powered by a Jumo 213 J, rather than a Jumo 222 E/F and had three MK 108s for armament. Other Dornier pusher-prop designs, as opposed to the push-pull Do 335 type, exist under the Do P 252 project number but these are significantly larger multi-seat night- and bad-weather fighters.

Based on the data presented, it would appear that the Dornier design was probably broadly similar in appearance to the Do P 247/6 – perhaps being one of the earlier iterations of the series.

COMPARISON MEETING

Focke-Wulf produced a report on September 20, 1944, retrospectively summing up a meeting held at the company's Bad Eilsen offices from September 18-20 to discuss the Jumo 222 E/F-powered Hochleistungs-Otto-Jäger designs submitted up to that point.

The three contenders were listed as Blohm & Voss, Dornier and Focke-Wulf itself. Representing Blohm & Voss were Hans Amtmann and Behrmann. Representing Dornier were Schüttel and Hueber and representing Focke-Wulf were Herbert Wolff, Stratenhoff, Lüpping, Voigtsberger and Eick.

The introduction to the report stated: "At the instigation of the Luftwaffe High Command and Air Ministry Technical Office, the companies Blohm & Voss, Dornier-Werke and Focke-Wulf came together in Bad Eilsen from September 18-20, 1944, for a working conference. The task was to compare and coordinate the existing projects with one another in terms of performance.

"The present designs correspond to the technical specification for the high-performance fighter with the Jumo 222 E/F from July 21, 1944."

The Dornier design was as mentioned above. The Blohm & Voss design was certainly a P 208-with-Jumo 222 variant but slightly larger than the one that appears as P 208.01-01 from August 1944 – having a wingspan of 10.5m and a wing area of 22sqm. Like the Dornier and Focke-Wulf designs, it was armed with one MK 103 and two MG 213s, rather than the two MK 103s and two MG 151/20s shown in Blohm & Voss's earlier drawings.

The Focke-Wulf design is the only one of the three which can be positively identified – being identical in both wingspan and wing area to the cruciform-tail fighter – and even then the design differs mildly from the known drawings. It would appear that Focke-Wulf's bid for this competition was scrabbled together in a hurry, since the drawings presented for it tended to feature dimensions and other minor details which did not always quite marry up with the text they were supposed to illustrate.

The chief finding of the meeting in terms of weights was that the Dornier design was somewhat heavier than Focke-Wulf's despite being more or less the same size otherwise. The report notes that "the difference in weight between the Focke-Wulf and Dorner designs is partly due to the choice of tyres, which were specified by Focke-Wulf as 880x250 (new development) and by Dorner as 935x345. The corresponding nosewheels are 630x220 for Focke-Wulf or 740x210 for Dornier".

In terms of performance, "based on the joint calculation of the companies involved, the following differences emerged between the individual designs: compared to the Focke-Wulf project, the Blohm & Voss project is on average 10km/h faster and the Dornier project is 6km/h faster". Focke-Wulf had estimated the maximum speed of its fighter, using methanol water injection, as 640km/h near the ground and 800km/h at 11km altitude.

But "according to Dornier's calculations, these values are on average 30 km/h higher, and according to B&V calculations, they are 15km/h higher". Focke-Wulf attributed this discrepancy to a failure on its own designers' part to account for "the laminar effect on the wing" making "the total drag area of the three designs lower than according to their calculations".

The P 208 had the lowest drag thanks to its small fuselage and wings and "the differences in the absolute values of the maximum speed are solely due to this".

In terms of climbing speed, the Dornier design marginally came out on top at with a rate of 22m per second at low altitude. All three designs could manage a 500m take-off run but there were big differences in landing speed, based on take-off weight minus 80% of the starting fuel load. Blohm & Voss's design required a rather dicey 195km/h, Dornier a more acceptable 170km/h and Focke-Wulf a relatively pedestrian 165km/h.

ABOVE: Page from a Focke-Wulf report dated November 1944 which includes a reference to the 'Viktoria-leitwerk' with illustrative sketch.

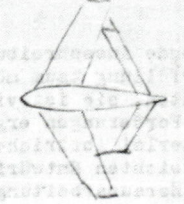

FOCKE-WULF VIKTORIA-TAIL FIGHTER PT.2

Quite why the Hochleistungs-Otto-Jäger meeting had concentrated solely on the Jumo 222 E/F designs is unclear. Perhaps the As 413 was now viewed as less desirable? In any case, Focke-Wulf did not immediately drop its Viktoria-tail fighter design. Instead, it expanded Kurzbaubeschreibung Nr. 16 Hochleistungsjäger mit As 9-413 with additional text and reissued it on October 3, 1944.

The aircraft itself was as previously described but the text now included an explanation of the design in prose rather than as a bullet point list of data.

This said: "The draft is based on the RLM tender of 21.7.44. Selected design: Due to the required high speeds, the lowest possible drag had to be aimed at. For this reason, the overall surface area was kept as small as possible and additional protrusions were avoided.

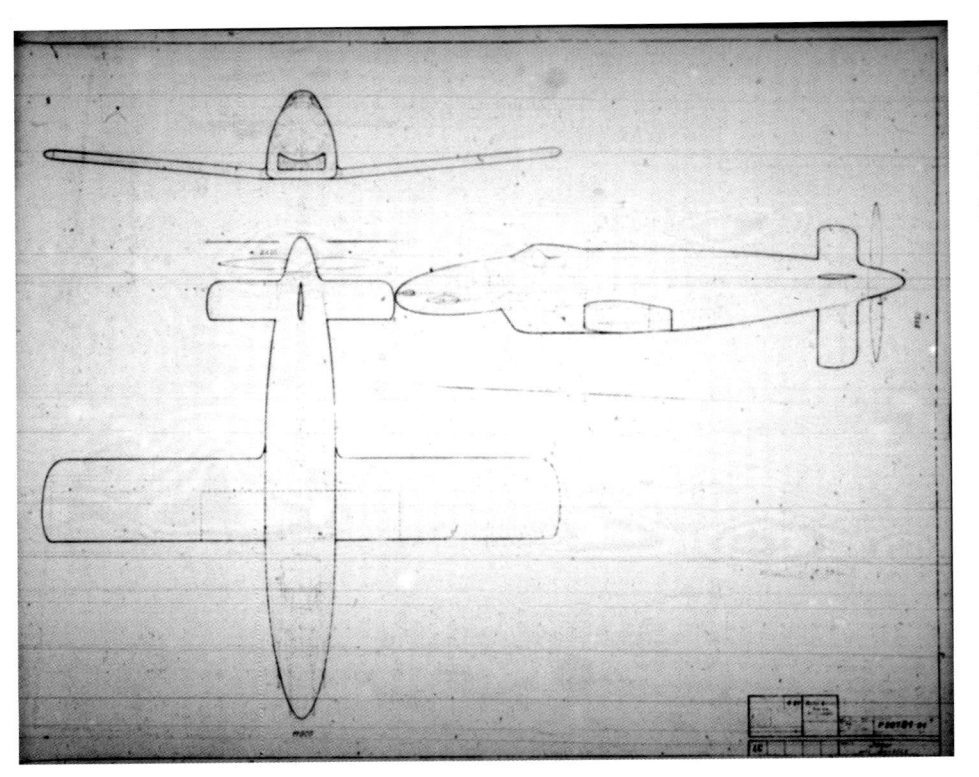

"Fuselage: The spindle-shaped fuselage, which has an almost circular cross-section throughout, is kept as short as possible for reasons of low drag. Its diameter is determined by the engine installation and is dimensioned in such a way that the engine is enclosed with the least possible clearance. The greatest fuselage thickness is about 40% of the fuselage length.

"In order to achieve good accessibility to the weapons and the ammunition boxes, the static structure of the fuselage front section is formed by two vertical supporting bulkheads as in the Ta 154. Large flaps and removable cover panels ensure easy access to all parts that require constant maintenance.

"The cockpit is one-seater and can be made pressure-tight according to external friction without changing the devices. An extension to a two-seater version for bad weather fighter operations is possible.

"Landing gear: According to the technical requirement, the design is equipped with a nose landing gear. The main landing gear is designed in such a way that the wheel stands upright in the fuselage when it is retracted by pivoting it in relation to the strut. Simply swinging the landing gear into the wing or

ABOVE:: Blohm & Voss worked on two basic airframe designs to meet the Hochleistungs-Otto-Jäger specification. This is the Jumo 222-powered P 207.01-01. It may look relatively conventional but the constant-chord wing was designed to rotate along its length – a feature not readily apparent from this appallingly low quality image.

BELOW: Combining the heavyweight As 413 engine with the diminutive dimensions of Blohm & Voss's P 207 concept resulted in the corpulent-looking P 207.02-01.

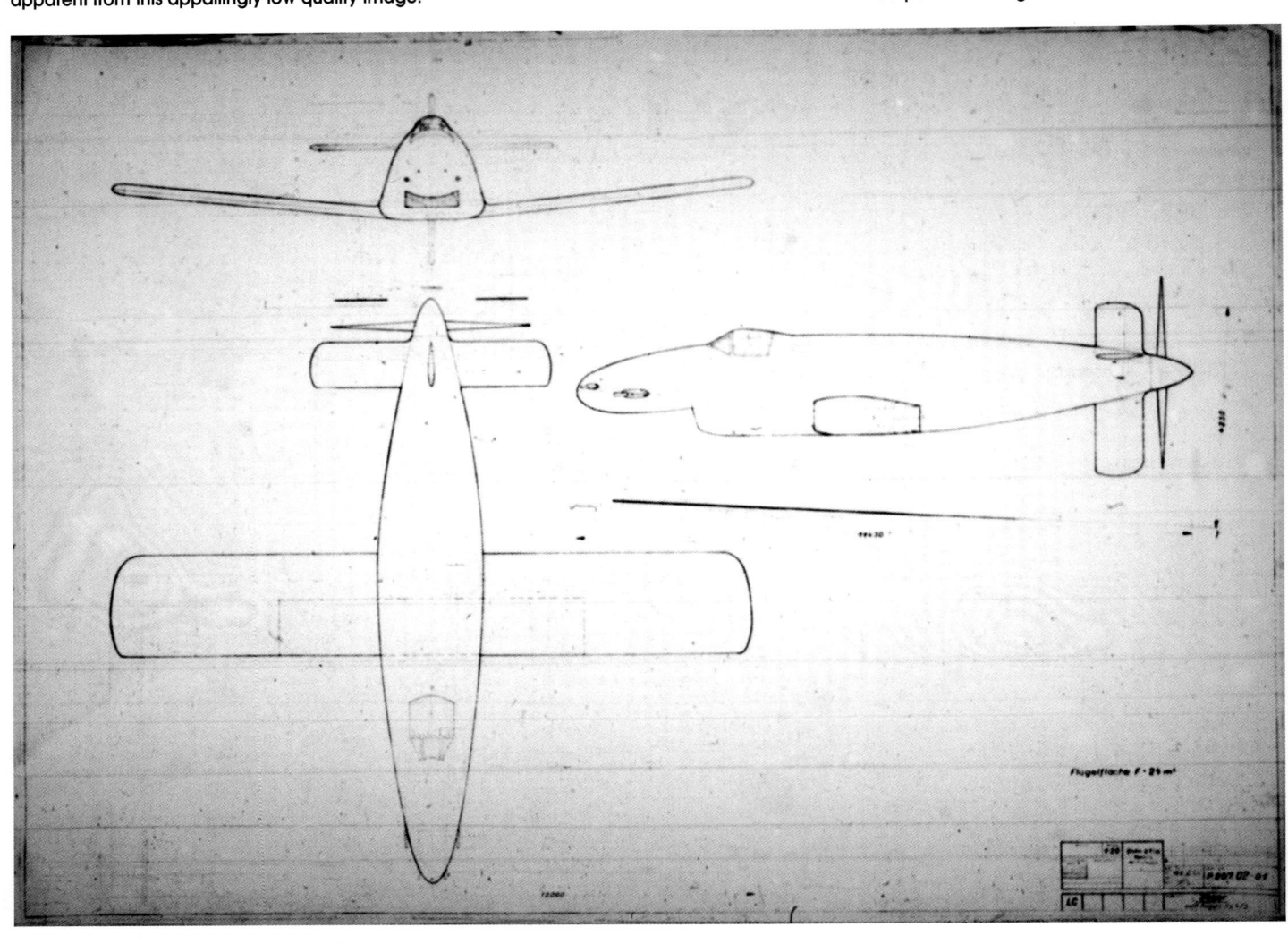

98 Secret Projects of the Luftwaffe

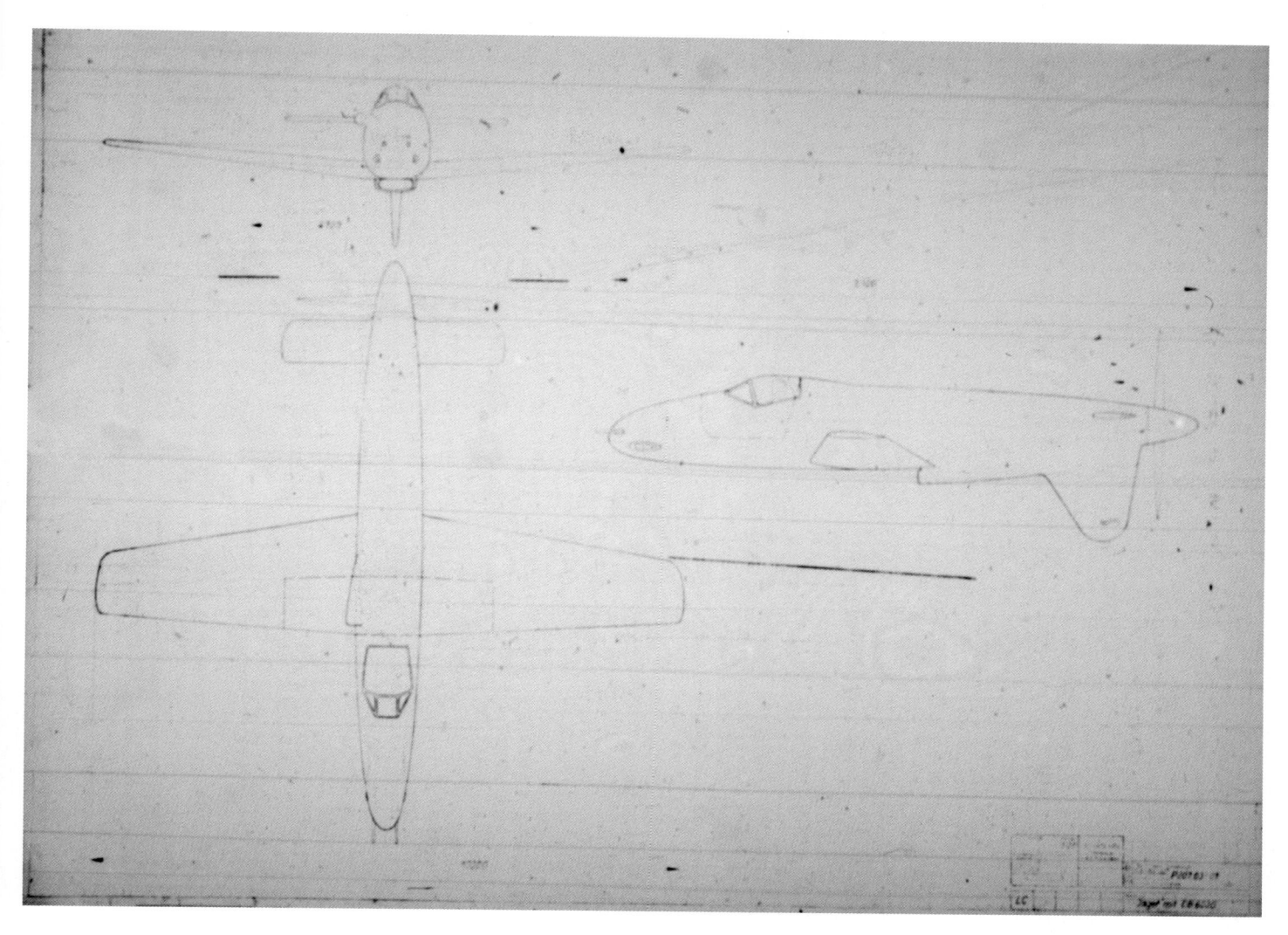

ABOVE: The last design in the series, P 207.03-01, featured the somewhat more compact DB 603 G engine – resulting in a pleasingly slender fuselage.

fuselage in the usual way would have required bulging of the airframe at the wheel location. The nose landing gear is pulled backwards into the fuselage in the direction of flight.

"Tail: The elevator has a size of 6.3sqm. In order to keep drag low in high-speed flight with high Mach numbers, and to ensure sufficient tail unit effectiveness, a sweep of 35 degrees was chosen – a little larger than that of the wing. Tail spar weight and surface area has been saved by attaching the negatively swept tailplane to an extended wing rib. For the purposes of adjustment, the connections on the fuselage and wing are rotatable.

"The rudder is located above and below the fuselage. The lower fin is necessary to protect the propellers from damage during take-off and landing. The upper fin can be blown off to protect the pilot from injury during an emergency exit. By dividing the rudder into two practically equal portions, above and below the fuselage, the torsional stresses on the fuselage from the tail forces have been reduced to practically zero.

"The ailerons with a total area of 4.7sqm are divided into outer and inner ailerons. They have the same depth and are interchangeable. The flaps in the inner wing area have a total area of 2.2sqm and are interchangeable."

The wings, designed for laminar flow, had a sweepback angle of 31 degrees and the

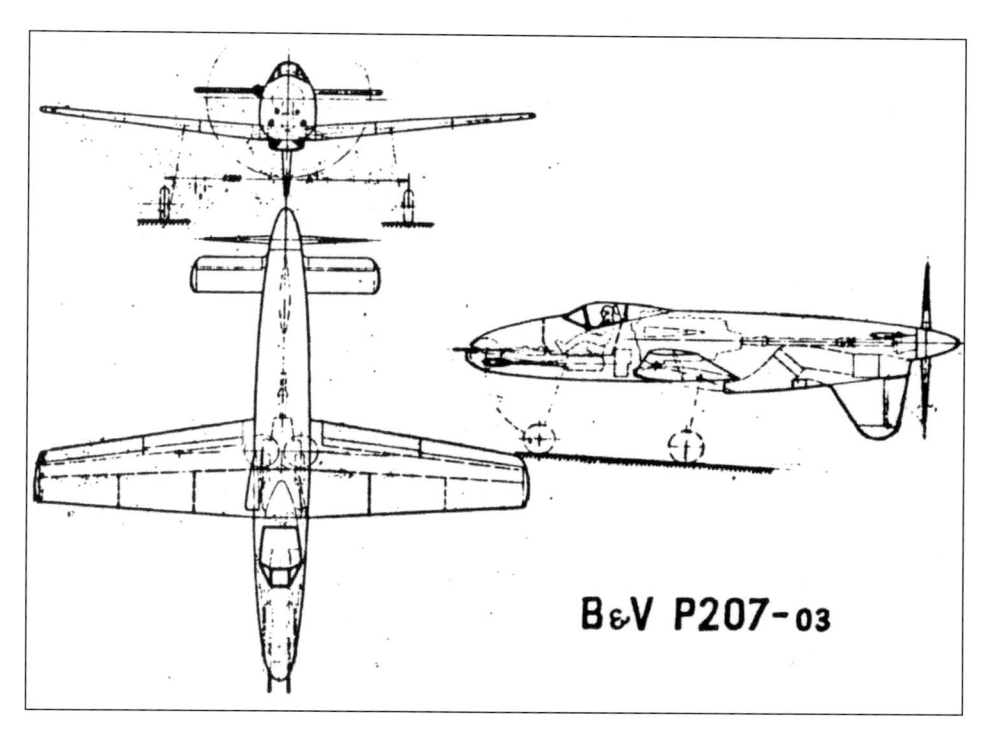

ABOVE: This alternative version of the P 207.03-01 drawing, reproduced from the original for an Allied report in 1945, shows how much detail has been lost in the preceding three 'grey' images, which are all that remains from Blohm & Voss's P 207 image archive today.

Secret Projects of the Luftwaffe

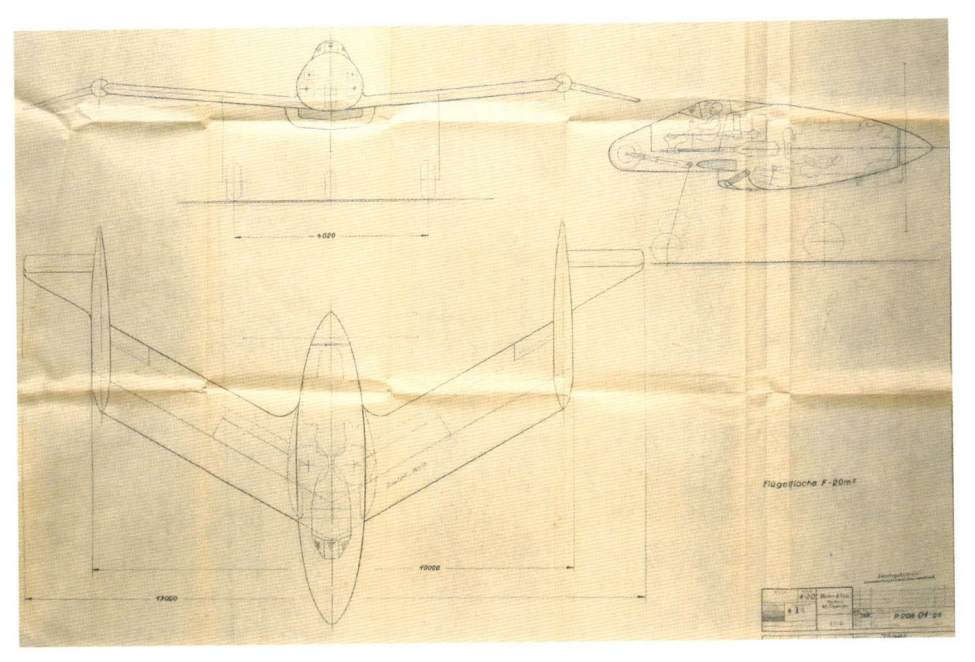

dihedral was 2.5 degrees. Profile thickness at the root was 13%, decreasing to 9% towards the wingtip.

The counter-rotating props each had four blades and were driven by the As 413 via a 2.5m long driveshaft. The report pointed out that "the counter-rotation results in a further improvement in efficiency compared to a simple propeller. For the safety of the pilot during the emergency exit, the propeller is blown off together with the upper fin.

"The radiator layer consists of a four-part annular radiator, which is arranged in front of the fuselage. In addition to the normal water cooler, it also contains a low-temperature cooler to dissipate the heat from the charge air. The arrangement of the cooling system results in the lowest possible drag. A fan is installed for warm-up and taxiing, which is switched off in flight. The front cross-section of the fuselage is not increased by this radiator installation. The radiator system is controlled by expanding flaps on the cooling

ABOVE: The first design in Blohm & Voss's radical tailless P 208 series – the P 208.01-01. This drawing is dated August 30, 1944, but data sheets suggest that the first drawing of P 208.01-01, with different dimensions, was made more than two weeks earlier.

BELOW: Diagram showing revised form for the nose of Focke-Wulf's cruciform-tail fighter, dated September 15, 1944.

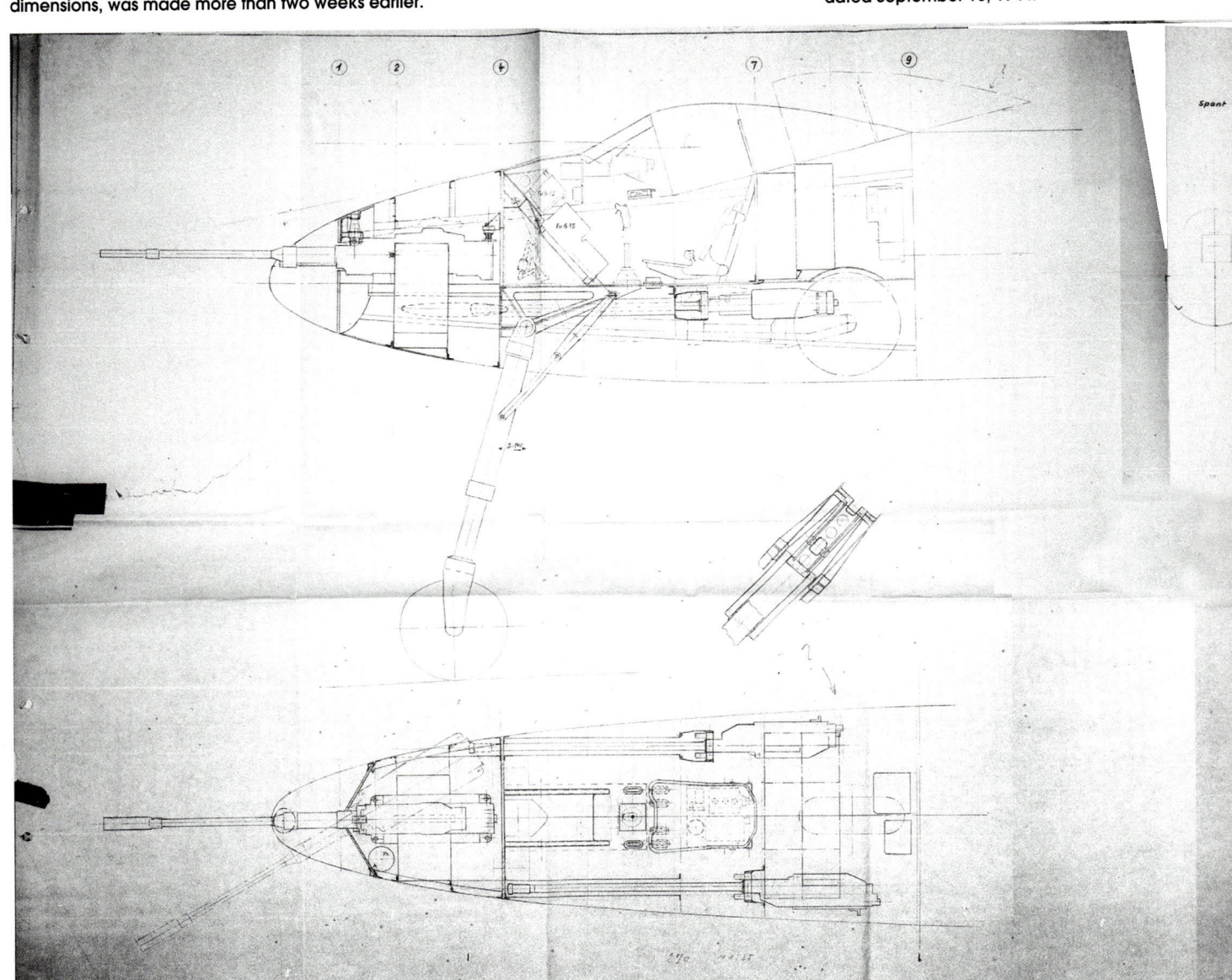

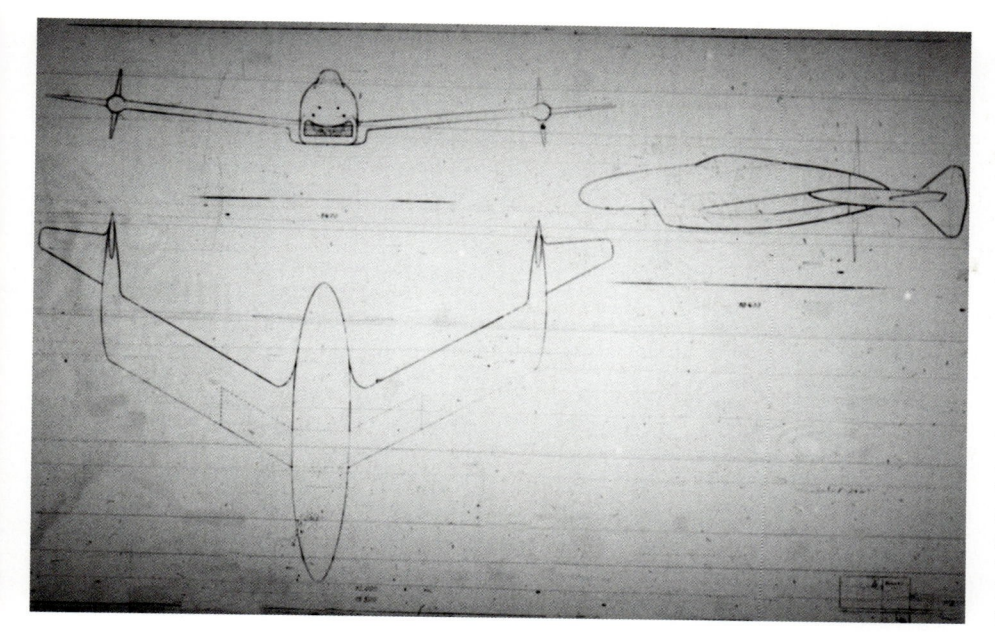

ABOVE: Blohm & Voss P 208.02-01 with redesigned wingtip booms. It was also larger in every dimension than the P 208.01-01 to accommodate its As 413 engine and its armament was moved into an elongated nose, with the cockpit being more centrally positioned.

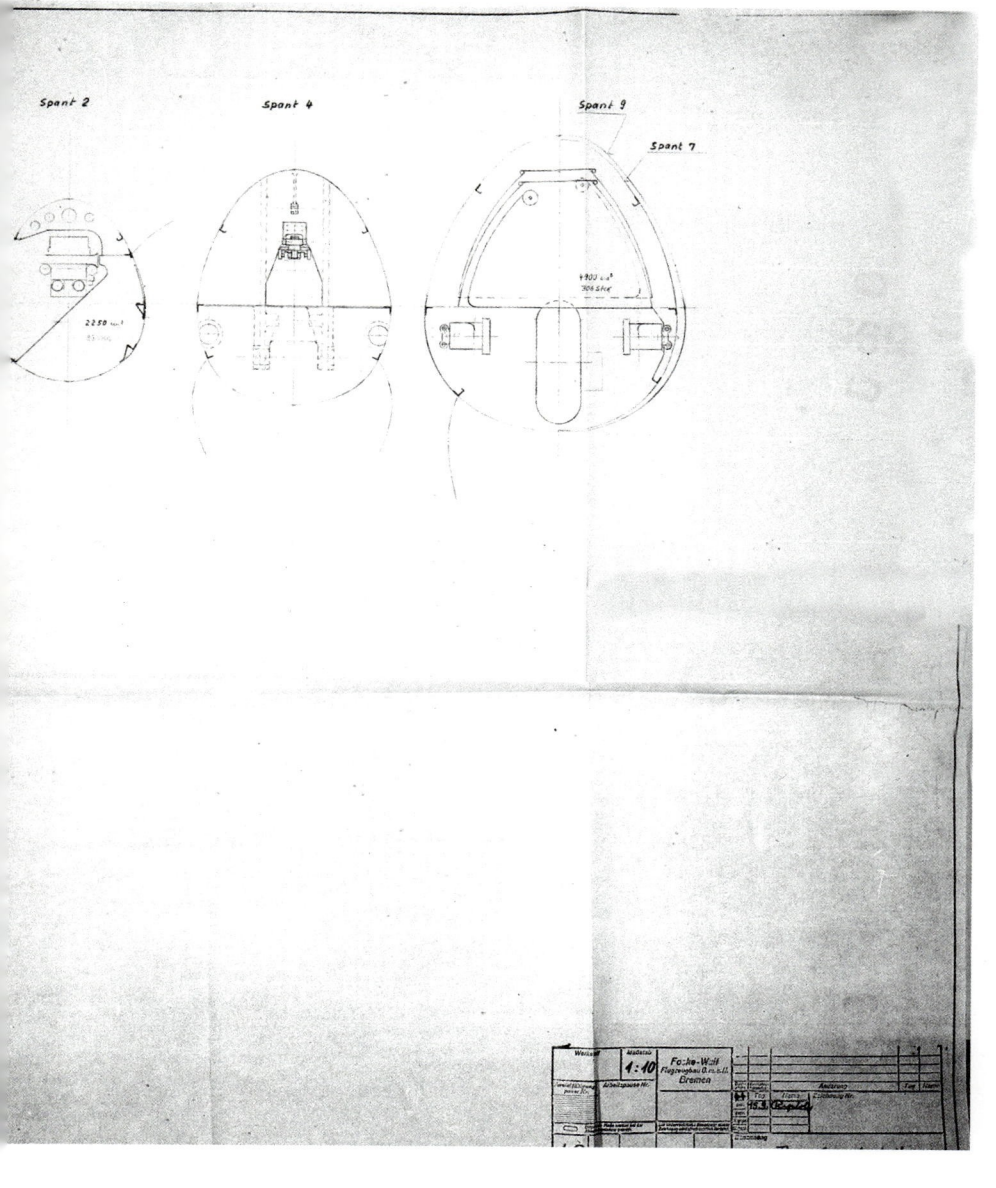

air outlet. In order to avoid disruption, the charge air is ingested through openings in the wing leading edge.

The fuel system consists of an approximately 1,200-litre protected tank in the fuselage and two protected 300 litre tanks in the wing. According to the tender, the entire fuel supply is sufficient for two flight hours with the maximum permissible continuous power at an altitude of 10 km including a 15-minute climb.

"The lubricant container is located in the fuselage in the landing gear bay and has a capacity of 130 litres."

There was frontal armour for the radiator, the ammo boxes and the pilot, with armour against 20mm fire incoming from the rear for the pilot. The aircraft's two MG 213s had 125 shells each while the pair of MK 102s had 46 shells each. All empty casings and belt links were collected within the fuselage rather than being jettisoned in order to prevent damage to the propellers.

FOCKE-WULF CRUCIFORM-TAIL FIGHTER PT.2

On the same day, October 3, 1944, Focke-Wulf also published a description of the cruciform-tail fighter design as Kurzbaubeschreibung Nr. 17 Hochleistungsjäger mit Jumo 222 E/F. Unlike Nr. 16, there is no known earlier version of this.

Oddly, it included the original 0310 025-501 drawing, which gave the aircraft's wingspan as 12.5m, alongside two newer drawings – 0310 025-505 and -506, the latter giving a wingspan of 12.8m.

Like the description of the Viktoria-tail fighter, the description of the cruciform-tail fighter included a section of text which explained more about the decisions made during the design process.

It said: "The requirement for high speed was decisive for the design. The fighter was designed as mid-wing, swept wing, laminar aerofoil. The sweep of the tail unit was chosen to be greater than that of the wing in order to ensure control effectiveness even at high Mach numbers. The arrangement of the propeller increases the propulsion efficiency considerably.

"Fuselage: The fuselage has an approximately circular cross-section. Since the propeller at the end of the fuselage requires the engine to be installed in the middle of the fuselage, the cross-section of the fuselage is adapted to the engine. The propeller is driven by a long elastically mounted shaft. A major innovation compared to other models is the radiator arrangement. The radiator is in front of the engine and the air is supplied through two flat inlets in the wing leading edge. Since a fan is required for the throughput of cooling air when taxiing and at the start of the take-off run, it is driven by the rear output of the engine.

"This arrangement was used to achieve a reduction in the frontal surface area of the radiator. The benefit of this design is the protected position of the radiator and the possibility of installing the weapons centrally in the nose of the fuselage. A good view for the pilot is also achieved.

Secret Projects of the Luftwaffe 101

"Maintenance of the engine is possible from all sides. The fuel tanks are also in the fuselage. Behind the cockpit, after the ammunition boxes for the two MG 213s and the radio compartment, there is a protected fuel tank with a capacity of 850 litres. In order to maintain centre of gravity, there are two unprotected tanks at the end of the fuselage to take the remaining fuel and MW50.

"The lubricant tank is also protected and is located between the front protected fuel tank and the radiator system. Its capacity is selected according to the entrainment of additional fuel tanks. The entire fuselage structure has the advantage that all important parts can be easily protected against fire from the front. The 140kg of armour provides protection against 12.7mm caliber ammunition when fired directly from the front.

"Landing gear: The nosewheel is swivelled backwards, the main landing gear transverse to the direction of flight. A large part of the wheel is in the fuselage, to the side of the cooling system.

"Tail: The tail is arranged in a cross shape, which keeps the torsional moment on the fuselage very small. The lower fin is used to protect the propeller when landing with a large pitch angle."

There were 80 rounds of ammo for the single central MK 103 and 240 rounds each for the MG 213s. Again, casings and belt links were collected within the fuselage to protect the propeller. And as with the Viktoria-tail fighter, the propeller and fin could be blown off in the event of an emergency so that the pilot wouldn't hit them on his way out.

FOCKE-WULF TA 152 H WITH JUMO 222 E

It can be no coincidence that a third construction description was also published on the same day, October 3, 1944 – Kurzbaubeschreibung Nr. 19 Ta 152 (H) mit Jumo 222 E.

Using as much of the existing Ta 152 H airframe as possible as a mount for the Jumo 222 E, assuming the engine could even be put into production, would seem to have been an eminently more sensible idea that building either the Viktoria-tail fighter or the cruciform-tail fighter.

Therefore, the creation of a report detailing a Jumo 222-powered Ta 152 H may have been Focke-Wulf's commendably subtle way of suggesting that an all-new piston engine fighter might not be such a great idea at this stage of the war. Or it might simply have been drawn up on the orders of the Air Ministry – which presumably also included a fair number of individuals who questioned the sanity of pursuing the design of a bespoke Hochleistungs-Otto-Jäger at this particular juncture.

In fact, Focke-Wulf had evidently proffered a 222-powered Ta 152 back in early 1944, albeit based on the regular 152 A/B/C airframe. According to the text of Kurzbaubeschreibung Nr. 19: "The Kurzbaubeschreibung No. 13 deals with the installation of the Jumo 222 for the Ta 152, which has a wingspan of 11m and a wing area of 19.6sqm. With regard to the higher full pressure altitude of the Jumo 222 E/F compared to the Jumo 222 A/B 3, the installation tests were extended to the Ta 152 H (high-altitude fighter with 14.44m wingspan and 23.3sqm wing area). Basically, the same installation conditions and changes apply here, i.e. due to the higher connection forces, reinforcements are necessary on the fuselage side, which include fuselage connection fittings and fuselage straps. The larger dimensions of the engine require a modification of the fuselage fairings, as well as a shift in the location of the fuselage weapons.

"In terms of airframe and cooling, the design of the engine is matched to the Jumo 222 E/F. Taking into account the timing of this engine model, the Jumo 222 A/B 3 will be installed by the time it is delivered. This measure eliminates the design changes when replacing the engines."

Total fuel load was 790kg – somewhat less than that of the Viktoria-tail fighter and cruciform-tail fighter – and armament was four MG 151s, two in the nose and two in the wing roots, but this was at least an aircraft nearly ready for full series production and the MG 151 was already in full production, unlike the MG 213.

B&V CARRIES THE TORCH

Following the first – and only – Hochleistungs-Otto-Jäger comparison meeting, interest in the project appears to have died down, though whether it was ever cancelled outright is unclear. Once its three short descriptions, Nr. 16, 17 and 19, had been completed, Focke-Wulf appears to have set all work on the project to one side while it pressed on with design work on single-jet day fighters, twin-jet day fighters and mixed-propulsion night fighters.

Dornier similarly appears to have deferred further work on its design for the time being. That left only Blohm & Voss to continue carrying the torch.

In early November 1944 the company published a new description of the P 208 based on an equally new variant – the P 208.03-01, which was to be powered by a Daimler-Benz DB 603 L. The report's foreword, which took preexisting familiarity with the project as a given, began: "Assuming that the aerodynamic questions to be clarified in the wind tunnel receive a satisfactory answer, then the present design can claim to have the following properties:

1. The simplest rear engine system without a [drive] shaft extension, i.e. light, cheap, easy to maintain and reliable.
2. Lowest overall surface area, due to the short fuselage, small wings and tail units, i.e. the highest possible speed that can be achieved.
3. Lowest overall weight, due to the light engine system, small wings and short fuselage.
4. The simplest possible production, since the wings are constant chord, the fin and its rudder are omitted, and the fuselage is not interrupted in its supporting structure by a built-in motor.
5. Low proportion of duralumin in the airframe weight with extensive use of sheet steel in easily manufacturable thicknesses."

The report went on to explain that dropping the requirement for a lengthy drive shaft was desirable, hence the short fuselage, and relocating the tail surfaces to the wingtips saved weight and reduced complication.

It explained that the tailplanes could be used as ailerons, making it possible to extend the aircraft's landing flaps over a large proportion of its wingspan. This in turn resulted in improved lift on landing – allowing higher wing loadings "in contrast to the notorious wing complexity of conventional tailless aircraft". And by "tilting the tailplanes – they must be set down in a way that makes sense and is effective – the elevator can also take over the function of the rudder. This results in a saving of fin surfaces, which has the effect of reducing drag and is advantageous in terms of production. So, as you can see, there are a number of reasons that all speak for the expediency of the wing and tail unit arrangement we have proposed".

The wings would consist of a steel shell braced by welded-in profiles, which could also double as a fuel tank. This would comprise about 50% of the wing chord, starting at the leading edge, with the rear part of the wing being made from riveted duralumin. The fuselage, meanwhile, would be a duralumin shell with the armament of three MK 108s in the nose. Below them would be the nosewheel bay. The nosewheel itself would retract forwards on take-off in front of the radiator inlet. The cockpit was separated from the engine by the horizontal radiator arrangement in the centre fuselage – air from the radiator exiting through vents on the upper fuselage behind the cockpit canopy.

The report stated: "In order to make the inlet cross-section as small as possible, a fan is provided. This fan can either be driven by an electric motor or, more economically, by a gearbox that branches off from the engine." Exhaust gases were vented via the trailing edge wingroots.

Dimensionally, the P 208.03-01 was certainly compact, with a length of 9.2m from the tip of its nose to the ends of its wing booms; wingspan of 9.5m and wing area of 19sqm.

Just over a month earlier, on September 29, 1944, Blohm & Voss had actually sketched out a P 208.03-02 which had presumably failed to make the cut for the November report. This design shifted the aircraft's radiator to a position inside the fuselage, between the cockpit and the engine. It was fed by a pair of broad rectangular wingroot inlets – resulting in a reduced frontal area and a clean underside. It had the same wingspan and wing area as the P 208.03-01 but was actually 10cm shorter overall at 9.1m.

HENSCHEL P 132

On or before November 3, 1944, Henschel Flugzeugwerke came up with its own Hochleistungs-Otto-Jäger design – even though the company had not been among those initially invited to tender and even though the competition had all but stalled by this point.

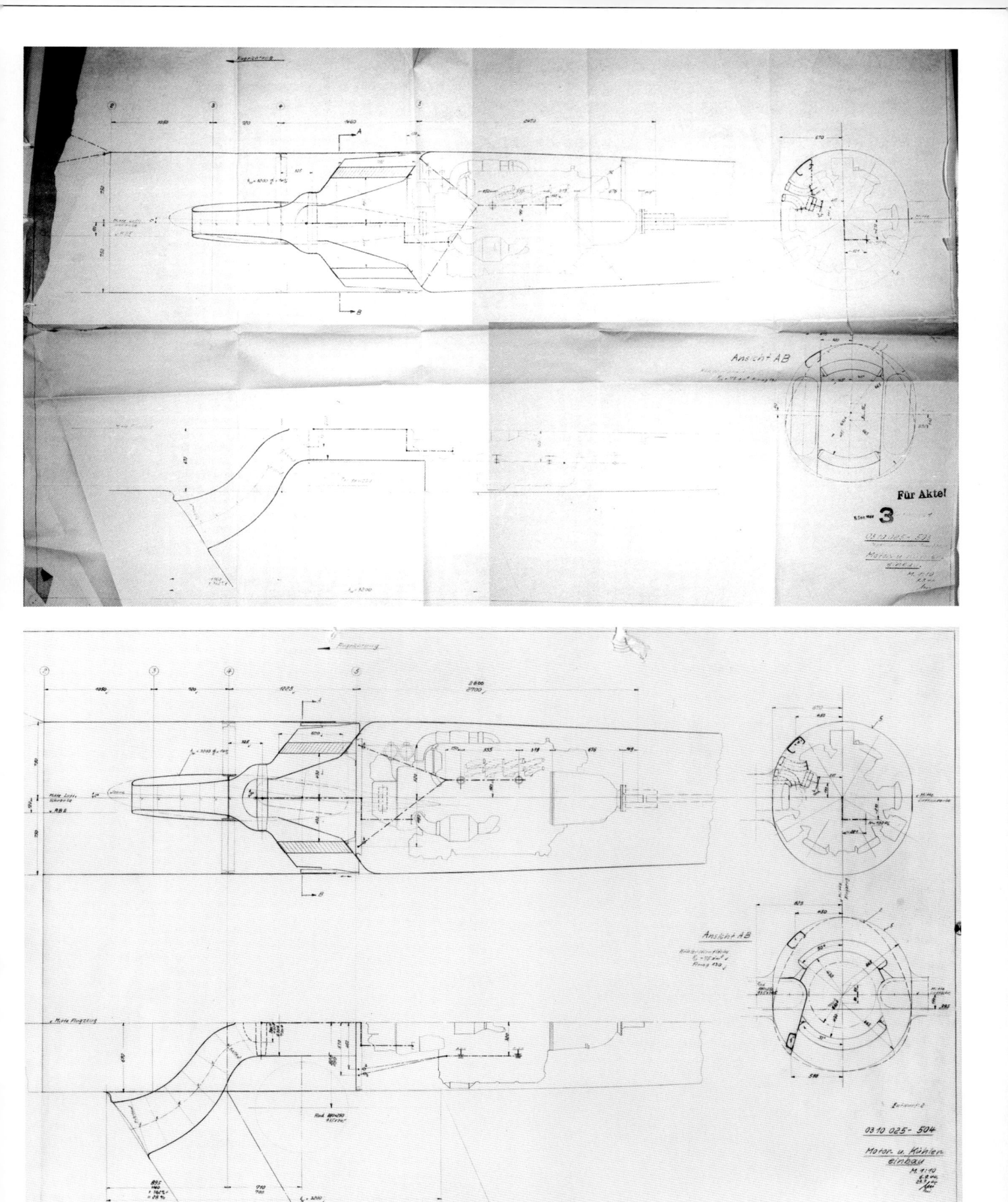

ABOVE: These images show Focke-Wulf considering whether to position the mainwheels of the cruciform-tail fighter vertically within the fuselage (drawing 0310 025-503) or horizontally in the wingroot/fuselage (drawing 0310 025-504).

The P 132, not to be confused with the Henschel Hs 132 jet-propelled ground-attack aircraft, is described on a company document as a 'Zerstörer' powered by a single Jumo 222 E/F driving contra-rotating 3.3m diameter propellers in a pusher configuration.

It had a wingspan of 16m and a wing area of 46sqm but measured only 8.2m long. Armament was two MG 151/20s with 500 rounds each and two MK 103s with 240 rounds each. Take-off weight was 7,300kg and top speed was estimated at 815km/h when flying at 13km altitude.

Unfortunately no further information exists on this design, nor has any drawing of it ever been found.

LUCHT THE CHAMPION

Roluf Wilhelm Lucht must have seemed to live a charmed life. Born on August 17, 1901, he studied engineering at Berlin Technical College and never had to go to war. He was hired by Blohm & Voss from 1923 to 1924 before getting his diploma from Kiel University and moving to work for Rohrbach back in Berlin. He entered the military in 1926 and trained as a pilot before going to work for the government. He was transferred to the newly formed Luftwaffe in April 1933 and had worked his way up to hold the rank of chief engineer in the Technical Office by July 21, 1937.

He was then promoted to the rank of Engineer General in July 1939 and later joined the General Staff as Luftwaffe Chief Engineer. He survived the downfall of Ernst Udet unscathed and appears to have been

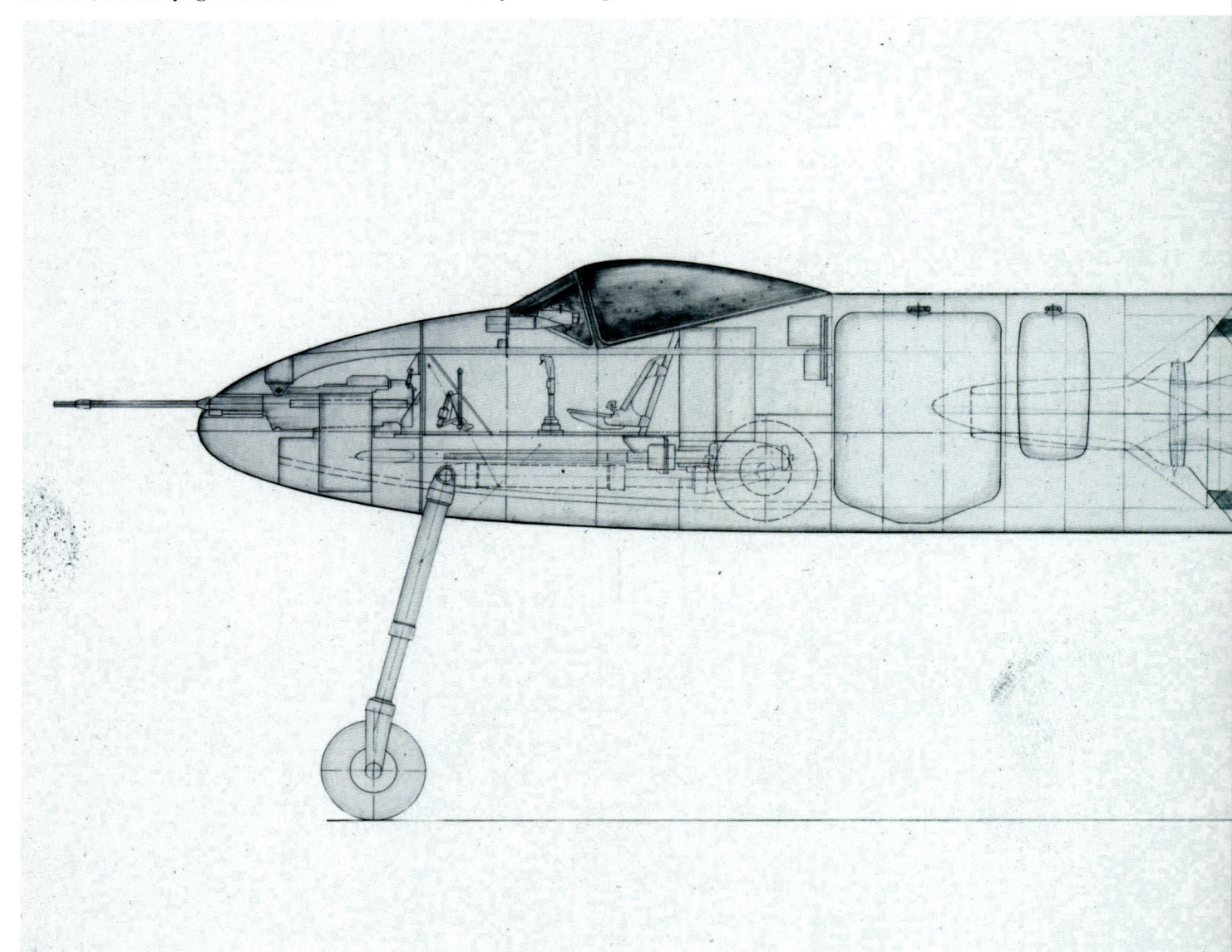

ABOVE: The cruciform-tail fighter as it appears in drawing 0310 025-0505.

one of Erhard Milch's closest allies. It might have seemed that his luck had run out when, aged 41, he was officially retired on January 31, 1943. But instead, he went to industry and became the Betriebsführer for Messerschmitt's Regensburg plant – a position equivalent to Kurt Tank's role at Focke-Wulf. This despite the fact that, a year earlier, he had come up with the idea of dismissing Willy Messerschmitt from the top role in his own company and had then been sent there by Milch to deliver the news to Messerschmitt personally. It seems highly unlikely that this appointment was something Messerschmitt himself had been given any choice about.

Even this might have been the end for Lucht – but not so. In August 1944, the German Air Ministry (Reichsluftfahrtministerium or RLM) was reorganised as the Chef TLR (Chef der Technische Luftrüstung). It had largely the same functions but was now subordinated to Albert Speer's War Production Ministry and controlled differently, being overseen by a series of special commissions. The commission responsible for making decisions on aircraft development was the Entwicklungshauptkomission Flugzeuge (EHK), established in September 1944, and the man appointed to chair it was… Generalstabsingenieur Roluf Lucht.

Lucht now had considerable power and found himself nominally overseeing the likes of Willy Messerschmitt, Kurt Tank, Junkers' Heinrich Hertel, Arado's Walter Blume, Lufthansa's Rolf Stüssel and, indeed,

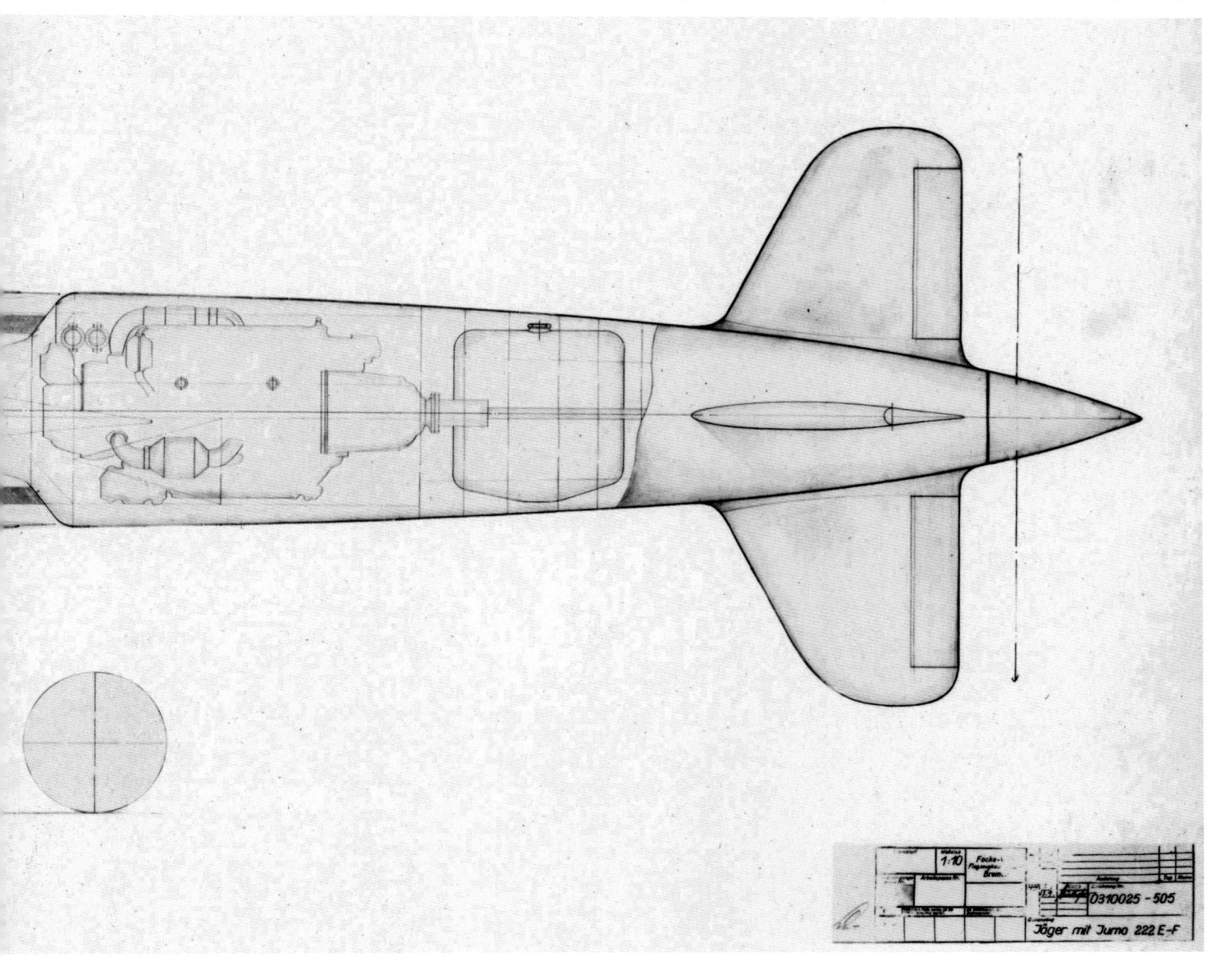

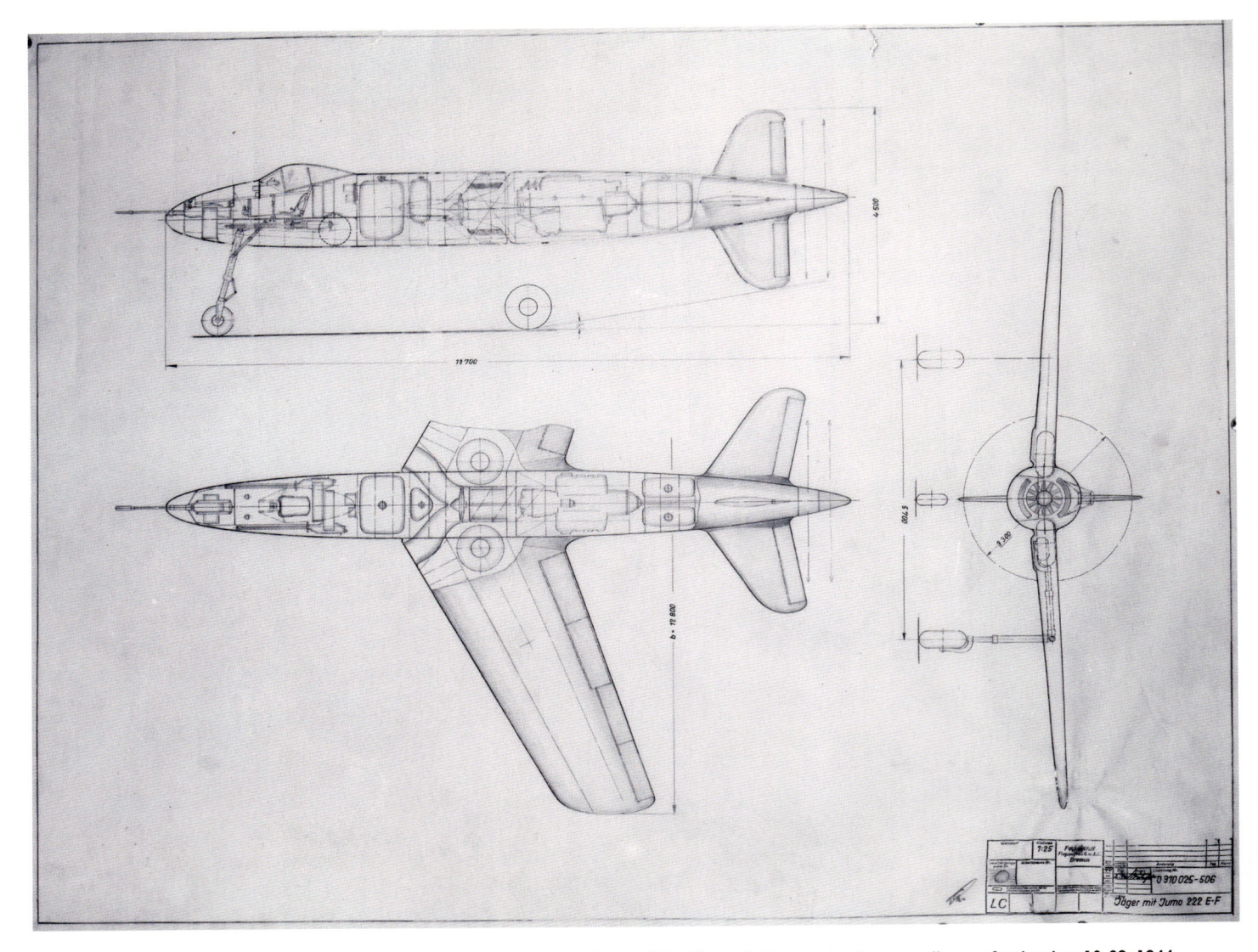

ABOVE: Focke-Wulf's cruciform-tail fighter as presented at the Hochleistungs-Otto-Jäger design comparison meeting on September 18-20, 1944.

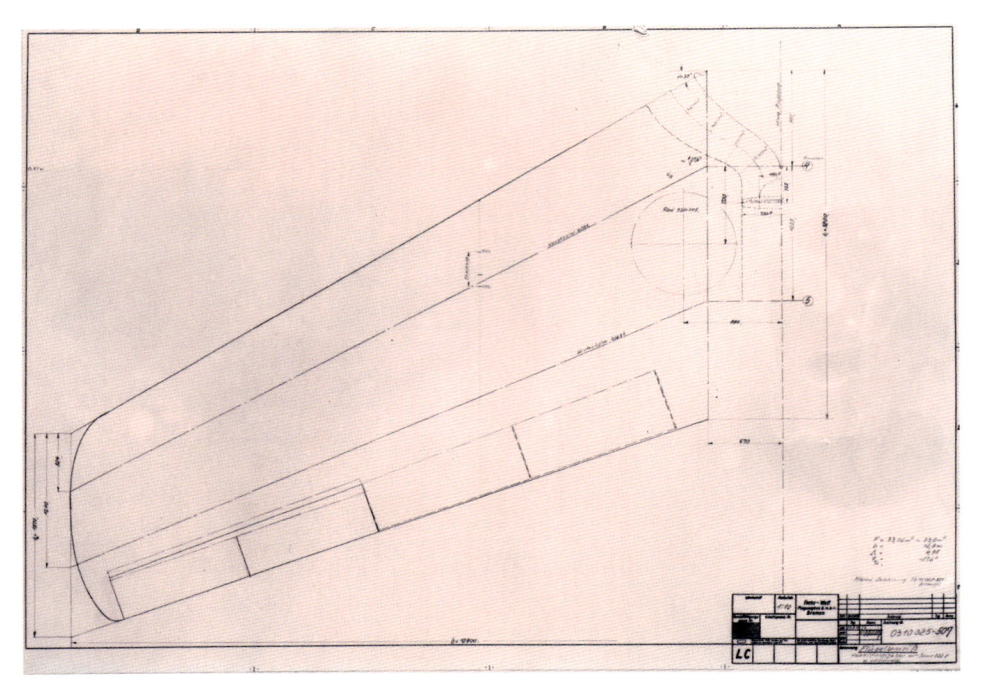

ABOVE: Focke-Wulf drawing 0310 025-507, dated September 29, 1944, further elaborated on the horizontal mainwheel positioning for the cruciform-tail fighter design.

Blohm & Voss's Richard Vogt. Each of these larger-than-life characters had been made the head of a subordinate 'special commission' – Messerschmitt taking on day fighters, Tank got night fighters and so on.

He also appears to have been the greatest champion of continued piston engine aircraft development at what was still functionally the Air Ministry – even as all his new colleagues were busily working on jet types. German historian Walter Schick, writing in his 1994 book Geheimprojelte der Luftwaffe Jagdflugzeuge 1939-1945, reports Lucht as saying on September 18, 1944, the first day of the Hochleistungs-Otto-Jäger conference: "On the basis of the aforementioned advantages and disadvantages, the single-engined pusher-propeller Otto fighter, which can perform the role of the Do 335 at approximately half the cost, is very economical for use against bombers at all altitudes.

"It is equally suitable for deployment against enemy Otto fighters at all altitudes. Thanks to its endurance the Otto fighter is the type most suited to protecting any given area of airspace. And due to its economical cruise capability, the Otto fighter performs better at all altitudes in bad weather and

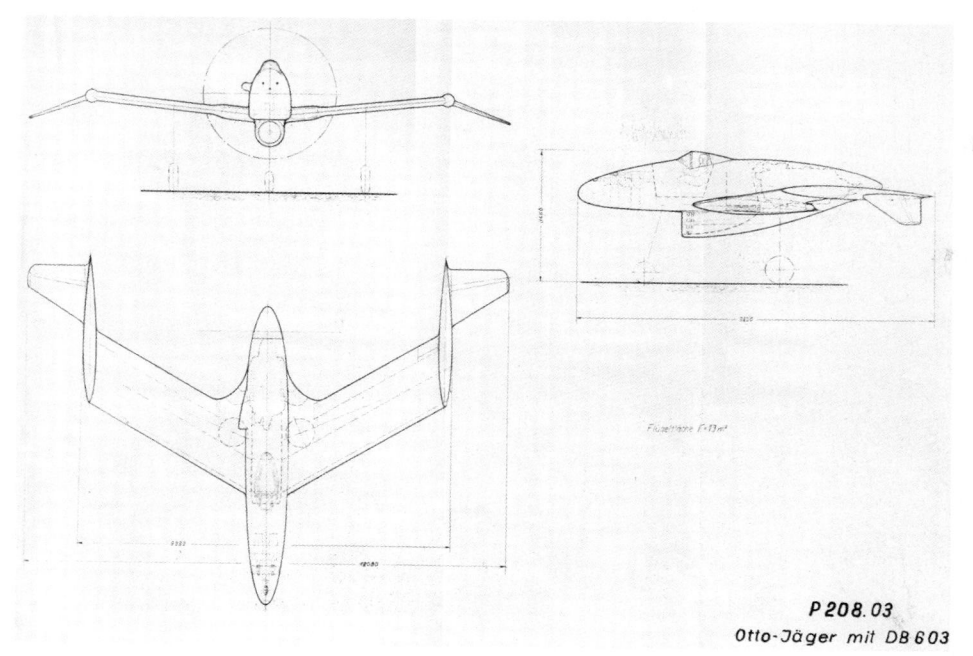

ABOVE: Blohm & Voss P 208.03-01 as it appeared in the company's November 1944 description report. The design incorporates elements of both P 208.01-01 and P 208.02-01 while introducing a new radiator inlet form complete with built-in fan.

blind flying conditions than would a jet-powered aircraft. Furthermore, it is the most suitable fighter for operation in greater numbers when circumstances call for massed formations.

"In our opinion, and in the light of the above, the Otto fighter at its most advanced stage of development with pusher propeller is indispensable for aerial defence duties above and behind the front lines. And thanks to its being less susceptible to ground fire, it also lends itself to use in the fighter-bomber and ground attack roles."

Those with at least some sympathy towards this viewpoint included Oberst Ulrich Diesing, formerly Göring's adjutant and now head of the Chef TLR, and Vogt.

Some time prior to November 9, 1944, Lucht wrote to Vogt and asked him to come up with a report explaining the advantages and disadvantages of the piston engine fighter. It was to be entitled 'Warum Otto-Jäger?' or 'Why the Otto fighter?'

Vogt did as he was told and the report was ready by November 9.

He wrote: "Although on the whole the decision already taken as to the absolute necessity of its [the piston engine fighter's] further development appears justified, a more detailed comparison shows that on some points the result is not so completely in favour of the piston engine fighter as a more general view of the matter might suggest.

"Our own people having during the past months been very busy on plans for high-speed fighters on both lines of development, piston engine as well as jet lines – and the projects having therefore reached an equal stage of maturity, it seemed appropriate to answer the above question by simply comparing the operational efficiency of both types.

"The [two] models in question are: P 208.03 Otto fighter with DB 603, pusher propeller and outer tail unit. P 209.02 jet

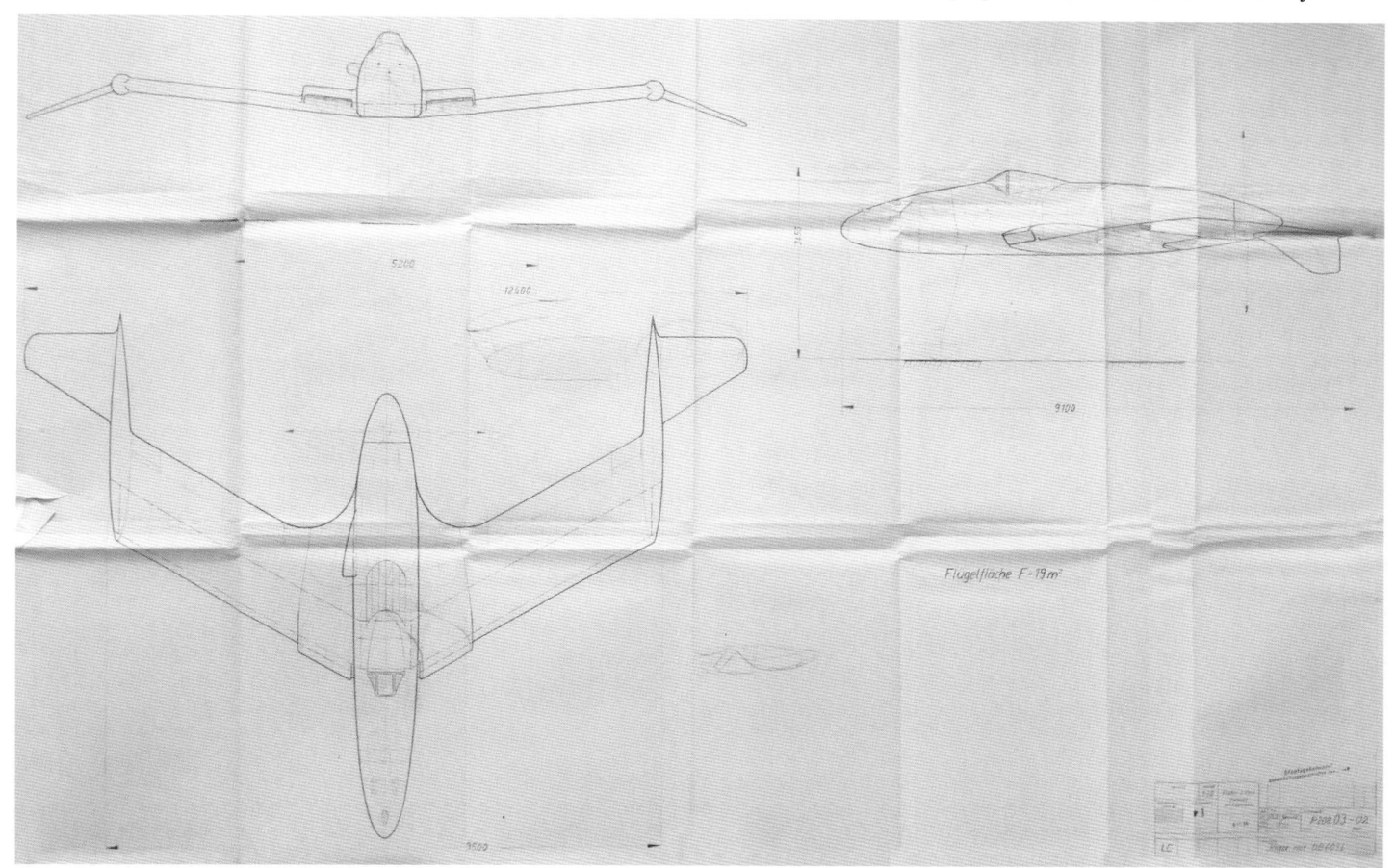

ABOVE: Blohm & Voss P 208.03-02 with over-wing radiator inlets. This design of September 29, 1944, appears to have been rejected in favour of P 208.03-01.

ABVOE: Generalstabsingenieur Roluf Lucht – a loyal follower of Erhard Milch who spent much of the war making life difficult for Willy Messerschmitt.

fighter with built-in HeS 011 engine and central inlet pipe connection. One series of diagrams includes the Kleinstjäger [another name for the Volksjäger, Blohm & Voss having competed against and lost to Heinkel – which would go on to build the He 162] P 211.01 jet fighter with BMW 003, detailed projects for it having been worked out.

"Finally, the operational efficiency of the extreme high-altitude fighter BV 155 is referred to on several occasions, in order to indicate its technical possibilities which go far beyond the scope of this investigation."

Vogt noted that piston engine fighters were invariably slower than jets fighters at low altitudes but the piston engine fighter was faster than the BMW 003-powered fighter at its maximum altitude. That said, "the extreme high-speed fighter with HeS 011 engine [P 209] is much more efficient at all altitudes".

The climbing speed of the piston engine fighter was best at altitudes above 2,000m and the piston engine fighter had "superior efficiency" in take-off, though "it should … be remembered that the initial thrust of the propeller will proportionately drop off, with subsequent gradual decline in superiority". The jet aircraft could equal the piston engine fighter's performance on take-off through the use of rocket boosters, he said.

When it came to range, "given, for example, a fighting time of ten minutes, at an altitude of 6km, the range of the piston engine fighter P 208 works out at 540km and that of the jet fighter P 209 at 290km. It is obvious that a comparison of non-combat flying times results even more conclusively in favour of the piston engine fighter. This applies especially to throttled flying which enables the aircraft to remain on station. That is important for mass formation work as well as for night fighting. But it is of equal significance at high altitudes which involve long climbing periods and where the handling of fighter aircraft may, in certain circumstances, become more difficult".

Fuel consumption was also a killer for jet fighters: "In view of the difficulties of sufficient fuel production the rate of consumption plays an important part. Near the ground the jet fighter uses about four times as much. At a height of 9km this additional consumption is reduced by half". As such, providing jet fighters with sufficient fuel "remains difficult even though it does not demand the highest quality fuel".

Furthermore, "as the piston engine fighter uses smaller quantities, its fuel tanks can be armoured more economically and with less waste of space. But it should be remembered that the faster rate of consumption of the jet fighter permits it, under certain conditions, to carry a large part of its fuel in the wing, without any protection. Most of the difference, therefore, cancels out".

BLOHM & VOSS PRESS ON

Vogt received a memo from the EHK on November 26, 1944, presenting him with the latest performance figures on the Jumo 222 E/F and asking him to "supplement the performance data of your project P 208.01 with these engine performance data". Clearly, P 208 was still a concept that some within the Air Ministry's leadership wanted to pursue.

Focke-Wulf was, meanwhile, going in a different direction – concentrating on its mixed propulsion night and bad-weather fighters. Presumably this shift in focus was inspired by Tank's newfound responsibility as head of the night fighter special commission.

The company also pushed the Jumo 222-powered Ta 152 concept again with a third report on the topic – Kurzbaubeschreibung Nr. 25 Jagdflugzeug Ta 152 mit Jumo 222 E und Laminarprofil, dated December 4, 1944. With the introduction of laminar flow wings to the project, it edged even closer to becoming a Hochleistungs-Otto-Jäger analogue.

The text for this report began: "The Ta 152 fighter aircraft with Jumo 222 E is developed from the Ta 152 H airframe. Because of the limited space, a Jumo 222 E engine specially developed for the Ta 152 has to be installed. This engine can be exchanged for a Jumo 222 A engine at any time."

Evidently new calculations had shown that the Ta 152 H's wing was unsuitable for use with the Jumo 222, so "there is a need to develop a new wing". This would "take into account the latest aerodynamic findings" by introducing a laminar profile, but that wasn't all. The fuselage would need to be reinforced around the engine connection fittings, with consequent modification to the aircraft's skin. The existing undercarriage, rear fuselage and tail were fine, however.

The new wingspan was shorter at 13.68m (compared to 14.44m in Kurzbaubeschreibung Nr. 19), wing area was larger at 23.7sqm (compared to 23.3sqm) and overall aircraft length was 10.77m – the same as before. There were two armament options – the four MG 151s previously offered or two MG 151s in the fuselage and two MK 103s in the wing roots.

December 6, 1944, saw the Aerodynamische Versuchsanstalt (AVA) at Göttingen publishing a report on radiators for fighters with pusher-props that its engineers had worked on in conjunction with Blohm & Voss. The introduction noted that it was "not intended to provide a complete answer to the question of which radiator installation is best. Only the possibilities that seem worth debating are presented and roughly evaluated based on the documents available. We would also like to point out the report Contribution to the Question of Radiator Installations by H. Reiniger (Heinkel report from October 25, 1944) which deals with the same issue".

Kurt Reiniger at Heinkel, having written this report on radiators, had by now turned his attention to other projects detailed elsewhere in this publication.

The AVA went on to caution that when it came to pusher-prop installations, "the lack of design documents and in-depth research is particularly noticeable in this case. In order to reach a conclusion at all, we refrained from making a general comparison and based our estimates on a given airframe of certain dimensions, whereby we were kindly advised and supported by the company Blohm & Voss. In this way, however, absolute dimensions come into the considerations, and it is quite conceivable that the situation would be different with other dimensions (e.g. a larger airframe or a larger frontal surface area)".

It was clear from the images accompanying the report that the P 208 had served as a basis for the AVA's study. First up, a variant with a nose-mounted radiator similar to that employed on Focke-Wulf's Viktoria-tail fighter was examined. This had "a particularly favourable aerodynamic shape" which allowed air to flow evenly over the radiator's entire surface area. Weapons could be fitted which fired around it and drag would be "relatively low … since there is no additional frontal area" and its small diameter would not impair the pilot's visibility.

However, "the disadvantage of this system would be that there can be no question of cooling while stationary and that forced ventilation would cost a considerable amount of effort. In addition, there are relatively long cooling water pipes, and therefore greater weight, and ultimately the space in the nose of the fuselage is no longer free for other installations (such as the nose wheel). Overall, these disadvantages are such that any advantage that such a system has, according to our estimate, is partially or completely cancelled out, though this of course cannot be estimated in general".

Next up was a ventral radiator arrangement – similar to what had actually been designed into the P 208.03-01. This had the advantages that airflow would be good and there would be "no particular restrictions regarding the depth of the radiator; the shape of the [radiator] block can be rectangular, which simplifies production". Furthermore, the freely emerging jet of cooling air [from the rear of the aircraft] should not cause any interference drag".

But there were some significant disadvantages: "the drag of such a belly cooler is relatively high, which is due to the large additional surface area as well as the additional frontal area and the associated shape". Worse, "in this form, the belly cooler will be relatively sensitive to [enemy] fire. Contamination is also to be expected, especially if there is a nose wheel. Ultimately, the cooling will be very inadequate or even non-existent when stationary".

For the third arrangement, "we thought of a radiator built into the fuselage, the flow of which takes place via two pipes and inlets in the wing roots. This was essentially the previously rejected P 208.03-02. In this instance, "the overall drag of this cooling system can be described as low. In terms of the radiator depths and shape, the fuselage radiator is just as favourable as the belly radiator. The location is characterised as completely bulletproof".

A design not illustrated in the report involved fitting very low, very wide radiators directly into the wings – an arrangement that had been worked on by Messerschmitt. But this resulted in long, heavy piping to the engine, vulnerability to battle damage and the potential to affect the aircraft's handling properties due to changes in the airflow around the inlet.

Lastly, there was a design where the radiator was positioned at the rear of the aircraft close to the propeller. The report said: "In all previous installation arrangements, the radiator was practically separated from the engine and there was no unitary engine cooling system similar to that used with tractor propellers. However, such a cooling system in the rear is not outside the realm of possibility."

A note of caution was sounded, in that "any drag values cannot be specified … [and] with this arrangement, an attempt would have to be made to overcome the boundary layer difficulties, for example by means of suction. In addition, as an important point, the propeller would have to take on the function of a cooling fan, for example through special profiling of the blades or through shaft covers, if one does not decide to install a cooling fan directly, which is structurally possible with this arrangement".

On the other hand, providing an outlet for air exiting the radiator would be simple: "You can try to get by with a fixed, unregulated outlet from the radiator cowling. The exit can be relatively large, which allows for a good shape of the outside of the cowl. In this respect, the situation is fundamentally the opposite of that in the normal standard engine, where achieving a large exhaust opening always causes difficulties."

Evidently, with the right design, adequate cooling could be achieved even when the aircraft was stationary. The propeller could also power a centrifugal pump for boundary layer suction.

Finally, "the additional frontal area for such a cooling system would be relatively small and the space required would be small, since you can hardly fit anything else in this place anyway. Visibility to the rear may be slightly impaired. Sensitivity to [enemy] fire is not great. Overall, it seems worthwhile to pursue such a radiator installation, as it at least has the great advantages of the standard engine [cooling system]".

222/413 IN THE BALANCE

The EHK met on December 7, 1944, specifically to discuss the Jumo 222, the Argus As 413 and the 'Gruppenmotor' designs of Professor Wunibald Kamm. These latter designs, consisting of high-power, multi-cylinder, multi-shaft piston engines, were being worked on at the Forschungsinstitut für Kraftfahrwesen und Fahrzeugmotoren Stuttgart (FKFS for short).

Among those present were Lucht, Messerschmitt, Tank, Gottfried Reidenbach from Dornier (a former Luftwaffe chief engineer who, like Lucht, had been 'retired' to industry), Friedrich Nicolaus from Henschel, Hertel from Junkers, Ferdinand Brandner from Jumo, Fritz Nallinger from Daimler-Benz and Dr Manfred Christian from Argus.

According to a post-meeting report, the Jumo delegation "reported on the status of the Jumo 222 motor. It was stated that this engine had been in development for a very long time, but that this development had dragged on mainly because of the lack of development capacity. The technical difficulties are not that great".

A discussion followed as to "whether this engine, given its fundamental handicap of the connecting rod bearing, can have any prospect of a corresponding performance development".

Brandner thought that the 222's development was coming along well "but the other gentlemen, especially Mr Bifang of BMW, have serious doubts about it. Mr Bifang briefly explains the great difficulties that BMW has with regard to the bearing of the connecting rod and explains that he considers an increase in speed, to the extent that Jumo is planning, to be hopeless.

"In the end, the formula was found that the engine currently has about 20% more power than the existing engines DB 603 and Jumo 213 and that this 20% more power could probably be retained for further development. The question arose as to whether it was worth building this engine with 24 cylinders

BELOW: AVA drawing showing a P 208 design incorporating a nose-mounted radiator.

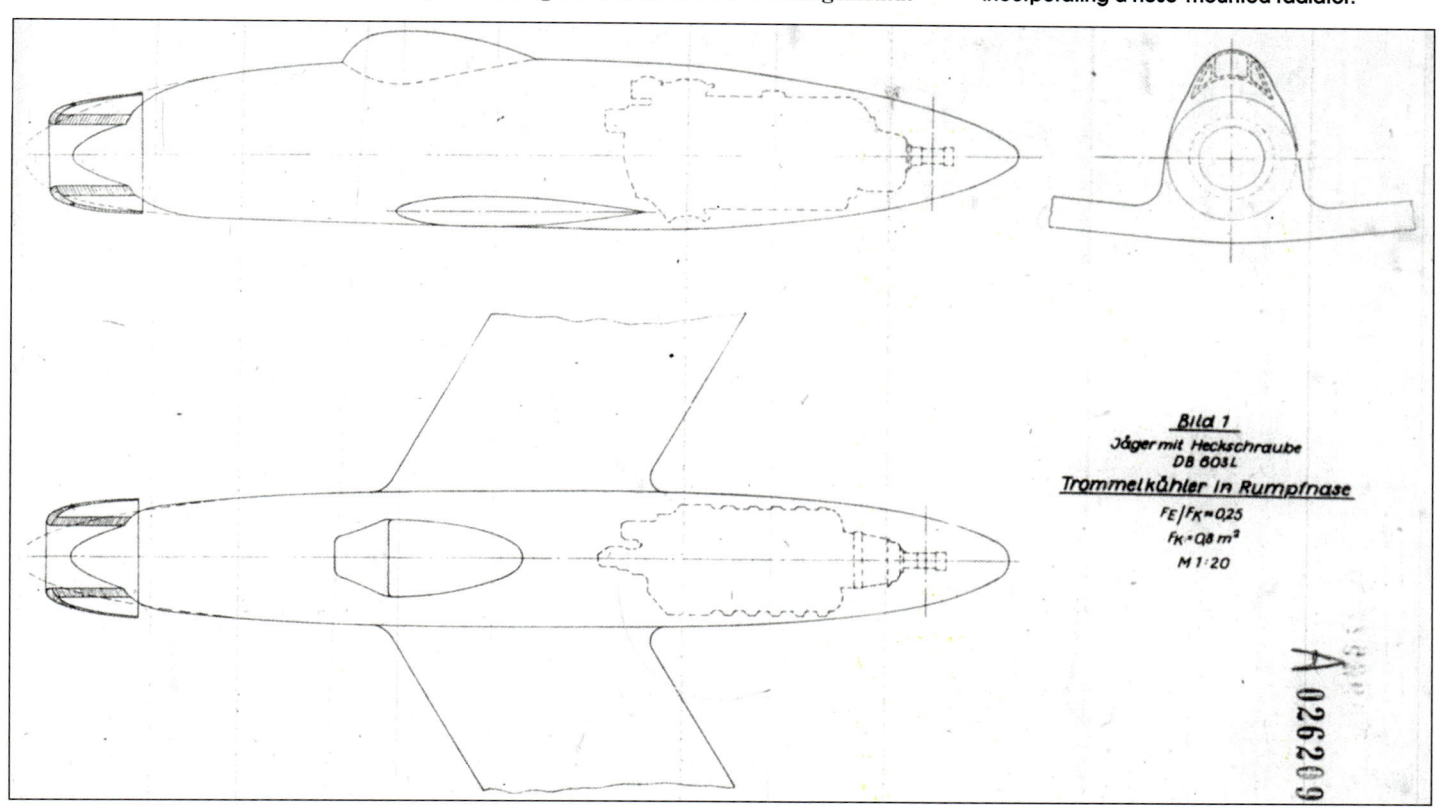

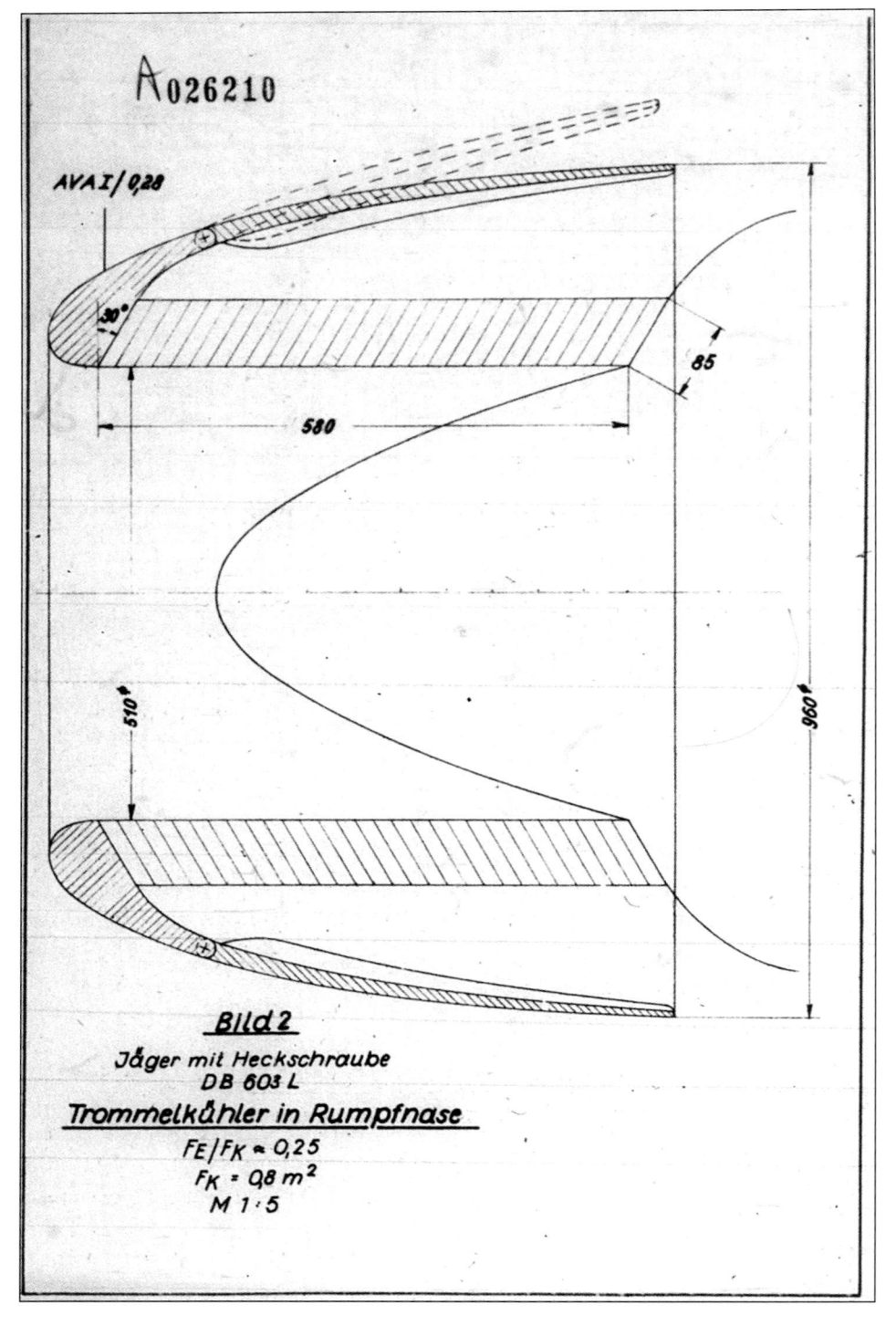

ABOVE: Diagram showing how the P 208 nose radiator's dimensions in detail.

and other new equipment because of the 20% increase in output".

The airframe companies chimed in and it was explained that while "a new project of a piston engine fighter could very well have an engine in the power class 3,000-3,500hp, fighter projects with a tandem engine design using two existing engines also had great prospects of success".

And "the following opinion emerges from the three fighter-building companies: Focke-Wulf/Prof Tank is probably interested in this engine [the Jumo 222]; Dornier/Director Reidenbach is not interested. The tandem design is developed there. Messerschmitt/Prof Messerschmitt has no interest at all, because he explains that it is nonsense to build a new fighter based on the piston engine".

Otherwise, "for the other projects, the engine was only suitable for the Jumo 388, which would be 40km faster as a result. Prof. Hertel explains that the engine must be there now and that it is a sin of omission that the engine was not built. It must be built as soon as possible".

Air Ministry staff engineer Schwarz presented some calculations on the Jumo 222 and "came to the conclusion that this engine would not make much sense compared to the existing 12-cylinder engines and compared to the further developments". The DB 603 L produced less power than the 222 but was lighter – resulting in no advantage for the 222. Schwarz's "remarks culminated in the fact that it didn't make much sense to build this engine".

Nallinger then presented his detailed conclusions: for the further development of existing airframes, "the two 12-cylinder engines, the DB 603 and Jumo 213, are undoubtedly the best choice, because these existing airframe designs are also primarily dependent on a centre cannon [mounted in the engine, firing through the spinner], which cannot be installed in the Jumo 222. The Me 109 example shows how much you can keep such a machine on a usable and equal basis for years to come by increasing the performance of the engine. This is exactly how one could imagine the further development of the Fw 190 and the Do 335".

As far as any new piston engine fighter, such as the Hochleistungs-Otto-Jäger, was concerned, Nallinger thought it was "wrong to speak of a 222 versus 603/213 competition here. The 222 would have to be viewed on a very different basis due to its weight and manufacturing complexity. If the engine is not at 3,500-3,800hp soon then in his opinion this motor doesn't make much sense.

"If new fighter projects with piston engines are already being developed, then it would probably make sense to go straight into a higher performance class, for example based on the 413, 613 or tandem design. The latter appears to be very favourable, since existing engines could be used and since this design is particularly suitable for a pusher-prop configuration, resulting in an extraordinarily slim fuselage and a favourable weight distribution".

It was decided that Speer's deputy Hauptdienstleiter Karl-Otto Saur should make the final decision "with a small group" on whether to proceed with the Jumo 222.

The Argus As 413 was then discussed in detail and "also discussed above all with regard to new fighter projects. Dr Christian gives a brief overview and describes the schedule in such a way that the engine will run for the first time in April 1945, that the prototype series will begin in autumn 1945 and that this engine can then be brought in [into series production] at the beginning of 1946. Parts from the [Jumo] 213 such as connecting rod, connecting rod bearing, cylinder head and piston are used. Everything else on this engine becomes practically new.

"Those present ... very much doubted the optimistic dates. It hardly seems possible that the series could come at the specified time, beginning in 1946. [But] General Diesing's deputy, Herr Obersting. Herrmann, explains that Luftwaffe High Command wants the engine".

Once again, the airframe companies entered the discussion and "explained that the engine, given its size, was not very suitable for a fighter because it required a very thick fuselage. Furthermore, the installation of this engine with a pusher-prop configuration is also uncomfortable, because you have to put it quite far forward for reasons of centre

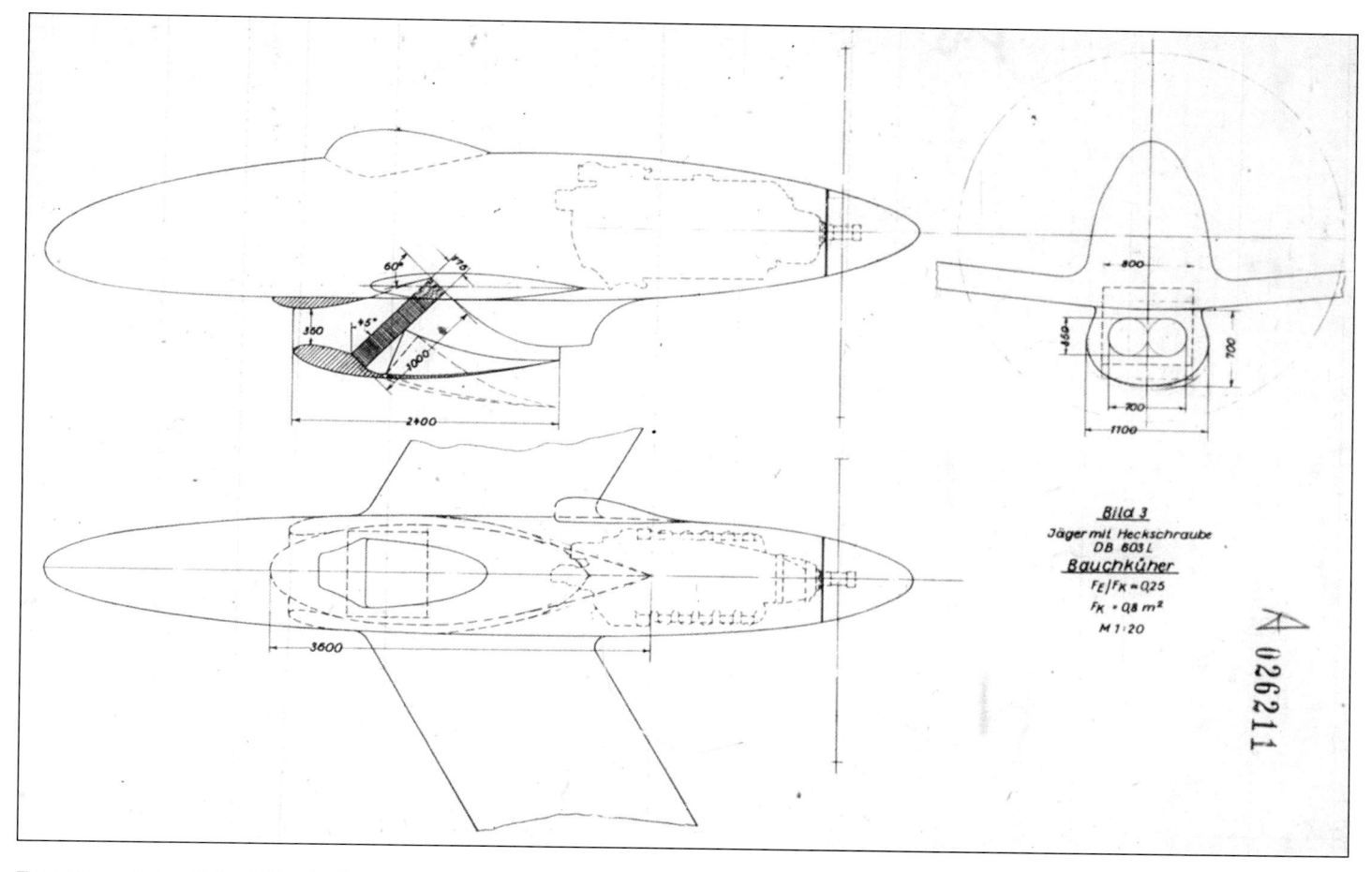

The radiator design Blohm & Voss had actually chosen for the P 208 – a ventral inlet arrangement.

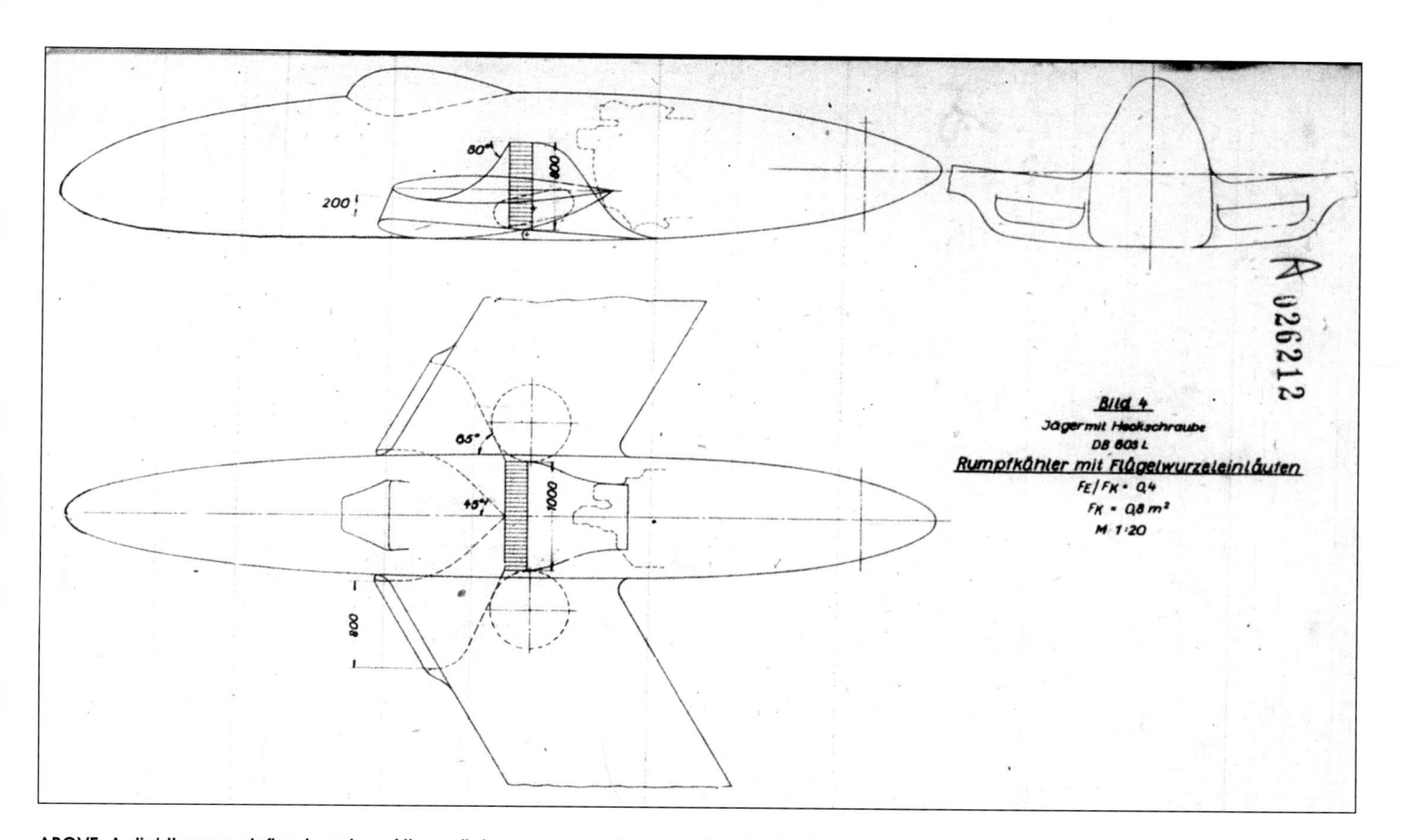

ABOVE: A slightly more defined version of the radiator arrangement designed for the P 208.03-02, with wing root inlets.

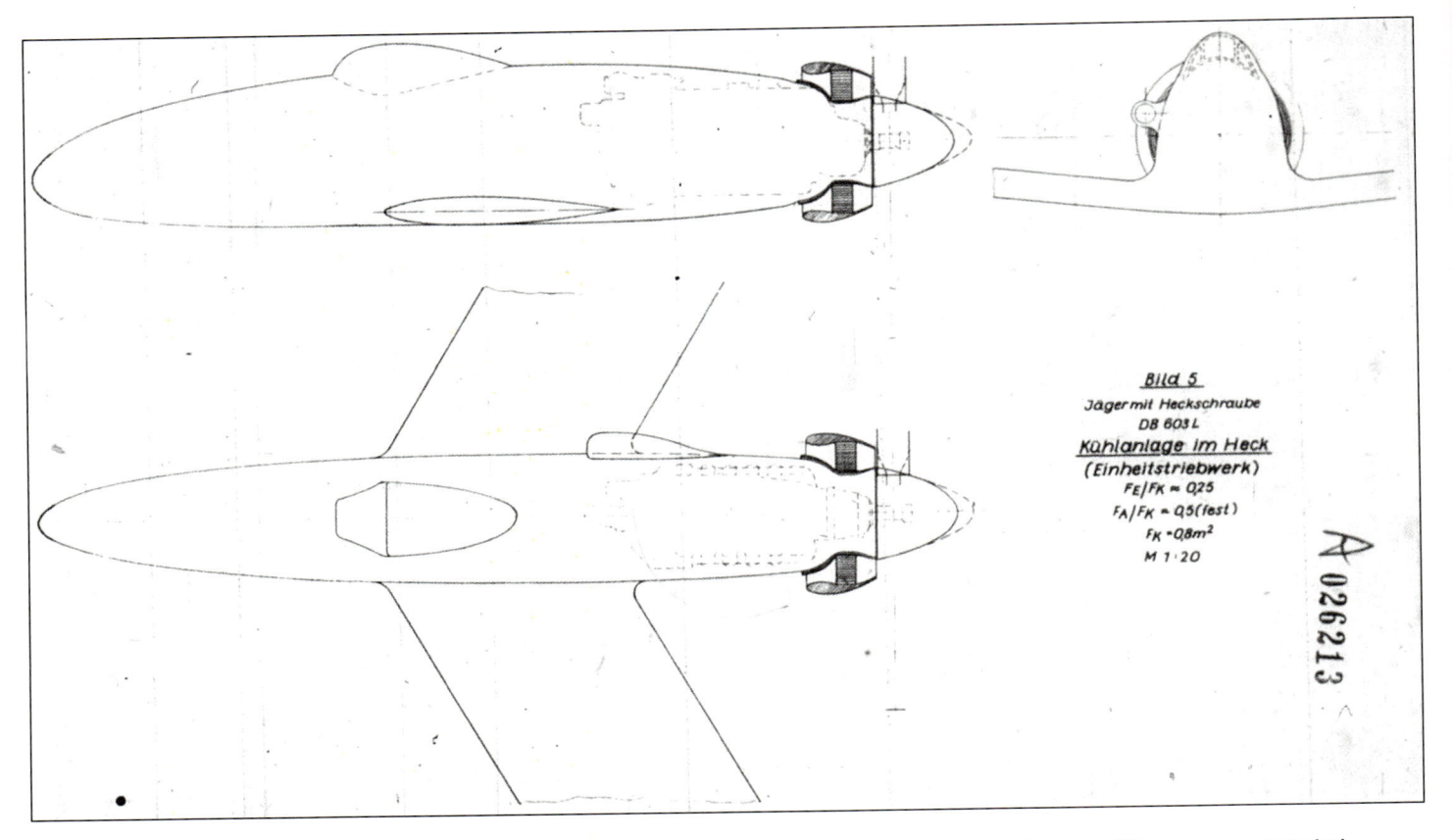

ABOVE: Having assessed Blohm & Voss's ideas for radiator installation on the P 208, the AVA evidently suggested one of its own: a rear-mounted annular radiator.

of gravity, which means that the drive shaft becomes very long. If you put it further back to get a shorter drive shaft, you would have to build a very long forward fuselage for weight reasons. Exhaust discharge is also difficult.

"In summary, Mr Schilo [Walter Schilo, BMW director, but here representing the Ministry] states that the airframe industry is not interested in this engine, since it can easily be replaced by the tandem design of two existing 12-cylinder engines, which, according to the explanations, would also result in more favourable installation conditions".

Incredibly, in spite of all that, it was concluded that "the engine should be further developed and only then can a decision be made as to whether it should be built or not".

Kamm then explained his Gruppenmotor developments but said they amounted to "student research that is readily available to industry. Of course, he could not carry out the full development of such an engine in his institute. He will send the documents about his engine to the individual aircraft engine companies". In other words, his research had produced nothing of note for the future of piston engine fighters.

CRUNCH MEETING

Another much more wide-ranging meeting of the EHK was held on December 19-20, 1944, during which all new fighter developments were discussed and concrete decisions on the way forward were reached.

The conference opened, apparently, with a presentation from Willy Messerschmitt entitled Otto and Jet Fighter or Only Jet Fighter? According to the official minutes of the meeting, in addition to a decision to push ahead with plans for a single-jet fighter powered by an HeS 011 turbojet, it was noted that "since previous frontline experience has not yet clearly shown whether the jet fighter is sufficient for all operational tasks due to its special properties compared to the piston engine fighter, further development of the piston engine fighter cannot be dispensed with for the time being.

"Decision: The further development of the aircraft type [Ta] 152 must be continued on both the engine and the fuselage side by all means in order to keep up with the performance of foreign piston engine fighters in the near future. The Day Fighter Special Commission (Messerschmitt) must also independently check at the beginning of January 1945 whether the new development of a piston engine fighter still makes sense in terms of performance and effort compared to further development of the 152. This requires a clear determination of how long and to what extent the performance of the 152 can still be increased compared to corresponding new piston engine fighter designs".

A more detailed account of the meeting comes from handwritten notes made by Arado's Walter Blume, typed up and issued as a memo two days later. He recorded: "Professor Messerschmitt rejects piston engine fighter, without giving detailed information, only with reference to speed superiority, also with regard to anti-bomber operations, where he considers a top speed of 1,100km/h possible".

Blume himself then reported on the results of a two-seater jet fighter study and noted that it took three times as much effort to build a twin-piston engine Do 335 as it took to build a twin-jet Ar 234.

Then, "General Diesing refuses to put everything on the jet card, as there are still too many risks and ambiguities of a tactical and technical nature – formation flying, acceleration; inferiority of the jet fighter against piston engine fighter in those respects".

Dr Vogt "is interested in piston engine fighter, apparently has project in that area". And then, "Decision: Ta 152 should be pushed as far as possible, new piston engine projects. An O.-J. [Otto Jäger] should be developed if capacity of the industry allows it".

Later on, as Messerschmitt was discussing the latest jet developments, Diesing pointed out that he shouldn't rely on boosters to get his proposed new jets off the ground since there was no longer any powder available for the rockets.

The last item on the meeting's agenda was entitled 'Series production Jumo 222?' and was prefaced with a lecture by Schilo, who had been appointed head of the EHK-subordinated special commission for aero engines.

According to the official record of the meeting: "a) There is general agreement at the EHK that the 222 is not required for the aircraft currently in series [production] and under development, since the engine is not available as standard today, and secondly, while it promises interesting performance, it only appears in the second half in 1946 at the earliest. Up to this date, the intended increase in performance of today's airframes can be

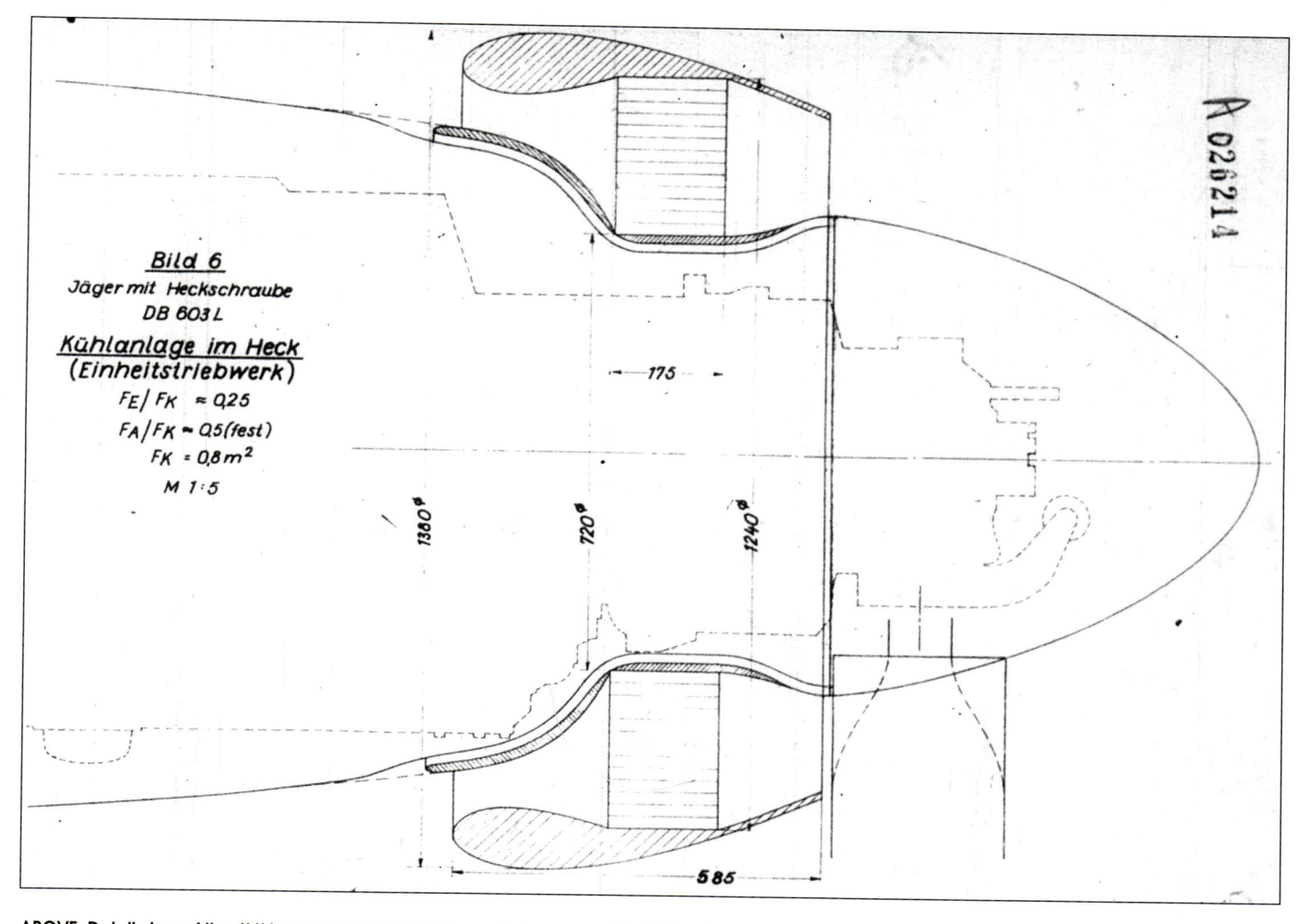

Bild 6
Jäger mit Heckschraube
DB 603 L
Kühlanlage im Heck
(Einheitstriebwerk)
$F_E/F_K \approx 0.25$
$F_A/F_K \approx 0.5 (fest)$
$F_K = 0.8 m^2$
$M\ 1:5$

ABOVE: Detail view of the AVA's rear-mounted annular radiator concept for Blohm & Voss.

covered with the motors (DB 603 and Jumo 213) which are also available today and which can also be upgraded.

"b) For future projects, in addition to the more powerful 603 and 213 engines, the As 413 under development is also in question, as well as tandem or other arrangements of several 603 or 213 engines. c) The performance improvement of the 222 compared to the 603 and 213 for the next two years is so small that it is not worth installing such a completely new engine model. This applies to all the piston engine aircraft types in question, namely 388, 335 and 152.

"d) In the opinion of the EHK, apart from a case that is still being clarified (night fighter), it is disputed whether the 222 offers significant advantages for new aircraft designs. e) The effort for series preparation, resources, etc. is very large in comparison to existing engines because of the completely different design and does not appear to be justifiable in view of the low usability for existing and future aircraft types.

"f) Decisive for the question of 222 series production is the entire existing or achievable capacity on the development and manufacturing side. In the case of the development of the 222, Junkers said that further development of the 213 and the 004 jet engine would be decisively impaired, since the capacity for all these tasks together is not available today and cannot be made available. So you have to decide to discard one or the other development either way.

"Decision: the introduction or carrying out of Jumo 222 series production is currently not justifiable in view of the greater urgency of a number of other developments and the lack of sufficient capacity. For this reason, all work on the 222 must, at least for the time being, cease in favour of other important tasks."

OTTO-JÄGER REVIVAL

The Jumo 222 appeared to be dead but against all odds the requirement for a new piston-engine fighter had survived. And on January 11, 1945, the Luftwaffe High Command's Quartermaster General issued a new requirement sheet which read: "The EHK meeting on December 19-20, 1944, defined and designated three fighter types for development priority, as replacements for the current day and night fighter aircraft."

The first of these was the HeS 011-powered single-seater and the third was a three-seater mixed propulsion jet/piston engine night and bad weather fighter, both requirements being highly detailed. The second was as follows: "2) Development of a single-seater propeller fighter with a performance-enhanced, possibly air-cooled piston engine as a replacement for the Ta 152 with suitability for bad-weather fighting and extensive automation of bad-weather landings. Top speed 800-850km/h at 10km altitude. Flight time at least three hours at the maximum permissible continuous power (excluding flight time when using external fuel tanks)". Half of the aircraft to be built needed to have a trio of 3cm cannon – MK 108s and/or MG 213s – and the other half needed to have four 3cm cannon.

A set of general requirements which applied to all three aircraft was also listed. This included: "a) In principle, the performance requirements listed are to be applied excluding external tanks, which must be provided separately in exchange for at least 500kg of droppable payload (fighter-bomber). b) Possibility to take 8-344 [Ruhrstahl X-4 air-to-air missile], R4M, Jägerfaust or larger calibre rockets filled with incendiary shrapnel. c) Possibility of interchanging the 2 and 3cm barrels with the MG 213. d) As a targeting device EZ 42 or its further development. e) Autopilot. f) Front and rear armour to protect against 20mm ammunition. g) Pressure-tight cabin. h) Nosewheel. i) Ejection seat. j) Blind flight instrumentation. k) Sufficient strength of the chassis and the tyres for overload starts. l) Possibility of taking off and landing on sites that are not specially prepared in terms of size and nature (use of take-off and landing aids only in exceptional cases)".

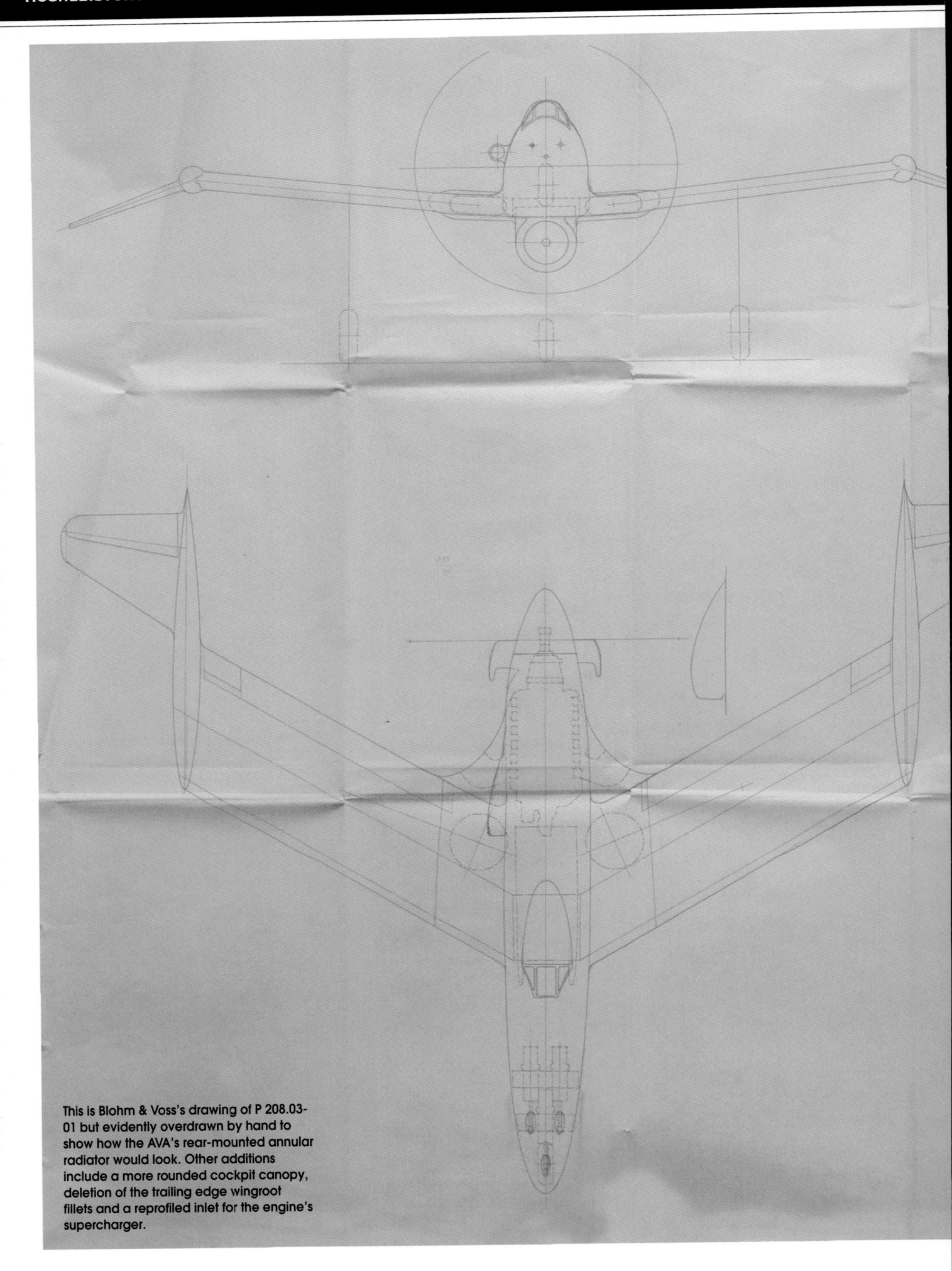

Hochleistungs-Otto-Jäger

This is Blohm & Voss's drawing of P 208.03-01 but evidently overdrawn by hand to show how the AVA's rear-mounted annular radiator would look. Other additions include a more rounded cockpit canopy, deletion of the trailing edge wingroot fillets and a reprofiled inlet for the engine's supercharger.

Flügelfläche F=19 m²

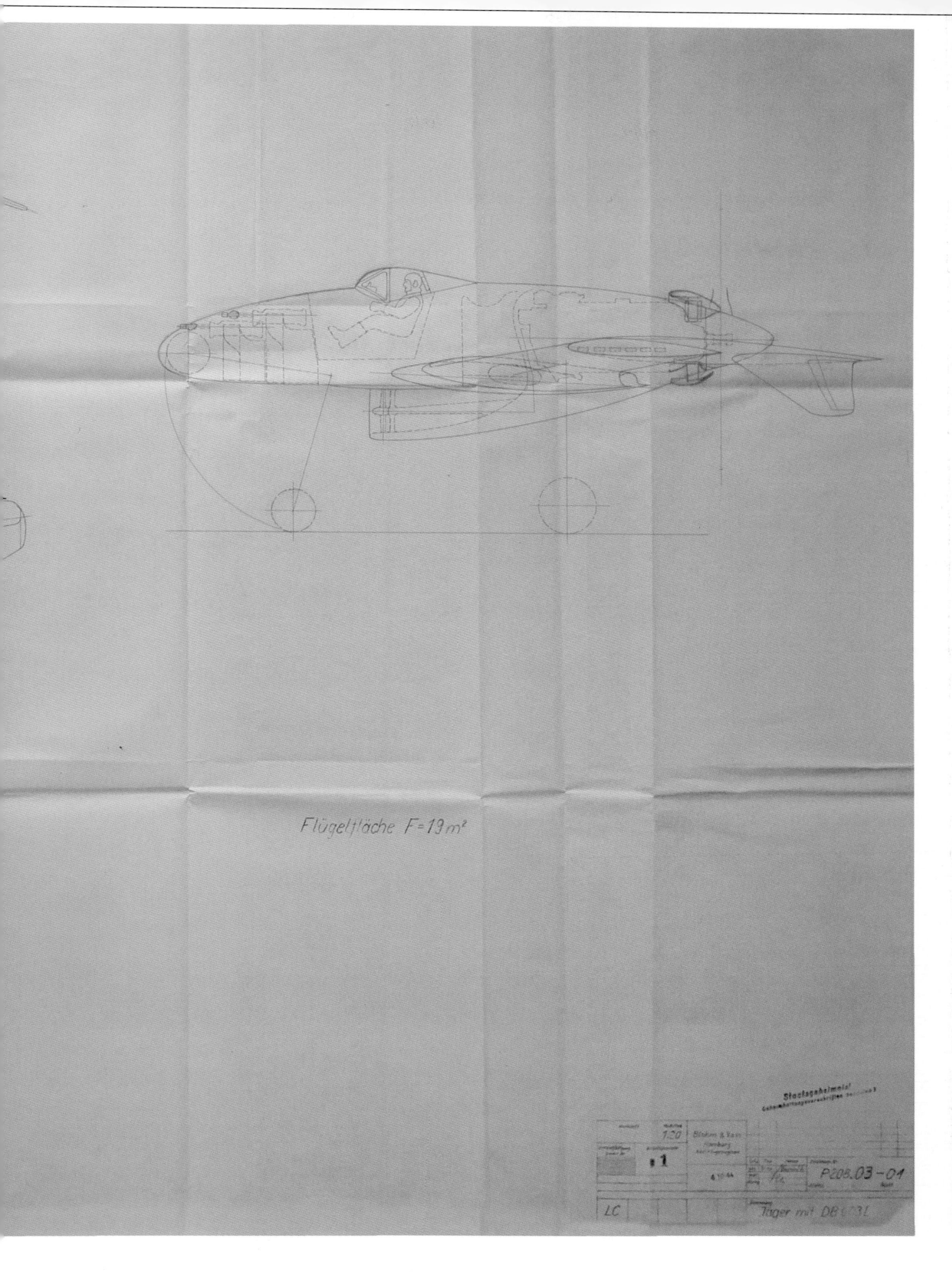

P208.03-01

Secret Projects of the Luftwaffe 115

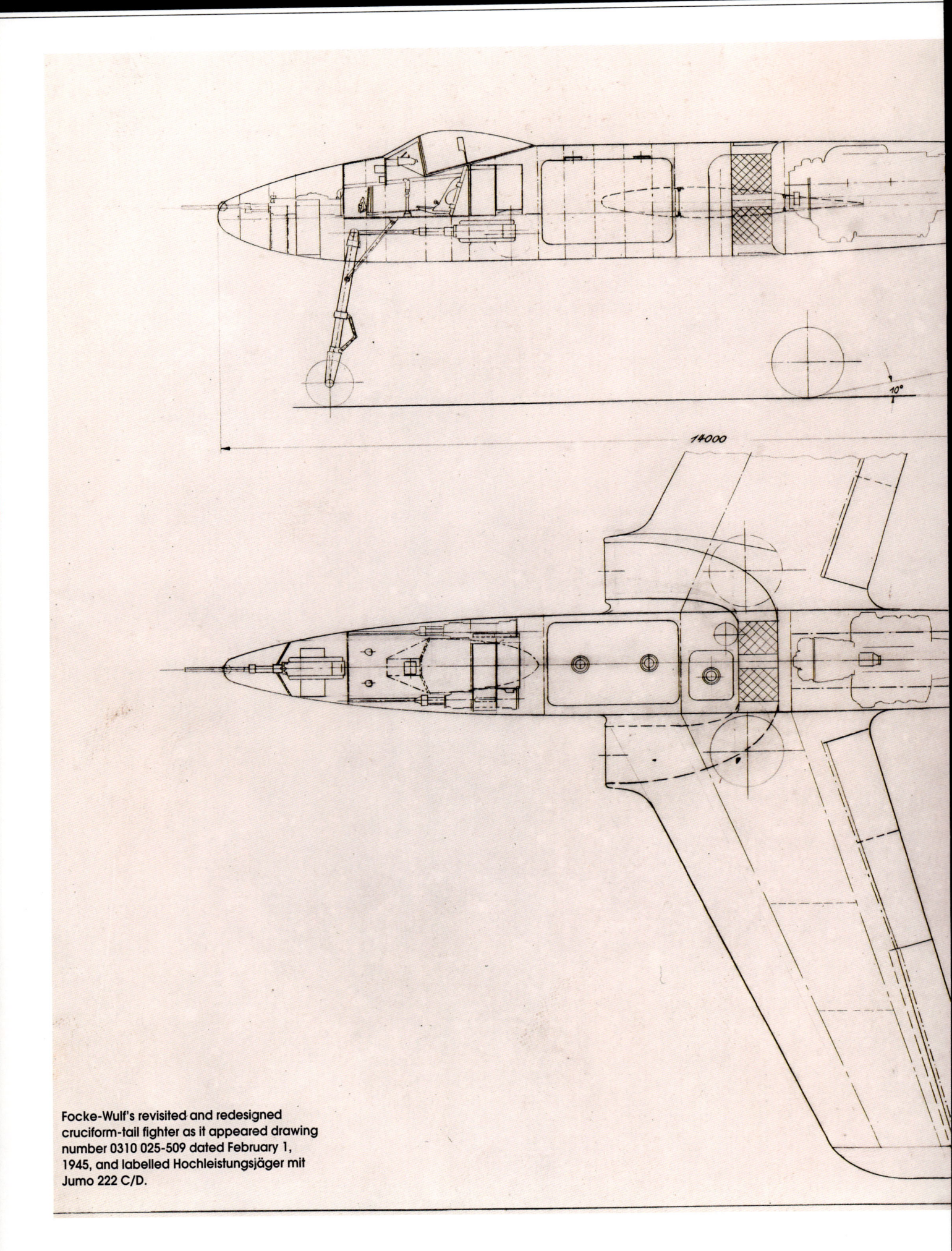

HOCHLEISTUNGS-OTTO-JÄGER

Focke-Wulf's revisited and redesigned cruciform-tail fighter as it appeared drawing number 0310 025-509 dated February 1, 1945, and labelled Hochleistungsjäger mit Jumo 222 C/D.

Secret Projects of the Luftwaffe 117

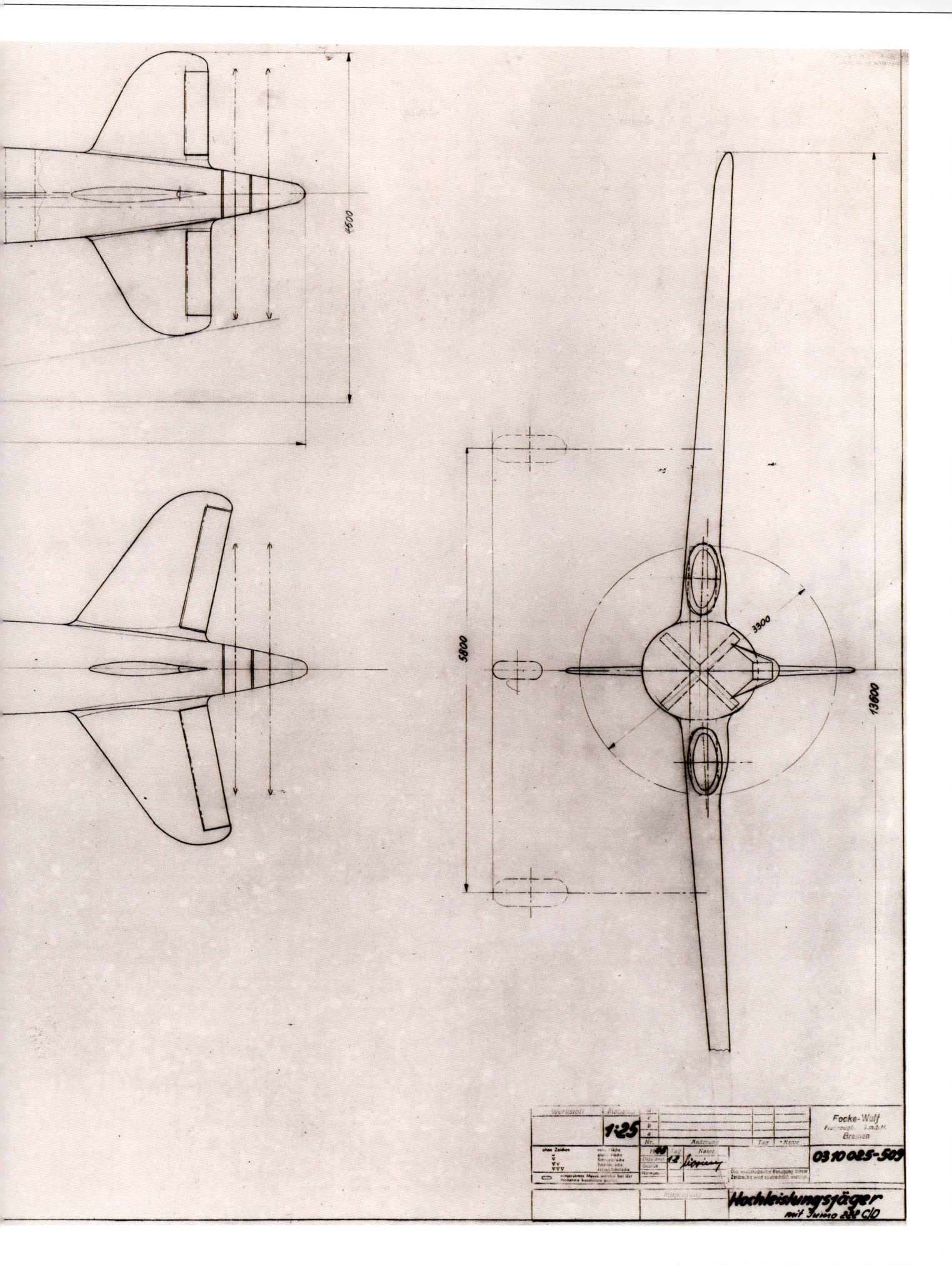

One final caveat was included at the bottom of the sheet: "The development requirements listed above are only to be regarded as a guide. The new tactical-technical knowledge that come up during the development period must be continuously checked and taken into account for its applicability to the use of these aircraft."

Then, on January 24, 1945, the Air Ministry sent Focke-Wulf a telex to say that, "re: Hochleistungs-Otto-Jäger, new demands from the General Staff significantly increase the military load, contrary to the previous announcement. In the opinion of the Technical Office airframes division, meeting these requirements is not possible with the DB 603 or Jumo 213 in their final stage – 2,800hp. You are therefore asked to investigate whether a high-performance piston engine fighter with two 213 or 603 engines or with a Jumo 222 in the second performance level – 3,500 to 4,000hp – meets the requirements. The following military load is to be provided: at least three hours of flight time with maximum permissible continuous power at 8-10km altitude without the use of external tanks, three MK 103s with 150 shots each, bad weather landing, bad weather fighting with extensive automation of bad weather landing, i.e. electronics set weighing approx. 100-120kg, top speed at 10km altitude 800-850km/h, armour front and rear against 20mm, pressure-tight cabin, take-off and landing on unprepared strips, nosewheel, carrying external loads of at least 500kg. We ask you to submit the results of the investigations as soon as possible."

It was as though the wealth of clear and obvious reasons why the Jumo 222 had to be cancelled, presented by Schilo at the December 19-20 meeting, suddenly no longer mattered. There was no capacity to build it, and even if there had been it offered no tangible benefits in the short term; even its utility in the longer term was doubtful. Yet against all reason… the Jumo 222 was back and once again being specified for the Hochleistungs-Otto-Jäger programme.

FOCKE-WULF'S LAST DESIGNS

While much of the requirement appears to be the same, the switch from MK 108s and/or MG 213s to MK 103s was certainly new. And each MK 103 weighed 141kg compared to 58kg per MK 108 or 96kg per MG 213.

Focke-Wulf consequently came up with yet another Hochleistungs-Otto-Jäger design, which appeared in drawing number 0310 025-509 dated February 1, 1945, and labelled Hochleistungsjäger mit Jumo 222 C/D. This appears to have been the first new numbered entry to the sequence since October 2, 1944 – a gap of four months. The last known full aircraft design had been depicted in 0310 025-506, Jäger mit Jumo 222 E-F, the previous last-in-line of the cruciform-tail fighter series.

The new design was similar in many respects to its predecessor but measured 14m from end to end, compared to 13.7m for the 1944 variant. Wingspan had also increased, from 12.8m to 13.6m. Mainwheel track was slightly broadened from 5.7m to 5.8m and there were a host of detail changes besides the switch to three MK 103s as armament. The most significant of these concerned the radiator. Previously, air had entered via lozenge-shaped inlets set flush within the wing roots before being funnelled into the fuselage to meet the radiator face, which was set pointing straight ahead towards the cockpit.

Now air entered via oval-shaped inlets set forward of the wing leading edge at the root. It was then funnelled through the wings to meet two radiators set sideways on. This necessitated the undercarriage mainwheels being moved further out into the wings but it also freed up a huge amount of space within the fuselage – allowing the main fuel tank to be significantly increased in size.

A second new design, Hochleistungsjäger mit As 413, followed on February 28, 1945, appearing in drawing number 0310 025-512. Given that the engine was somewhat larger than the Jumo 222, the aircraft's dimensions had had to be appropriately enlarged. Overall length increased to 15.35m and wingspan rose to 15.2m. Mainwheel track remained the same at 5.8m but the diameter of the contra-rotating props had risen from 3.3m to 3.5m.

Squeezing the enormous As 413 into the basic cruciform-tail fighter layout posed other problems too. The engine wouldn't fit perfectly horizontally, so it had to be positioned at a slight angle – which meant that the propellers could not be entirely vertical. The engine's mass was such that the centre of gravity was skewed, meaning that the wings had to be moved significantly further back on the fuselage. One benefit of this was that the wingroot inlets, now circular rather than oval, were almost next to the radiator. This shortened the inlet tube, which was bifurcated so that cooling air would be pushed directly into the engine as well as to the radiators.

Both the Hochleistungsjäger mit Jumo 222 C/D and the Hochleistungsjäger mit As 413 of drawings 0310 025-509 and -512 were set to be included in a new description: Kurzbaubeschreibung Nr. 29 Hochleistungs-Otto-Jäger, dated March 9, 1945. However, the only known version of this is handwritten and whether it was ever typed up and published is unclear. It would appear, however, to have been Focke-Wulf's final description document of the war – making a piston engine fighter, rather than a jet, the company's last wartime design.

The text is somewhat difficult to decipher but it can be said that the report was divided into two sections, one for each design. The Jumo-powered variant had a calculated wing area of 36.84sqm and there were three armament options despite what was depicted in the drawing: four MK 108s, three MK 103s or four MG 213/30s. The fuselage tank could hold 1,580 litres and two more tanks in the wings could take 360 litres each – getting the endurance time up to the requisite three hours. Take-off weight was around 8,250kg.

The Argus-powered variant had a wing area of 41.84sqm and an armament of either four MK 108s, three MK 103s or four MG 151/30s. The fuselage tank could hold 1,900 litres while the wing tanks could hold 600 litres each. Take-off weight was roughly 10,500kg.

B&V AND DORNIER

It would appear the Dornier's Do P 247/6 design was an attempt to meet the January 1945 requirement for a Hochleistungs-Otto-Jäger. The Jumo 213 J engine and armament of three MK 108s would certainly seem to support this idea. Again, however, little more is known about the design and there is no evidence to suggest that Dornier attempted further variants based on the late January revision of the specification.

Blohm & Voss also appears to have done at least some further work in relation to the Hochleistungs-Otto-Jäger concept but perhaps more in connection with the radiator investigation work that had been carried out by the AVA. A drawing was created either on January 23 or February 23, 1945 (the month part of the date is unclear) which showed a radical reimagining of the P 208 as a tractor prop design.

The engine had been shifted to the front of the short fuselage, with the cockpit being relocated towards the centre-rear. The radiator now appeared as a much more conventional chin arrangement – similar in appearance to what Blohm & Voss had in mind, at this time, for the production variant of the BV 155 high-altitude fighter, the 155 C.

No details were given as to any wing structure changes, though the overall concept of a tailless fighter with wingtip booms appeared unchanged. Similarly, there were no details of how the armament would be incorporated since the small fuselage leaves little room for anything but the engine up front.

THE HANDYMAN

In his notes on the December 19-20 EHK meeting, Arado's Walter Blume mentions a 'two-seater study' then Diesing later refers to this same enigmatic project as a Mädchen für Alles which, although it literally translates as 'girl for everything' actually means 'handyman' in German.

There are two further Hochleistungs-Otto-Jäger projects from this period which, while they fit most other requirements of the specification, are two-seaters with tandem engine installations: Dornier's Do P 252/1, from a drawing dated January 20, 1945, and described as a 'Zerstörer – zweisitzig' (two-seater heavy fighter), and a Focke-Wulf design described as a 'Höhenzerstörer'.

Dornier's design is outlined in the company's 'Baubeschreibung Nr. 1608 DoP 252/1 Dornier – Zerstörer für Tag- und Nachteinsatz mit Tandemtriebwerk 2 x DB 603 LA bezw. 2 x Jumo 213 J', dated January 27. It begins: "This design is to be viewed as a consistent further development of the pusher prop system used for the first time in the Do 335 series, with the elimination of the nose propeller and the use of counter-rotating propellers resulting in a number of advantages, which primarily affect speed.

"These advantages can be summarized in the following points: 1) Best efficiency of the propellers. 2) Perfect flow at the airframe due to: a) Elimination of the nose propeller, which eliminates the disruption to the flow pattern on the airframe caused by the propeller

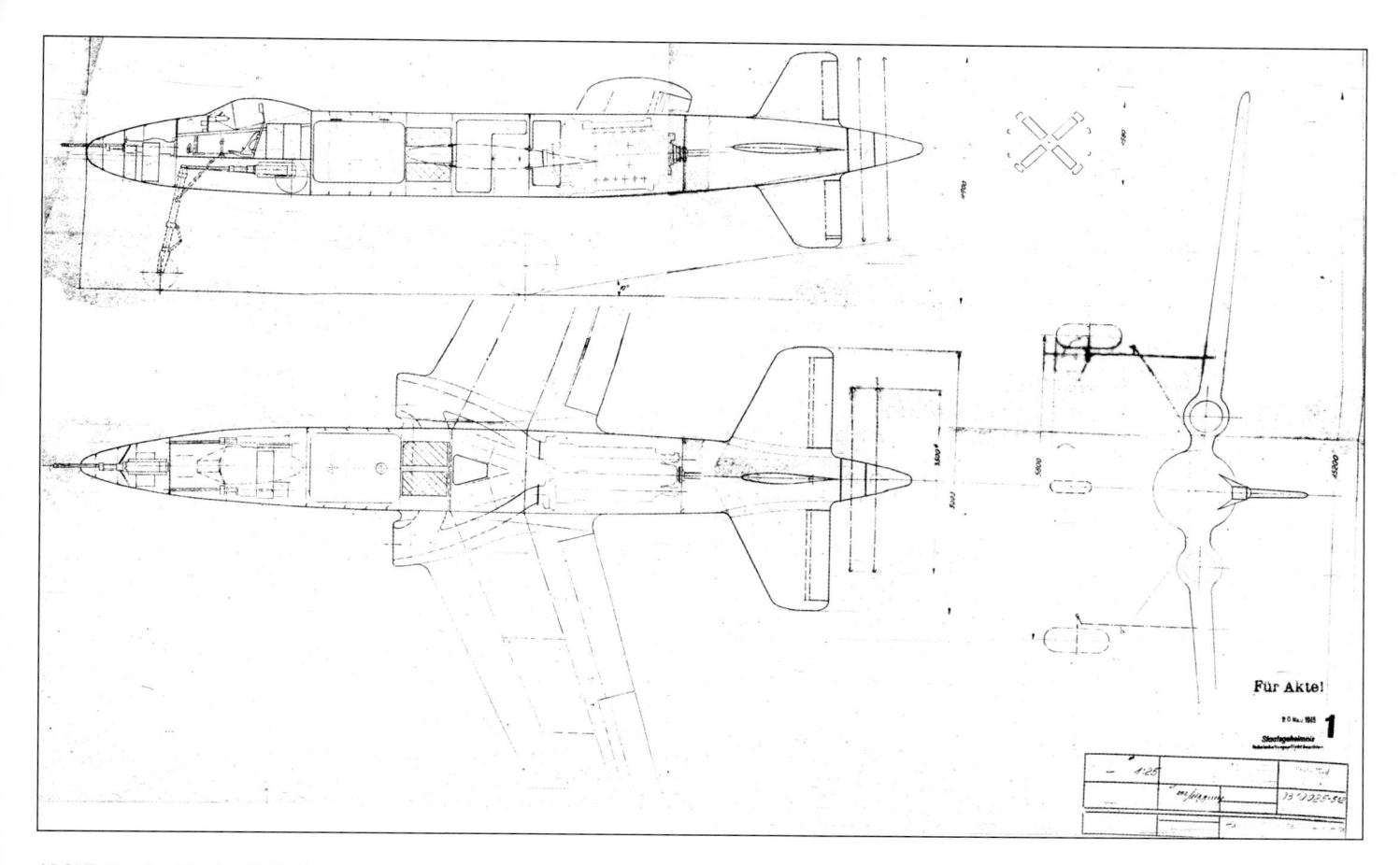

ABOVE: The final Focke-Wulf single-seater cruciform-tail fighter design was labelled Hochleistungsjäger mit As 413, appearing in drawing number 0310 025-512 of February 28, 1945. Note that the wings have been moved further back towards the tail.

wash. b) Elimination of the nose radiator and instead a favourable arrangement of the block radiator at the root of the wing leading edge.

"This achieves the highest level of aerodynamic quality. The maximum speed of 900km/h, which hardly seems credible for aircraft with piston engines, is proven by precise mathematical documents. In addition, the absolute aerodynamic optimum would be achieved by sweeping the wing (35 degrees) and the tail unit backwards, as well as using swept propellers (50 degrees), whereby the maximum speed would be 950km/h.

"The tandem arrangement of the engines also results in special advantages in terms of space, namely: 1) Best visibility for the crew, especially the pilot. 2) Interchangeable weapon nose, also suitable for installing night fighter equipment. 3) Best protection of the radiator blocks against incoming fire. The equipment in this description is intended for use in the fair weather heavy fighter. With its two-man crew, this model is also ideal as a night hunter or bad weather heavy fighter."

The Do P 252/1 measured 15.2m long, with a wingspan of 16.4m and wing area of 43sqm. It could be powered by either tandem DB 603 LAs or Jumo 213 Js and could carry could carry a payload of two 250kg bombs if desired – one under each wing. There were three armament options: three MK 108s in the nose and two MG 213s in the fuselage, or two MG 213s in the nose and two more in the fuselage, or three MK 108s in the nose and two more in the fuselage.

Focke-Wulf's two-seater Höhenzerstörer took the cruciform-tail fighter concept to its limit by extending the fuselage to 18.83m and the wingspan to 16.2m – resulting in the company's largest ever piston engine fighter design. The triangular wings and low-set tailplanes were more sharply swept than those of the other Hochleistungs-Otto-Jäger designs, the fins had a different profile and the radiator system most closely aped that of the cruciform-tail fighter design from drawing 0310 025-506, with flush leading edge inlets.

Unlike the other designs, the near-cylindrical fuselage cross section was abandoned in favour of a broader, flatter shape akin to that of the Messerschmitt Me 262 – presumably for the same reason of encompassing the retracted undercarriage

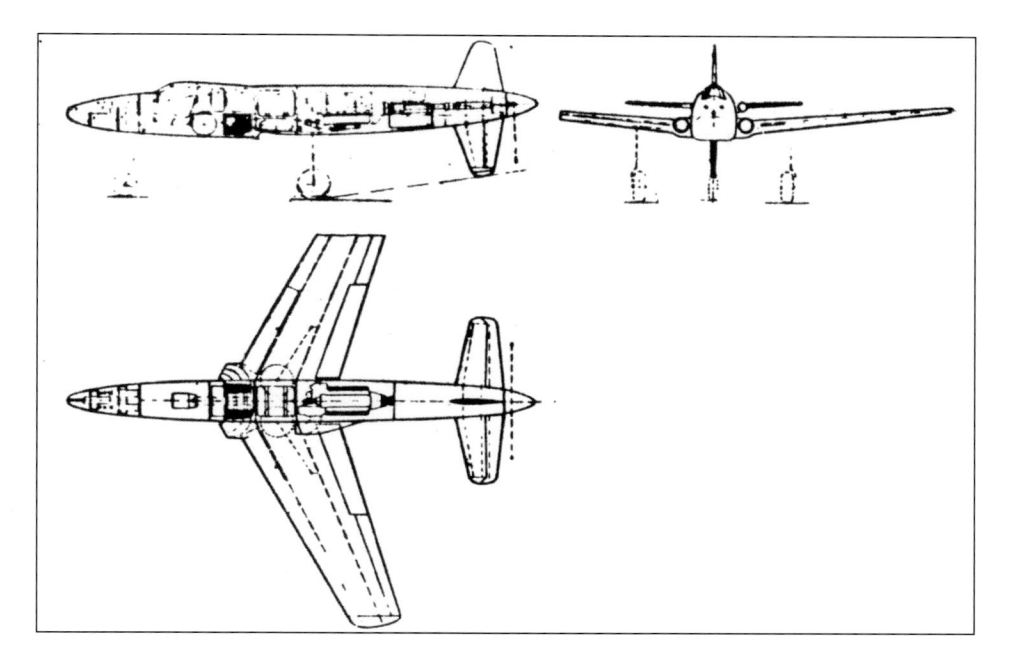

RIGHT: Little is known for certain about the background of Dornier's Do P 247/6-01 but it would have met the January 1945 specification for a Hochleistungs-Otto-Jäger.

Secret Projects of the Luftwaffe 119

HOCHLEISTUNGS-OTTO-JÄGER

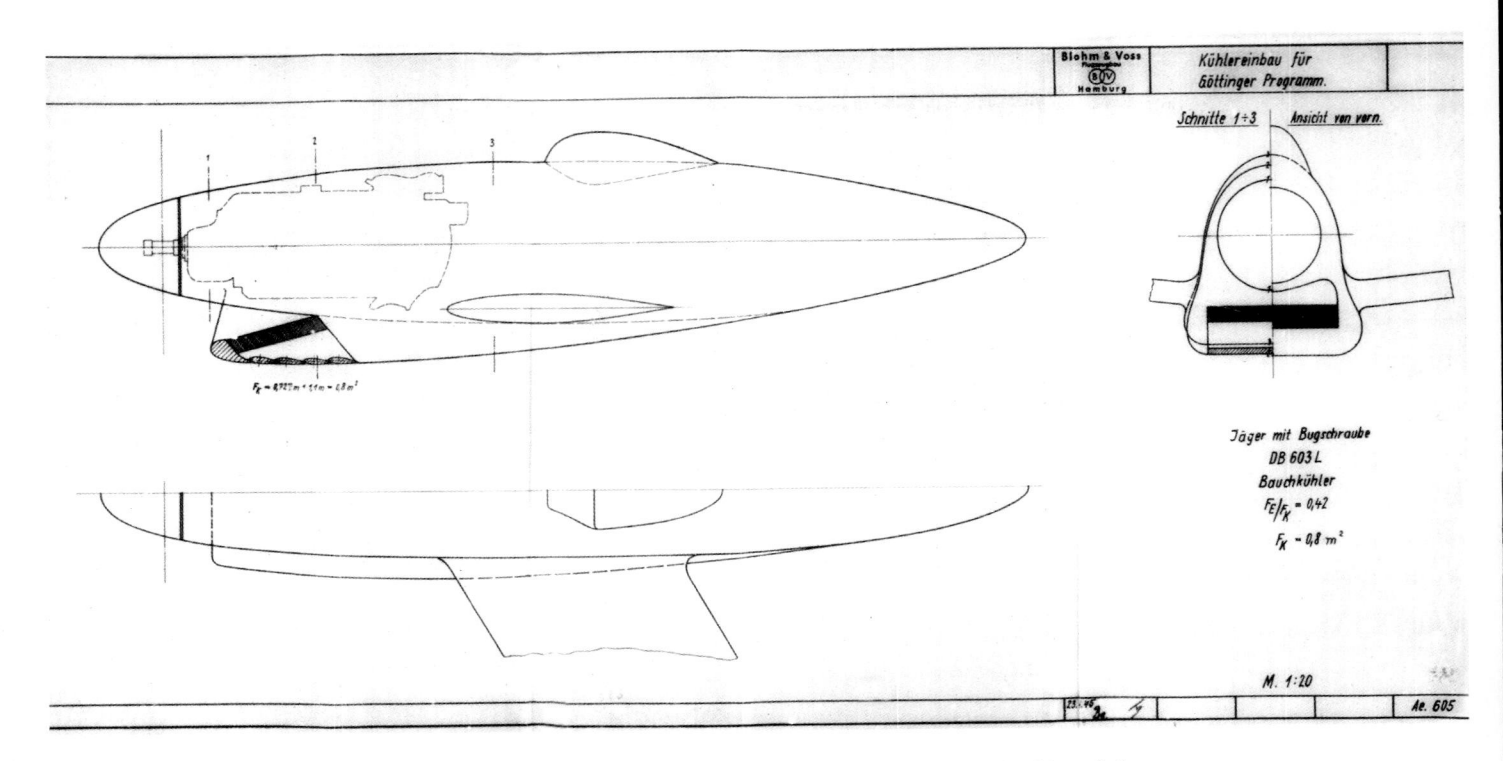

ABOVE: Blohm & Voss's last redesign of the P 208 from 1945 – featuring a tractor prop with BV 155 C-style chin radiator.

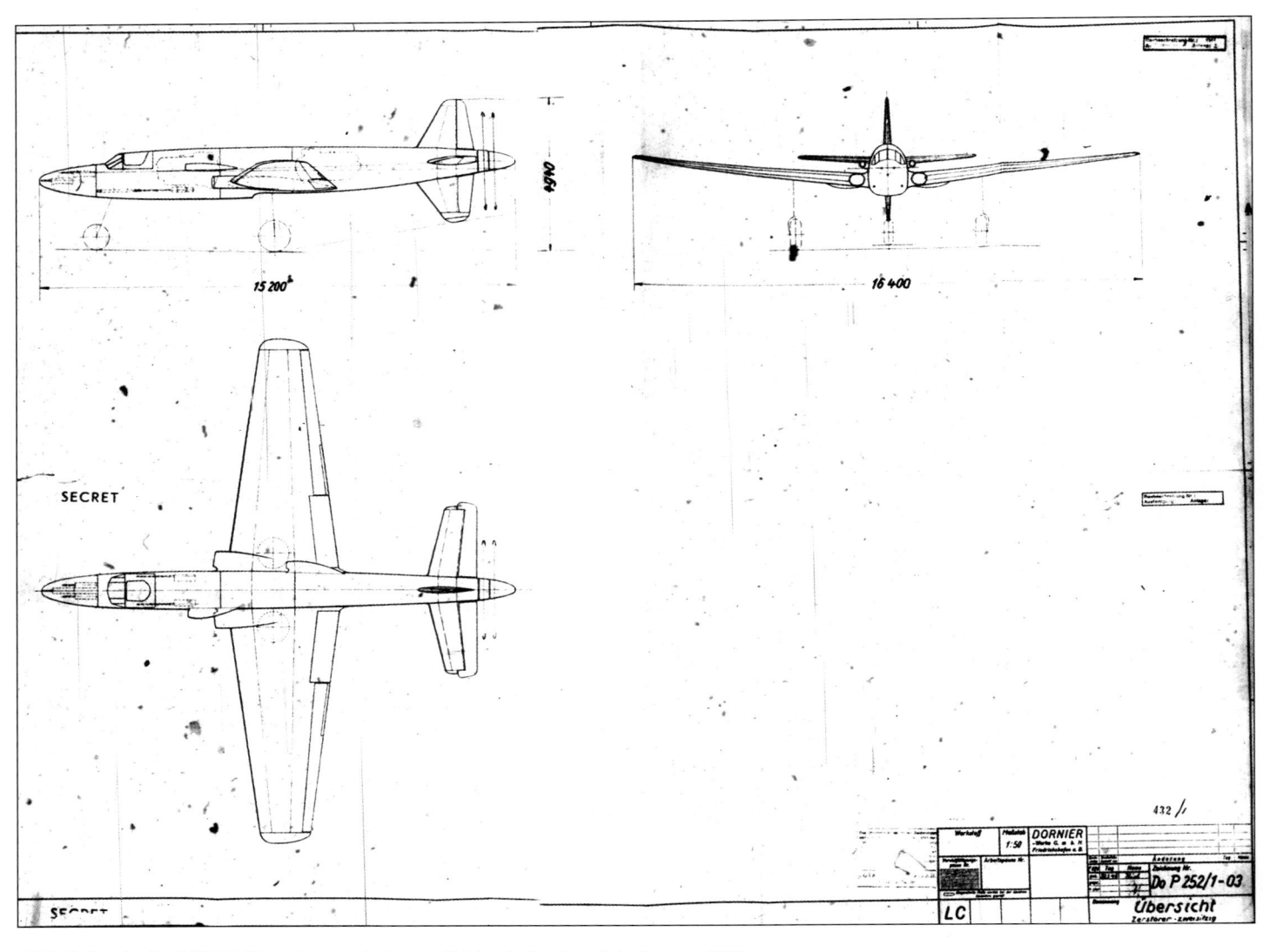

ABOVE: Dornier Do P 252/1-03 – a two-seater heavy fighter design from late January 1945.

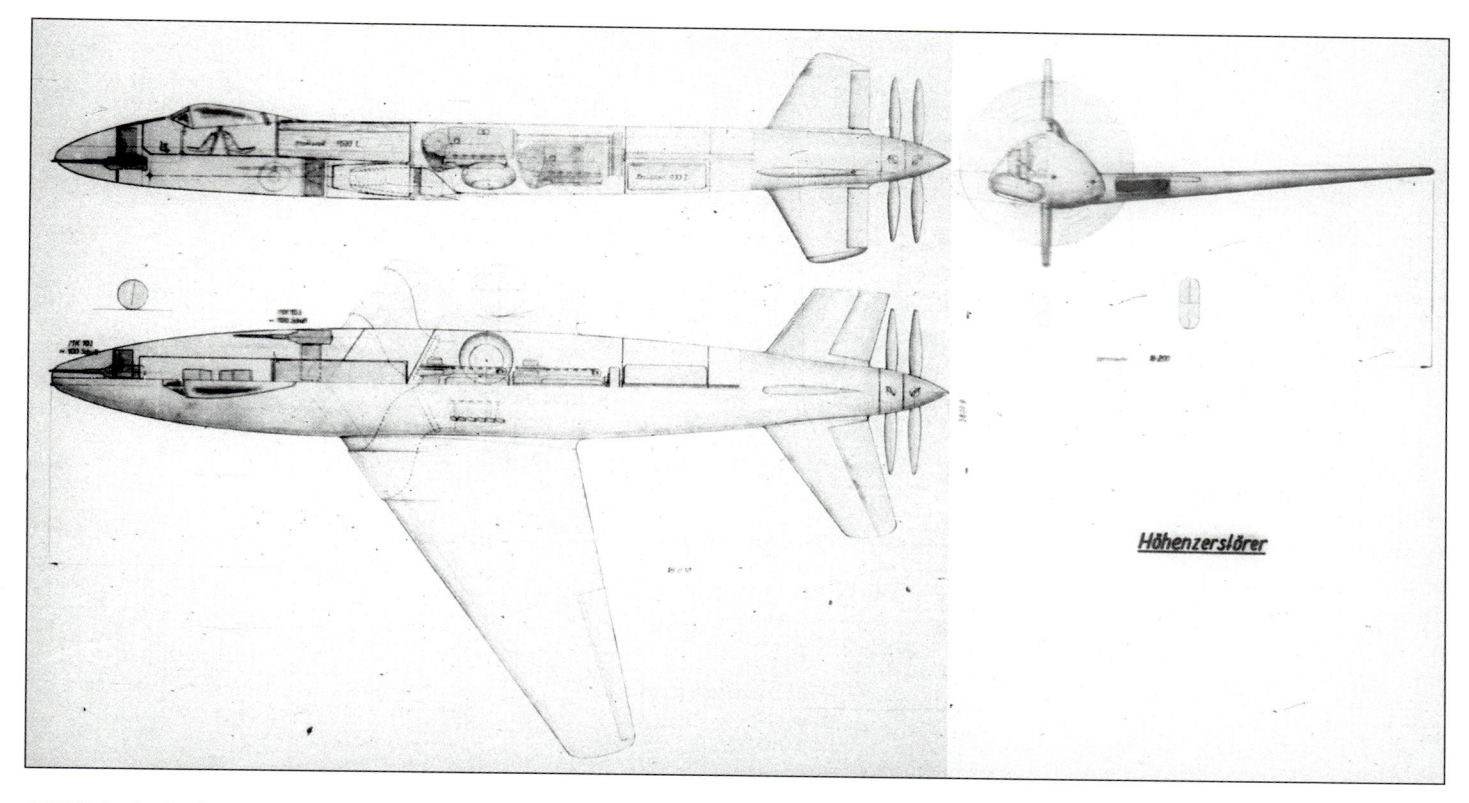

ABOVE: Focke-Wulf two-seater heavy fighter design – undated but probably from January 1945.

mainwheels without leaving a bulge. Armament was three MK 108s and the second crewman was seated back-to-back with the pilot. Overall height is not given as a dimension on the one known drawing of this design but it was extremely tall and some sort of boarding ramp/ladder would presumably have been required to get the crew onto and off the aircraft.

CONCLUSION

With hindsight it is clear that the Hochleistungs-Otto-Jäger competition was doomed from the very beginning. Perhaps, in fact, it was clear even at the time. The whole contest may well have been little more than a political tool whose real purpose was never the design and eventual construction of a pusher-prop piston engine fighter for the Luftwaffe.

Indeed, the Jumo 222 and the Jumo 213-based As 413 never looked like particularly viable prospects for production given Germany's war situation. BMW had been made to cancel its heavyweight engines, the 802 and 803, since there was no capacity to develop them and Junkers being given permission to keep the 222 project going albeit on the back burner would seem to suggest political influence. Certainly, there were plenty of high-ranking individuals who appear to have had some sort of financial or business interest in Junkers – far more than was the case with BMW.

Of the three airframe manufacturers that bothered to respond to the requirement in the first place, Focke-Wulf evidently did so because being under the Air Ministry's thumb it could hardly say 'no'. As soon as the opportunity to shift focus away from it arose, the company swiftly did so – only returning to it when compelled to do so. Dornier appears to have been entirely half-hearted in its involvement, perhaps seeing it as an unwanted distraction from the Do 335, much as Focke-Wulf no doubt did with its Ta 152.

Only Blohm & Voss seems to have been earnest in its efforts to design the Luftwaffe's new Hochleistungs-Otto-Jäger. Chief designer Richard Vogt was single-minded, however, in his determination to push radical design concepts that no decision-maker in his right mind could ever authorise for mass production. It must have been obvious to everyone, except perhaps to Vogt himself, that the P 208 was never going to see service with the Luftwaffe.

So why was the Hochleistungs-Otto-Jäger competition launched and how did it survive right up to the end of the war? The most likely answer appears to have been the influence of Roluf Lucht. Lucht and his boss Milch appear to have held a disdain for Willy Messerschmitt which bordered on the pathological. Lucht had been sent to dog Messerschmitt's footsteps as the unwanted manager of his Regensburg plant and in August 1944 he was once again well positioned, presumably at Milch's recommendation, to cause Messerschmitt discomfort.

As described earlier, Messerschmitt had by this time become a true believer in jet engines as the future of fighter aircraft – which he had not been just a year earlier. He saw absolutely no point in wasting further resources on developing entirely new piston engine aircraft types. And he was in the process of being made head of the special commission for day fighters, which gave him oversight of and responsibility for all day fighter development programmes.

Lucht's relentless insistence that Hochleistungs-Otto-Jäger would continue despite all objections both technical and tactical forced Messerschmitt into the awkward position of having to oversee the progress of something to which he was diametrically opposed. There was a genuine case to be made that jet aircraft were not, at that time, capable of covering every mission that the Luftwaffe might require but there were existing airframes with years of development progress behind them which could cover those missions. The decision to keep going with Hochleistungs-Otto-Jäger, particularly given the situation faced by Germany in January 1945, makes absolutely no sense except as a means of needling Willy Messerschmitt – though there were those within the Luftwaffe High Command who seem to have thought it was a genuinely good idea.

It might seem far-fetched to suggest that precious resources were being squandered on a personal vendetta at the highest level of the Nazi leadership at such a desperate time for the German war effort – but perhaps Lucht and his allies believed that getting one over on Messerschmitt was something at least that could be accomplished when everything else was failing and falling apart.

Messerschmitt's irritation, from this direction at least, came to an abrupt end on April 10, 1945, when Lucht's luck finally ran out. He was a passenger in a Fieseler Fi 156 Storch being flown by his personal pilot, Gefreiter Kurt Schnittke, when they were shot down by American anti-aircraft fire in the area of Vienenburg, near Goslar, Lower Saxony, Germany. Lucht was killed in the ensuing crash, Schnittke surviving with severe burns. ●

Late risers

Heinkel Ringflügel-Projekte

When it comes to radical German WW2 'secret projects' there can be few more outlandish than Heinkel's vertical take-off and landing (VTOL) fighters: the piston engine Lerche I, II and III plus the turboprop-powered Wespe.

The gas dynamics department of Focke-Wulf, led by Dr Otto Ernst Pabst, began studying ramjets during 1941 and by February 1944 work had commenced on designs for fighter aircraft powered by these revolutionary new engines.

One avenue of development resulted in a design known as the Strahlrohrjäger, a somewhat strange-looking but otherwise relatively conventional fighter with a pair of ramjets mounted on its thick tailplanes. The other avenue of development resulted in the Triebflügeljäger. This aircraft was designed to sit vertically on the ground, resting on four 380x150mm outrigger wheels on the ends of its cruciform tailfins with a single 780x260mm wheel housed within a fairing on the tip of the tail itself – creating five points of contact with the ground.

At the front, or top, of the 9.35m long fuselage was a pressurised single-seater cockpit, with the aircraft's four cannon positioned around the pilot – two on either side. When the aircraft was on the ground, the pilot would be lying on his back with his legs in the air above him. Behind, or below, the cockpit was a ring section with three wings attached to it, each tipped with a combination ramjet and 300kg thrust solid fuel Walter starter rocket.

For take-off, the rockets would be fired to get the wings spinning around like the blades of a helicopter. The ramjets would then be fired up at the appropriate speed and the aircraft would rise vertically into the air. At a certain altitude, the aircraft would transition from vertical to horizontal flight – with the pilot now in the normal flying position. When the time came to land, the aircraft's tail would be dropped until the aircraft was once again vertical and the pilot would have to guide the aircraft to the ground while, again, lying on his back.

Early drawings of this design are dated July 1944 and a preliminary description of the proposed aircraft and its systems was produced on September 15, 1944. The project continued for at least another couple of weeks after that, with the last known drawing being made on October 4, 1944. After that, it appears to have been abandoned.

RIGHT: Focke-Wulf's Triebflügeljäger as it appeared in drawing 310 0240-02, dated July 16, 1944 – some three months prior to the start of Heinkel's work on Ringflügel-Projekte.

Meanwhile, over at Heinkel, engineer Kurt Reiniger was busy working on a report about radiator installations for advanced piston engine aircraft – which was published on October 25, 1944 (see the Hochleistungs-Otto-Jäger chapter of this publication). With this completed, Reiniger appears to have been at a loose end and so, along with his colleague Gerhard Schulz, he began work on a new vertical take-off aircraft design project apparently inspired by the Focke-Wulf Triebflügeljäger.

In a letter to historian Steve Coates dated November 7, 1980, Reiniger wrote: "I did the VTOL work at Heinkel, where I joined the project office in 1939 after a few years in the aerodynamic research institute in Göttingen. They were studies motivated by the vulnerability of normal takeoff aircraft in the last years of the war. The projects weren't ready for production yet, and the RLM [German Air Ministry] wasn't informed about it either. The work had only started half a year before the end of the war."

Coates had asked Reiniger about the Triebflügeljäger directly and he responded: "I cannot give you any details about the Focke-Wulf projects you inquired about. I recommend that you contact Dr Otto E. Pabst, who was with Focke-Wulf during the war and is about to bring out a comprehensive book on short and vertical take-off aircraft."

Reiniger noted that his full report on what he called the Ringflügel-Projekte or Annular Wing Projects had run to 70 pages and included "four versions of the 'Lerche'

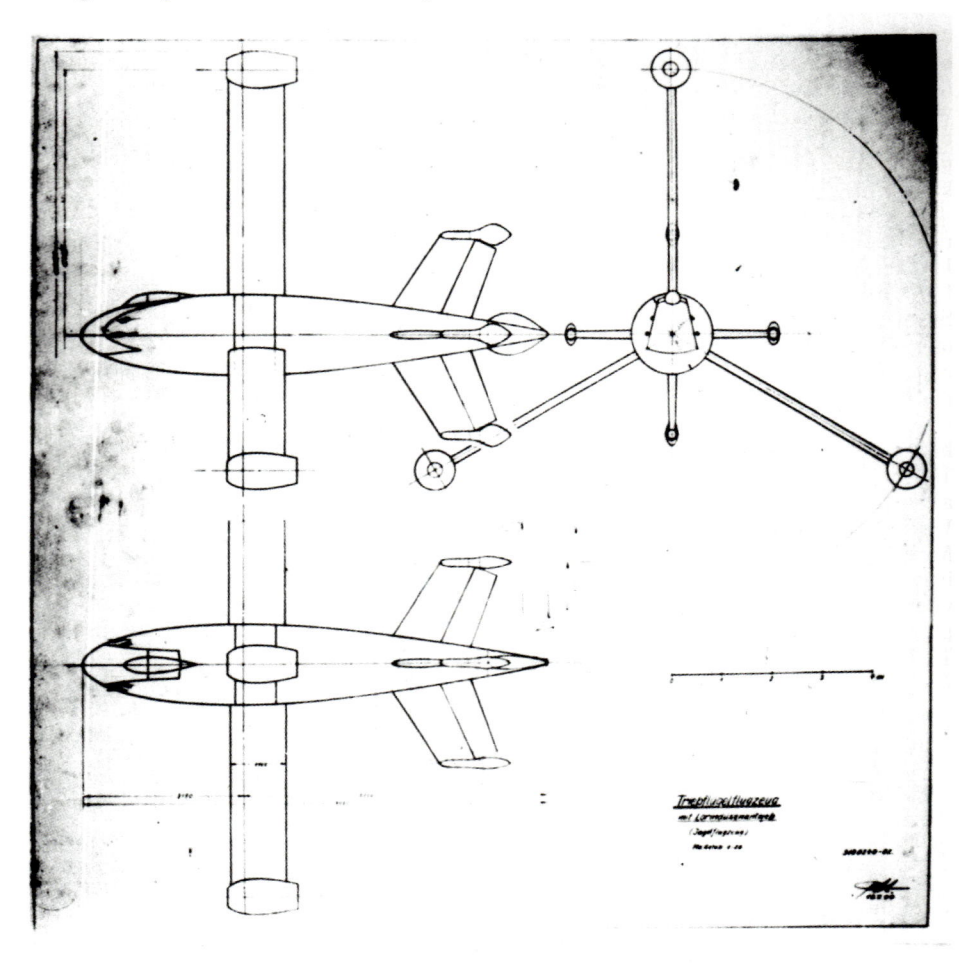

(with Otto engines) and one version of the 'Wespe' with PTL (propeller turbine jet engine)". Lerche means 'Lark' and 'Wespe', unsurprisingly, means 'Wasp'.

Coates also wrote to Schulz, who replied in English on July 7, 1981, as follows: "It is true that I made the performance calculations of the projects in 1944/45. I joined the Heinkel company in 1939 and worked there during the whole wartime as a project and wind tunnel engineer. I was engaged in most Heinkel projects e.g. He 280, He 177, He 219, He 162 and others.

"In 1944/45 the Heinkel crew was very busy in VTOL designing, as you know from Mr Reiniger. For my feelings these things were sometimes a bit too much 'future-minded' (new engines, rockets, jets) and the VTOL technique and its adherent marginal problems). So we tried whether it could be possible to do the VTOL techniques with well-known engines too, preferably constructed for take-off thrust.

"Measurements directly aimed at the special projects were not always available. The performance calculations were based on annular wing theory (which appeared then quite recently), on cooling systems inlet measurements, jet engine inlet measurements and a modified airscrew theory, where the induced drag of the blades had been reduced because of the annular wing shroud covering the blade tips (the so-called Kramer-Driggs one-cross section method). All these components had been combined more or less successfully under time pressure.

"The results showed that a vertical take-off of the vertically placed aircraft was possible, but with the engines available at that time, the transition flight into the wing-supported state was still a problem. Therefore we planned to let the aircraft rise sufficiently high, then turning down and by a short nose-dive getting speed enough for the wing-supported phase."

Coates queried several points of Schultz's response and asked directly whether the Heinkel Annular Wing Projects had been a follow-on from Focke-Wulf's Triebflügeljäger. Schultz replied, rather more curtly this time, on September 19, 1981: "There were indeed other groups at Heinkel designing VTOL projects: The project 'Julia' (a tailsitter) which you know probably. But there is hardly a person of that staff still alive. The project did not get ready. 2. I was not aware of the Triebflügel projects at Focke-Wulf. 3. The tunnel [ducted] propellers (= Mantelschrauben) have been measured in a wind tunnel, but I do not remember in which one. The theory of the tunnel [ducted] propellers was then rather well developed. "4. The VTOL work was initiated by ourselves (i.e. Mr Reiniger and me) and after a short while supported by our chief, Mr Siegfried Günter. He died in 1969. I suppose that I could hardly give you more information."

REINIGER'S REPORT
The full 70-page report on Heinkel's Ringflügel-Projekte, Proposals for Increasing the Speed of Piston Engine Fighters by Using a Propeller Shroud as a Wing With Vertical Take-Off, is currently unavailable. However, a few extracts from it have certainly survived. The two-page summary, signed by Reiniger and dated March 8, 1945, stated: "The present report proposes using a propeller shroud as a wing at the same time and thus, in addition to achieving a considerable reduction in the surface area of ducted propeller aircraft, vertical take-off and vertical landing.

"The resulting airframe structure deviates greatly from that of current fixed-wing aircraft, so that an exact determination of weight and centre of gravity was necessary and certain aerodynamic assumptions were used as a basis, the experimental confirmation of which is still required. The advantages and difficulties as well as the possible applications and flight performance of the proposed arrangement are examined on the basis of four examples:

Lerche I: light fighter with 1 x DB 603 E (take-off weight ~3.5t) or with 1 x DB 603 N (take-off weight ~3.7t)
Lerche II: attack aircraft with 2 x DB 605 D (take-off weight ~5.6t)
Lerche III: heavy fighter (night fighter) with 2 x DB 603 N (take-off weight ~7.4t)
Wespe: light fighter with PTL-021 (take-off weight ~3.7t)

"For each design, the requirements on which the performance calculation is based, as well as design proposals, are reproduced and a type sheet, data sheet and weight plan are attached.

"With vertical take-off and vertical landing, the landing gear can be dispensed with and the wing loading can be increased beyond the limits usually accepted for take-off and landing. This results in a compact construction of the airframe combined with a low airframe weight, a primary requirement for vertical take-off. In accordance with the high power-to-weight ratio (< 1.5kg/hp), exceptionally good climbing performance and good top speeds are the result.

"The limitation of flight times to 45 minutes to one hour including combat seems justified given the intended purpose and the possibilities of vertical take-off and landing. In general, a sensible limitation of the area of application to intercepter-like use, with a short flight time, is the prerequisite for a promising realisation of the configuration. In addition to good flight performance, the decisive advantage lies in the aircraft being able to operate independent of airfields and terrain (mountain and ship use)."

ENTWURF A-B: LERCHE I
The first of the Ringflügel-Projekte was designated Lerche I and came in two very similar forms both represented in the same drawing, which is dated February 24, 1945. The Entwurf A: Lerche I light fighter with DB 603 E was intended for "deployment close to the ground up to full pressure altitude of ~6.5km as a ground-attack aircraft to support ground troops (infantry fighters)". The engine's output on startup was 2,400hp with MW50.

The Entwurf B: Lerche I light fighter with DB 603 N was intended for "use as a day fighter up to a full pressure altitude of ~11.5km". The DB 603 N was expected to provide an output of 2,800hp with MW50. Within the fuselage there was a tank able to hold 400kg of fuel plus a second one for 200kg of oil.

Apart from their engines, the designs were otherwise identical. Overall length was 7.15m, fuselage diameter was 1.2m and the diameter of its single six-bladed propeller was 3.2m. The propeller shroud had a chord of 1.2m. It was attached to the fuselage by a trio of triangular 'fin' structures which protruded slightly beyond its rim, each of which had a control surface on its trailing edge.

Armament consisted of two MK 108 cannon, one either side of the pilot who lay on his chest (or stood upright, when on the ground) in the nose. His 'canopy' consisted of a transparent dome which formed the forward tip of the aircraft. The narrow fuselage meant bulged fairings were required on either side of the exterior in order to accommodate the gun bays. The aircraft had three tail fins and the landing gear consisted of three oval-shaped 'feet' on shock struts on the fin tips.

ENTWURF C: 'LERCHE II'
The second design was designated Entwurf C: Lerche II. This was a dedicated ground-attack aircraft powered by two DB 605 Ds and the drawing is dated February 25, 1945. Engine power on startup was 2,000hp from each unit for a total of 4,000hp with MW50. And like Entwurf A: Lerche I light fighter with DB 603 E, the full pressure altitude was around 6.5km.

Overall length was 9.4m this time and space within the fuselage was slightly more generous thanks to a diameter of 1.25m. The propeller shroud had a 1.5m chord and had the same sort of fin structures as those featured on Lerche I. The nose/cockpit arrangement remained largely the same, with the prone/standing pilot beneath a transparent dome and flanked by an MK 108 on either side – but the extra room meant that no bulges were needed on the sides of the fuselage to accommodate the cannon.

Unlike the Entwurf A-B: Lerche I, this design had contra-rotating twin propellers. The rather ingenious internal arrangement of the fuselage had the two DB 605 Ds facing one another, which meant that they could function simply as ordinarily configured individual engines without any complicated gearing or extension shafts.

This arrangement, however, left very little room for fuel and the single tank was relegated to a position at the tail end or base of the aircraft. Its woeful capacity of just 350kg would have meant for extremely limited endurance, particularly given that this was for two engines rather than just one.

The tailfin/landing gear system was largely the same as it had been for Lerche I but with unswept rudders on the fins.

ENTWURF D: 'LERCHE III'
The final piston engine Ringflügel-Projekt was Entwurf D: Lerche III – a heavy fighter with two crew that could also be configured as a night fighter. It was to be powered by two DB 603 Ns positioned to face one another in the fuselage just as the DB 605 Ds had been

in Entwurf C: Lerche II. They were expected to deliver 2,800hp each at take-off for a total power output of 5,600hp with MW50. Full pressure altitude was 11.5km. The drawing showing this design was dated February 24, 1945 – a day earlier than the Lerche II drawing.

Overall length was 10m while each engine's six-bladed propeller had a diameter of 4.1m. The main fuselage had a diameter of 1.2m and the propeller shroud had a chord of 1.7m. Like the smaller designs, the Lerche III had a trio of triangular 'fins' attached to its propeller shroud/annular wing. But while the dorsal fin terminated just beyond the rim of the shroud, the side fins transitioned into short outer wings. These gave the aircraft an overall wingspan of 8m.

The pilot was positioned, as usual, in a prone/standing position in the nose but next to him was a regular seat for the second crewman. Rather than the familiar transparent dome, both crew looked out of a much larger teardrop canopy with an additional bulge above the second crewman to accommodate his more upright position. On the underside of the cockpit was a fairing which housed a trio of MK 108 cannon. Between the rear wall of the canopy and the engine bay was a slender fuel tank with a 500kg capacity and a second, 400kg, tank sat in the tail.

ENTWURF E: 'WESPE'
Powered by a Daimler-Benz DB 021 turboprop – essentially a Heinkel HeS 011 jet engine driving a propeller – the Entwurf E: Wespe light fighter was physically the smallest of the Ringflügel-Projekte. Appearing in a drawing dated February 25, 1945, it had an overall length of just 6.2m and the shroud of its single 2.8m diameter propeller had a chord of 1.2m. Its fuselage had a 1.25m diameter, the same as Lerche II, and like Lerche III it had short outer wings resulting in a span of 5m.

The aircraft's nose/cockpit arrangement was unique in featuring a wide intake for the turbojet, with air being funnelled to it via a tube running beneath the pilot. Surrounding this tube, behind the cockpit, was a fuel take with 550kg capacity. As with Lerche III, the pilot was positioned beneath a teardrop-shaped canopy rather than a dome and the aircraft's twin MK 108s were, as usual, either side of him.

PRACTICALITIES
In addition to the aircraft drawings and basic data, Reiniger's report of March 8, 1945, also included a diagram showing how the VTOL types were intended to take off, transition into horizontal fight, transition back into vertical flight, shave off horizontal speed, then land. It must go without saying that these manoeuvres would have been extremely tricky to master, particularly for an inexperienced pilot expected to fly solo.

While Schultz denied any knowledge of Focke-Wulf's Triebflügeljäger, Reiniger does appear to have known about it judging by his correspondence with Coates. Given the timing of the Heinkel project – just a month or so after Focke-Wulf's project had concluded and final reports on it had become available – it is difficult to imagine that Reiniger and Schultz came to work on such a similar concept without knowing about it at all.

Indeed, the Heinkel concept appears to have addressed several critical flaws in the Focke-Wulf design. Perhaps most importantly the Heinkel designs, with the exception of the Wespe, used engines which already existed and were already being mass-manufactured, albeit perhaps in lower-powered variants. Focke-Wulf's ramjets/rocket combination relied on technology which did not exist in any practical, usable form. And the stresses and strains on its rotating wings, not to mention their unique rotating characteristics were unknown quantities which would have required extensive testing.

The Heinkel designs relied on ducted fan or propeller technology which had already been extensively texted albeit for other applications far removed from its use as an annular wing for a fighter aircraft.

Providing the pilot with a standing, rather than seated, position for take-off was also a huge improvement on Focke-Wulf's seated arrangement. Standing upright, the pilot would find himself easily able to orient both himself and the aircraft during the take-off and landing phases – even if actually controlling the aircraft would still be incredibly taxing. The Triebflügeljäger's pilot, lying on his back, would likely find it near impossible to correctly position the aircraft for landing. Including a standing/prone pilot position also main sense since it was a key feature of Heinkel's rocket-propelled interceptor project, P 1077 Julia. The Heinkel Julia, as mentioned in the Coates/Schultz correspondence, was a ramp-launched vertical take-off, horizontal landing aircraft which was worked on throughout the autumn of 1944.

For all their improvements over Focke-Wulf's design, however, the Heinkel designs were lacking in at least a couple of areas. The undercarriage was a substantial downgrade from Focke-Wulf's spring-loaded fairing-covered wheels. What remains of Reiniger's report does not address the undercarriage issue at all and the drawings depict only acorn-shaped blobs on the ends of the fins. Where it would be possible to wheel the Triebflügeljäger into a take-off position, the Ringflügel-Projekte would presumably need some sort of wheeled launcher or trolley to get around on the ground. Either that, or the blobs were actually intended to house wheels but that element of the design was never fleshed out.

Secondly, as several modern day examinations of the piston engine Ringflügel-Projekte have pointed out, no provision appears to have been made for radiators. This is rather odd, given that Reiniger started work on them immediately after having completed a report specifically on the topic of radiators, yet such a key aspect of the design is simply not addressed. It has been suggested that perhaps the propeller shroud might have incorporated the engines' radiators – or an evaporative cooling system – but the drawings appear to give no hint of such an arrangement.

RINGFLÜGEL-PROJEKTE FINALE
Reiniger and Schultz's VTOL projects appear to have been started on their own initiative and without the knowledge of the German Air Ministry. The worked lasted about six months – presumably from late October to early April 1945 when Heinkel's engineering and design personnel were evacuated from their base in Vienna ahead of the advancing Soviet forces.

Reiniger told Coates in his letter: "I do not know whether the Russians found the documents left behind in Vienna during the occupation. At that time, our departure from Vienna was very sudden, without being able to take or destroy all the documents. I myself saved two copies of the report I just completed when I escaped and still have an original. More copies are left behind."

Over the years since, various low quality copies of the Ringflügel-Projekte drawings have surfaced and circulated though little of the accompanying documentation appears to have come with them – leading to much speculation and confusion as to their background and technical details. Today they remain somewhat enigmatic and perhaps will continue to do so until a complete copy of Reiniger's 70-page report, assuming it still exists, appears. •

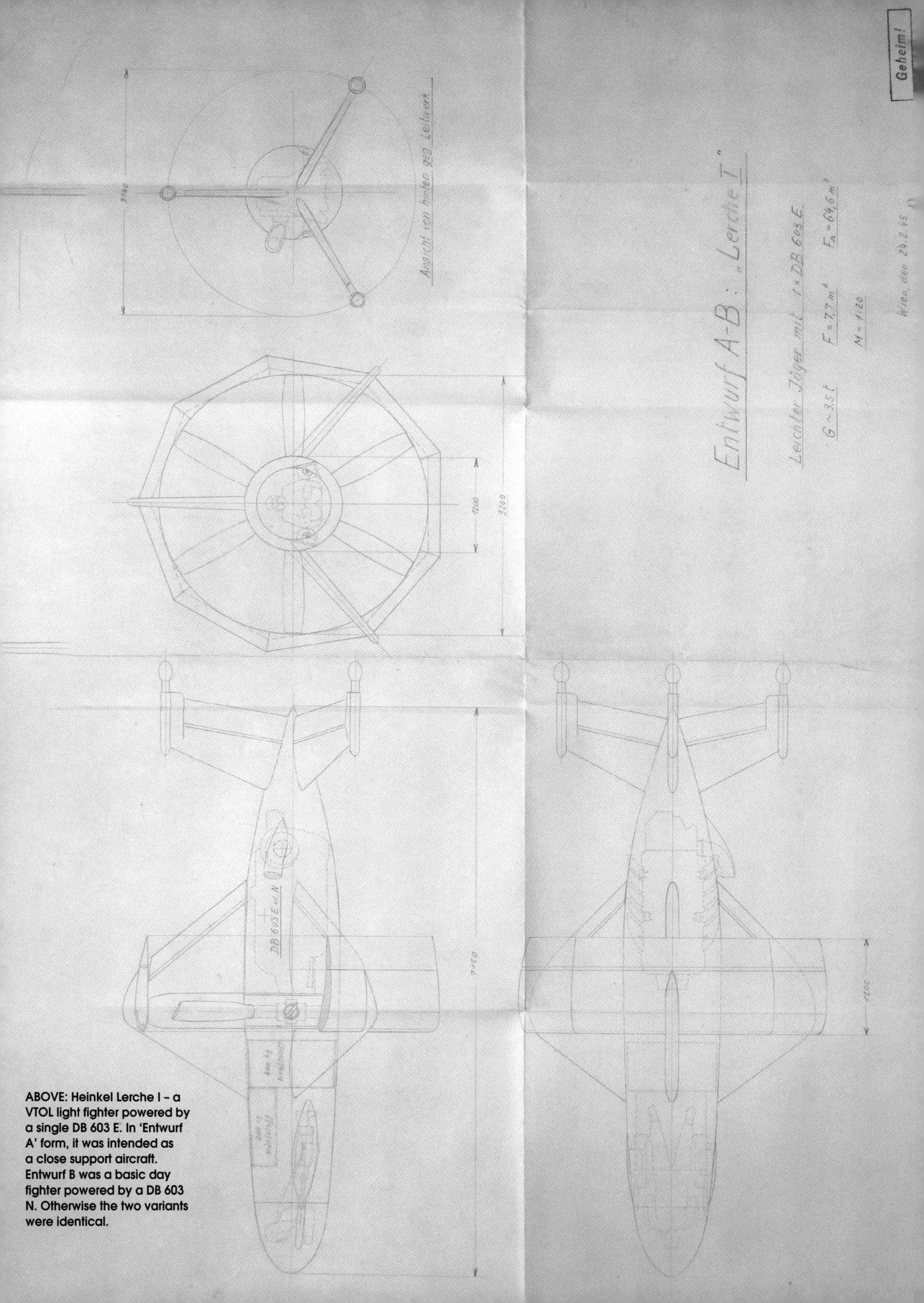

ABOVE: Heinkel Lerche I – a VTOL light fighter powered by a single DB 603 E. In 'Entwurf A' form, it was intended as a close support aircraft. Entwurf B was a basic day fighter powered by a DB 603 N. Otherwise the two variants were identical.

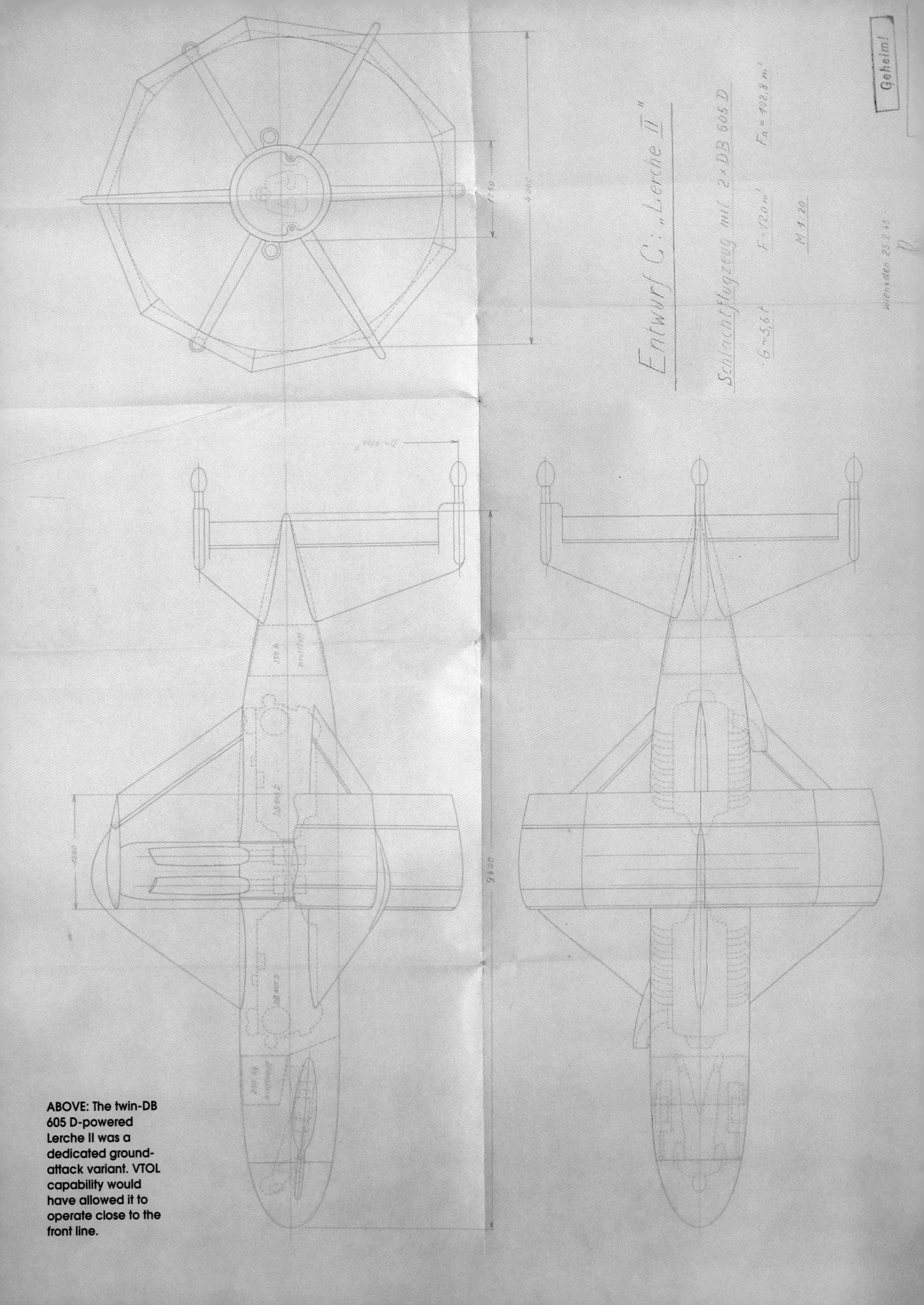

ABOVE: The twin-DB 605 D-powered Lerche II was a dedicated ground-attack variant. VTOL capability would have allowed it to operate close to the front line.

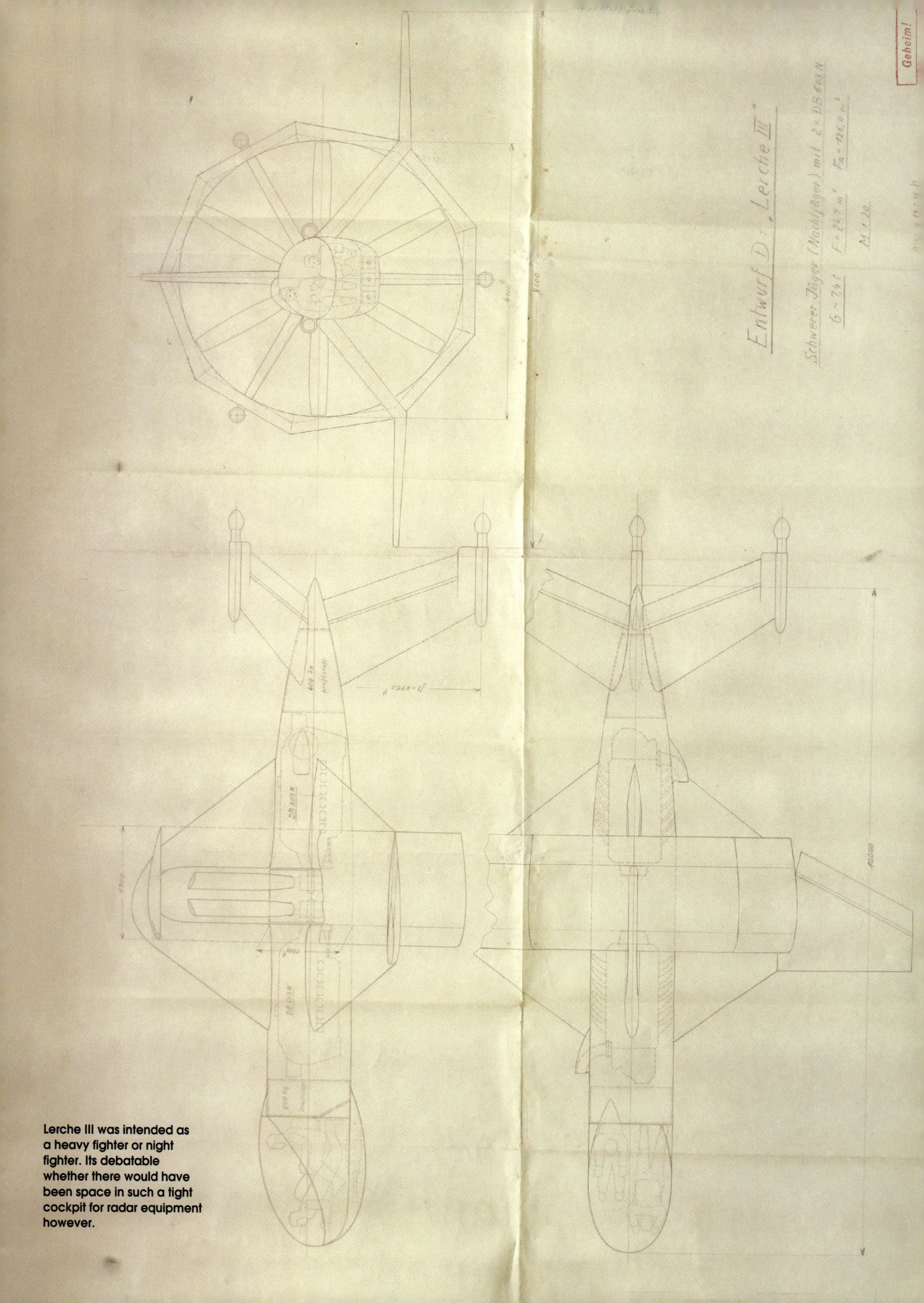

Lerche III was intended as a heavy fighter or night fighter. Its debatable whether there would have been space in such a tight cockpit for radar equipment however.

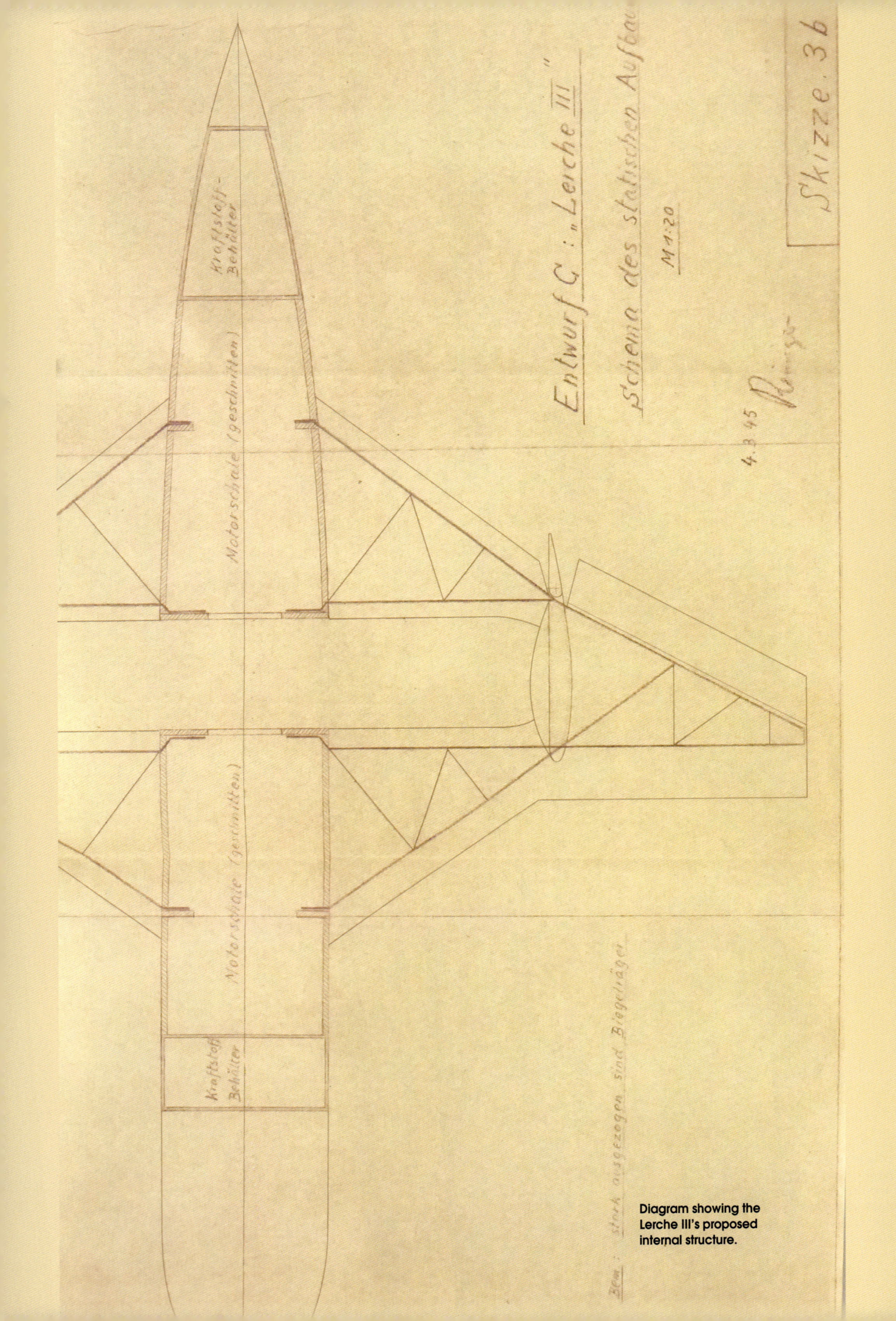

Entwurf C: "Lerche III"
Schema des statischen Aufbau
M = 1:20

4.3.45

Skizze. 36

Kraftstoff-Behälter

Motorschale (geschnitten)

Motorschale (geschnitten)

Kraftstoff-Behälter

Bem.: stark ausgezogen sind Biegeträger

Diagram showing the Lerche III's proposed internal structure.

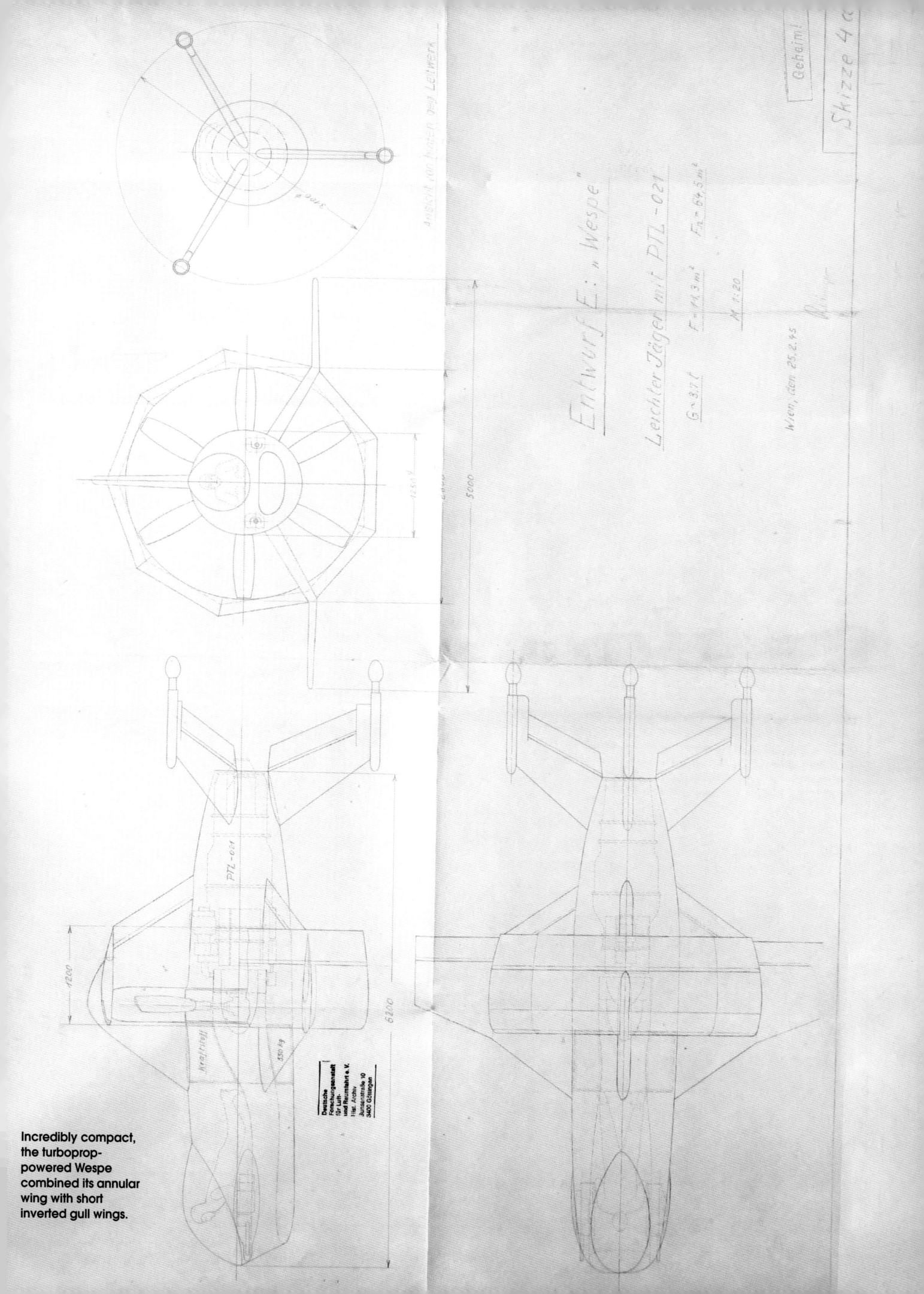

Incredibly compact, the turboprop-powered Wespe combined its annular wing with short inverted gull wings.

HEINKEL RINGFLÜGEL-PROJEKTE

Aus dem Heinkel-Bericht vom 8.3.1945

Schema des Start- und Landevorganges

Bremsen — Landung — Ca > Ca max — Bahnneigungsflug — Start

Reiniger

Abb. 8

Reiniger's plan for how his VTOL designs would take off, transition to horizontal flight, transition back to vertical, brake and then land.

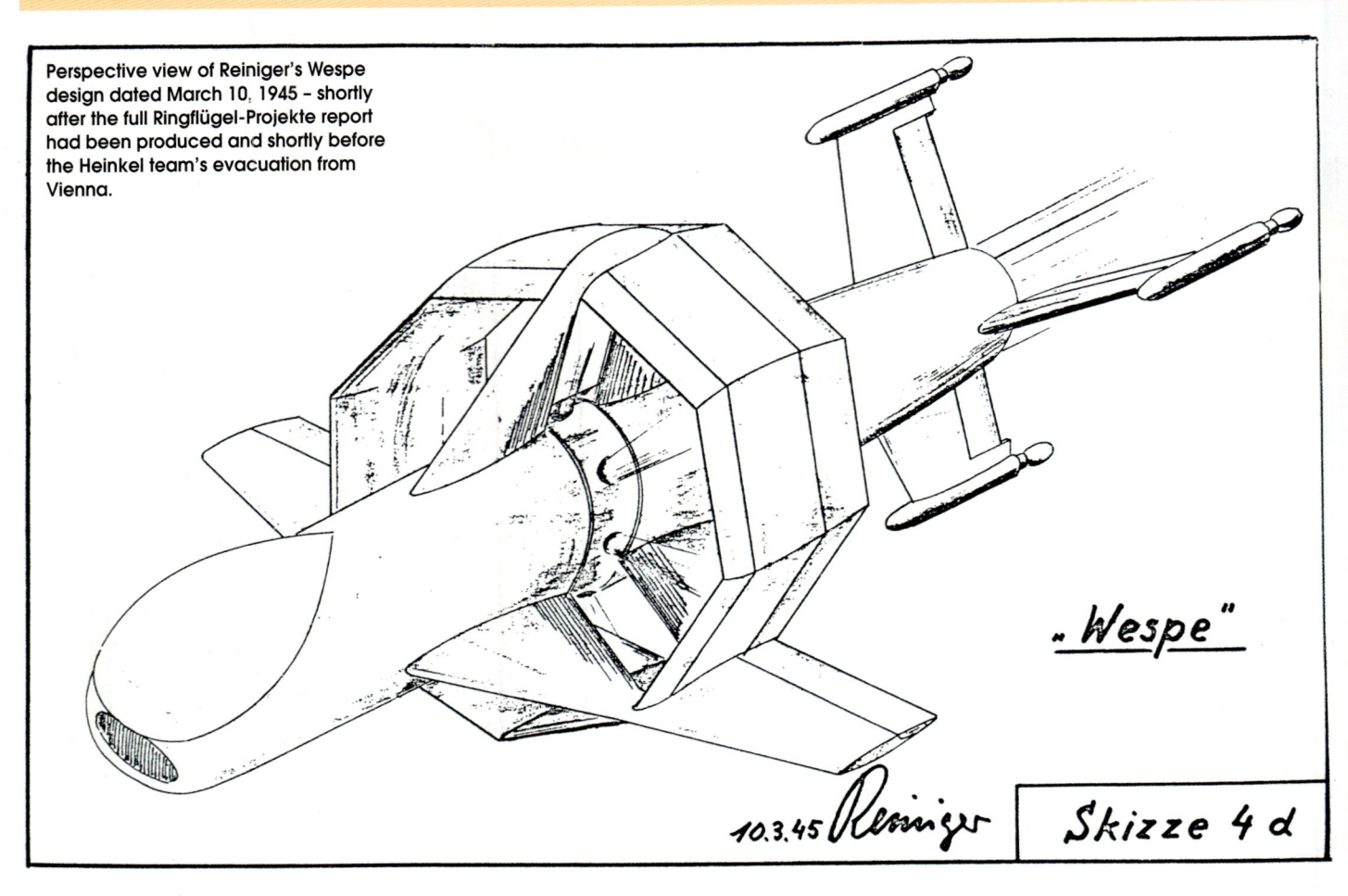

Perspective view of Reiniger's Wespe design dated March 10, 1945 – shortly after the full Ringflügel-Projekte report had been produced and shortly before the Heinkel team's evacuation from Vienna.

„Wespe"

10.3.45 Reiniger

Skizze 4 d